JOURNEY INTO
THE MIND'S EYE

JOURNEY INTO THE MIND'S EYE

Fragments of an autobiography

Lesley Blanch

LONDON

To my Russian friends, everywhere

First published by Collins in 1968
This edition published February 2005 by Eland Publishing Ltd,
61 Exmouth Market, London EC1R 4QL

Text © Lesley Blanch 1968

ISBN 978 0-907871-54-5

Cover shows a detail from a Palekh laquer miniature, *Troika*, from
Russian Laquer Miniatures and Fairytales by Lucy Maxym, published by
Corners of the World Inc.

Cover designed by Rose Baring, text by bk design, typeset in
Schneidler and printed by GraphyCems

Chaque homme porte en lui sa dose d'opium naturel
Baudelaire

CONTENTS

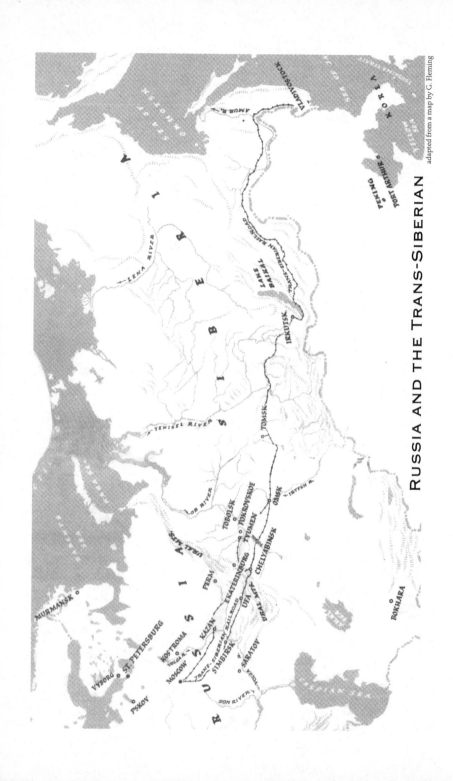

RUSSIA AND THE TRANS-SIBERIAN

adapted from a map by G. Fleming

PART ONE

THE TRAVELLER

Who is the lonely Traveller
Racing the moonlight to my door?
Racing his troika over the steppe
Pacing his steeds with the wind in the forest.
The North wind that harries
The South wind that tarries
Who the lone Traveller come to my door?
— Lonely no more.

Siberian song - Trans-Baikal region

CHAPTER ONE

I must have been about four years old when Russia took hold of me with giant hands. That grip has never lessened. For me, the love of my heart, the fulfilment of the senses and the kingdom of the mind all met here. This book is the story of my obsession. In her essays, *The Sentimental Traveller*, Vernon Lee wrote of her emotion for Italy thus: 'There are moments in all our lives, most often, alas! during childhood, when we possess the mystic gift of consecration, of steeping things in our soul's essence, and making them thereby different from all others, for ever sovereign and sacred to us.' So Italy became to her – so Russia to me.

~

The Traveller had come to rest in the rocking-chair. The clumsy folds of his great fur-lined overcoat stood round him like a box, while a number of scarves tangled under his chin. His tight-skinned Chinese-yellow face seemed to glow, incandescent, in the light of the nursery fire where we made beef-dripping toast together. Even this warming occupation could not persuade him to remove his overcoat.

'You'll catch your death of cold when you go out,' my nurse would always say.

'Not after Siberia,' the Traveller would always reply. It was a ritual.

Of all the lands he had known, his own, Russia, seemed to me the most fabulous. He was from Moscow, 'a Muscovite', he said, but later I was to learn he was of Tartar blood; and unmistakably, the Ta-tze or Mongol hordes had stamped their imprint on his strange countenance. The dark slit eyes, the pointed ears, the bald, Chinese-bald skull, the slight, yet cruel smile which sometimes passed across his usually impassive face – all these spoke of Asia, of the Golden Horde, and the limitless horizons of Central Asia, where he roamed, in spirit, and in fact.

Whenever he came to Europe, he would visit us, and then, reaching my nursery, sit beside the fire, his huge shadow spread-eagled – a double-headed Russian eagle to me – across the rosy wallpaper. Shrugging and gesticulating with odd, unexpected movements, his long, bent-back fingers cracking, the nail of one little finger sprouted to astonishing length, he would spin a marvellous web of countries, cities, people and things, conjuring for me a world of shimmering images. Fishing for serpents in the lakes of Central Asia. How pomegranates (which at that time I had never even seen) were said to contain one seed from Eden... The sort of food Mamai the Tartar ate sitting in his brocaded, fur-lined tent. The Trumpeter of Cracow, the private lives of reindeer, his grandmother's house in the Ukraine, where the vast entrance-hall was paved like a chess board in squares of blue-john and jasper; how, when he was my age, he used to jump the various moves on it with two aged dwarfs, who had been part of the household of his grandmother's mother, and had remained on, capering up and down stairs with messages, and preparing the special violet-scented cigarettes the old lady puffed incessantly.

Or he would tell of Tarbagan Bator, the Marmot hero of Mongol legend, one of my favourite characters, who, in the beginning of the world, shot down several of the twelve suns which then blazed on high. 'The brave little marmot used a bow and arrow, and that is why, to this day,' said the Traveller, 'no Mongol will shoot at a marmot with such a weapon.'

'So you see, since there are very few guns either, in Inner or Outer Mongolia, the marmots live happy lives there,' he added reassuringly, seeing what was known in the family as my 'Black Beauty Face' threatening. This was always the prelude to an outburst of uncontrollable sobbing brought about by any mention of animal suffering, such as Anna Sewell's story of that name, the poem entitled *The Arab's Farewell to his Steed* or any other reminder of dumb distress.

Along with an amber chaplet which he fingered abstractedly, the Traveller always carried a squat little agate spoon. 'For my caviare,' he said, 'it tastes so much better from a spoon.' He never met with this delicacy at our table, unless he brought it with him, which he sometimes did, appearing unexpectedly, with a lavish pound of the great, grey-grained Beluga kind.

'Fish jam,' cook called it, sniffing suspiciously. But I took to it from the first.

Sometimes he told me fairy stories – Russian legends, Ilya Mourametz the heroic, or Konyiok Gorbunok, the little hump-backed horse who brought his master such good fortune; or the magical cat, chained to a tree, who sang verses when he circled to the right, and told fairy tales when he went to the left... Best of all, he would tell of the great train that ran half across the world – the most luxurious and splendid train that ever was – the Trans-Siberian.

He held me enthralled then, and today, a life-time later, the spell still holds. He told me the train's history, its beginnings (first mooted, it seemed, by an Englishman, a Mr. Dull by name); how a Tzar had said, 'Let the Railway be built!' And it was. He told me of its mileage, five thousand (to the Canadian-Pacific's three thousand); of its splendours: brass bedsteads instead of bunks; libraries, hot baths, and grand pianos to while away the hours. (From Moscow to Irkutsk, barely a half way point to Vladivostok, was nearly a week's travelling.) Of its miseries; of prison wagons, iron barred trucks hitched on at some wayside halt where the shackled lines of wretched creatures could be heard clanking their chains, often five pounds of wooden logs added to the heavy irons, and singing their traditional exiles' begging song, the Miloserdnaya, a sort of funeral chant of doom and despair.

'How did they learn it?' I asked. His face changed terribly. Another mask, of pure hatred, suddenly succeeded the habitual one of Asiatic impassivity.

'Those who went on foot sometimes took over a year to reach Tiumen – not even half-way,' he said, 'two miles an hour – twenty miles a day was good going in chains... They had plenty of time to learn the begging song. And to learn how to suffer, and die,' he added. He shrugged. 'Life teaches.' It was one of his favourite dictums. Then, wrenching himself from Siberia to London, he became suddenly autocratic. 'More tea!' he demanded, and I hurried to the tea-pot.

He always insisted on having his tea, Russian-style, in a glass. He liked a spoonful of cherry jam in the saucer, beside it. Sometimes he showed me how the peasants held a lump of sugar in their teeth, and sucked the tea through it, noisily, for sugar was a great luxury among them, and not to be dissolved prematurely. The Traveller always drank his own tea in a strange fashion. He never held the glass in his hand, but would leave it on the table, then bend his head down to it, rather like a camel drinking. And all the while his wicked-glinting little eyes would range round the room. If anything so narrow could be said to roll – they rolled ecstatically. He particularly savoured the China tea my mother obtained, and he strongly approved of her allowing it in the nursery. Even more, he admired her for giving me a beautiful old Worcester tea-cup for my own use.

'When I was your age, I drank from Tamerlaine's jade drinking-cup,' he said, and I believed him.

How I loved him! How I loved his Traveller's tales and the way he brought the Trans-Siberian railway thundering through the house. There was a chapel on the train, he said; a candle-lit ikon-filled chapel where the long-haired, long-bearded Orthodox priests ('Popes we call them') gathered the pious together before a gilded iconostas, praying and swaying as the great engine snaked across the steppes. Piety ran the length of the train. Piety and patriotism: love of a country. As the train rattled across the bridge over the Volga, every man stood up and doffed his cap to Mother Volga.

I knew it all by heart. Every Wednesday and Saturday, the Trans-Siberian train pulled out of Moscow and for seven days ate up the eastward miles to Irkutsk, and farther, into the heart of Siberia, through the Trans-Baikal provinces, edging the Mongol steppes and the yellow dust-clouds of the Gobi desert. There was a branch line to Outer Mongolia – another, along the Amur, to bandit-infested Manchuria, and at last, ten days later – Vladivostok, Russian outlet of life and death on the Sea of Japan. One extension of the line led to the Forbidden City.

'The gates were scarlet lacquer, a hundred and fifty feet high, and stuck with the heads of malefactors,' said the Traveller, spreading beef-dripping with a lavish hand.

~

For me, nothing was ever the same again. I had fallen in love with the Traveller's travels. Gradually, I became possessed by love of a horizon and a train which would take me there; of a fabled engine and an imagined landscape, seen through a pair of narrowed eyes set slant-wise in a yellow Mongol face. These Asiatic wastes were to become, for me, the landscape of my heart, that secret landscape of longing which glides before our eyes between sleeping and waking; a region I could not fathom, but into which I was drawn, ever deeper, more voluptuously, till it became both a challenge and a retreat. It was another dimension where I could refuge from the rooms and streets about which I moved, docile but apart. From the first, the Traveller had understood my infatuation for Asia, and every time he came to see me, he brought some object which told of those horizons. A chunk of malachite, or a Kazakh fox-skin cap (which smelt rather rank) and once, a *bunchuk*, or standard, decorated with the dangling horse-tails of a Mongol chieftain. I was enraptured.

'Nasty dangerous thing,' said Nanny, holding it at arm's length and depositing it in the umbrella stand. 'Why can't he bring you dolls, dressed up in national costumes? You could have quite a collection by now.'

But the Traveller knew better.

True, he had turned a deaf ear to my plea for a Samoyede dog, or at least a pair of Pharaoh's mice, the curious little creatures that swarm over Siberia, a kind of prairie-dog, which emerge from their burrows to sit up on their haunches in attitudes of interest and amazement every time the great train rolls past. But by way of compensation he brought me the malachite, which I sank in my goldfish tank, and this now became, in my mind's eye, a miniature Lake Baikal. The violet and emerald coloured shrimps which lurked in the lake's depth were something I had also set my heart on acquiring although, in the matter of live-stock, the Traveller was not as accommodating as I could have wished. But I consoled myself by the thought that no other nursery of my acquaintance boasted the horsetail standard of a Mongol chieftain. Nor, I thought, did anyone else I knew put down a plateful of pudding for the *Domovoi* in the manner recommended by the Traveller.

The *Domovoi*, he explained, was a gnome-like creature of Russian legend, a self-appointed spirit of the house, inclined to be touchy, but gratified by such attentions. He was certainly somewhere about our house – knowing how much I loved Russia. It did not do to neglect the *Domovoi*, or bad luck would follow. Traditionally, food for the *Domovoi* should be placed beside the front door, but in our household this practice had to be abandoned when my father stumbled over a saucer of roast lamb, spinach and mashed potatoes (for I saw no reason to deny the *Domovoi*). After that my offerings had to be confined to the nursery threshold, where, for the most part, they were eaten by the cats.

Gradually, the Trans-Siberian journey became an obsession. But how to make it? At that time, my journeys were circumscribed: family holidays to Sussex downs or Cornish beaches (gingerbread biscuits after an icy dip, sand-shoes drying on the window-sill, along with strips of seaweed). But there were travel-books to comfort me, and whole worlds to be explored by turning the pages. The top shelf of my toy-cupboard turned bookcase now assumed a most business-like air, and was labelled SIBERIA, while I waited for donations. I had learned to read very young, so that by seven I was experimenting with any book I could lay hands on. When my father, who believed in children reading anything, at any age, cynically produced Dostoievsky's *House of the Dead* my mother suggested Jules Verne's *Michel Strogoff* would have been more suitable, to which my father replied that he had no doubt wading through Dostoievsky's miseries would finish my Siberian craze for good. My mother contributed Xavier de Maistre's *La Jeune Sibérienne*, in the hope it would improve my French, while Aunt Ethel produced Harry de Windt's fearful accounts of a journey across Arctic Siberia, among the convict settlements and political prisoners. But still my enthusiasm grew.

I thought my Siberian collection looked particularly impressive, above a shelf full of the *Bibliothèque Rose*, the E. Nesbitt books and *The Wind in the Willows*, and I preened, becoming a topographical snob, a weakness which I have never wholly outgrown. Presently I acquired some odd volumes of Prishvin's *Russian Natural History*. The Traveller, on learning of my budding library, sent me a sumptuously bound edition of Atkinson's classic, *Travels in the Regions of the Upper and Lower Amoor*, with the most romantic early nineteenth-century illustrations of perpendicular granite cliffs along the shores of Lake Baikal, of Tartar and Kirghiz horsemen, and the fluted roofs of Buddhist temples. '*Pour votre Bibliothèque Noire*' was inscribed on the fly-leaf, in his sprawling hand.

'Siberia! I'll give you Siberia – you with your chilblains,' said my nurse, when I whined to go out in the brown-edged, slushy London snow. I was hardening myself, in preparation for journeys to Omsk and Tomsk (later I named two kittens after these towns) and the mysterious, icy-sounding places along the Trans-Siberian's way. Verkhné-Udinsk, Chita and Chailor Gol were names round which the tempests of Asia howled. Nevertheless Nanny, who had now left us, showed an understanding of my peculiar passion, and next Christmas sent me a purple-bound volume (a come-by chance, off a barrow in the Portobello Road) entitled *On Sledge and Horse-back to the Outcast Siberian Lepers* by Kate Marsden - New York 1892.

'Must have been off her rocker,' said cook, when I read her the more dramatic passages. Moreover she was adamant in her refusal to make *pelmeni*, pieces of stuffed pasta, a celebrated Tartar dish, of which the Traveller had given me the recipe.

'Staple Siberian diet,' he said. 'Filthy, but filling.' He also added it was very hard to make.

'Which is as maybe,' said cook darkly, basting the roast in a crimson glow of professional complacency.

Nor was she any more co-operative when I dwelled on the habits of Jenghis Khan's troops who were required to carry a sheep's stomach full of desiccated dried meat, and another of powdered milk flour under their saddles, thus being ever at the ready to gallop off on some foray.

'But it would only be like getting a haggis,' I pleaded, when she refused to supply a sheep's stomach. I had planned to attach it to my tricycle, and thus provided, pedal furiously off down the path to Asia.

On my seventh birthday there was a party. 'Seven – a MAGIC number, the mystic number of all Asia,' said the Traveller portentously. But the joy of cutting my cake was clouded by his telling me about the birthdays of his niece, Sofka Andreievna, in Tomsk. *She* had always been given the traditional Siberian birthday sturgeon: a six-foot-long giant fish, frozen stiff, garnished with ribbons. After the caviare had been ripped from its belly it was stuffed with special herbs, and cooked in a huge iron dish. 'Big as a coffin,' said the Traveller. And, suddenly, all the jam sandwiches and éclairs turned to dust. I craved a Siberian sturgeon.

Although a sturgeon was no more forthcoming than the sheep's stomach, the Traveller always knew how to console and intrigue me. When, a week or two later, I came out in spots and measles was diagnosed he was all sympathy and imprudence, brushing aside any talk of contagion or quarantine.

'I've had it and I don't believe that rubbish about spreading germs, or I should have brought every kind of Asiatic plague into this nursery long ago,' he said. All objections were useless. He installed himself beside my bed and launched into a flow of the most distracting stories, of how, when he was my age, and had measles too, he had been sent to a Bashkir camp in the Urals, to take the *Koumiss*, or fermented mare's milk cure. 'Pretend it's *Koumiss*,' he would say, when I turned away from a bowl of some despised Anglo-Saxon pap.

But my temperature was raised, rather than reduced, following his accounts of how, had I been stricken in Moscow, he would have gone to fetch the Miraculous Ikon of Iverskaiya no less. This most sacred of images was housed in the Iversky chapel beside the Red Square; Holy of Holies, the Ikon of the Mother of God was driven about the city in Her own carriage and four. Lackeys in livery, but hatless, even in a blizzard, as mark of reverence, conducted it to the bedside of the sick or dying, or to bless some family fête. (When demands were too numerous there was a stock reply: 'The blessed Mother of God is a trifle fatigued and cannot come today.')

'Your spots would have disappeared as soon as they carried the blessed Mother of God upstairs,' he said, crossing himself, 'but as it is, you'll just have to go on being spotted for a while... Though I shall bring you a little ikon all for yourself, tomorrow, so don't be too sad, Spotichka,' he said, embracing me, spots and all.

He had come into my life very early: indeed I can hardly recall a time when he did not dominate it, when I was not gripped by an infatuation for all things Russian. And then, as if to set the seal on my childish obsession, there had been that fatal encounter with the Grand Duke...

At the time of which I write, the beautiful Palladian building now known as Chiswick House (then Burlington House) was a luxury lunatic asylum for a small and particularly wealthy group of unfortunates. The place was run by a distinguished alienist, and the lunatics lived in considerable freedom and style. There were dinner parties in the lofty ornamented rooms and where once Georgiana, Duchess of Devonshire, had been adulated by Whig society, delicate dishes were served – but with wooden spoons. No cutlery was allowed, for some of the inmates were dangerous. Childlike, I took a keen interest in stories of these wretched beings. Nanny knew the lodge-keeper's wife, and sometimes, as they chatted at the gate, I could watch one who spent his days constructing huge bird-like structures, flying machines, out of branches, twigs and lengths of sheeting. Aided by an apparently enthusiastic keeper he towed these structures along an open stretch of grass. 'But they never fly – they never will!' he said sadly when once I strayed near, eluding Nanny's vigilance.

On the day of my fatal encounter (I must have been about five at the time) I was bowling my hoop along the quiet road that ran beside the walls of Burlington House, when the gates swung open and from the ilex groves within an elegant equipage emerged, drawn by a pair of bays. (Horse-drawn carriages were, already, becoming something of an exotic legacy of the past – arresting spectacles.)

'Careful now!' called Nanny, as I went trotting on after my hoop. But at that moment, a gigantic ogre-like figure leapt down from the open carriage and dashed past us, swerving to avoid my hoop. Every detail of his appearance is graven on my memory. He wore a fawn overcoat, and a top hat, and a white flower in his button-hole. He had a dense black beard, and his general appearance was one of the utmost ferocity and fascination. The coachman had sprung down in pursuit, but already the keeper had caught up with the madman and they were locked in a desperate struggle. The madman's black beard was flecked with foam and he roared terribly, unintelligible, like some great wild beast, before he was overcome and carried unconscious inside the gates. The top hat lay glistening in the dust near my hoop. I felt suddenly sick. A man came out of the gate-house and led the horses inside the grounds. They had been standing quietly throughout this alarming scene. As we passed him he smiled reassuringly and winked at Nanny. 'It's that Grand Duke again,' he said, 'I never saw such a one for giving trouble. Foreign, of course.'

Russian, of course.

The whole episode was saved up to be recounted later to the Traveller, and only served to confirm me in my belief that Russians were the most interesting people in the world.

Pursuing my passion, all things were better Russified. Herrings, called *siliodka* tasted more delicious. Raspberry jelly, melted down, became *kiciel*, and much nicer. The spurned cabbage was redeemed, in soup, as *stchee*. With the same ardour I collected old Russian superstitions, spitting to neutralize bad luck if I saw a parson, until smacked out of this affectation. And I recall a scene at the luncheon-table when I denied myself a slice of ruby-fleshed water melon, recounting how in some Russian villages people thought it unlucky, because it looked like the severed neck of St. John the Baptist. This robust simile disgusted my mother to the point of nausea.

'Morbid lot,' remarked my father, cutting himself another slice.

I possessed a fine dolls' house, a three-storeyed red-brick mansion with a classic portico. Nothing would do but I must transform it into some kind of Slav edifice.

My mother plunged into this ambitious project with delight and together we modelled the onion-shaped domes of the old Russian churches. Ours were made of clay, and baked, before being glued over the chimney stacks. We painted them in the lollipop stripes, stars and harlequin effects of the Vassilii Blajennii Cathedral in Moscow, which we took as our model. The façade of the dolls' house was painted a brilliant blue – 'to show up in the snow' – and we added curlicues of plaster-work round each sober window. The cupolas were topped with little gilded cardboard crosses rising over a crescent, as the old prints showed. It was neither cathedral nor palace, but it was unmistakably Slav, and I loved it, keeping it for many years, at last transforming it into a hat cupboard (berets in the attic, straws in the dining-room and so on). During the bombing of London, in 1944, it suffered considerably, and at last, taking up too much room to house and time to repair, was given away. But I mourned its fantasy and the past it had evoked.

Even my first essays in sewing were conditioned by thoughts of Russia. My kindergarten school had been a very old-fashioned one, kept by two elderly ladies, the Misses Peeke, who between them taught us the rudiments of music, water-colour painting, and sewing. We reeled off a few dates, recited poetry, were taught simple arithmetic, and to curtsey and waltz. Once a week, a decrepit retired Marine, known as the Serjeant, came to give us 'drill', which consisted of swinging Indian clubs rather wildly. Over the years batches of children came and went, but the Misses Peeke had never thought of changing or advancing their curriculum. Thus, we learned to sew on an antiquated looking red flannel bedjacket known as a Nightingale. This was named after the redoubtable lady who had designed it while running her hospital at Scutari, and it had been a period-piece even when the Misses Peeke had tried out their 'prentice's hands on it. Along with a peculiar knitted helmet, a 'Balaclava', these two garments had once been destined for the Misses Peeke's long-dead father, who as a young man had fought in the Crimea, but, laid aside in grief, they had at last come to serve as a practice-ground for several generations of uninterested little pupils. Until my advent; for on hearing the magic word 'Balaclava', my fervour was aroused. Inkerman and Alma, Sebastopol and Eupatoria were all living epics to me. I had heard the Traveller airing Russian views on the invasion of the Crimea and, much as I thrilled to the Charge of the Light Brigade, I was even more enthralled by Admiral Nakhimov's stoic decision to sink the whole Russian fleet in Sebastopol harbour. Thus I fell on the flannel Nightingale, running, hemming and feather-stitching it with ardour.

~

At this time, my view of Russia was simple. I saw it all under snow; winter and summer alike, the forests and the cities were seen through a whirl of snow-flakes, just as I saw the entire population – the Traveller apart – as hirsute, bear-like creatures smothered in full-length fur-lined shubas. Men wore shaggy furs merging with their beards and long locks; women were even more spherical, toddling and toy-like, bright-coloured handkerchiefs framing their round red cheeks. These were the images of a child's picture-book, and they lingered: it was some years before I could visualize Russia under the torrid midsummer sun that strikes down so briefly. My first readings of the Russian classics were conditioned by this childish vision too; it was as if I had shaken one of those glass paper weights that produce a flurry of snow-flakes. Through this, the plot developed against a background of universal whiteness. The burning noon-tides of Gogol's Ukraine, Turgeniev's autumn woods, fields of wheat at harvest time, or the opalescent summer nights of St. Petersburg were all seen through this perpetual snowstorm. It was only after a considerable effort to re-focus my vision that I could admit, or appreciate the infinite variety, the nuances of climate and landscape which Russian writers evoke so wonderfully: or, for that matter, the range of figures within the landscapes.

I now began to ask the Traveller to take me back with him to Russia. Generally he would reply: 'Of course – if you will learn to speak Tartar by Tuesday or Friday,' or whenever he was leaving. But I had no gift for languages, he well knew. It had taken him two weeks to teach me a Russian rhyme about a crocodile walking down the Nevski Prospect. While the Kyrillic alphabet had been mastered laboriously during my convalescence from some childish ailment, along with the names of the Kremlin's towers and gates, the Sunday Gate, the Gate of the Saviour, the Trinity, and more, I was painfully slow to construct even the simplest sentences correctly. At which he would call me *Douraka-Glupi*, little fool, *Stupidichka*, or even *Numskullina*, a blend of Thumbelina and numskull. He always showed a most inventive turn for such names, and over the years I acquired many, my favourite being *Rocokoshka* – which might be translated roughly as my little Rococo pussy-cat. But this came later, when I began to show signs of those elaborate ambiguities known as femininity. At the moment of which I write, I was still comparatively straightforward. And certainly single-minded, even for a short while going so far as to stir butter into my tea in faithful imitation of the Mongolians who, I had learned, enjoyed yak-fat in theirs.

Once, learning he was leaving for Siberia the next day, I became desperate.

'*Please* take me with you. *Please!* I want to ride in *our* train. Can't I, this time? Why not?' I burst into tears of longing.

The Traveller was stretched out on the old nursery sofa. He still kept to his fur-lined overcoat, but now it was flung over his feet. He was reading *The Times* leader and disapproving. There were guests in the drawing-room and he had not wished to join them, for he was not sociably inclined.

Ermyntrude, my pet black and white rabbit, had climbed inside his jacket for a nap, as she liked to do with my father. Her long, pink-lined furry ears could be seen, emerging from the lapels of his coat. Sounds of conviviality reached the nursery; the chink of glasses, high-pitched talk, and a piano began to accompany a soprano. Ermyntrude's ears twitched apprehensively. The Traveller laid down *The Times* and sighed, listening more attentively, it seemed, to the song, than to my plea.

'Less than the dust beneath thy chariot wheels,' sang the disembodied soprano, with dramatic emphasis.

The Traveller scowled. 'A lot she knows about that sort of thing.'

I must have looked puzzled for he took my hand, looking suddenly melancholy. The slit eyes stared, seeming to reach the brain behind my eyes.

'Don't cry, my funny little Nursery Traveller... How can I take you to Siberia tomorrow? I doubt I can ever take you there... But you have such violent desires... I've no doubt you will get yourself there one day. And you may even find me there.' He sighed.

'Where?' I asked, breathlessly.

'Anywhere,' he replied casually, and picked up *The Times*.

As an afterthought: 'As a matter of a fact, we're probably there now, having never left it. Magic of magics! Don't be so finite. "*Je suis hier, je suis demain...*" That's an inscription on one of the Egyptian monuments to the God Horus. You must *think* yourself where you want to be. *'Païdium!* Lets go!' Since I continued to stand rooted to the nursery floor, he took my hand, smiling one of his rare soft smiles; then, assuming the proud stance of an archer, he told me how the Mongol warriors galloped across the Gobi, accomplishing distances which nothing less than magic could explain, racing after the arrows they shot into the air before them.

'I remember an old song of theirs,' he said, 'Fly! Fly! wherever ye be, for I am the Lord of the Arrows said he.'

'You must learn their secrets,' he went on. 'Magic is everywhere – in the Gobi – in this nursery too.'

And with that I had to be content.

So, despairing of human aid to reach Siberia, I turned to magic. Perhaps I could discover some spell which would whisk me there. Magic of Magics! Although the Traveller professed himself a believer it was not without some trepidation that I consulted him on the question. He listened attentively and promised to try and find a secret formula for granting wishes which he had been given, long ago, by a Siberian Shaman living, very suitably, on the Shaman's Rock, Shaman Kamen, on the Angara.

'And did it work?' I asked.

'Like a charm,' he replied, crossing himself and mixing his magics. He also suggested I should try to reach the Street of the Necromancers, in Prague, where, it seemed, I would encounter a number of helpful people. But from my nursery, Prague seemed as remote and inaccessible as Siberia.

In due course, a small yellowing square of white silk arrived, curiously folded and covered in cabalistic signs. This, wrote the Traveller, must be placed on the head during the first three nights of a waxing moon. If possible I was to drink the milk of a hump-backed white mare and (this may be tricky, he warned) sprinkled with three hairs from the beard of a centenarian.

Most of this proving indeed, too tricky to achieve, I fell back on a less exacting, home-made magic, the wishful thinking he had advocated and which for some while I practised hopefully. Having collected a number of my most vivid old Siberian postcards, dog-teams straining across the snows, the interior of the restaurant car on the Trans-Siberian train, a trading post, ice-breakers on Baikal, or the main street of Irkutsk, I would take the pictures to bed with me, and then, by the aid of an electric torch concealed under the bedclothes (for reading in bed was forbidden), I would place each image in turn under a glass paper weight which magnified the scene, bringing it into stereoscopic reality. Then, holding my breath, crossing my fingers, and counting up to ten in Yakute (a piece of exoticism it had amused the Traveller to teach me, one wet Sunday), I had to project myself deep into the magnified scene. *Bir, iki, ous, tar, bar, ali, sekki*, I counted, plunging into some marvellous white and glittering world where the far northern names on the map sounded like bells tinkling on the reindeer's antlers as the teams posted between Tsissibas and Yuk-Tak, Sarak-Kalak and Beté Kül. Whichever picture I fell asleep over would be the one in which I would find myself when I awoke... or at least, would live in during my sleep my home-made magic told me. But in the morning I was still in bed, unable to remember my dreams, still not in Siberia.

How to get there? How to reach Moscow, Tash Kurgan or anywhere else, either side of the Urals, on the strength of my desires alone? On New Year's Eve I still scrupulously observed the Russian tradition of writing my wish (naturally to attain Siberia) on a piece of paper which I then burnt, ceremoniously eating the ashes. It was dusty fare to choke down, but I managed it – that way you could rely on your wishes coming true: but it left a rather grubby smudge round the mouth, and was not encouraged by my family. Since none of the spells worked, I began to think of making off in an easterly direction. But even my accumulated pocket-money would not have got me farther than Dover, although I had read, in some out-of-date periodical, that in order to encourage immigration, the Russian Government had drastically reduced tickets to Siberia, whole families travelling a hundred miles for a few pence. I was enthralled by accounts of the manner in which the peasants were transported in box-cars, hugger-mugger with their farm-yard, two or three cows, geese, some sheep, the dogs, the children and (being Russian), the baboushka-grandmother, along with the pots and pans, while bales of hay were corded on to the roof for cattle-fodder en route. This I saw as some protracted picnic, a country outing on wheels – and surrounded by all those darling animals, too... Perhaps it could be arranged that in next summer's holidays I could go along?

I decided to lay this plan before the Traveller, as soon as possible, and waited, fuming with impatience, for a suitable moment. I was learning that he, like all men, was more approachable after he had eaten well. We had been spending the afternoon at the British Museum, where, in the Print Room, the Traveller had been studying a collection of Tibetan paintings, gold-leafed scrolls, intricate cloud formations, bamboo thickets glowing with tigers, and holy figures meditating on sacred mountains.

From my earliest childhood I had been accustomed to long hours spent in museums, for these were my father's natural habitat, and I accompanied him to them several times a week. My stamina for such outings was therefore established; but the Traveller was plainly flagging when I injudiciously suggested we should leave by way of the Ethnographic Department, taking in the Aztec crystal skull and the Persian porcelain section on our way out. Not that I cared at that time for Persian porcelain, but in the same room there were some life-sized Kadjhar Court paintings of dancing girls whose crimson-stained hands and feet emerged from stiff jewelled and brocaded garments, their side-long glances flashing beneath beetle-brows as they postured invitingly, holding a rose in their teeth, or offering a goblet of sherbet while balancing on one leg, or even upside down, in acrobatic attitudes. They must, I thought, resemble the legendary dancers of Shemakha, on whom the Traveller had expanded, so that Gobineau's fiery character Oum Djehane was now one of my favourite heroines, whom I liked to impersonate, dressing up gaudily, having stained my fists with red ink.

But the Traveller had no heart or no feet left for further dalliance, and dragged me away, without so much as a glance for the Asiatic charmers. By way of consolation he proposed a restorative tea. This was the moment I had been waiting for. After a rich tuck-in I would unfold my plan for going to Siberia in one of the migrant box-cars. Infinitely cunning, I suggested Buzzard's in Oxford Street, a long-vanished caterers which high-lighted my childhood by its sumptuous spreads. Towering white sugar wedding cakes, looped in garlands, were displayed in its long, low window. Lesser glories, christening cakes, birthday cakes and ornate puddings flanked the wedding cakes, promising unimaginable delights within. Tea at Buzzard's never disappointed; it was my usual half-term treat after a matinée at the Coliseum, or the climax to a day's Christmas shopping and occasionally, as now, an unexpected extra.

In a religious hush we applied ourselves to the spread. Plum cake, wine dark and accompanied by a thick layer of marzipan, the whole encased in dazzling white icing. Chocolate éclairs, coffee éclairs, marron-cream tartlets, brandy-snaps, cream horns, the whipped cream bursting from the puff pastry shell, meringues, petits fours, strawberry layer cake, rose icing, violet icing...

At last the Traveller was left by the way, a gastronomic casualty. Lighting a cigarette he ordered another brew of China tea with lemon.

'They say lemon helps,' he said gloomily.

'Helps what?' I spoke through a glorious last assault on the plumcake.

'Stomach-ache,' he said curtly, and added, 'It's all a question of what one's used to eating. I was brought up on pickled cucumbers and salted fish – all the things your mother believes would ruin your digestion; but you can eat any of this' – he waved his hand to the depleted spread – 'while I'm feeling worse every minute.'

Clearly this was not the moment to broach the question of the journey.

'There's nothing for it, we shall have to walk it off,' he said, turning up his coat collar and plunging out into a raw foggy twilight. He had a highly personal way of walking – a prowling, catlike tread, made more so by the soft leather boots he always wore. These were quite different to the regular Russian boot, and I have never seen their like in Europe. He could only obtain them in Irkutsk, he said: they were, in fact, an adaptation of the Torghut boot worn by the Mongols. The upturned, blunt toe he wore was less pronounced, but on the heel there was the classic appliqued pattern resembling the prow-like line of the toe. This was said to commemorate a ruse by which a Mongol army defeated another, wearing their boots back to front on a march, and thus throwing their enemy off their tracks. The Traveller's boots walked soft as slippers, and were, I thought gratefully (for children are self-conscious about such departures from convention), not too apparent beneath the trouser leg. We had crossed the park and were cutting through the little squares and terraces between Knightsbridge and South Kensington before I judged it judicious to raise the question of the box-car journey, or, failing that, the possibility of leaving with him on his next journey to Siberia – for I never imagined he was anywhere else, when he was not with us.

'Children under ten travel free,' I added hopefully.

But no doubt those same jumbles, meringues and slices of plumcake which lay so light on my stomach still tormented him; in any case he was unusually severe in his refusal even to discuss the project.

'Out of the question. Ridiculous! Have you no sense of reality? Don't go on about it. I *cannot* take you with me. I've told you a hundred times. What's more, *I don't want to!* Not now, anyway,' he added, softening as I burst into tears.

It was all so hopeless, I sobbed, no one understood, not even he. And now he was angry. How much longer would I have to wait? I would never get to Siberia by myself – I wouldn't be grown up for years. I would die first. I still had years and years of school to get through... I choked despairingly.

'Hush, Doushinka! Hush!' he whispered as my sobs redoubled. He looked round the quiet square apprehensively.

'You mustn't cry in the street – it's not allowed. Look!' He pointed to a notice attached to the railings of the gardens which read MUSICAL INSTRUMENTS AND STREET CRIES STRICTLY PROHIBITED.

CHAPTER TWO

Presently, I moved to another school, a big muscularly-inclined establishment considered to provide an excellent all-round education; but this merely meant that hockey (and cricket too) counted more than learning, and many exhausting hours were spent in the gymnasium. I loathed everything about my school days; especially the vaulting horse and parallel bars upon which I wobbled like an unset blancmange. Even the discovery that the gym-mistress had been born in Siberia could not diminish the miseries endured in these unheated, echoing vaults of athleticism.

It was said that Miss Volkhovsky was none other than the child of that celebrated Russian liberal writer, Felix Volkhovsky, who had been exiled to Siberia in 1878, upon vaguely worded charges of 'belonging to a society that intends, at some time in a still distant future, to overthrow the present form of government.' He had been imprisoned in the dread fortress of Petropavlovsk and later given a life-sentence to Tomsk. His young wife had followed him there but, at last, falling ill and believing herself a burden, she had taken her own life. Disasters pursued Volkhovsky: a daughter, Kate, pined and died; and he was sentenced to a further exile, in a small forgotten town on the Mongolian border. But from there, leaving his remaining daughter Vera in charge of friends, he succeeded in making a most daring escape to America, via Japan. The child, dressed as a boy, was smuggled out of Siberia to London and her waiting father.

That same little Vera was now the brisk, springy figure in a gym tunic, black plaits bound round her head, Russian-peasant fashion, who rapped out marching orders and chivvied us on to gymnastic feats. Even the nimbus of Siberian origins could not blind me to the fact she made my life thoroughly uncomfortable. Yet, hanging sullenly from a trapeze, I would forget my indignities and, watching her as she squirmed effortlessly through a pair of dangling rings, see her transformed into some legendary heroine of the Siberian snows. As she swarmed up and down ropes, I invested this exercise with the glamour of an escape from some prison stockade. Michel Strogoff, the Courier of the Tzar, no less, was hidden in the shadows, with a pair of fast-paced Mongolian ponies, and an unsheathed knife... Together he and I would flee the Khan's torturers, and gallop to freedom across *taïga* and steppes. Yes, Miss Volkhovsky had known those vast and mysterious regions I craved... And then her voice would pierce my reverie, whip-lash sharp.

'Well, going to hang there till tomorrow morning?'

My mind, like my body, thudding heavily down to earth, I would slink off to the pitch-pine-partitioned lavatories, my only refuge, where, having concealed a copy of Atkinson's *Travels in the Regions of the Upper and Lower Amoor*, or better still, *Michel Strogoff* under my gym-tunic in a squared-off bust effect, I would spend an hour or two in unmolested calm. Ignoring the thunders of adjacent flushings, or regarding them as the rapids of the Angara, I read:

'"Your name?"

"Michel Strogoff, Sire."

"Your grade?"

"Captain in Your Majesty's Courier Corps."

"You know Siberia?"

"Sire, I *am* Siberian..."

"Here is a letter," said the Tzar. "Give it to my brother, the Grand Duke, and no other! But you will have to cross a country up in arms, in the grip of rebels, and invaded by the Tartar tribes, who will at all costs try to intercept this message... Can you reach Irkutsk?"

"Sire, I *shall* reach Irkutsk!"'

And twenty-six chapters later, by way of tortures and innumerable trials, he does.

Lovely stuff.

~

As my obsession gained in strength it coloured everything and, to my mother, appeared to distort my education (whereas, in fact, it merely developed it in an unusual direction). The Houses of Plantagenet and Stuart were meaningless to me beside those of Rurik or Romanov. America's abolition of slavery in 1862 was for me only an echo of Russia's liberation of the serfs, a year earlier, in 1861. The year 1479 was suddenly of particular consequence, because of the Tartar invasion of Russia, which befell that year, and, I thought, must have swept the first of the Traveller's Mongol ancestors down on Moscow. Some odd numbers of the *Penny Cyclopedia*, published by the Society for the Diffusion of Useful Knowledge, 1837, which I had unearthed among a cupboard full of musty old yellow-backs, part of a collection of Victoriana my father had made, promised infinite bliss, for to me, 1837 was a fatal year – that of Pushkin's duel and death. But there was no mention of the dark drama in the *Penny Cyclopedia* and when I complained of this omission to my father he merely suggested I should start my own Society for the Diffusion of *Useless* Knowledge.

'Changeling!' he called me when I enlarged on my obsession, but he spoke with comprehension, for he too loved Pushkin's tales and also lived withdrawn in his own world of reveries, immobile for the most part, in a bluish haze of his favourite Latakiyeh tobacco, the daylight of daily life filtered fitfully through a heavy Moorish moucharabia he placed across the window of his dressing-room.

Between us both, my poor mother fought a losing battle for those practical issues she felt necessary, useful, correct, but which she too, in secret, detested. In short, ours was not a conventional or practical household.

The tone of my school reports was disquieting. 'Seems to be daydreaming...' 'Oddly lacking in team-spirit...' 'Moody, secretive,' were recurring phrases. The Head Mistress, a majestic figure hedged with self-importance, who was occasionally glimpsed sweeping down the corridor, her academic gown billowing in the blasts of fresh air to which we were so ruthlessly exposed, was more specific when discussing me with my mother. That is, when stating her views; she had cowed my mother with one look. A child of my age, she said, was not expected to know about anything so specialized as The Old Believers sect – a grounding in the Old Testament would be better – nor should I interrupt the history lesson on Queen Elizabeth to ask about Tzar Ivan's matrimonial intentions: it was simply showing off. I spent far too much time in the Library, and was always trying to get out of Games and Gym. And how regrettable it was that I had refused to be Confirmed... really quite outside the Head Mistress's experience! My mother had nothing to say to this, for she too, had found my obstinacy incomprehensible. All the girls of my age-group were being prepared for confirmation that term; some pompous talks were given by visiting clergy, in preparation for the ceremony itself, conducted by a Bishop of the Church of England. But I had taken a stand and flatly refused to be received into the fold. It would be Orthodoxy or nothing I told my mother, who, for once, lost all control and boxed my ears. I held firm, sustained by my father who refused to exact pressure in the matter; for to him it was of no consequence. This was just another example of my *wilful* nonconformity, said the Head Mistress. 'No team spirit,' she hissed, and my mother wilted at this dreadful taunt. And then, to cap it all, I had chosen such a particularly unpleasant subject for my half-term essay...

Did my mother know of this? asked the Head Mistress sternly. But on learning it was the assassination of the mad Tzar Paul I, my mother breathed more freely.

She had found it, from the beginning, quite impossible to control or steer my reading. That term, *Resurrection* had been my favourite book, one she viewed with mistrust, comforting herself with the belief (perfectly correct) that I did not understand half of what I read. She obtained no support from my father in the question of selected reading for he insisted I should be allowed what I liked, regardless of suitability. This naturally led me to the world conjured by Russian novelists, that immoderate world populated by so many characters considered inadmissible in the schoolroom.

~

Once, on holiday in North Devon, we were unexpectedly joined by the Traveller. The telegram announcing his imminent arrival had been brought up to the house before breakfast by a sweating Post Office boy on a red bicycle, who, in my eyes, appeared to be some messenger from the Gods announcing bliss too great for mortal compass.

My parents received the news with mixed emotions. 'Pity he doesn't play golf,' was my father's reaction, while my mother sighed over the prospect of catering for so exotic a guest. The presence of the Traveller always seemed to make her nervous: she fussed over both the food and her own appearance: yet she welcomed him warmly, as did my father. They had both known him from some remote past, or so I thought it, before they were married.

I myself was consumed with anxiety lest I should not be allowed to go to the station to meet him, wearing my new party dress.

'By all means if you want to look ridiculous,' said my mother who, being the most feminine of women, sometimes appeared to cede before gaining her point: still, six o'clock found me in the pony-trap, outside the little yellow Victorian-Gothic station, gloriously attired in Liberty silk, and of course cutting a ridiculous figure.

The Traveller, an adept at pleasing when he chose, fell back before my splendours saying it was quite the loveliest dress he'd ever seen and made me look years older (a phrase which, at that time of life, gave infinite pleasure) and so I returned to the house in a glow of triumph, hanging on his arm.

He slipped into our ways 'as into a goose-feather bed', in his own words; eating buns, junkets, shepherd's pie and other innocent foods with gusto. Even those I thought least agreeable, such as rhubarb, were gilded by the unexpected light he cast upon them.

'Rhubarb! You don't like it? You would, if you knew what the name signified,' he said cunningly. 'Rha is the dialectic name for the Volga. All along its banks this plant grows hugely. So since my country has always been considered barbarous by others, the Latin – barbara is tacked on. There you have it – Rhubarb – a plant grown in the barbarous regions of the Rha, or Volga. Yes. I thought you'd want a second helping after that.'

Sometimes we shrimped or collected glistening sea-weed; or there would be a family outing in a trap, to Bude, for a Cornish Cream tea where, seated in the tea gardens, spooning clotted cream into dollops of golden syrup or home-made jam, he would listen attentively to the talk at other tables, savouring the innumerable variations of the English accent. The niceties of Kensington English, Oxford Cockney, East-Ender Cockney, and all the rest fascinated him: he was particularly intrigued by certain homely phrases and would try to trace their significance and origin. The Cockney rejoinder, 'the same to you with knobs on', baffled him; but the nannies' classic 'ta-ta!', employed either as a farewell formula or in the sense of an outing - 'going ta-tas', 'going for a ta-ta', derived, he was convinced, from some Elizabethan fur-traders' expedition to High Tartarie.

'It's obvious,' he said, and planned to write a monograph on the subject.

I had discovered a hiding place on the cliffs where, crawling under tropic-sized bracken, I could spend hours hidden in the green gloom. Here, reading the story of Yermak's conquest of Siberia, I listened with relish to the anxious voices of my family, calling for me on the other side of the headland. This promontory was known as Gallantry Bower, and it was supposed to have been a smugglers' lair. There were caves in the cliff-face but I never discovered them, having no head for climbing. Gallantry Bower was something I kept to myself, until the Traveller's arrival. Then we shared its green secrecy. We would scramble up the pebbly paths where tiny pink shells had been washed up among the fox-gloves. Sometimes the Traveller would ask the name of a tree or a flower. 'Forget-me-not,' I would say, 'Love-in-idleness, Love-in-a-mist, Love-lies-a-bleeding, Heart's Ease.'

'And they say the English are not sentimental!'

In return, I would ask him the names of Russian wild-flowers, but it was plain he had never known a country childhood. After much thought: 'There was one I remember in the Ukraine, green and white striped. I think we called it Snow on the Mountain...' Then I would persuade him to tell me of the over-heated, exotic winter-gardens which every well-to-do house boasted in the Russia of his childhood: conservatories where gloxinias, stephanotis, orchids, and full-sized orange trees bloomed exuberantly, glowing against the whiteness of the encircling snows, and lit, on the night of a party, by hundreds of festive candles.

Crawling under the tunnels of bracken we would reach the heart of Gallantry Bower and, plagued by midges, spend the rest of the afternoon 'talking Russia' and, sustained by currant or 'squashed-fly' biscuits, play the Run-Away Game, something we had invented in the early days of our friendship when our Russian bond was first cemented. This game allowed our imagination full rein and permitted us to talk Russia by the hour. One of us would imagine some incident and place, in Russia of course, where we had run away together. The other would have to find us, in three guesses.

'We are at the Fair at Nijni-Novgorod?' the Traveller hazarded.

'No. One guess gone.'

'Mmm... We're Jenghis Khan's guests of honour at the Festival of the Banners?'

'No... but you're getting warm.'

'Then we're in Siberia... I know! We're in a sleigh – we're dashing through the forest pursued by wolves – but it's all right, because the Cossacks arrived in time!'

Siberia! It held us both in thrall.

'Why do you want it so much?' he asked, but I could not explain.

'Isn't Gallantry Bower enough? I suppose you'd rather be in a Mongolian *yurt*? Or on the Trans-Siberian?'

Much rather.

I had been reading the travels of Huc and Gabbet in Tartary, the two Jesuit priests who travelled in the Mongolian hinterland, and whose accounts of the high-priest, the Kutukthu, stirred my imagination. Sometimes I persuaded the Traveller to speak some sentence in a Mongolian dialect, and thought it marvellously exotic to the ear: but when he wrote the characters down I agreed with Gilmour the Scottish Missionary – 'Gilmour of the Mongols', my nursery hero – that they looked like a piece of knotted string. Soon I had built up another fantasy life beyond Siberia, in one of the Gobis, in a splendid *yurt* hung with yellow silk and furnished with scarlet lacquer boxes. Here the Kutukthu and I had set up house together. I was his constant companion, queening it over the Mongols. Wrapped in snow-leopard skins we rode out over the wind-bitten plains, galloping our blunt-nosed little ponies towards the buried treasure of Kara Korum. As the dusk fell, we returned to the *yurt* where saffron-robed monks played to us on conch shells and, blasting on gigantic copper and silver trumpets, summoned the encampment to watch the sacred dance of the Burkhans, or a wrestling contest. We had our own stable of wrestlers, which I knew was a mark of stylish living in Mongolia. Carpets were spread before the *yurt* and beside a heavy brass samovar we settled down to the entertainment. I brewed green tea – the best he'd ever tasted, said the Kutukthu, whose features remained shadowy. But as he crowned me with an intricately worked turquoise and coral tasselled headdress, he naturally became the Traveller.

This Asiatic idyll was soon confided to him and he countered with a jingle set to the tune of some current popular air:

'I want to elope with the Kutukthu
If he won't oblige, kind Sir, will you?
I must have you or the Kutukthu
If I can't have him, then you will do.'

'If you only knew how much you'd be shocking the Mongols! The Kutukthu is considered a particularly holy figure... You might as well imagine setting up in sin with the Archbishop at Lambeth Palace... However, it's a nice idea, you and the Kutukthu...'

Pleased with his versifying he had suddenly begun to caper about with astonishing agility, stamping and kicking with all the abandon of the three Ivans in Tchaikovsky's ballet.

'I didn't know you could dance.' I was enthralled by these violent leapings.

'All Russians can dance,' he said curtly, and stopped as abruptly as he had begun. I never saw him dance again. He was entirely unpredictable.

He loathed snobbery, pretension, and all the protocol of convention. Yet, when annoyed by what he considered the lack of consideration, or the impertinence (a favourite accusation) of post-office officials, taxi drivers or anyone else, he would always relieve his feelings by a long-winded plaint reeled off in a muttered undertone. 'And-to-think-that-when-my-great-grand-father-arrived-in-Kiev-the-Metropolitan-had-to-be-at-the-gates-to-receive-him-in-person-and-all-the-bells-were-rung!'

We never discovered why his great-grandfather merited this obsequious reception. 'Perhaps some prophetic vision told them how illustrious the old man's great-grandson would be,' said my father, nettled by some of the Traveller's exigencies.

Under the curled bracken fronds and fox-gloves of Gallantry Bower he lay on his back, the yellow shaven skull of the Chinese djinn cushioned on dried grasses and little speckled mauve flowers. The slit eyes stared up, unblinking, at the sun's rays which pierced the bracken fronds overhead. As usual, he was fingering the beads of a Moslem chaplet, and as each bead clicked past he was singing, very low, a Russian song I tried to follow. The deep smoky tones of his speaking voice which, as with so many of his fellow countrymen, had a vitality and depth associated with basso-profondos, was retained when he sang; although that unmistakably national, smoky timbre veiled every range of voice, melting yet puissant, with nothing of the Italian treacle tones, even in the lightest tenors.

'What are you singing?'

'An old Russian song – nothing for you, miss – not yet, anyhow.' He lay there, staring up at the bracken roof above us, smiling his secret smile.

I have heard the song many times, since. It is the song of the pedlar going to the fair bargaining his wares with a girl - a piece of red velvet for a kiss... Only the night knows how they settle their bargain. 'Grow high,' says the pedlar to the wheat-field. 'Grow high to hide our secret.'

~

Now the Traveller was more often in England. Yet his comings and goings were more mystifying than ever. No one knew from where he came and to where he went. In 1918 Revolution and counter-Revolution had flamed across Asia. The Romanov family met their end in a cellar in Ekaterinburg. Bandit warfare raged in Manchukuo; the tracks of the Turk-Sib railway were being dug with bayonets. Pale-eyed fanatic Baron von Ungern Sternberg was terrorizing Outer Mongolia and trying to raise his Corps of militant Buddhist monks. White officers and Red Commissars were hidden among the Mongol ranks. 'He is certainly among them,' said my father, when we had not seen the Traveller for some while. Had he returned there – on a longing, on an order? The Asiatic hinterland was his true setting, and away from it, he always seemed in exile.

'I do believe you are more homesick than I,' he had said in a rare admission of his exiled state. Can one be homesick for something one has never known? But then, had I never known it? Was it not once my setting too?

'I can see you there very clearly,' he said. 'And when you *do* get there, you'll be home, I fancy.'

'Don't go putting ideas in her head.' My mother's voice sounded an unaccustomed note of sharpness. The Traveller and I were seated on the sofa, sharing a Russian picture-book together, and he was translating the titles under each picture. Perhaps it was the Tretiakov collection. Years later, in Moscow, I was to find there the originals of many of these pictures. Vereschtschagin's Uzbek warriors gathered in Samarkand. The three giant *Bogatyri*, mythical horsemen, dominating the steppes. Portraits of Pushkin... I pored over them all.

Sale of a young Serf, translated the Traveller patiently. *Tsarevitch Ivan on a Grey Wolf. Execution of the Streletzi...* He turned the page and stopped, studying another picture attentively, going from it to my face and back again.

'Look!' he said triumphantly. 'It's you! You see. You do belong there!'

I thought there was, perhaps, a flick of malice in the glance he shot my mother out of his sidelong eyes. 'You'll never have a better likeness.' He spoke with finality.

'You're there for ever. Magic of magics! Now you have only to step into the picture-frame to be there whenever you wish. *Chort!* It's better than the Run-Away Game.'

'Please don't teach her to swear in Russian,' said my mother. *Chort,* the devil, was a mild enough expletive beside the rich resources of Russian swear-words he might have employed, and which, later, I sometimes heard in all their bawdy vigour. But oddly, the Traveller seldom exploded in Russian, employing the niceties of French more often. 'French,' he would say, 'is the language of elegant spite – of fury politely expressed – although that's a contradiction in itself. Politeness has little to do with emotion: French is all right for hatred, though. When I hate, I find French phrases admirable – like poisoned darts. But it is *not* the language of love, whatever they may say - and how *much* they say about love! A national obsession! *The tender passions...* They don't know the meaning of the phrase. The English now, have both passion and poetry... But when I love, I return to Russian. Russian is the loving tongue.'

A silence fell over us all. The Traveller thinking of love; my mother too, no doubt. But I was, as usual, thinking Russia; straining to go on with this new variation of the Run-Away Game. Ostentatiously, I lifted the cumbersome picture-book from the table to my knee. The Traveller's inward-turning stare shifted forward once more on the world around him, and the open page.

It showed one of those early nineteenth-century *genre* paintings at which the Russians excelled. I peered into the charming snowy scene. On the outskirts of a town, a fur-capped young man is dragging a little sledge loaded with household goods, baskets, pottery, and a brass samovar. His long *caftan* is bordered with fur, his top-boots crunch the snow. He gazes ardently at the girl beside him. Is he her lover or her husband, and are they setting up house, or is he a saucy merchant importuning her? She wears a voluminous cloak under which her hands seem to be holding a muff. Her smooth young face is turned towards him hesitatingly. It is an intriguing picture, full of that static, yet compelling quality peculiar to the best *genre* paintings, making them *tableaux vivants* in which we long to participate. I could see the girl's likeness to myself.

'But where are you?' I asked, lonely in my new dimension.

'Ah! Who knows? Perhaps we shall find ourselves together in another picture, racing out of the frame in one of those troikas you love. "*Gaïda troika!*"' he sang, his voice sharp as the cracking whip. '"*Gaïda troika!*" Go on looking while I'm away,' he commanded, and vanished in a clap of thunder. Or rather, soon after disappeared on another recondite absence – a long one this time. We never discovered where he was when he was not among us, for he was an adept at side-stepping questions. The Arab saying, 'conceal thy tenets, thy treasure and thy travels,' might have been his. We had heard he was in some way connected with the export business; but exporting what? Slaves, biscuits – guns? And from where, to where? The combinations were limitless. My parents inclined to believe he was a secret agent. Particularly now that war was on us. *Agent provocateur?* Double agent? They breathed the sinister words unwillingly. For – against?

We were never to know. They loved him in spite of themselves, accepting his comings and goings like the flight of some strange bird, a rather disturbing creature whose irruptions into their life brought drama, colour and confusion. I loved him unreservedly: for his strangeness and for the climate of danger that I sensed around him – as adventurer, and as the man of whom, even unconsciously, in my earliest childhood I had been desperately aware. So, loving him, I loved his background, everything that had surrounded and formed him, and I sought to penetrate that enigmatic and remote limbo-land of the Slav where, I felt, my roots had been planted in some unfathomable past. It seemed I had always known and loved him, and in his world I would at last come home.

CHAPTER THREE

The presents which I received from the Traveller in such erratic but gratifying quantities seemed, by comparison to the boxes of chocolates, work-baskets or suède covered prayer-books which most of my schoolfriends were receiving, to possess a quality of mystery worthy of his djinn-like personality.

A string of enormous amber beads with a faded silken tassel proved to be a Moslem chaplet from the Holy City of Meshed. Richly embroidered Turcoman saddle-bags were, I thought, worthy to have been slung across the winged back of El Borak, Mahommed's miraculous horse, and for a moment my loyalty to the Trans-Siberian wavered in favour of some Bactrian camel caravan, plodding across the Central Asian steppes, one of so many Moslem links in the Russian chain. Once, after we had heard nothing of the Traveller for a long while, a most romantic and grown-up gift arrived, and I took particular pleasure in producing this from my satchel in order to impress the fifth form, for it was a cigarette case, its dark steel and silver inlay work peculiar to the Caucasus. Besides the Traveller's initials in gold, it bore a number of symbols and Russian regimental crests. No doubt it was, as I heard people say, a very odd present to give a schoolgirl.

'Why not? By the time other people are giving her cigarette cases I may not be around to give her mine,' he snapped. I have it still; and I have never defiled it with anything other than the Turkish or Balkan tobacco which it seems to demand. As for the Traveller, he broke all my preconceived notions of his epicurism, by preferring *mahorka*, a fearful rank stuff, the sweepings of third-rate Bessarabian tobacco generally found only among the soldiers or lower depth of *moujik* life. When I first remember him, he used to roll his own cigarettes from a tin of this *mahorka*, part of a large supply with which he always travelled. Later, when it seemed he could no longer come and go from Russia as he pleased, it was the loss of *mahorka*, he maintained, which irked him more than anything else he had left behind.

Every Easter, I received the lovely painted eggs of Russian tradition; some were in *papier mâché*, elaborately decorated with the Imperial eagle or some regimental insignia; some were gaily painted with peasant designs. When I was six he had sent a tiny one in dark blue enamel with a ribbon of pin's-head diamonds around it, a lavish Faberge' toy.

'Diamonds for a child! It doesn't seem *natural*, does it?' sniffed Nanny, putting it out of reach, until my mother appropriated it for her dressing-table, where it hung beside the looking glass, on a blue ribbon. One egg I particularly liked was in deep mauve blue-john, its bland surface veined in golden brown. This I was allowed to keep, placing it in a carved wooden sleigh, drawn by three prancing horses – another Russian acquisition. One red-letter day he gave me an ikon, and a *lampada*, or silver lamp, to hang before it.

'Very decorative,' he said, for he always shrugged off spiritual implications and often quoted an inscription over a Confucian temple, in the Master's words: 'Listen! You must revere and oblige the Gods, for all the world as though they existed.' But he was careful to see that I hung the ikon in the proper fashion – in the eastern corner of the room. Russian children, he told me, used to read by the little *lampada* long after they were supposed to be asleep. They were never afraid of the dark, for the ikon was always there, shining for them, keeping them company all night long, the long nights of a Russian winter... And now, I too had this sustaining image to shine down on me in London.

The companionable aspects of the ikon were not, however, apparent to our window-cleaner, Mr. Bates, an old friend, to whom I proudly displayed my new treasure as he sat swaying giddily on the window-sill.

'My word! Them eyes follow you round. Fair gives you the creeps! Religious, is it? Looks 'eathen to me. I wouldn't 'ave it in my room of a night, I can tell you.'

~

All night long the Trans-Siberian raced through the nursery; past the rocking-chair and through the rose-patterned walls it sped on its way, carrying me into the steppes, to Omsk, and Vera Andreievna's birthday party, where the giant sturgeon adorned with ribbons dominated the feast. Wearing my white party dress, I was just taking my place at the table when a door banged somewhere downstairs, and I woke, hurtling back through space, to see the wavering red glow of the *lampada* swaying gently before my ikon... just as it had been doing in Vera Andreievna's room. I turned over, and went back to Siberia, to blizzards and wolves, and a highly-coloured tale I had much enjoyed, lately, about a noble-hearted Siberian lad who rescues the beautiful but priggish daughter of an émigré French aristo turned dancing-master in Irkutsk. Alas! Feodor is but a serf, and Geneviève is a haughty patrician: between them the social gap looms as large as any fissure in the ice-floes over which Feodor leaps to snatch her from the arms of a polar bear.

Although the niceties of social distinctions were something of which I was not then aware, I relished the story for its local colour, and thought Geneviève soppy as she wept and swooned her way through the book. Didn't she know how lucky she was to be on the Siberian ice-floes with a handsome serf and a polar bear?

I lay in my warm London bed and wished ardently that her lot might be mine... Siberia! Russia! RUSSIA... the last thing I saw before I slept was a pin-point of light swaying before the shimmering silver casing of the ikon which the Traveller had brought back for me from Moscow.

Not all his presents were Russian or rare, like the ribbon knot, garnished with coloured stones and seed pearls, from which a miniature copy of the Koran dangled: this was a *bouti*, an ornament once favoured by the well-to-do Tartar ladies of Kazan, which I treasured accordingly. Packets would arrive from all over the world, particularly when we had heard nothing from him for some while: a blown-glass Christmas-tree cherubim from the Christkindlmarkt in Vienna, all gilded curls and fat pink cheeks 'because it reminds me of you'. For my mother, an austerely beautiful bronze Buddha from Tibet. For myself post-cards, some not in the best of taste as my governess pointed out. (On one, a coloured reproduction of Fragonard's *La chemise enlevée*, he had scrawled across the seductive pink rump, 'Miss you, Miss'.) Curious *papier-mâché* animal masks from some Central American carnival, purple and white monkeys, or scarlet deer's heads would arrive in battered hat-boxes still bearing the label of some celebrated Parisian milliner. A beautiful mother-of-pearl Victorian tea-caddy, containing six separate compartments, arrived on another birthday and is still in my possession, having survived the bombardment of London and all the successive *déplacements* of my life. Each compartment was filled with a different kind of tea: green tea, gunpowder, Lapsang, smoked on tarred nets, orange Pekoe and jasmine teas... A rather grubby Tarot card accompanied the box; across it he had scrawled another succinct message: 'It is as important to know about tea as about wine.'

The Traveller and I shared a craving for possessions – for things; though in his case, having so far as I knew no fixed home, his belongings were scattered all over the world. Some remained in packing-cases for years, in storage, others bulged his pockets, being transferred from one suit to the next, without explanation as to their particular significance to him, at that moment.

In the course of conversation he was apt to say: 'That reminds me – I've got something you'd love – a *khalat* from Bokhara... Nice for a dressing-gown. I must get it to you. Now where did I leave it?' Or, 'I bought you a painted Persian looking-glass when I was last in Kazvin...' But why he was in Kazvin he did not say.

He would remain abstracted, trying to place these objects, and then shrug off the matter. But months or years later they would turn up, the crimson and violet padded silk of the *khalat* crushed into a battered paper parcel bursting at the corners, and scattered with illegible customs markings, the cards, perhaps stuffed into a little tin tea-pot from Morocco.

Thus my naturally acquisitive bent was fostered. From an early age I collected *things* – objects rather than *objets d'art*, and took them about with me, even on the shortest journeys. I have never understood the dictum 'always travel light'. Like the Traveller, I have always travelled heavy. In the school-room, as the objects multiplied, my parents dwelled on the dangers of accumulating. And of course there were constant fretful references to dusting. But the Traveller understood my profound craving.

'Things are loyal. They remain when people go,' he said, investing *things* with a life, an entity of their own. This was something which I also felt to be true. From my childhood I was always conscious of this unity with what are described as inanimate objects. To me, the adjective has never applied. No brass-bound Arab coffer or sagging arm-chair but it cries aloud to me of its past.

Marie Bashkirtsieff, so uncontrollably romantic, knew this sense of unity with things; writing of her childhood home in Tcherniakov she says: 'One laughs at people who find memories, charm, in furniture and pictures, who say to them: Good morning, good-bye; who look on pieces of wood and stuff as friends, which by being useful to you and constantly seen... become part of your life...'

Peering through the dusty windows of a junk shop or at the litter of a street market, I have always been aware of this unity with *things*. A sale-room, or a warehouse, is both a meeting place and a burial place. I feel a surge of recognition as my eye lights on some apparently unexceptional object, but it has spoken to me above the clamour of all the rest. Then, if I am able to acquire it, it comes home, finding its place in the hierarchy of my possessions, setting itself among other things which have come to me. Come *back* to me, perhaps. For who can say where, and in what other moment of time, things, as well as people, or the essence of an individual which we call the soul, was once known to us, or was part of ourselves, on our other passages through eternity?

Thus, with what was perhaps an atavistic urge, I was, above all, set on acquiring anything Russian. I would long, with equal fervour, for a strange brass samovar of the type used in the encampments of the Eastern tribes, or for a *kokoshnik*-shaped tiara of gigantic emeralds, brutal in their splendour, with that unmistakably excessive effect so characteristic of Russian taste.

~

It was 1920. The war was over and in those first post-war years the Traveller appeared among us again. Djinn-like as ever, he suddenly materialized, but brooked no questioning, even from my parents, who continued to speculate about him to each other. 'When I am here, with you, you know all about me – why do you want to know all about me when I am elsewhere?' he would say, turning our innocent curiosity into something sinister. And he would launch into tangled theories of time and place, and the non-existence of persons, or objects, except when in direct contact with other persons or objects. It was all very confusing, but his meaning was clear: don't pry.

There were, at this time, a number of bazaars for Russian Charities, to which I tried to lure him, but he remained aloof. 'All those old Grand Duchesses selling off other people's treasures in the name of charity!' he said, rather unjustly, for many of the objects were their own possessions salvaged from the débâcle, and now gladly given. But he was not to be won.

'Go, then. Go and find yourself a Palekh box... but I remember Fedoskino, the village where they painted them, and the hard bargaining that went on in the Stchoukin Dvor, the thieves' market in Moscow. I'm not going to turn treasure-hunting into a benevolent or social occasion, not even for your blue eyes, Miss.'

'But my eyes are green,' I reminded him, laboriously literal. 'Turquoise then,' he replied, being in a poetic mood; he shuffled about in his pockets, producing an uncut stone, which, having held beside my eyes, he carefully re-pocketed, remarking it would be a reminder when he was far away.

Later, I learned he had raised a storm among the Russian Relief Organizations by refusing to contribute anything whatever; worse still, on the mere mention of Lenin's name, (anathema to the émigrés), he was in the habit of remarking:

'Such a delightful couple!'

'How *can* you be so aggravating?' said my mother.

'Praise where praise is due,' he replied. 'I used to see them when they were exiled to Minusinsk. It was a dull hole – right up in the middle of Siberia. His talk was first-rate. So was her cooking,' he added, on an after-thought. 'I was very grateful.'

When my worldly Aunt Ethel spoke sharply of the improbability of good cooking among anarchists, he had his answer ready.

'Don't imagine the Devil doesn't know how to eat well. I've no doubt Faust seduced Marguerite with lobster soufflés. And if you imagine the wilder parts of Siberia were not full of temptation let me tell you, life among the Yakutes was considered more immoral than in Bucharest.'

What he himself was doing in Minusinsk we never discovered.

~

When I was fourteen, 'twice seven – double Magic!' said the Traveller, he gave me my first samovar, a squat brass affair, which I found rather complicated to manage; but it had come from him and it was the unchanging symbol of Russia – of 'All the Russias' I craved – that *he* had made me crave, so I mastered the business of charcoal and boiling water, and was rewarded by its purring sound. However soft, this purring of the samovar always seems to dominate the room, bestowing an unequalled sense of companionship and reassurance. It is something so dear to the Russian heart that few will journey without it; even now, in the sternly purposeful pattern of their lives, some board trains or planes with their samovar to bring them the comfort no electric kettle or thermos flask could do.

About this time I acquired a treasure which has remained one of my most cherished possessions: *Murray's Guide Book for Russia, 1893*. The time and the place. This fat little crimson book, crammed with what have now become romantic and inaccurate statements, has remained my favourite bedside reading. Now, as in my schoolroom, I open the overcrowded pages, to read, with a sense of intoxicating excitement:

KOURSK. 20 mins. stop. Buffet. Station 3 versts from town. 50,000 inhabitants. 23 churches. 5 convents. Bogoroditsky-Znamensky (Apparition of the Virgin) commemorates retreat of Polish Hetman Jolkevski, 1612. Situated at confluence of rivers Koura and Touskara. Surrounded by fertile lands. Centre for water melons which are exported as far as Chinese frontier. Celebrated Fair of Koursk held annually, 10th week after Easter. Cathedral (numerous interesting ikons). Hotel Poltoratsky (single rooms 4 roubles per day). Restaurant recommended for *petit déjeuner*. Public garden Demidov (band Wednesdays and Saturday evening in summer). Headquarters of the District Governor and Seat of the Bishop. Many public buildings include Lunatic Asylum and House of Correction. Bottled or mineral water advised.

Now although on first reading this and other similar statements might not appear of great significance, they were so to me. Koursk! I yearned for it. Koursk, where the Russians used to say the nightingales sang twelve different songs... Perhaps destiny was priming me for that remote future when I should marry Romain Kacew, or Gary, as he became known, a naturalized Frenchman whose Russian roots sprang from the Owczinsky family of Koursk.

Or was it simply that I found every entry magical, whether telling of train timetables to Baku, the contents of the Hermitage, or the Fair at

Nijni-Novgorod if it conjured the landscape of my mind's eye – the landscape of my heart's desire?

~

While I achieved the Russia of my imagination through the Traveller he too was able, through my childish enthusiasm, my credulity, to reach again a Russia he had lost – or perhaps, had never even known, as he described it. Looking back, I think he too was taking journeys into the mind's eye to reach the heart's desire. Some atavistic craving for a memory or an echo of a faraway land, long gone, drew him.

He too had his spells and magic formulae, and sometimes, holding my hand in both his own as if it were a talisman, his eyes clouding into that inward-turning stare which meant he was 'thinking Russia', he would repeat a traditional Siberian song with its haunting refrain:

'Who the lone Traveller, come to my door?

Lonely no more.'

Come at last, to the door of my nursery, he was lonely no more.

~

When the Traveller reappeared among us he simply resumed his place in our house and lives, rebuffing all questions with his usual skill. I was never able to assess, properly, my parents' attitude towards him. My father appeared to enjoy his company, but in a detached manner: observing the dramatic exits and entrances and the highly flavoured monologues as from a seat in the stalls. My mother was less detached. She listened spellbound, but sometimes seemed oddly unsympathetic, especially concerning Siberia.

'It must have been so *inconvenient* – I really don't know what he liked about it,' she would say, as she wrestled with a shopping list, or the day's menus. I asked her once why she had not gone to Russia – long ago, when she first knew the Traveller, and was grown up and free to go anywhere she liked.

'One is never really free,' was her enigmatic reply. But it did not satisfy me, for I had begun to discover that my mother rather enjoyed restrictions: they saved her the strain of making adventurous decisions. Ill-health, lack of money, her duty to others, all these things gradually became her allies: she had opted for quiet.

Now there were my overflowing bookshelves to be discussed. The original Siberian collection had expanded impressively, boasting rarities such as *Revelations of Siberia by a banished Lady, 1852*, or *Gilmour of the Mongols*, besides numbers of less localized subjects, spreading south to Gogol's Ukraine and the romanticized Caucasus of Bestoujev-Marlinsky's tales. The Traveller eyed them with his usual impassivity.

'*Ammalat Beg? En Esclavage chez les Tartares?* Dear me! You should read Leskov and Perchersky-Melnikov if you want to penetrate the real old Russia,' he said. 'Golovliev, too, and Herzen is one of the most interesting of all our writers. An Olympian figure... Did you know he was forbidden in my youth? Our censorship was particularly thorough. Lenin was very much influenced by Herzen I believe... A great mind – a very great man...' He lapsed into silence, his shoulders hunched, his eyes staring blankly with that curious gaze that always baffled me.

'A *great* man? Lenin? Not Lenin surely,' shrilled Mademoiselle Lavisse, a sniffling pinched little Dieppoise who came twice a week to coach me in French and arithmetic, subjects for which I showed no aptitude.

The Traveller shrugged:

'It's a matter of opinion; it's from where you stand, what you have to lose or gain.'

He stared out of the window morosely, watching the well-heeled passers-by, and uniformed nannies pushing immaculate prams, their pink-faced occupants brandishing expensive toys, cheerful-looking dogs following nicely to heel.

He pointed an accusing finger at me.

'It's all according, as your nanny used to say. You have much to lose, here... We – most of us in Russia – had much to gain. Even at that price... And don't forget, we were at least four hundred years behind you Europeans,' he continued, once again ranging himself and his race in Asia.

It was one of the few occasions I had heard him speak politically and it was quite wasted in the schoolroom.

'Where is my tea?' he demanded, and, watching us – his serfs – scuttle round, he assumed an air of complacent anticipation. When the ritual of the glass of tea and the spoonful of cherry jam was achieved, he was persuaded to talk of Siberia. Again, of those wastes by which he knew me to be possessed.

But now he told how they were streaked by long lines of émigrés, dispossessed White Russians, who fell back, retreating day by day farther East, before the Red tide. They trudged, came in carts, on horseback, or however they could. The Trans-Siberian's last run east had been in 1917, but the dispossessed had struggled on for years, across this landscape of desolation. The little Siberian towns never offered much, except space – and quiet: in some, you could hear your watch ticking in the main street at noon, it was so still; and so dull that anyone receiving a telegram was expected to circulate it as reading matter – distraction. Puddles as big as ponds, lowering skies, dust or mud, a fly-blown shop or two, a little green-domed church and a street lined with ramshackle wooden houses dominated by one yellow-plastered building, the police headquarters: such was the scene. Now the *gendarmerie* stood empty, its doors flapping, the Imperial eagle, its symbol of authority, defaced by some passing band of liberated convicts.

The new order took a long while to reach Siberia; at that time, it was still forming in Moscow. Meanwhile, the dispossessed were still moving eastwards; their ranks decimated by famine or typhus. Some fell by the way, some stayed: Generals turned keepers of slipshod wayside inns, their daughters plying for hire among the flotsam of adventurers, Chinese merchants, or the ragged, untamed bands of former prisoners that the Revolution had freed but who had not yet been organized or utilized by the new Russia. Some of the émigrés reached China and the outer world with their jewels, obtained Nansen passports and a new life. Some reached the frontiers with nothing, to become taxi-drivers, or waiters, or just princes, bringing that rank to an almost professional status. These Russians were the first of that legion of émigrés who were to become the twentieth century's problem and shame: displaced persons whose lot we have now become accustomed to accept as inevitable.

'The emigration – the mass exodus of the immediate post-war period – was a unique chapter in Russian history,' wrote the Grand Duchess Marie Pavlovna. The exiles fled North – to Finland; East – to Siberia and beyond. Over a million made that particular migration. They went westward, too, to the Polish frontier and South to the Black Sea, and Turkey. Military and civilians were evacuated together. Chaos, despair, bewilderment, disease and terror – these were the exiles' lot. A British cruiser took off the Dowager Empress Marie Feodorovna and her suite. Suddenly there were three hundred thousand sick and destitute Russians flooding into Constantinople. English, French and American Missions struggled to relieve the misery. Epidemics raged, typhus took hold. Spanish influenza decimated the exhausted masses, who lacked food, clothing, shelter... The Traveller told of all this.

In 1920, the last stand of anti-Bolshevik forces was crushed in the Caucasus and the Crimea. Now, entire military units streamed into Turkey; sixty thousand or more of these battered and hopeless men were evacuated to Gallipoli alone. Cholera spread. Those who survived were centred round General Wrangel who, with his disbanded Kuban Cossacks, held firm beside them throughout the time they were waiting to be absorbed into the Balkan countries, or to scrape a living farther afield. All of them now fought new, more bitter battles of unemployment and disillusion. Groups of men from the same regiment would find work as a whole unit – as miners or agricultural workers. One such military unit was in Paris, where I was later to know some of them. They retained all the discipline and dash of their regiment, forming colonies, living in barrack-like wooden huts, in the railway yards, working as porters, or freight men.

'As long as they don't become signal-men, or engine drivers,' said the Traveller dourly. He had no faith in his compatriots' mechanical abilities. I have sometimes wondered, since, how he would have responded to the scientific and mechanical triumphs of a later generation of Russians – of Soviet citizens.

~

While one of the Traveller's voices was denouncing the horrors of the Revolution, where, it seemed, many of his friends had perished in terrible circumstances, he spoke glowingly of Revolutionary ideals, and pointedly avoided the society of the more aristocratic émigrés. Those who turned their titles to profit and married, because of them, into security, and flourished, aroused the Traveller's particular fury. One such nobleman had shown a particular understanding of London's credulity, for having wed the daughter of a vastly wealthy man of business, he proceeded to acquire two Russian bodyguards whom he was careful to dress up in dashing Cossack uniform. They accompanied him everywhere and were to be seen standing, with arms folded impressively, behind his chair at dinner parties (one can imagine their effect, below-stairs, on susceptible parlour-maids), or flanking him in his box at the theatre. Such flamboyance, said the Traveller, would have been almost out of place for any Romanov and was certainly nothing to which the prince in question was accustomed in Russia, for he was a minor princeling, mentioned somewhere in the hierarchy of the *Livre de Velours*, though scarcely ranking a Cossack bodyguard. But his effect in London society was electric, which was what he intended, after all.

This was the sort of opportunism against which the Traveller always railed. Such princes and their kind had brought down the country, he said; and he would set-to, attacking the Court and Government for the last hundred years, ranging from the soured glories of Alexander I's last years through the despotism of Nicholas I's reign to Alexander II's abortive liberalism, Alexander III's reactionary rule, and finally, to the cumulative disasters, the inertia and ineptitude of the last Romanov, the irresponsibility of his family circle, and the Court in general. 'Why, the all-powerful top-crust in Russia had no sense of moral obligation, as your landowners possess. They thought only of one thing – their pleasures. It wasn't arrogance – you English have the monopoly of that. You are all born *sahibs*, colonizing the rest of us. No, it was something quite different among the Russians. No laws existed for the princes – only their whims. There were a few exceptions, of course; Prince Kropotkin was one – so was Prince Khilkhov, who once worked as a linesman on your Trans-Sib. But you see why the revolution had to come.'

There was another circle of the Russian emigration to which the Traveller sometimes took me, and where he was generally in a gentler vein. This was the intelligentsia, a shabby, brilliant lot who still believed in liberalism, still quoted Herzen. They congregated in frowzy basements or A.B.C. tea rooms, smoking and coughing furiously. They, just as much as the aristocrats, were survivors from another world: but my obsession, my reading, made it possible for me to follow them a certain distance into their Slav world. They were at home in many languages and cultures and would talk to me of Plato or *Peter Schlemil*, the Golem, and Gamlet, as they pronounced the gloomy Dane. And I would question them about the Russian autocrat who spoke only in verse, and forced his entire household to reply in kind: or the Guards officer who used to walk about St. Petersburg exercising his pet wolf: or I would beg them to recite me some of Lermontov's *Demon*, which theme (the illicit passion of a Dark Spirit for

41

a pearly-pure young girl), I found indescribably romantic. I did not question them on Siberia – that was something apart, between the Traveller and myself.

The exiles displayed a remarkably wide knowledge of the most specialized kinds of English literature, discussing *The Paston Letters*, the works of John Stuart Mill, *Alice in Wonderland* or the Restoration poets. Chatterton they admired particularly, and they spoke of him as a martyr. Perhaps it was the attic death-bed which struck a familiar chord. They talked among themselves in French, but I observed that whenever it was a question of politics (which it was, more often than not) they reverted to their mother tongue, as if no other could express the urgency of this theme. Besides, as the Traveller reminded me, it was always a mark of the best-educated Russians to be able to speak such pure Russian: generally, it was considered chic to speak French and German – English too, proving your nursery had been ruled by an English nanny – the height of snobbery, but Russian was apt to be of the careless, ill-educated kind, culled from the servants, with no great value set upon it.

I was always intrigued by the vitality of their voices, in contrast to their wan faces; yet the barely perceptible play of emotions across these immobile masks lifted the most unintelligible exchanges to the realms of some dramatic spectacle.

Wan or not, they showed extraordinary stamina. Both work and play were attacked with whole-hearted emotion. Their lives were hard. The men scraped along on tutoring or translating; the women took in sewing or worked in small restaurants or private houses. They had reached England at the first moments of its economic upheaval when, after the First World War, the disagreeable phenomenon of a domestic shortage was beginning. English women had tasted economic independence working in munition factories or on the land, and never again would they willingly go back into domestic service. Thus the era of the daily-help dawned. Never again were there to be basements full of ill-considered and unquestioning slaveys (the British version of serfs). Upstairs, distracted housewives struggled to keep up appearances in antiquated, inconvenient houses. In such households, many of the Russian women found work which, in the main, they were as unfitted to do as their employer. But both were glad of the arrangement.

I knew that the Traveller admired the unquenched courage of these émigrés, but he also deplored the intellectuals' inherent political ineffectuality. He enjoyed baiting them, denouncing Tolstoy, and Gorki too, as hypocrites, monstrous *poseurs*. With relish, he would quote Lenin on Tolstoy: 'A Tolstoian is a snivelling, worn-out hysteric known as a Russian intellectual, who beats his breast, publicly announcing that he is bad – disgusting – but that he is working to achieve perfection, having renounced meat in favour of rice.'

This never failed to irritate them, for they generally admired Tolstoy, had renounced meat from motives of economy, and one and all abhorred Lenin. Having scored his point, the Traveller would resume his baiting, condemning writers who engaged in politics.

'Tolstoy, the seigneur of Yasnaya Polyana – Gorki, enjoying the view of the Bay of Naples – both of them carrying-on about political and agrarian reforms? Bah! Neither of them meant a word they wrote by the end... when the soap-box had taken over. *Littérature engagée*. It ruined them as artists. It always does. "The meaning of poetry should be poetry – nothing more," as Pushkin said. Politics are not a fit subject for literature.'

He was impatient of the interminable political discussions which were the intelligentsia's breath of life, and had no sympathy with those of them who saw the Revolution as a temporary state of affairs, or those others who planned to follow Marshal Pilsudski on his white horse, riding into Russia, believing they would reconquer it for themselves.

He saw very clearly that the Russia he had known had vanished, but that another would one day emerge triumphantly he did not seem to doubt. While he knew it would in no way resemble the world he had known, he believed profoundly in the strength of the Russian people, in their great destiny. Waxing mystical he would sometimes pace up and down the school-room, quoting Dostoievsky, who claimed that on the brow of each *moujik* the Archangel of the Apocalypse had inscribed the destiny of the world. And then, forgetting his condemnation of writers who involved themselves in politics, he would strike attitudes worthy of André Chenier, to thunder out Dostoievsky's visionary speech at the unveiling of the Pushkin memorial: 'Beyond all doubt the destiny of a Russian is pan-European and universal. To become a true Russian, to become a Russian fully, means only to become, if you will, a universal man... our destiny is universality, not by the sword, but by our fraternal aspiration to unite mankind...'

Swept along by such fervour, I acquired *Pages from the Journal of an Author*, in which Dostoievsky's tribute is included; heady reading for the school-room, but naturally I absorbed my politics, like all my tastes, via the Traveller. I think the habits of a self-indulgent life had caused him to remain faithful to the outward patterns of a vanished world; but I had the impression that each time he reappeared from one of his unexplained absences, or disappearances, he was further from that easy way of life he had first known, and nearer to the newer one then forming far beyond our own periphery.

~

Returning to the gentle ambiance of my mother's hearth, so far from politics and worldly preoccupations, he would speak contemptuously of 'the decaying remnants of a corrupt Byzantine Court', meaning the handful of sad Romanov relatives and their suites, gathered round the Dowager Empress Marie Feodorovna, then staying with her sister, Queen Alexandra, the Queen Mother, at Marlborough House. The doings of the more princely Russian refugees were much discussed in London at that time, on account of the British Royal family's ties with the Romanovs, and I would pore over photographs of them, in *The Tatler*. After the Dowager Empress and her daughter, the Grand Duchess Marie Pavlovna and her brother the Grand Duke Dimitri headed the Imperial circle, while the Yussoupovs and many others close to the Imperial family had not yet transplanted themselves to Paris.

Those Russian Charity Bazaars which plunged me in such acquisitive frenzies were also in the nature of elaborate social functions, for now increasing numbers of the Russian nobility were to be seen there conspiring with their British peers to raise money for needy compatriots. While spending my pocket-money recklessly, borrowing far ahead to acquire any Russian trifle, I would stare hungrily at the bearers of historic names – names that were bound up with their country. A little *piroshki*, or pie, and a glass of syrupy *kvass* from the refreshment stall presided over by one of the several Galitzin Princesses seemed sacred to me, a sort of Communion bread and wine: although, for the sake of historic continuity, I could have wished it had been a Menshikov, rather than a Galitzin hand from which I took my *piroshki*. Had not the first Prince Menshikov begun as a pie-seller, and risen to glory as Peter the Great's statesman? From my *piroshki*, to those faraway ones, by way of a descendant's hand would have held an especial meaning for me.

So, steeped in Russia's past, I ignored its stupendous present, concerning myself little with history then in the making, with Rasputin, the Ipatiev house at Ekaterinburg, the Cruiser Aurora, Admiral Kolchak's betrayal by the Czech and French Commanders, famines, Five Year Plans, Lenin's rule, or any other landmark of Russia's fall and rise.

I moved in an imagined limbo-land, chasing souvenirs – *memento mori*.

PART TWO

Gallantry Bower

In matters of affection the Russians are the gentlest wild beasts that are to be seen on earth, and their well-concealed claws unfortunately divest them of none of their charms.

de Custine

CHAPTER FOUR

I was seventeen when I first saw Paris, owing this, like so many other perspectives, to the Traveller. It seemed that he owned an apartment there, filled with his furniture and the accumulation of many years' wandering. It was generally let, but now he was inhabiting it himself and, having briefly come to a standstill, he wrote to my mother saying it would be good for me to spend my Easter holidays there; and so, rather in the manner of the chattel which I was to him, my family duly dispatched me, with Mademoiselle Lavisse, the small beetle-black figure who had coached me so inadequately and who still sniffed incessantly. Except for some years in London she had never left Dieppe and knew no more of Paris than I, but she had stipulated we should stay at a small hotel in the Rue de l'Arcade run by an old friend of hers. To this, the Traveller had been obliged to agree.

When our train steamed to a standstill at the Gare du Nord he was waiting for us at the barrier with two bouquets. Mademoiselle had resisted the whole project, being profoundly suspicious of the Traveller, but now appeared mollified. The Traveller was one of those rewarding men who can, on occasions, display deep emotions in public. Now his usually inscrutable Tartar face betrayed him. He was flatteringly, touchingly delighted to see me; I thought there were tears in his narrowed eyes as we embraced.

'Pussinka moiya!' he said. 'At last!' But almost at once, those same narrowed eyes fixed coldly on my hat, a rather pretty straw one – hats were still worn, then. Tearing it from my head he flung it on the ground, kicking it down on to the rails as a passing porter attempted to return it to me.

'Never let me see you in a hat again!' he said, stroking my ruffled hair which he admired. Mademoiselle glared, the softening effect of the bouquet considerably lessened. Eschewing a taxi, the Traveller piled us into a *fiacre*, the kind that still existed in Paris at that time.

'I knew you'd want to ride in a *fiacre*,' he said, and began whistling Yvette Guilbert's song of that name which so enchanted my parents when she gave her rare recitals in London. He launched into the words, eyeing Mademoiselle mischievously. They were not the sort of thing she cared to hear and, in retaliation, she declined his invitation to stop for an apéritif at a café under the chestnut trees. At which the Traveller, getting into his stride for the battle that these two were to wage for the rest of the holiday, countered by ordering the coachman to draw up just short of a small mysterious-looking iron-work structure into which most of him now disappeared.

'*Toutes mes excuses, Mesdemoiselles,*' he said politely, on rejoining us. 'Nature is so inconsiderate.'

Outrage was expressed by every angle of Mademoiselle's rigid form; it gathered on her face, and was to remain there for the rest of our stay in Paris.

Her real reason for selecting the meek-looking little hotel in the Rue de l'Arcade was soon apparent. Not only was it kept by an old friend, but it was within sight of the Chapelle Expiatoire, a dank-looking building in the Greco-Roman style, quite unsuited to its surroundings, but which commemorates the first burial place of the unfortunate King Louis XVI and his Queen. As an ardent Royalist, this melancholy monument was an object of special veneration to Mademoiselle and her friend, the proprietress of the hotel. My first outing, next morning, was to accompany them when they laid a hideous wreath at this shrine: however I managed, with the Traveller's connivance, to insist on a counter-outing to the cemetery at Montparnasse to lay a much prettier bunch of flowers on the grave of Muraviev – Count Muraviev-Amursky, Governor General of Siberia; he who acquired the Amur provinces from China, and whose name is for ever linked with the development of Siberia.

'A nice mark of respect,' said the Traveller, lingering purposefully when Mademoiselle fretted. 'We were always given to such gestures in Russia. I remember old-fashioned people in Irkutsk used to take off their hats, or bow, when passing Muraviev's statue. And in an earlier generation schoolboys were taught to speak of Great Novgorod, one of our most historic towns, as "*Sir* Great Novgorod."' But Mademoiselle was not charmed by such snippets of nationalism. Russia was an anathema to her, every manifestation an aspect of the Devil, barbarism incarnate, the Red Peril.

Although she was a stranger to Paris, she had drawn up a formidable programme for us. Notre Dame, the Louvre, the Jardin des Plantes, Versailles, the Invalides (in spite of her Royalist views) and the Panthéon were only a beginning. The Conciergerie was a harrowing outing, from the Salle des Pas Perdus to a hushed vigil in the cell occupied by Marie-Antoinette prior to her execution. Then there was the Sainte Chapelle and the Chambre des Députés, the Madeleine, and the Sacré Coeur at Montmartre, where the Traveller suggested we should also visit the cemetery.

'What about Heine's grave? You might lay another wreath there too. You seem to be getting the habit. He's someone worth remembering, German or no. While you're about it why not take a picnic lunch? The Turks spend whole days in their cemeteries, eating, sleeping, making love...'

I was kicking him under the table, fearful he would go on to recount how, in earlier times, the prostitutes of Constantinople used the cemeteries of Khassim-Pacha as a place of assignation and business... It was one of his more lurid tales and frowned-on by my parents. But for once, he was discreet and returned to safer topics.

~

In drawing up her programme, Mademoiselle had not reckoned with the Traveller, who instantly imposed or irradiated an Asiatic ambiance wherever he went. He knew Paris very well and it was not his fault, but rather his force, that I could only see the city as a frame for his compatriots, those strange and fascinating Russian exiles who were then centred there in their thousands, bringing with them their own special climate of inertia and violence, their legends and way of life, all with far more colour, it seemed, than in London, where they appeared damped-down. In Paris they adapted more easily, but they were not truly absorbed. No Slav, I think, can be truly integrated outside the Slav perimeter. Basically they remained untouched – uncorrupted, perhaps, by Western civilization, which they simulate, superimposing this simulation like a carapace, on their more vulnerable Slav selves. This was something I had not analyzed at the time, but I was aware of it subconsciously in the Traveller, and now I sensed it in his friends. There is an unaccountable element which lies below the surface in all Russians; it is a darkness or depth peculiarly their own. Perhaps it is the Asiatic in their blood; in any case, it remains mysterious to the west, and it is the Russians' especial strength; another dimension into which they retreat at will.

Everything about them fascinated me; the lives they lived in Paris; the lives they had lived in Russia, the dramatic stories of their escapes, and the stories of other, earlier Russians who had known Paris under other circumstances; Turgeniev, for ever sighing over Pauline Viardot, installed as a cuckoo in the Viardot nest; Tolstoy, fleeing from the seductions of a street-walker; Herzen and Bakunin deep in revolutionary ideology.

It was useless for Mademoiselle to tell me about Clovis, and his victories: I wanted to hear about the Tzar Alexander I and his generals meeting with Wellington and Blücher – Allied conquerors, in a conquered city. I could only see the city subjectively, in relation to the Russia of which the Traveller told me. Therefore, the expeditions I most enjoyed were those which took us about the streets, tracing scenes associated with the triumphant sojourn of the Russian armies there in 1814. Under Blücher, Barclay de Tolly, the Baltic Russian, and numerous princes of the allied staff, Paris was stormed. Montmartre fell to the Generals Kaptsievitch and Batsievitch who drove off 40,000 French and 150 cannon under Marmont and Mortier. On March 31st – 'Today is the anniversary,' the Traveller reminded me – the city capitulated.

When the victors entered Paris the curious-looking Russian army came by way of the Bonne Nouvelle Boulevard and the Porte St. Denis, the Tzar Alexander I at their head. And now, standing below the massive Porte, I listened to the Traveller describing the little shaggy horses of the steppes pulling supply wagons and gun-carriages, and the cavalry – some of the riders equally shaggy, in their fur caps and sheepskin paddings, with the flat-nosed, narrow-eyed countenance of the north, so that to the French crowds watching apprehensively, they seemed some barbarian horde come from the Great Wall of China or beyond.

There were men from all the Russias; Ukrainians, Kalmucks, Kirghiz, and Tungus tribes from Siberia carrying bows and arrows; Circassian chieftains with pointed helmets and chain mail, and Cossacks with fur caps and long lances such as the guard of honour which escorted General Osten-Sacken, the newly appointed Military Governor of Paris. He took little heed of appearances, and rode proudly enough in an equipage harnessed with ropes. But some of the young officers were dandiprat figures, with jewelled swords and sumptuous furs lining their cloaks; most of them wore their hair long, on to their epauletted shoulders, in a manner which seemed medieval to the fashion-conscious French.

Among these exotic figures were not only the nucleus of those idealistic hotheads who, eleven years later, were to become known as the Dekabristi (or Decembrists), making their heroic, if muddle-headed stand for a Constitution, but another, most remarkable figure, a Kalmuck prince who raised his own regiment to fight beside the Russians, and who commanded his Kalmuck hordes when they bivouacked along the Champs Elysées beside the Cossack regiments. The Asiatic prince had created quite a sensation in Paris, especially among the *ton*, and was a change from the blackamoor pages of the *ancien régime*. He had been painted by Isabey. The Traveller told me that, to the French portraitist, all Kalmucks were indistinguishable; the Prince or his orderly were both flat-faced, slant-eyed, with wide mouths and an impassive expression. When the Prince became restive at sittings, Isabey suggested his orderly should be substituted; and, on completion, the Prince's portrait was pronounced a striking likeness.

At that moment, to the 800,000 Parisians, there were 150,000 foreign troops about the capital, so that it appeared some huge military encampment, set down among the grandiose or the frivolous. Along the Champs Elysées, Russian army tents and Asiatic *kibitkas* were side by side under the budding chestnut trees, and this vast throng spread as far as the Porte Maillot. At Passy some of them had invaded a decorator's shop, for on seeing a screen of *papier peint* with a most life-like representation of a forest glade, they were about to seize it for firewood, when the proprietor was able to turn their attention to the near-by Bois de Boulogne, which suited their purpose better.

'Father Paris, you shall now pay for Mother Moscow,' said the troops; but they were good-natured in their victory, and proved themselves easy-going conquerors. The French soon forgot their dread, dubbing them *bons enfants*, preferring them to the German and English troops. Many women found them irresistible, and the young officers (generally a most cultivated lot, lusty for museums, picture galleries and new ideas) also led rackety lives, snatching at the proverbial pleasures of Paris. Between easy duties at their Grenelle headquarters, and the seductions of the Palais Royal, the opera, tête-à-tête suppers at Tortoni's, or even more generously expressed hospitality in the alcoves of the Faubourg, they savoured the pleasures of conquest while the ranks made as merry with the maidservants. But then, said the Traveller, all women like to be conquered.

At which Mademoiselle Lavisse snorted. She insisted on accompanying us everywhere, but rather in the spirit of a captive, attached to our chariot wheels, I told the Traveller.

'Precisely. She enjoys being conquered too, in another way. Such women make the happiest martyrs. Misery becomes quite a hobby with them.'

Rubbing salt in her wounds (or indulging her?), the Traveller now dwelt on the Tzar Alexander I's magnanimities. He had not wished to impose himself on Paris as a tyrant.

'Fear nothing,' ran his Proclamation to the citizens. 'Fear not for your money, nor your public buildings, your private houses or families.' ('Showing the proper order of things for the French,' muttered the Traveller, in an audible aside.) 'I take the capital under my protection,' ran the Tzar's words. 'I have no enemies in France – or only one, Napoleon – and he no longer reigns... I come to bring you peace.'

'After which, no one called us barbarians,' concluded the Traveller, and Mademoiselle appeared too stricken to argue.

~

Wherever we went, whatever we saw in Paris, the unfortunate Frenchwoman fought a losing battle to wean me from my Russian preoccupation, for walking along the noblest streets, confronted by the most grandiose vistas, my inner ear still listened to the sound of horses' hooves... those shaggy little blunt-nosed horses of the Tzar Alexander's army: men and horses from the steppes... the longed for, unattainable steppes.

'You remind me of the bird that flew backwards to see where it was coming from,' said the Traveller fondly.

It was Russia, Russia all the way. The Pont Neuf paled beside the Pont Alexandre III, while a matinée at the Comédie Française, *Phèdre*, I believe, was completely spoiled for me, by hearing that the Pitóievs had just opened in a Chekhov play. However, both Diaghilev and Rachmaninov were among the Traveller's circle, and once or twice Diaghilev, or Sergei Pavlovitch as he was to the Traveller, allowed us, O rapture! O rare privilege! to attend a rehearsal, flattened in the wings. But Mademoiselle Lavisse was never allowed beyond the stage door, and would be compelled to sit there for hours, not unnaturally sulking. The

Sakharovs, Alexandre and Clotilde too, sketched out their stylized dances for the Traveller's opinion, dancing to Fauré and Bach. Komisarjevsky presently joined this eclectic band, with projects for a production of an Ostrovsky play; and when Chaliapin appeared, and none of these lofty personalities seemed to object to the presence of a gaping school-girl in their midst, I was able to savour, first-hand, some of the greatest aspects of Russian theatrical genius. It was transplanted in its full bloom and, for a while, it did not wither.

Once I sat beside the Traveller when Rachmaninov was persuaded to play for his friends. He was always surrounded by compatriots. I cannot breathe without them, he would say. In his house at Rambouillet he had recreated the pattern of Russian country-house life. Here, when he was not shut away with his music, he would melt, play tennis and eat quantities of Russian delicacies, as a circle of friends and family gathered round the eternal pivot-point – a samovar. When he played, the strange stone mask never softened, never moved a muscle, as he stormed a Chopin *étude*, evoked some sad song from the Black Sea, or a Bach *toccata*.

In a more frivolous vein there was Nikita Balieff, whose family life was quite as stylized as his Chauve-Souris theatre, and Vertinsky, who was then enthralling the *boîtes de nuit* of Berlin and Paris with his craking voice and air of a disillusioned pierrot. And then there was Ivan Mosjukhine, the arch seductor of his moment, Mosjukhine of the silent screen – of countless heroes, Kean, Casanova, or the Courier of the Tzar. I only saw his films much later. But the seducer, in the flesh, I once saw at close quarters. He was in Paris to make a film there and, in the Traveller's rooms, I sat watching the drama, the melodrama, rather, these two Slavs conjured up. Both their faces were perfectly expressionless, yet both produced an overwhelming climate of emotion. The Traveller, with his flat-planed yellow face and slit eyes; Mosjukhine, paper-white, with his long nose, enormous, almond-shaped eyes, and his air at once dissipated and tragic, as if taunted by his own Casanova legend. They were flung back on the low Turkish divans which ran round the room; beside them, the samovar, humming comfortably; above them, one of the many glittering, silver-cased ikons which studded the walls. Tradition, superstition and religious observance were all things against which the Traveller railed, yet he remained captive to them.

Together he and Mosjukhine were partial to discussing the state of the French theatre – *pourri*, they said furiously – rotten through and through. After which they would turn to the hopelessness of life in general. They usually talked in French, so I was able to follow their almost voluptuous indulgence in the pure misery of existence... Then there was *tosca*, spleen, something which cropped up regularly in conversations between Russians, I noticed, like *dousha*, the soul. After which, it was the body's turn, and they went on to compare their respective livers and other organs, all of which, they agreed, were *complètetment pourris*.

I thought the Traveller's rooms the most extraordinary I had ever seen. Now for the first time I saw him in a frame of his own choosing: the dark, yet burning blue or crimson walls (like those of an old Russian *traktir*, or wayside inn, he explained) were hung with primitive prints of peasants hunting bears, or falling drunk from troikas plunging over the snows. The furniture was a mixture of Turkish and austere Russian Empire pieces in pale golden Karelian birch, while the squat little Turkish coffee-tables were encrusted with mother-of-pearl. The floor was padded with rugs, crisscrossed, and overlapping each other in that lavish manner I was later to associate with mosques.

The Traveller was never moderate in his tastes: it was a lot, or nothing. 'What's the matter with a lot?' he would say, jibing at my father's rather austere sense of decoration – one Persian rug and one Chinese bowl at a time. Some of his finest rugs continued up from the floor to surge across the divans in waves of colour. His favourite corner was massed with Daghestani carpets, upon which he had boldly imposed gros-point cushions of riotous Victorian roses, parrots and beadwork spaniels. Beside the samovar was a bronze and enamel Chinese opium pipe. This never failed to upset Mademoiselle Lavisse, who would purse her lips every time she saw it.

'Aspirin for you – opium for me, it's all one and the same really,' the Traveller would remark mockingly, at which she would take her revenge by saying it was time for us to leave: La Sainte Chapelle must be visited without further delay. She hurried me off before the Traveller could enlarge on his suggestion to visit the Musée Cluny, 'where all those mediaeval *ceintures de chasteté* are not to be missed... Come back for tea, and I'll tell you some amusing stories about them' was his passing shot.

~

In Paris, on that first unforgettable visit, the Traveller was to fulfil a long-held promise to take me to the midnight Russian Easter Mass. So, warming-up, on the last two Sundays before the Russian Easter which fell, that year, eighteen days after ours, the Traveller took me with him to the Cathedral of St. Alexander Nevski in the Rue Daru. 'Not that I hold with any of this white magic,' he said, as he bent to kiss the ikons. Each time he gave me a candle to light, and carried three himself; for whom, or what, I never knew. Together we would watch them flickering among the forest of other little flames lit by love and faith. Then, transported into the very heart of my longings, of the Traveller's Tales, I would stand beside him, rapt, listening for the first time to the sombre chants of Bortniansky or Turchaninov as they rolled upwards into the golden cupolas, piercing the bluish, incense-laden air, sung by voices as veiled, as smoky as the air itself. Here there were no mighty thunders of organ music, no disembodied flutings of boy choristers, but something simpler, warmer, the voices of men and women, earthly beings aspiring to their God with that mystical yet intimate fervour possessed by orthodox worshippers.

Such veiled, yet vital tones only issue from Slav throats. Or rather from Slav bellies. For while the French seem to sing through their noses, and the English through their teeth (the Italians, it must be admitted, singing straight from their lungs), only Russian voices issue directly from their guts – from their bellies and their hearts – like some centrifugal life-force, springing from the earth itself. Turgeniev has written of this quality of nationalism in Russian voices, describing the village singer Yakov, in a tavern competition: 'He sang, and each note breathed an inexpressible quality of nationality, of vast spaces; it was as if the steppe unfolded before us in all its infinity... A true, ardent Russian soul sounded there, and went straight to your heart...'

So they sang in the Cathedral, their melancholy eyes fixed on some remembered past, crossing themselves in a strangely urgent fashion, their fingers closed, as if plucking out their own hearts; and while the incense thickened headily, the candles guttered before the miraculous ikons, and the exiles prostrated themselves in supplication and acceptance.

For me, it was the affirmation of all my longings, the body and soul of Russia, and when we emerged into the emptied Sunday streets I felt myself an exile, too. The Traveller lingered to talk with the priests, sinister-looking figures, with their long hair and pepper-and-salt beards, or the black-wimpled nuns in their high *kloba* or headpieces, who might all have issued from some low-vaulted chapel of Ivan the Terrible's Kremlin. As he moved among the little groups of shabby, worn-faced men who gathered in the courtyard of the church, they all seemed to know him; I thought, perhaps, to fear him too; it was difficult to penetrate the Slav mask – his, or theirs. Even among these massed faces, so unmistakably un-European in both their ugliness and beauty, his seemed more quintessentially Asiatic.

In my nursery he had appeared the strangest-looking person I had ever seen, and, in memory, he remains so. I associated him with the illustrations to my *Arabian Nights*. The Chinaman's traditional pigtail and long wispy moustaches were missing but otherwise he resembled the djinn who vanished in a puff of smoke. Indeed his comings and goings always had a quality of magic about them.

But that Easter in the Rue Daru, watching him among the flotsam of strangeness washed up on this narrow Russian strand, I was suddenly aware of him as a person, a man, rather than the djinn of my childhood. Was it that I had grown older, or did he seem younger? In my nursery he had appeared a remote, even ancient figure, by reason of his egg-bald skull. In London, baldness had seemed a symbol of age. Yet here I saw numbers of bald or shaven pates having no connection with the years, but being rather the mark of many military men, or even some Asiatic religious organizations. For while all Orthodox priests wore their hair and beards flowing, there were, at that moment, a group of Russians who had arrived from Outer Mongolia, where they had been part of a militant-monastic order which imposed shaven heads. Some of these men were known to the Traveller, and watching him among them I now saw him truly, for the first time: a man in his forties, with something taut in his bearing. This I had not sensed before, for at home or in my nursery he was always sprawling on sofas or lounging in my rocking-chair in boneless abandon. Seeing the way the émigrés treated him, with this mixture of deference and perhaps even something of fear – seeing the way the men spoke to him, and the manner in which the women looked at him, I now became aware of him as a stranger – as a man. It was most disturbing.

I felt that I had spied on him unawares, catching the man beneath the Traveller's mask, and with a sense of impropriety, or intrusion, I turned away, to stare, once again, avidly, at the curves of the bulbous cupolas and the golden crosses high above me, trying to imprint them, for ever, on my mind's eye. I could not tell then that I should come to know them later, in their true setting, soaring above Rastrelli's churches, reflected in the still waters of the Don, or rising, lonely, from the steppes. Lovingly, I traced the swell of the domes, finding them indescribably beautiful; they rose up, like the fabulous fire-bird of Slav legend, confounding the bourgeois desolation of Baron Haussmann's Paris, which at once, and for ever, chilled me by its immutable French logic. Then, suddenly, the Traveller was at my side.

'Enough talking. Eating now, although according to the Church we ought to be fasting.' And he took me off to some tiny overcrowded Russian bistro for cabbage soup and poppy-seed cakes.

'The word *bistro* is Russian – it means hurry – quick,' he explained. 'Our troops brought it with them when we occupied Paris.' Once again, a tinge of unmistakable pride sounded in the smoky voice.

Although he was international in his way of life and Tartar in his remote ancestry, he was in essence, the most supremely Slav being imaginable. I use the word Slav rather than Russian, for how to define or pin down the prototype of this race which is the blend of a hundred different peoples from the Arctic to the Black Sea, from Poland to China? And just as he seemed a conglomerate of all these peoples, belonging wholly to no one of them, so he was impossible to place in any one milieu; too luxurious for a revolutionary – too cynical, also. Too active for an intellectual; too realistic, too openly in revolt, too free of all conventions for an aristocrat; and far too adventurous for a bourgeois. He was impossible to classify. There was something of each in him, besides an inertia recalling, at its worst, Goncharov's Oblomov, who rotted on a sofa; at its best, his immobile moods recalled the withdrawals of a Buddhist priest. Each aspect of his character contradicted or constrained the other.

Constraint is perhaps not a word to be applied to him, for he was entirely free. But secretive to a theatrical degree. Secrecy, with him, was a fine art, something he enjoyed practising for its own sake. The most devious motives of the Asiatic mind were understood by him and he attributed them to everyone else, adducing cunning labyrinths of behaviour to the simplest of his Anglo-Saxon friends: this they could not grasp and were often hurt by his seeming mistrust. But to take anybody on their face value would have been, for him, an insult to both his own intellect and the nature of his opponent – for he saw everybody, except perhaps myself and my mother, as a real or potential adversary. On the whole it was a mark of respect. English simplicity always baffled him. 'They're fools or hypocrites – there's no other explanation,' he would say.

He was proud of his Tartar blood. *Tartarskaya krov* was, it seemed, particularly recherché (like Red Indian blood in America). The Tartars had gradually become the rulers, the new aristocracy of Russia, he said. They had brought the power instinct, and a touch of perfidy besides, to the simpler Russian character. The Tartar princes were forcibly converted to Orthodoxy, but bided their time. Gradually, the great Boyar families intermarried with them, becoming Yussoupovs, Ourousoffs, Tchegodaievs and such. The Tartar strain was all-powerful; it is still to be traced in those high-cheekboned, flat-nosed, slant-eyed features so often regarded as typically Russian, by the west.

All this I found infinitely romantic. It fitted in with my snow-storm vision of an archetypal landscape, where Pushkin's Dubrovsky, and the Tzar Saltan, the nuns of the Novodievitchi Convent, the Hetman Platoff, and Yermak the Conqueror of Siberia were massed together beside Tolstoy's Prince Andrei on the steps of the Kremlin, chanting something from *Boris Goudenov*. Then, in a perverse mood, the Traveller would bait me, quoting the Marquis de Custine's *Voyage en Russie en 1839*, of which I possessed an early copy, but seldom read, detesting its carping tone: '*Savez-vous ce que c'est de voyager en Russie? Pour un esprit léger, c'est de se nourrir d'illusions...*'

'You have those illusions, Pussinka, though your *esprit* is not really *léger* as regards Russia... but you are wilfully romantic. I don't know how you are going to reconcile the lot when you do get there. You must realize that what you choose to imagine, and what is, are far apart. You see yourself driving about the countryside in one of those old-fashioned back-to-back carriages – a *dolgoushka* – or dashing from one golden-domed city to another in Tchitchikov's *britchka*, scarcely drawing rein, because you have an Imperial *padoroshna* – that's an equally out-of-date laissez-passer for fresh relays of horses. Let me tell you, only something as remote as a *padoroshna* could transport you to the realms you imagine. Today's visas – when you get them – will only show you today. And that won't tally with your mind's eye, Miss.'

And he would quote de Custine again, maddeningly apposite – '"*ces deux nations... la Russie telle qu'elle est, la Russie telle qu'on voudrait la montrer*" – in your case, *telle que vous voulez la voir.*'

There was nothing to be said to that, even if I had been so tactless as to remind him that he too seemed to wish to see Russia in his own, or rather, *our* manner – *telle que nous voulons la voir*.

~

Sometimes, sternly realistic, he took me with him to one of the many unpretentious little clubs run by the exiled White Army officers. These were the remnants of General Wrangel's forces, who lived and worked together in units, keeping much of their military discipline. Their morale remained high. This was a strange and now forgotten milieu I knew briefly. They preserved their regimental emblems, caressing them, carving them, painting them, even working them out in pebbles whenever they set up their camps. Sometimes they contrived a little church, or a modest *popote*, where memories of the old ways of life and thought were kept green. At the time of which I write, when I first encountered them, their lot seemed hard enough, but at that time they still hoped they would return to their own country; that is, to the country they had known. They were not, generally, endowed with political acumen. Few were trained to view political and international horizons in depth. So they still believed in a Holy Russia, a Mother Russia, which would, one day, shelter them again.

Few of the army in exile ever saw better times again. These were not the minority of princely opportunists, the dashing Georgians who stamped through their wild dances at the night-clubs of Pigalle, sometimes spring-boarding off into the arms of besotted heiresses. These were simpler men who, if they knew languages, generally found work in banks or commerce; those who did not usually turned taxi-drivers, and this unmistakable legion were for many years part of the Paris street scene. I write of them now in retrospect, knowing their ultimate decline; but even when I first encountered them, I sensed something of their tragedy. General Wrangel might have been composing their epitaph, when he wrote in his *Memoirs* that at the Unknown Soldier's Grave – the Memorial to the First World War – only the Russian Army was forgotten.

~

The Traveller had many friends among these men, as well as among the more eclectic circle of Russian artists and musicians. He had known them in those first days of exile, in Turkey, and had never lost touch. Now, working their way through plates of *stchee* together, they would recall old times and hold post-mortems on lost battles. 'Listen carefully,' the Traveller admonished me, seeing my attention wander. 'Listen to those men, they are telling history as few will choose to remember it.' So I listened, watching their faces leap to life, listening to their voices deepen with emotion. Unlike the voices of Western races, which tend to grow shrill under stress, Russian voices deepen to further, smokier depths. Always, they returned in indignation to those hushed-up pressures which, in the fateful year of 1919, were applied by the Allies, closing in on a decimated Russia.

While three separate White Russian Armies were opposing the Bolshevik forces, it seemed the Allies had been cynically planning their individual coups, north and south, to obtain ascendancy over the exhausted country. As the internal strife deepened they had watched it through spectacles tinted golden by greed. The British, who had been fighting the Turks in Persia moved north, landed in Baku and took over the fabulously rich oil districts. Batoum was pronounced a 'free' city under a British protectorate which supervised the shipping of oil and raw materials – to Britain. And who was there to stop them? The bewildered, exhausted country appeared to have no means of fighting back. The French sent two divisions to occupy the vital port of Odessa, while their battleships patrolled the Black Sea. The vultures were closing in.

Italians arrived in Tiflis, 'assisting at the formation of an Independent State of Georgia' as this manoeuvre was airily described by their High Command, but no doubt the proximity of the magnesium mines in the North Caucasus was not overlooked. Two Greek divisions next arrived, while there were Roumanians, 'even *Roumanians*' as the Traveller said witheringly, occupying Bessarabia and the Ukraine. A British fleet dominated the Baltic ports where the states of Latvia and Estonia were proclaimed, while American and Japanese troops landed in Vladivostok to 'run' the north. In the spring of 1919, nine independent states were organized on Russian soil and recognized by the Allied powers.

The Russian people found themselves isolated, more isolated than ever, within their separate ethnic groups and geographic boundaries, for now news travelled slowly if at all, impeded by enormous distances, wide rivers and mountains and, often, impenetrable snows. Telegraphic communications had, largely, broken down; the Ukraine did not know

what was happening in Bashkir country, the Caucasus was cut .
Moscow; all information depended on the chance arrival of a mess
As the talkers expanded on this state of affairs my mind would esc.
deliciously, to early and more romantic systems, such as that of tı
Cossack couriers – generally illiterate – who travelled at a speed dictated
by the seals placed on whatever letters they carried. Three pigeon feathers
indicated they must ride by day and night, at the gallop; two feathers, at
the trot; if there were no feathers they could amble along, taking their
time.

The trouble was, said the exiles, nothing had gone according to
plan. Those Bolsheviki were a most obstinate lot: they positively *would* not
collapse in the manner so confidently predicted by both the White Army
generals and the Allied High Command. The obstinate proletarians were
determined to keep their country for themselves.

In April 1920 the Americans pulled out of Vladivostok, and, one by
one, the Allied forces found it expedient to withdraw from the scene of
their operations. The two Greek infantry divisions were routed by
Bolshevik guerrillas. The crew of a French battleship mutinied, the ratings
refusing to fight their own kind – the people – Red Russians or no. Strains
of the Marseillaise sounded ominously from below decks and soon they
sailed for home waters while the French High Command ordered the
evacuation of their land forces. For the White Russians, as for the Reds,
that particular war was over. Now, for both, a new economic war had
begun; in each case, a struggle for survival. In Paris, as once in
Constantinople, General Wrangel stood beside the battered remnants of
his exiled army as they sought work of any kind, to keep themselves from
the ignominy of begging. They were trained soldiers but now they worked
as labourers; on the land, or handling freight, as did a group at the Gare de
la Chapelle, doing pick and shovel work. They accepted whatever they
could find, in France, in the Balkans, the Near East, or whichever countries
would harbour them. Some, more fortunate, formed a dashing cavalry
unit in Syria. In the General's words: 'The Army, not wishing to be a
burden to the countries which gave it a place of refuge, feeds itself by
working, till the day when it will be called to arms to do its duty to its
country.'

Among these lost legions were men from Siberia, who had moved
westwards on various fronts and were at last evacuated from the far

st. Siberian troops were always regarded as the ...withstood every hardship, and their requirements ...hey were usually the last to arrive at the battle ...Australian troops, they came from a great ... –' said the Traveller, admiration lighting his usual

...siberians,' he continued, thinking aloud. 'It's odd that in the war there were so many Siberians, children of those condemned to prison or exile there who had suffered and lost all by the persecutions of the Tzarist régime, children who grew up overshadowed by restrictions, who still flocked to fight in the White Armies, *against* the Reds. For adventure, rather than idealism, I fancy. Warfare broke the monotony of Siberian life.'

It was among these forgotten ranks who waited, and still believed, that I now sat, listening to them talking of Russia – the exiles' Russia, become now a myth, like the legendary city of *Kitej*, the vanished realm of Rimsky-Korsakov's opera, lying beneath the waters of the lake, from where its bells still sometimes sounded for those who loved it, to whom it still sometimes revealed itself, briefly, in all its loveliness. So, it seemed, the exiles saw the country they had lost, but which still gleamed for them, from afar.

CHAPTER FIVE

Mademoiselle Lavisse had been able to observe her own, more sober Easter celebrations well before the Russian ones. Indeed, I had been obliged to accompany her to *Le Temple Anglais* in the Rue Boissy-d'Anglas, where worshipping in tight gloves and a stern hat, in company with the British Ambassador and other members of the English colony, she had felt her duties, as my governess, to be honourably discharged. On the Russian Easter eve, she had been persuaded by the Traveller at his most solicitous not to accompany us to the St. Alexander Nevski service. The spiritual nature of this outing excused its lateness, he convinced her. Moreover, he said, he dreaded the amount of standing it involved for her (in Orthodox churches everyone stands or kneels). But it was the corrupting atmosphere of Orthodoxy, something which as a Protestant she regarded with even more suspicion than Papist rituals, which finally persuaded her, and she had gone to bed early, exhausted by our days of concentrated tourism.

Ten o'clock found the Traveller and myself leaving for the Rue Daru. He had come to fetch me at the hotel and was helping me into my coat. We spoke in whispers, for I think both of us were apprehensive that, at the last moment, Mademoiselle Lavisse would emerge from her room and forbid me to be out so late – even in such devout circumstances.

'One good thing about being an émigré,' he said, hanging his overcoat on his shoulders in his customary cloak-like manner, 'I don't have any more family evenings. Easter used to be an excuse for fearsome gatherings at home – family life at its most suffocating. But being English you don't know about that – you are all so detached.'

'I don't understand: you always say how much you love family life when you come to us.'

'Ah! That's quite different – it's not *my* family life. One must always take care to be the cuckoo in someone else's nest.'

Holding hands, an agreeable childish habit we had never foregone, we watched the bright-lit Paris streets through which our taxi threaded towards the Rue Daru. At the corner of the Rue de la Néva it came to a standstill, for large crowds were converging there making for the Russian Cathedral. At all the windows people were craning to watch the proceedings. Outside the church the crowds had thickened, so that it was some time before we could edge inside to stand among the hushed, exalted throng.

The symbolism of the Russian Orthodox Easter service is profoundly moving. Within the church, all is dark, anguished, still, as priests and people alike await the moment when Christ is risen. We lit our candles and inched our way to leave them before one of the loveliest, oldest of the miraculous ikons. Turning away the Traveller took my arm and began propelling me towards the door.

'We'll wait for the procession outside – you'll see, it's beautiful.' Docile but disappointed, I followed him, burrowing through the crowds, making for the door.

'The procession is what matters most, tonight,' he said, explaining how the circling of the church expressed the hesitation, the doubts of the Disciples, finding Christ vanished from the Sepulchre. Thus, the procession goes to search for Christ outside the walls, and the third time, accepts the miracle, entering again, to proclaim the Resurrection. Yea, verily He is Risen!

As we waited, the night air smelled damp and fresh, the scent of the early lilac in the courtyard overcoming the wafts of incense that floated from the church along with snatches of muffled chanting. At their windows the French householders stood silent, sharing something of the tension. Just before midnight the church doors swung open and in a flood of colour and candlelight the glittering procession emerged to circle the building three times, chanting. The long tapers they carried sparkled on the sumptuous brocaded vestments and the diamond-studded crowns of the Metropolitan and high clergy. Gold-coped priests and acolytes swung censers and carried the banners and ikons, all glowing out from the darkness. At last, with measured tread, grave in their joy, they re-entered the church, there to announce to the waiting throng that Christ was Risen. We heard a sudden burst of singing, rapturous music, and the bells rang out overhead.

Christos Vosskress! Christ is Risen! Yea, verily He is Risen! The crowds joined in the great cry, crossing themselves, prostrating themselves, kissing each other, friends and strangers, each saluted with the triple kisses of the Trinity.

The Traveller and I exchanged such kisses; but as he kissed me, his basalt-dark stare clouded. He held me close, kissing me once again, before turning away, pushing me from him, roughly.

'*The Resurrection kiss! You swore it me!*' He was quoting Pushkin, I knew, for I was familiar with most of the verses which had been translated. These poignant lines were occasioned by the poet hearing of the death of his mistress Amalia Rimich – a bitter outcry of the flesh against the tomb. I wondered why the Traveller spoke those lines now, and of whom he was thinking as he spoke them with such passion, over my head. A wave of vague, undirected jealousy enveloped me. It did not occur to me, then, that perhaps the Traveller was remembering an abstraction – a Russia that had vanished with his youth, when he uttered that bitter farewell: the exile's rather than the lover's cry. 'Gone is the Resurrection kiss! But yet to come: you swore it me!' But such metaphysical suppositions had no place in my reasoning at that moment. And soon, being absorbed by the scene around me, I forgot to be jealous of some imagined creature of flesh and blood, and returned to watching the Easter crowds embracing and congratulating each other as they dispersed to break their fast at the *Rozgoveni* – the traditional feast, a gargantuan spread of *paskha*, *koulitch*, caviare, multi-coloured eggs and much more or less, according to their means. Gradually the streets emptied, the French watchers banged their shutters closed, and the quarter resumed its habitual quiet. The Traveller had been silent, leaning against the railings, his coat collar turned up, his slit eyes staring at nothingness.

'In the old days' – he shrugged – 'as I told you, we should have been caught up in some frightful gathering.'

'But gone to the Gypsies later,' I prompted.

'Are you mad? The tziganes on *Easter* night? They were for other nights... Easter was something quite apart. In Holy Russia we took Easter seriously. Why, no one even made love to their own wives, let alone anyone else's, in Holy Week.'

His face darkened. 'D'you remember Liouba?' he asked, and seemed put out when I looked blank.

'Of course you don't – you couldn't. I forgot. They killed her off before you were born.' He spoke crossly and I felt disgraced. 'Bed for you, Miss,' he snapped, and hailed a passing taxi.

As we drove through the empty streets I ventured to ask why Liouba had been killed.

'None of your business.' He glowered ahead, the slit eyes like dark thread. Abruptly his face changed, lit by one of his most delightfully malicious smiles.

'There are a few of our Tziganes here, you know – they came in from the Balkans. They won't be keeping Easter – except as good business. I think we'll go and find out what they're doing. Shall we?'

'*We?*' I wondered how Mademoiselle would view this further excursion.

'It's educational,' he replied, and giving the taxi-driver (a fellow Russian) an address in Passy, we rattled off to perdition.

In my imagination, the Tziganes were a tawny band of savages, dancing fiercely round the camp fires, strumming guitars, stretched on bear-skins, loving wildly but chastely, nobly, as in Pushkin's *Aleko*, holding proudly to their tribal laws. If, however, they were what I thought of as the *indoor* kind, then, although equally tawny and savage, their setting was some crimson and gold restaurant, all mirrors and chandeliers. But now the foreground of this glittering scene was filled with even wilder figures. Here, Hussars drank from the satin slippers of beautiful ballerinas. Mysteriously masked men, still retaining their heavy, sable-lined overcoats, called for champagne, and more champagne, flinging bank notes in the air and, maddened by the music of the Tziganes, forced their mistresses to dance naked on the tables, while, equally maddened, the Tziganes broke their guitars and fiddles over each other's heads and rushed out into the snowstorm, leaving the *débauchés* to challenge each other to duels or blow out their brains. All this to the strains of *The Two Guitars*.

It was inevitable, then, that the unpretentious night club at which we now arrived should seem an anti-climax. I had never been to one before and I stumbled across the small darkened room with a faint sense of disappointment. The Traveller explained that he preferred this place because the particular Tziganes who performed here were worth all the rest of the already corrupted groups who were hired by more elegant establishments.

'That lot get themselves up in fancy dress – shiny satin *roubashkas*, shinier every year – and sing the sort of songs the French public like. These are different. You'll see.' He ordered *blini* for both of us, and warned the waiter to reserve me a double portion of *paskha* which he knew, with prophetic accuracy, would be my favourite food for evermore. Vodka and champagne now materialized; 'but no vodka for you, Miss,' he said, downing several tiny glasses in rapid succession and making short work of some *piroshki*.

'How d'you find the champagne?' he asked, his tone implying that I was at least knowledgeable, if not a connoisseur, instead of tasting it for the first time, as he very well knew.

'We had a saying in Russia,' he went on. 'One cannot live without champagne and Tziganes. And another: Only he who loves a Tzigane knows Paradise... I know – I loved one once, and Paradise it was – at a price. Tziganes are an expensive hobby. You're better off in England with pets. More champagne?' He bent forward to refill my glass.

Sipping with what I hoped was a negligent air, I began to think more kindly of my surroundings. Even the Niagara-like flow of a too adjacent W.C. did not dispel the waxing glow of dissipation which now seemed to illuminate the scene. It was, I thought, quite extraordinary how often the French seemed to need the lavatory. Wherever I went, in restaurants or cafés, I always observed a line of men, either buttoning or unbuttoning, perpetually hurrying past, colliding with waiters and blocking the narrow space between the tables. At this night club there did not seem to be a 'Ladies' marked anywhere, and I realized I would have to brazen it out, taking my place in the line, or 'manage', as Nanny used to say. In the England of my childhood, the lavatory was something to which we went or from which we emerged as inconspicuously as possible, a sharp, dividing line for the sexes.

'No thanks, I'm quite all right,' I replied, in answer to the Traveller's solicitous inquiries as to my needs.

'No, you're not – you can't be, it's hours since we left the hotel,' he said firmly. 'You'd better go and get it over. And,' he added impressively, 'the sooner you learn not to be fussy about that sort of thing the quicker you'll be able to stand the kind of Asiatic travels you're after! You'll have to do without the "Ladies" if you ever get to Outer Mongolia.'

I needed no second bidding.

When I returned the Tziganes were filing in and taking their places on a bench against the wall. They bore no resemblance to the wild creatures I had imagined. Although they were tawny skinned, with ink-dark hair, they were neither picturesque nor romantic looking. There were no bear-skins, no tambourines, no gaudy kerchiefs. The women wore shawls over their dresses; the men were unshaven, without collars, in dark, everyday suits, entirely without magic I thought, until I became aware of a compelling, animal force beneath the sullen mask.

The Russians in the room were now applauding their arrival and crying out for the songs they wanted to hear. The Tziganes remained immobile, staring straight in front of them.

'Poor things, they'd be better off in Montparnasse, they hate Passy,' said the Traveller, 'but they stay here because of the Grand Duke. They're waiting for him now; he usually comes in about this time.'

It was difficult to imagine any connection between the etiolated, sad-faced man to whom I had once been presented, and this rough-looking lot. I did not know that he retained here, in Paris, something of his former, St. Petersburg style, however reduced, combining his pleasure in the Tziganes' music with his patronage, which sustained them, and finally set them up in the little restaurant where we now found ourselves. In effect, the Tziganes had become his private orchestra; more wholly his, in exile, than when he had known them in his Imperial splendour.

Across the soupy darkness the Tziganes had recognized the Traveller and now came crowding round our table, greeting him with warmth. They stared at me with their unblinking black-blazing eyes, and then, smiling, showed wolfish white teeth, so that I had the impression they were in fact laughing at me. Probably they were: in my school-girlish pink dress I must have looked out of place. But they were very polite, bowing and asking what 'the *barishnaya*' – the young lady – would like them to sing. At that moment, one of the older women, a squat toad-like figure with matted hair, advanced on the Traveller, bearing a glass of champagne on a painted wooden tray. This she offered to him ceremoniously, singing what appeared to be a song of welcome in which the whole band joined. It was, the Traveller explained later, a ritual with the Tziganes.

To whom shall we drink it?
To whom shall we pledge it?
To him who is here.

The Tziganes gathered round and the toad-figure subsided beside the Traveller, laying a massive arm across his shoulder. Like several of the other women, she looked battered but not old: rather, she seemed timeless. He looked at her with affection. 'She was such a beauty... *Tant pis!* She can still sing better than all the rest.'

The Tziganes waved aside the drinks he offered; it was rare for them to drink alcohol, he said, though they generally inveigled their audiences into excesses. Soon, they filed back to their places on the banquette, and sat staring blankly out over the now overcrowded room. The Russians cried louder for their favourite songs, but the Tziganes still appeared indifferent, until a whispered message informed them that the Grand Duke would not be coming in that night. ('Caught up in a family party, no doubt,' said the Traveller, making a face.)

A very tall Tzigane with a shock of grizzled hair suddenly came to life and, picking up his guitar, began to sing on a long, drawn-out howling cry which cut across the smoke-filled room like a whip lash. With that one note the desolation of the steppes and the sound of a lone wolf in the forest closed round us, silencing the supper table chatter. I shivered, terror and pleasure struggling for place. Now the rest of the choir joined in, dutifully at first, but soon becoming one with their music, they flung the refrain at us, or relapsed into brooding minor chants where their harsh voices seemed to break with all the anguish of the world. Although they remained rigid, stony-faced, some of the women now began to sound another note, singing with a piercing sweetness and tenderness which I was to discover, years later, was something belonging to the Russian Gypsies alone. Spanish Gypsies, however fiery their flamenco, however melancholy their Arab cadences, would never sound this particular note of heartbreak.

Had I thought these Tziganes without magic? Now I understood the Traveller's descriptions of their magnetism, of whole nights and days and nights again, spent among them; of whole fortunes dissipated for their music. Now I understood the spell they cast over Pushkin and Dostoievsky, the young Tolstoy and so many more. Here in the stuffy little room there was no more time or thought – only feeling. Ten minutes to four said the phosphorescent dial of a waiter's wrist watch, as he settled another bottle of champagne into its ice-bucket. I realized with pride that I had never stayed up so late before.

The Traveller was silent, listening raptly, as if drugged. From time to time he roused himself and threw me a crumb of companionship or explanation. 'Russian enough for you here? Yes – it's the real thing, as regards the Tziganes... Listen! This is one of their most famous old songs... "You kissed my dark shoulders and I loved you for evermore." Mmm. No doubt she did. Not everyone admired a sunburnt skin when that was written. Your sort of sugar-icing was much more à la mode then. I think I shall call you Rhodopé. It's Greek: *Rhodopis*, rose-fleshed.'

It was the first time anyone had ever made an allusion to my flesh and I was overwhelmed. Growing up, I thought, offered the most fascinating possibilities.

The Traveller was speaking again, as if to himself: how curious, he said, that the Tziganes always held such a potent appeal for both the old merchant classes and the aristocracy – the Guards and the Princes – but never for the bourgeoisie.

'Monstrous lot, anyway. It's enough to make one dislike them more – as if more reasons were needed...' His voice trailed off. Again that inward-turning stare I knew so well, and hated, for it shut him away where I could not follow. No doubt he was thinking Russia, thinking love – the loves he had known there, set to music by the Tziganes. The choir sang on, gathering momentum, intoxicated by their own rhythms. Tragic, desperately gay or haunting, they sang of the troika which carried the lover to his mistress through a snow-storm: they sang of love 'stronger than fire or the sun', of the dark forest and the sleeping camp, of betrayals and partings: *Sertzé*, the Song of the Heart, and the Song of the Evening Star which had once moved Tolstoy to tears.

Perhaps my rapture was apparent to them, for now they came over to our table and repeated the ritual of offering champagne, but this time addressing themselves to the *barishnaya* – myself. ·

'To whom shall we drink it? To whom shall we pledge it?' they chanted.

'They ask what you would like them to sing,' prompted the Traveller and, overcome, I could think of nothing. For all my infatuation with Russia, I could only recall the most commonplace verses, *Black Eyes*, or, losing my head entirely, *The Song of the Volga Boatmen*, something to which I was never, in fact, attached, even when I heard Chaliapin sing it.

Seeing my confusion, the Traveller intervened: 'I'll choose for you,' he said, and the Tziganes sang me *The Black Shawl*, Pushkin's verses, and one of their most heart-rending melodies, all passions and partings.

It was past five o'clock. Grown as reckless on Gypsy music as champagne (though this was doubly intoxicating when the Traveller ordered it as *champagnskoye*) I joined him in a toast to the downfall of Mademoiselle Lavisse – and with another gulp, proposed a last toast: 'Our Trans-Siberian journey!'

'*Kama matout!*' said the Traveller abruptly, raising his glass to me, and smiling his sly teasing smile when I looked blank. '*Kama matout!* That's Tzigane talk, my little Stupiditchka, and if you were more of a linguist, you'd know what it means!'

Or more of a woman, he might have added. *Kama matout* – I love you.

~

Perhaps it was the fabled spell of Tzigane music, but that night had, I think, decided both of us – he to seduce me, I to be seduced by him. Looking back, I consider the Traveller acted disgracefully, abusing every canon of honour. He not only seduced a minor, but the daughter of old friends who had entrusted her to his care while abroad. Yet neither of us had the slightest qualm, nor were we ever found out. The Traveller conducted the whole affair with what was, I suspect, practised care.

We were walking dreamily along the empty rain-washed streets towards my hotel when he stopped, swinging me round, looking at me in his curious, intent manner, reaching and reading my mind, behind my eyes.

'*Pussinka moiya* – d'you want me to love you properly – improperly, I should say?'

'You mean...?'

'What else d'you think I mean, Stupiditchka?' He was kissing me now, wooing kisses, but I was already won – undone. 'And don't start asking what Mademoiselle Lavisse would say – she'd be speechless.'

I too was without words. My dream and my wish, the core of all my romantic longings was suddenly before me waiting to be fulfilled. Now I was not sure what I wanted, what I felt, except that the street and the sky and my head spun dizzily. The chimney pots, the Paris attics, the tree tops, the Traveller's face were all whirling round in fair-ground confusion. Gradually, they spun slower and came to a standstill, and I found myself walking along the same street once more. But it should have been a Russian street... I sighed, thinking of my old fantasy – the Trans-Siberian honeymoon. The Traveller read my sigh.

'Yes, I know, you want us to be in our train – but that's impossible... As a matter of fact, I think you're in love with the train – not me... Wait, though... You've given me an idea...' A curious look of elation passed across those generally inexpressive features. '*Pussinka moiya!* You shall be ruined in a train! We'll turn it into the Trans-Siberian...' He looked at his watch. 'Six o'clock. I can't imagine what sort can be running at this hour – nor where they are going. One thing is certain. I absolutely refuse to ruin you on a workmen's train... O *Pussinka moiya*, my angel child, if only you knew how wonderful it is to steal a march on time! You ought to be older – I ought to be younger... *tant pis!* We've won. We've tricked time. To Siberia!'

He pushed me into a passing taxi and told the driver to go to the Gare de Lyon via the Rue de l'Arcade.

'For my luggage?' I was clutching at straws now, swept along by the racing tides of my desires.

73

'Don't be ridiculous – we're not eloping. And you don't need clothes for this sort of thing. On the contrary. I'm going to leave a message for Mademoiselle Lavisse.'

'What on earth are you going to tell her?'

'Quite simple – that we left early for a day in the country with old friends I met at the Cathedral last night – an unexpected invitation – interesting for you to visit their historic château – knew she'd agree. We didn't want to disturb her so early. You'll see, it will work out perfectly.'

And so it did. We caught a *rapide* to Dijon which was almost empty and soon, with the rustle of a lavish tip, the contrôleur was persuaded to lock us in our compartment. The Traveller snapped down the blinds in a business-like manner. 'We are in the Trans-Siberian,' he announced, with finality, and set out to convince me. Locked in with love and caviare... the perpetual day-dream... There was no caviare, although we had tried to get some at the station buffet, but there was love, all love. My childish imaginings merged with the present, the urgent, brutal and obsessive kingdom of the flesh which was now revealed to me. There were no more hesitations, no doubts nor any terrors. Only loving, only happiness.

'*Kama matout,*' I whispered, but my words were lost in the roar of the wheels.

So we loved, as the train hurled itself across the flat fields of France that should have been the Steppes and, to me, seemed so.

The Traveller reached out and jerked up the blind of an outside window.

'I want to see you in daylight – at your age you don't need pink-shaded lights and all that fiddle-de-dee.'

I lay on the prickly red velvet banquette watching the telegraph poles and signal-boxes rushing past above my head. Grey streaks of poplar that should have been birches; rain that should have been snow. But it no longer mattered. The Chinese-yellow head came closer. The slit eyes stared down, as inscrutable as ever, but the harsh voice was soft.

'So – how do you like being ruined in a *rapide*, my funny little Nursery Traveller? Don't bother to tell me. You look remarkably happy. But then you never did have any sense of moral values. That and a good digestion are two of your most endearing qualities... Now get dressed quickly! We're almost there!'

We scrambled for respectability. As the Traveller fought with his tie and I groped under the seat for a stocking I saw the side-long eyes turned on me with a particularly sly gleam. 'You know,' he said ruminatively, 'I always liked that bit in your great Duke of Marlborough's journal when he returns from the wars and rushes at the Duchess Sarah: "Pleasured my lady twice, with my boots on." It's so perfectly expressive of how one wants a woman. Women are different – they waste a lot of time subjugating their desires (and ours) to the setting and their appearance. Come here, *Pussinka*, come here this instant! I want you *now!*'

The train was slowing down, was sidling to a halt and had stopped dead before we collected ourselves. Crumpled and confused and suppressing hysterical laughter we emerged weakly on to the platform among the uproar of trolleys and scurrying figures.

'We shall go to a hideous-looking hotel I know that understands comfort. The restaurant is excellent – *renommé* all over France. We shall sleep until tea-time, and then we'll see,' said my lover.

He took two rooms, escorted me to mine, ordered me a *café complet* and expressed the hope that I would sleep well.

Now launched on the path of depravity I felt slighted – rejected, even – that no double-bed was forthcoming. The Traveller, as usual, read my mind.

'Don't be so greedy – all in good time. Besides – I can't have you getting blasé; sleep now. Later – we'll see.'

Later saw the Traveller in my room explaining that we were not in Dijon for tourism, so it was unreasonable of me expecting to visit the city. 'What d'you want to see – the mustard factory? Look out of the window – you can see the Cathedral quite well from here... it's nothing extraordinary, in my opinion... We'll go down and have a splendid dinner presently.'

Meanwhile, trains thundered and flashed past the windows. Signals fell with a shattering clang, whistles blasted, porters yelled, steam puffed angrily. The whole hotel seemed to rock, like the trains, for it was built beside the station, sharing and having its whole being within that of the S.N.C.F. But it was supremely comfortable, its crimson carpeting and white antimacassar-trimmed plush armchairs echoing the décor of the train; and, as the Traveller pointed out, the beds were as excellent as the restaurant. He studied the impressive menu long and silently, before ordering a meal composed largely of regional dishes.

'This is a materialistic city. We are in a world of the senses,' he said, falling-to with relish.

'You *are* unromantic.'

'Not at all. I'm practical. I'm not in Dijon every day. It's a *centre gastronomique*. Besides, I don't seduce girls in trains every day, either. Emotions need feeding. Pass that *ravigote*, will you? It's particularly good.'

Mademoiselle Lavisse had been reached by telephone earlier, her bleats of protest silenced by the Traveller's flow of explanations. Such perfect weather – staying on another day, the Baronne simply insists. The gardens at their loveliest just now. It was, he added, such an opportunity for me to see something of French country life at its best. An unforgettable experience – here he had caught my eye. Yes, we should be back tomorrow evening. No, he couldn't say exactly when, everything depended on the trains, he added, catching my eye again, and ringing off before she could ask our whereabouts.

We spent that night and all next day in Dijon, or rather, in the hotel, and I never succeeded in visiting the Cathedral or seeing anything of the city.

'Time enough for tourism later in your life. First things first,' said the Traveller, burrowing under a yellow satin eiderdown and inviting me to join him in his Mongolian *yurt*.

The magic of the Run-Away Game triumphed over the shunting uproar of the near-by goods yard and the conventional setting of a hotel bedroom. We were alone in the infinite snowy silence of the *taïga*, listening to the soft thud of snow falling from a branch above us, to the crackle of a twig, as some unseen beast prowled near by.

'I love you! I love you!' Which of us spoke? The crescendos of passion are seldom suited to words, but our bodies spoke for us.

It was Siberia, it was a Mongol *yurt*, it was a troika speeding through the forest, it was Gallantry Bower made perfect. It was how I had imagined love-making would be when, long ago, I had crouched beside the Traveller under the bracken fronds on a Devon headland. It was as I had always known our loving would be.

'It will always be Gallantry Bower as long as we are together, shut away like this,' said the Traveller when I reminded him of that first green hide-out. His voice sounded strange, and suddenly, there were tears in the dark, slit eyes. With one of his abrupt changes of mood he laughed sardonically. '*Doucinka* – d'you realize I'm a monster of depravity? I'm over forty and you're under eighteen. You've turned me into an insatiable satyr.'

I opened my mouth to tell him I thought it a horrid way to speak of our love, but he cut me short.

'Come here, you silly romantic miss, I can't let you alone.'

CHAPTER SIX

The following autumn I was sent to Italy. It was better than my first athletic prison, but I did not fit in there, among the girls who dreamed of a season, a husband, and two or three frilly babies. I had other ideas of adult life.

'Finished? That's just about what you will be, if you stay there much longer,' snorted the Traveller. He had come to see me, unheralded. One of the nuns was sent to fetch me from the library, a room darkened by cypress trees, where I was supposed to be reading Pater's *Renaissance*, but was, in fact, revelling in a smuggled copy of Dumas' *Le Maître d'Armes* and fancying myself as the French-born heroine who follows her lover to Siberia – Dumas' worst book and a libel on the truth, according to the Traveller, to whom every aspect of the Dekabrist tragedy was sacred.

'There is a signor waiting for you in the parlour,' she said. 'Your mother has written that you may go out with him.' It could be no one else, I knew, although I had not seen him for nearly a year, and I rushed through the icy stone corridors and into the parlour, to find him telling Sister Maddalena that Tamerlaine's twelfth ancestor was said by the Mongols to have sprung from the immaculate conception of a virgin.

'Nothing like *your* Virgin of course,' he added, anxious to avoid causing Sister Maddalena any possible offence. She smiled at him serenely, knowing there had been no wish to offend, and so left us, sailing away under the wide white coif.

As we walked through the olive trees, towards the gates, we passed Luigi, the old gardener, working among the tubs of oleander and box. He straightened himself to wish us a fortunate day. The sun shone overhead, as it usually did. But to me it now blazed in tropical splendour. The Traveller stopped, listening intently.

'Nightingales at noon! In October?' he said, '...like the Krim.' He always called this region, the Crimea, by its Russian name – Krim – which I thought far more exotic, besides having for me, no associations with the agonizing Crimean campaign, which haunted me by reason of an engraving I had once seen, where English men, and – oh, horror of horrors – innocent English horses, writhed and perished under *Russian* guns.

'The Krim! Have you managed to go back there? What about the Fountain of Bakhtchisarai? And what about *Siberia?* Tell! Tell all!' The Tuscan landscape faded, and I saw only Tartar bazaars, or the great steppes. The Traveller laughed. He seemed in a gay mood.

'You never think of anything else, do you? Anyhow, today's different. It's here and now, and I've got a surprise for you.' He looked slyly amused.

'Something to eat, or to wear?' I asked. Last Christmas he had sent me caviare and a muff.

'Neither to eat or wear – rather to love or to hate,' he replied, enigmatic as ever.

Outside the ornamental stone gates two young men sat on the balustrade overlooking the valley. One was about my age, I judged, the other a few years older. Both were unmistakable in their likeness to the Traveller, with the same dark, slanted, slit eyes, but with this difference – this welcome difference, I might have said, had not everything about the Traveller appeared irresistible to me – both young men had the thick, blue-black thatch of the Asiatic, plumage rather than hair. Both wore their overcoats as he did, flung over their shoulders in the manner of cloaks, which gave them a dashing air.

'My sons,' announced the Traveller.

'But I didn't know you were married,' I said, foolishly.

'I'm not – whatever made you think I was?' he replied, rapping my conventionality over the knuckles.

'Kamran! Sergei! This is Charlotte Russe.' It was one of the names by which he liked to call me, in reference to my Russophile inclinations, and also my infinite capacity for eating an English pudding of that name.

The two young Slavs bowed ceremoniously, and fell into step beside us. They said nothing but, as we walked, we all eyed each other furtively. The Slavs had an advantage over me, for their eyes were set so sidelong that it was clearly easier for them to look out of the corners than for myself, with my round, doll-like Anglo-Saxon gaze.

'Well, what shall we do?' asked the Traveller, who had, of course, no intention of listening to any suggestions we might have made. 'Shall we go and eat very rich cakes? (Something he knew I found irresistible.) Shall we make a state call on the Grand Duchess?' He named a celebrated old Russian princess who lived in pinched state outside the city. 'Or shall we run away? To Siberia of course,' he added, catching my eye. 'Though since you've become such a convent-miss, perhaps you'd expect to get *married* first? Then you could play stepmother to my sons... Mamasha!' He laughed diabolically seeing my crimson face. 'Yes, it's quite an idea,' he went on, 'I always say every woman must be married at least three times. You'd better start off with me... You could do worse... *Chort!* I could do worse... Well, that's settled then. Kamran! Sergei! What do you think of Charlotte Russe for your stepmother? She'll spoil you abominably. Perhaps you can teach her to speak Russian. I've never succeeded. However, you can still count up to ten in Yakute, can't you, pet?' he asked anxiously, appearing delighted when I began the uncouth syllables, *bir, iki, ous, tar, bar, ali, sekki...*

Thoroughly over-excited, I began to explain to my future stepsons that the Siberian tribe of Yakutes are said to be of Turanian stock, their language resembling Turkish. The two young men looked bewildered, more so, when to illustrate my point I began rattling off the similar Turkish numerals – *bir, iki, utch, dort, besh, alti, yedi...*

'I love you, but that's enough culture for today,' said the Traveller.

'Kamran, Sergei! Welcome your father's fiancée!' *Fiancée!* In a daze I saw the young men – my ready-made Russian family – bend over my hand – the hand of their future stepmother, I thought rapturously. It was the first time anyone had kissed my hand, although this bliss was short-lived.

'What! Kissing a young *unmarried* woman's hand! Don't you know that's not done?' snapped their father. 'I'm surprised at you. No *tenue!* And anyhow, all that hand-kissing is corrupt Petersburg rubbish. You should have dropped such salon stuff – it won't fit tomorrow's world. And neither will you, Mamasha,' he continued, enjoying my new name. 'You never ought to be here, now. You ought to be in Russia – twenty years back. There's been some accident in time...' He suddenly looked pinched – old even. The long, bent back fingers began to snap: he stared, that curious, inward-turning stare which always meant he was remembering a vanished world, trying to summon its shadows round him once more.

'*Ah! que nos désirs sont sans remède.*' He sighed. 'That's Saint Theresa of Avila. Do they teach you that at your finishing school?' The old mocking tone had returned and now we were bundling into a hired car, which was waiting for us on Mussolini's splendid new highway.

'*I Promessi Sposi* will sit in the back and hold hands,' he said, cramming his sons in beside the chauffeur, a stout man who groaned dramatically as he manoeuvred the hairpin bends of the Tuscan hills.

'Now – about the wedding,' the Traveller began, as, later, we sat eating *gelati* in the piazza. 'I suppose you expect the whole traditional business – angelic choirs, the Metropolitan in person to pronounce the blessing, and those ridiculous golden crowns held over our heads? I knew you would.' He seemed much amused by the whole idea. 'You two can hold the crowns,' he said to his sons, who remained as monosyllabic and deferential as ever. I noticed they were almost extravagantly respectful towards their father and, indeed, although they were what Nanny would have described as likely-looking lads (likely for what, she never explained) they immediately faded into insignificance beside the Traveller. Much as I rejoiced at the notion of acquiring a ready-made Russian family, I could not find them of interest, at that moment.

To be married in a Russian church, with all the splendours of Byzantine symbolism, had long represented the sum-total of my romantic aspirations. There, the crowned bride and groom become king and queen, too. The honeymoon, I thought with rapture, the *real* honeymoon this time, mystical consummation of my love for Russia, *must* be spent on the Trans-Siberian, locked in with love and caviare. At last! This time he could not refuse me. The fact that the Trans-Siberian, if it was still running at that moment, was unlikely to have been accessible to us did not occur to me. Politics were something to which I had never applied myself – or rather, had never felt applied to myself. Politics were newspaper headlines, and in any case no newspaper penetrated the convent. So far as I was concerned, the Trans-Siberian, like the Pumpkin Coach, would materialize magically for this magical occasion. Alas! there was a cloud on the glowing horizon, for I was offended by the Traveller's mocking tone. Later, when Kamran and Sergei had been packed off to the cinema to see *The Four Horsemen of the Apocalypse* I told him sulkily that he had spoiled everything, bringing up the subject – such a subject as our marriage – in front of other people. Particularly, in front of his sons – his sons by another woman.

'Another woman? Other *women*, you mean.' He laughed his rare thunderous laugh. 'My poor Numskullina, can't you see those two boys are of quite different stock? Sergei's mother was a Georgian, from Tiflis. Kamran's mother was half Turki – don't go confusing Turki with Turkey, there's a big difference – all Central Asia between them. Georgian women are great charmers, born to please – hot-tempered, as well as facile however. Nothing facile about Turki women. Kamran's mother was a beauty too, but different – *difficile*... like her father. He was a Kirghiz chief – one of the Kara, or Black Kirghiz – they're a swarthy lot. He was worth over a thousand tents. They reckon wealth by tents, you know. He was said to be descended from one of the Khans of the Little Horde – the Ktché Dj, which, by the way, is the largest, and one of his wives – my mother-in-law, I suppose you'd call her, politely – although as I said, I never married – was descended from Tamerlaine, I believe. Don't ask me to explain Asiatic *snobisme*: and don't go imagining they were all savages. A chieftain I knew used to pack Verlaine into his saddlebags when he went on the summer migrations. I found Kamran's mother when I was looking for the Tombs of the Tartars beyond Semipalatinsk, which, for your edification, was once the Capital of the Province of the Seven Tents. Got that? I like travel as much as I like children. Plenty of both suits me. Don't look so prim. And while I am on the subject, I've two more sons. My eldest was by a Manchu girl – he's in Vladivostok, I believe. Haven't seen either of them for years. The mother of Shamgon, the youngest, was from the Tien-Shan mountains (I usually find Asiatic women irresistible), but I've lost all trace of her, and the child too. Pity. He was such a funny little boy... I always have boys, so be prepared for sons.'

Seeing my look, he added: 'Perhaps you'd better go back to the finishing school after all. You're not ready for the world. You ought to have been at Smolny.' (This was the Institute for Noble Young Ladies at St. Petersburg: it had been founded by the Empress Elizabeth, and was housed in a former convent, the most sumptuously ornate building imaginable.)

'They were much more worldly at Smolny... one of the pupils set her cap at the Tzar Alexander II. Katia Dolgorukaya. You know the story? She was finished all right – and so was he... And so are we all, one way or another...' he added sombrely.

We went to sit in a café on the Tornabuoni to await Kamran and Sergei, who presently joined us, demanding to be fed, and describing the tempests of emotion aroused in them by the love scenes between Rudolph Valentino and Alice Terry. It was getting late by convent standards, and soon I was obliged to leave this fascinating new-found Asiatic family life. The Traveller accompanied me to the convent gates, where our farewells were whispered in the shadow of the wall. Against the fast-fading lemon-coloured sky, the pointed leaves of the orange-trees were silhouetted sharp as cut-out black paper.

'I hate to leave you here like this, *Pussinka* pet.'

'Not as much as I hate to be left,' I replied bitterly, crushing down a wild hope he might suggesting eloping there and then.

'No, Greedy.' He was reading my mind as usual. 'We can't be together as we want to be, for a while... But we'll write – d'you know, I've always kept your first love-letter to me? Probably your first *love* letter. You wrote it when you were six. It said: "Please come back I love you I love you yours sinserley." I've not kept anybody else's letters, by the way. That ought to satisfy you... And – damn it all! I've proposed marriage to you! That's more than I've ever done for any other woman. It will have to do, for now.'

Over the wall, the chapel bell suddenly clanged, with rusty insistence. He kissed me violently and turned away, driving off without looking back.

~

After that, the Traveller disappeared for nearly a year and I heard no more of the radiant matrimonial prospects he had dangled before me: nor did I hear anything of Sergei and Kamran. A future stepmother who was still at school and appeared proud of counting up to ten in Yakute had no doubt intimidated them. I felt myself abandoned – marooned on an island of conventional living – and sulked accordingly. I admired the determined girl who had followed her love, Thomas à Becket, across Europe, on foot, without any means or language but her own, and at last ran him to earth in London, by the simple process of repeating his name to every person she encountered on her long march. Could I undertake such a search into the hinterland of Asia, repeating the Traveller's name as I inched into those wildly desired horizons? But I knew I should be quickly lassooed by telephone and telegraph, frontier controls – the networks of civilization. In despair I dropped Dumas' Siberia and applied myself to Russian history.

When the Traveller told of treaties, ideologies, mystics or villains concerned with Russia, all sprang to life, alive, alive O! Which aspect of Russian history would find most favour in his eyes, I wondered, imagining how I would dazzle him with my learning. I had not yet realized that, in women, specialized knowledge is likely to chill rather than charm, and should always be cunningly concealed if the object is to please. Thus I weighed up Potemkin's foreign policies against the Dekabrist rising or Russia's annexation of the Central Asian Khanates. The last stand of the Tekké Turcomans was a serious rival to the eternal magnet pull of Siberia and the Dekabrists' incarceration there. Desert or steppe?

As I wavered, Bokhara's mud-walled fastness rose before me, vibrating in heat and wickedness as the Traveller had told. I saw the Ark, the Emir's fortress palace. Here, on a balcony hung with carpets and rainbow silks, I saw the Emir, a scowling, turbaned figure, pawn in the Central-Asian power game, for Bokhara lay on the Russian route to India and was only twenty-three years away from its annexation by Russia. Crescent, Cross, Hammer and Sickle. The age-old struggle for supremacy. All the colour and violence of Central Asia flamed round me in the cool dark library where I brooded. Many years later, I achieved these Turcoman territories, and stood before the Ark, entering its blunt-towered gates to hang over the prison pit, now displayed by Soviet custodians as an example of the combined abuses of both Emirate and Tzarist rule.

But in the convent library, no crystal foretold my future travels for me, and I was still weighing up the respective merits of Central Asia or Siberia for my studies. Inevitably, Siberia won. With voluptuous abandon I floated away, out of the barred windows, across the trim box hedge of the garden, above the cyprus-speared hills of Fiesole, north, over the Apennines, northwards again, and backwards in time, till I reached the great grey blocks of granite surrounding the Senate Square in St. Petersburg, on that fateful December day in 1825, where the Dekabrists were making their stand – that heroic piece of clumsiness that led them to execution or a lifelong Siberian sentence.

~

The Dekabrist Revolt, 'the Revolution that stood and waited', took its name from the month in which this forlorn gesture was made. It was in the nature of an abortive stand for freedom, rather than a revolution. Its aim, among other reforms, was to obtain a Constitution – something Russia had never known. But the whole affair was conducted with such amateur folly that it was doomed from its inception. All was bravura and hurrahs; daggers were brandished but with no definite plan as to whom they should slay. Above all, there was too much talking. Those interminable nights of idealistic hyperbole beloved of the Slav politico-intelligentsia led nowhere then, just as they led nowhere when I listened to them among the Russian exiles of Paris or London.

The movement had begun among a young army elite, an aristocratic, cultivated milieu. The Guards officers had returned from the Napoleonic campaigns quite dizzied by the freedoms they had tasted abroad, in those heady days of triumph, occupying Paris in 1814, where they had frequented the intellectual salons as much as *le beau monde*, and been amazed, and awakened by the winds of liberty which blew through every stratum of French thought and life. Now, all over Russia, secret societies on Masonic lines sprang up. Their aims were admirable. A Constitution, a more humane army administration, and the suppression of the twenty-five years' military service then imposed, together with the freeing of the serfs and other liberal reforms were some of the things for which they stood, collectively. Individually, many among them set about liberating their own serfs, or organizing agrarian reforms on their lands. The Union of the North, the Society of United Slavs, and the Southern Secret Society mustered an impressive aristocracy: the Princes Volkonsky, Troubetsky, Obolensky and Bariatinsky were all would-be reformers, stemming from the noblest stock. Great fortunes, limitless estates and privilege surrounded them, so that they were, potentially, wielders of decisive power.

Nothing decisive was done, however, and the talkative visionaries continued to meet for the next five years, (the young Pushkin among them, though he was never deeply involved) planning more and more impractical means of overcoming the growing climate of reaction around them. When, in 1825, the Tzar Alexander I died without a direct heir, the succession was obscure. For his brother, the Grand Duke Constantine, living in Poland as Viceroy and married to a Polish woman, had, some time earlier and in secret, renounced his claim to the throne. It was not generally known that his younger brother, the Grand Duke Nicholas, was to succeed him. In this state of confusion, when the army was called to swear the oath of allegiance, it was not clear to whom it should be made, and some oaths were nullified by being made to Constantine.

This was the moment chosen by the secret societies, to make their stand demanding a Constitution, before they would accept Nicholas as their Tzar. It seems a simple enough decision: yet fearful confusion and agitation prevailed.

At last these idealists, so touching in their innocent beliefs, so exasperatingly ineffectual in their actions, decided to make their stand in St. Petersburg on the Senate Square, beneath Falconet's equestrian statue of Peter the Great. It was December the fourteenth; the young Grand Duke Nicholas had taken the oath of succession and now, become Nicholas I, awaited his Court, his Ministers and his troops to take the oath of allegiance to him. This icy tyrant was to show, from the first, that ruthless force which now served him, but was to make him an abhorred symbol of oppression, in particular to the families of the Dekabrists, to whom he was never to show the slightest mercy.

He believed in the Divine Right of Kings: he was, in his own eyes, God's anointed, Autocrat of All the Russias. Rebellion was blasphemy. He ordered all available troops forward. Three thousand forlorn rebels faced three thousand cavalry, nine thousand infantry and a thousand of the artillery. On each side of the vast square, they stood and waited. Their rebel ranks seemed pitifully insufficient for the great ideals they represented. They had no prepared plan of battle. It was all in their hearts.

When the Chevalier Guards pranced out to take their places behind the Tzar, fourteen members of the various secret societies were among them. There was still time for them to support their rebel associates. But they too seemed frozen into immobility. The crowds, who also stood waiting, became impatient, and began taunting the Tzar's troops, throwing stones and bricks: their sympathies were all with the rebels, to whom they now brought vodka as protection against the fearful cold. This had an unfortunate effect; some of the ranks falling drunk, their rifles clattering to the frozen ground. The short winter's day was darkening as one of the more hot-headed rebel leaders, Kakhovsky, suddenly galvanized, fired his pistol at General Miloradovitch, Governor of St. Petersburg, who fell from his horse mortally wounded.

The Tzar, his terrible pewter stare taking in the scene and noting each conspirator's face for future persecutions, now ordered the artillery to open fire. But no one moved. The order was given again, but again the gun-crews hung back from firing on their fellow ranks. There was still time – a last, desperate chance – for the rebels to storm the guns trained on them. A civilian, Pushchin, urged action; yet, curiously none of the rebel officers seemed able to give the command. Again the Tzar ordered his troops to fire, and now, at last, rebels and civilians scattered or fell under a raking fire. Too late, a handful of insurgents attempted a last-ditch stand, meaning to retreat across the bridge, and storm the fortress of Peter and Paul, there to hold out against the rest of the army. But the Tzar ordered the guns up to the embankment, and shot them down as they raced across the ice-bound Neva. The ice was shattered by shot and shell, and gaping holes received many bodies which were seen no more till, with the spring thaw, they floated to the surface, ghastly reminders of this day. 'The Revolution that stood and waited' was over. The vengeance of Nicholas had not yet begun.

This was some of the intricate background to that moment in Russian history which I now set out to study, being certain that one day I should come to know the terrain of its Siberian sequel.

All that winter, the biting cold of Florence was warmed by the Traveller's letters. He wrote to me often – guarded letters, but sometimes we now employed a peculiar code, or cypher, which he had once explained to me when describing the strange beliefs and habits of the Old Believers, snug in their forests beyond the Volga. In the seventeenth century this cypher had been used in diplomatic exchanges, but falling into disuse, had been adopted by the Old Believers for their secret correspondence between the monasteries and prelates, obstinately defending their Schismatic doctrines against the Patriarch Nikon's reforms. Now, in a modified system we lisped our own secrets to each other in this juggled Russian alphabet.

Although no one read my letters, the nuns not being empowered to do so, I think both the Traveller and I enjoyed this exercise in stealth. It heightened our agreeable sense of guilt, and besides, since we often recalled our expedition to Dijon in detail, we really did have something over which to be secretive. The *tramontana* might howl across the Apennines while I slept in an unheated, stone-walled, stone-flagged room in a bed inadequately warmed by a contraption of charcoal known locally, and bawdily, as 'the priest in the bed'; yet I glowed, re-reading the Traveller's cryptic letters, recalling another, warmer couch. Thus, although far apart, an illusion of closeness was preserved. I needed this solace, for my remaining months at the convent were stultifying. An occasional cinema, tea-parties among the English colony, long-distance flirtations with young officers at the Fortezza... these were not for me. I had tasted wine and now sipped water.

Perhaps my restlessness was reflected in my moodiness, my lack of interest for my studies, or anything around me. Perhaps the nuns complained to my mother and she drew her own conclusions. Even though she knew nothing of my true relationship to the Traveller she had always been aware of my infatuation. When the Sister, who supervised our out-going mail, reported I was writing to him three or four times a week, my mother wrote back to me, fond but firm. My studies were suffering. She feared he was becoming too disturbing an influence in my life... (*Becoming?* He had been that since I could first remember him, toasting bread and beef dripping by the nursery fire.) I wondered if my parents knew of the four Asiatic sons or had, somehow, learned of our project – the golden-crowned wedding. This, I sensed, would not be viewed with sympathy.

'Our Traveller is off on his travels again,' said my mother's letter, 'and perhaps it would be better not to write for a while. He is planning a trip to Afghanistan, where there is Trouble.' During the Trouble, she suggested, he would have no time to write and I should be careful not to bother him with too many letters. Although we both knew how irresistible Trouble – especially if situated in Asia – always proved to the Traveller, I believed he would continue to write, and so he did. But I resented my mother's attitude, feeling she had tried to come between myself and my Slavic destiny and I bore her a grudge for this, which lingered, hardening gradually from resentment to distrust. I also resented her referring to him as *Our* Traveller. He was mine, mine, entirely. I now became aware that no one was to be trusted wholly.

~

'It is frightfully hot here,' wrote the Traveller, 'but they know how to make good tea.' The letter was headed 'September, southeast of Kabul.' It went on:

'Not much going on, so I have had time to look at the country: reminds me of the Caucasus. Rough-going for picnics. *Wish you were here, Pussinka moiya*. Your insatiable tourist appetites would at last be satisfied. There's everything. Danger, beauty, innocence, corruption, small-pox, syphilis, stagnation... My vocabulary is giving out – it's Asia, all right. I can see you sitting sketching under a green umbrella, not noticing bursts of cross-fire from the hills. I suppose you'd tell the tribesmen not to be so silly, if they closed round you. Quite a good method, on the whole. I am writing from a *tchai-hana*, a sort of tea-house, with a little bridge across the stream; we sit on the bridge to drink our tea and watch the water flowing below.'

'We?'... My heart was pierced by a barb of jealousy. Who was with him in the *tchai-hana?* Another traveller? Some henna-fingered Persian houri? One of the legendary dancers of Shemakha?

'Tell your mother that I have discovered a new way to cook rice,' the letter went on. 'It requires a copper cauldron at least 3ft. across. Better try Harrods. By the way, prisoners are worse off here than they used to be in your adored Siberia. They stick them in iron cages, and leave them to perish, hanging from a rock. The last Prime Minister was swinging over a ravine for almost two weeks before he died. But they gave him a splendid funeral – full dress. I had to wear my tails. In this heat!'

The letter then went on to ask for some laundry to be reclaimed and a number of books to be returned to the London Library – books that had, of course, been borrowed in someone else's name. The atmosphere of the *tchai-hana* seemed to have induced total recall for everything except the golden-crowned ceremony round which all my thoughts were now centred.

PART THREE

THE BORROWED LIFE

My love was much
My life but an inhabitant of his

Thomas Beddoes

CHAPTER SEVEN

B y summer the Traveller's adventurous mood must have passed, for he had returned to London, where he soon conquered my mother's resistance to a plan that I should join him, with his two sons, for a holiday in Corsica, 'because it reminds me of the Caucasus. My mad Montenegrin aunt, the old Countess Eudoxia, will be there too,' he wrote, 'just a family outing...' Although my parents interpreted family outings in other terms than mad aunts from Montenegro and illegitimate sons (the Traveller had, it seemed, boldly proclaimed their bastard birth, no doubt aware of my family's large views on such matters), it seemed that, for them, the educational benefits of foreign travel outweighed most other considerations and, since they were still in happy ignorance of our excursion to Dijon, where my education might be said to have been conducted along dangerously liberal lines, they agreed to this Corsican expedition. And so, once more it was written that I should hang on his words, lie in his arms, and fall even deeper under the Russian spell.

Our journey was not without incident, for we had assembled early one morning at the Gare de Lyon under a torrid sun which shortened tempers dangerously. We were to take the *rapide* to Marseilles; even so, we should not get there till nearly midnight. The Traveller laid no trust in the comforts of the *wagon-lit* or the dining-car. We would go by day, and we would picnic, he decreed. Mademoiselle Lavisse was escorting me to the train and, as we drew near the compartment, we heard him shouting angrily at the porters who were, he said, mishandling a large samovar he had brought along. Mademoiselle seemed rather disconcerted on finding that the Traveller was wearing dark blue silk pyjamas and grey suède gloves.

'I always change into something of this sort for long journeys,' he said, catching her embarrassed stare, and I wondered what he wore when crossing the Gobi desert.

I was now introduced to the mad Montenegrin aunt. Her exuberant curves were moulded into a silk dress splashed with brilliant coloured flowers; a number of pearl necklaces were wound in a strangle-hold round her plump throat and, in spite of the heat, a rather shabby fur cape kept slipping off her shoulders and was clutched into place again. She appeared to be drenched in some particularly exotic scent for, at every movement, wafts of fragrance flowed about the compartment – something I found particularly delicious, remembering how my mother and most of her friends practised the utmost restraint, holding that anything more than the merest hint was a sign of vulgarity. I now perceived that, on many other counts, Aunt Eudoxia would not have met with their approval. She was boldly rouged, the colour painted high and wide, in the manner of a Largillière portrait, and her hair was that rich orange which derives from unstinted applications of henna. It was bound round her head in tight plaits, forming a high tiara or *kokoshnik* which immediately proclaimed her Slav origins. Her eyebrows, carelessly slashed across her face, were an uncompromising black, like her small, almond-shaped eyes, set, like the Traveller's, at an Asiatic slant. Yet with all the pearls and paint and overpowering perfume, there was nothing vulgar about her, and it was with an air at once majestic and agreeable that she greeted me.

'So – I am seeing you at last. I have heard very much of you.' I wondered what, exactly, she had heard... The hand she held out was beautifully shaped, small, white, cushioned, and heavily ringed; a pampered nineteenth-century hand, recalling a portrait by Ingres.

She smiled, gravely, thoughtfully, as if weighing me up, and then, having made up her mind about me, turned back to her preoccupations. An air of brooding melancholy settled round her and seemed oddly out of place since her sharp little nose turned up in the most cheerful fashion. She appeared to be a creature of contradiction, and I observed her with particular interest for she was the first member of the Traveller's family I had encountered. Somehow, I did not regard his sons in the light of true family – of Russian roots and all that vibrant Muscovite past which I believed Aunt Eudoxia would be able to reveal. Sergei and Kamran were off-shoots, adjuncts, echoes – but Aunt Eudoxia must inevitably have shared much of the Traveller's early background.

I sat contentedly, already preparing in my head a list of leading questions I would pose at suitable moments.

Aunt Eudoxia was now focusing her attention on a complicated-looking object placed on the floor beside her. This, she explained, was a *tchibouk*, or Turkish water-pipe; its coiled tubing stemmed from a graceful ruby cut-glass jar which, since she was installed in a corner seat next to the corridor, caused anyone entering or leaving the compartment to trip over it, scattering the silver paraphernalia where the tobacco and charcoal were placed and jerking dangerously at the amber mouth piece attached to the tube through which the rose-water was already bubbling.

'My *tchibouk* never leaves me – never,' she said emphatically. 'It is of such soothingness.' But I was to discover that in the matter of trifles she was singularly agitated. The weather, the cards (she read them every day for guidance) or a lost hairpin appeared to be of more consequence than graver trials upon which she sometimes dwelled – her lost youth, her vanished wealth, or her murdered relatives. Like the Traveller, she seemed to find a certain pleasure in major disasters.

There was no sign of either Kamran or Sergei, which I thought threatened a disastrous start to our journey.

'If they miss the train I shall disinherit them – bastards though they are,' said the Traveller angrily, at which a meek English couple who were trying to insinuate themselves into the middle seats looked startled and left the compartment.

Just as the train was moving, the two young men flung themselves aboard. Their father's face fell. He always enjoyed drama or suspense and had been hanging out of the window, beaming with anticipation as the platform emptied and it seemed certain his sons had been left behind.

They were leading an enormous woolly white dog, the largest, woolliest, and most curious animal I had ever seen.

'Ah, so Hondi had to come too,' said the Traveller indulgently. 'But I won't have him put with the luggage. You know how difficult it was to get him over.'

'Hondi', I learned, was an abbreviation of Hondof – 'Hondof the Baskervilles' as Sergei explained, adding that Sherlock Holmes was his favourite author. The creature was a Komondor, said the Traveller, the rarest breed of Mongol sheepdog, seldom seen outside Asia, although the Magyars brought some back with them to the Hungarian plains a thousand years ago, and Hondof had been born in the *puszta* and brought to France last year.

The Komondor's matted white coat hung in long woolly stalactites, and his loving brown eyes shone out through a thick fringe.

'That coat is what protects them against attack by wolves and the frightful cold,' said the Traveller, 'and then it makes them acceptable to sheep – the ewes think it's a sort of guardian angel.'

93

He asked me for my comb and began to untangle some of the most clotted portions of Hondof's coat.

The Komondor whimpered neurotically and tried to climb on to my lap for protection.

'He weighs eighty and three pounds,' said Kamran fondly, eyeing the picnic basket. 'Papasha, please, could he...?'

'Certainly not,' snapped the Traveller. 'I did not know you were bringing him and I have nothing fit for him to eat. Chicken bones would be dangerous. Lobster is out of the question. Pâté would be constipating.'

The Countess looked up from the pack of tarot cards she was now dealing and said she thought this might be most desirable on a long journey. But this question was shelved by the *contrôleur* arriving to punch our tickets and working himself into one of those legendary Gallic uproars over the presence of a dog in the compartment. The animal had no ticket and, in any case, must travel in the luggage van, he said. A furious scene ensued.

Although Russian invective is held to be of an unimaginable violence, I observed that in moments of fury the Traveller held to his opinion that the French language best expressed hatred. Sometimes, however, he had recourse to those homely English phrases he so much enjoyed acquiring. Now, after a tirade in his mother-tongue which left his family gasping, and which the *contrôleur*, at last stung beyond officialdom, countered with the more homely *'Foûtez-moi la paix!'* the Traveller capped it with 'and the same to you with knobs on'. Although this phrase was no doubt incomprehensible to him the *contrôleur* grew even more livid, lost all semblance of control, and striking an attitude worthy of Talma, hissed: *'Mes compliments à Mademoiselle votre mère!'*

The Traveller had now worked up to a histrionic degree of rage, and, being almost asphyxiated by the fumes of garlic which the *contrôleur* diffused about the compartment, threatened to open the outside door, and fling himself or the *contrôleur* on to the line if a hair of the dog's head was touched. A rush of air, soot, sparks and noise overwhelmed us. The Countess was clutching the *tchibouk* to her bosom, while the samovar overturned, hot water cascading over the plush seats. In spite of the silk pyjamas and the grey gloves, the Traveller contrived to appear an intimidating figure and, when Kamran and Sergei closed menacingly round, the official turned tail. The Traveller sat back, looking purged, while I righted the samovar. Hondof had taken advantage of the battle to apply himself seriously to the picnic hamper, his head and ears buried deep among the debris of a cold chicken. The Countess, I noticed, now had tears in her little eyes.

'I saw it in the cards this morning,' she moaned. 'No good will come of this journey. We are under a dark star.'

The guard had not given up so easily. He returned with a notebook, still glaring malevolently but calmer, being secure in his official rights. Ignoring Hondof who growled half-heartedly, he now prepared to prosecute by taking down the Traveller's name and address, both of which presented almost insuperable difficulties, for after the Russian patronymic came a long, and probably apocryphal address in Central America, full of Xochimilco-like words. This was the Traveller's revenge. But the *contrôleur* won the last round, for having announced that he would also prosecute for the use of insulting language, he went off, to return with some elaborately uniformed higher official of the *Compagnie des Chemins de Fer*, who bowed most civilly to all of us, and proceeded to lead Hondof away with an air of implacable authority amid shouts and threats which rose above the clatter of the train. The Traveller, who was now positively distorted with rage and frustration, yelled a last, and thoroughly Gallic insult on the lines of: '*Va, rentre dans ta mère que je peux te refaire!*' while a number of passengers now stuck their heads out of their compartments and looked along the corridor with expressions of approval. A foreigner who possessed such a command of the French language was to be respected – doubly so, since he had come to blows with the officials, something the uniform-respecting French admired whole-heartedly.

'*Scandalist!* He was always a *scandalist*,' the Countess was whispering with sibilant force, explaining that in Russia, in the old days, this term was generally used to describe those whose wild behaviour invited criticism and provided food for gossip of a censorious nature. 'Some people made quite a hobby of it,' she concluded.

I always noticed that such uproars, while leaving those around the Traveller in a state of nervous prostration, had the most tonic effect upon him. He found them at once stimulating and relaxing. All passion spent, he now assumed an air of beatific calm, and was easily persuaded to recount other journeys – the sort I liked to hear about; of gliding down the Don to Astrakhan, legendary Tartar city – 'Star of the Desert'; day after day, on a steam-boat filled with water melons and concertina-playing steerage passengers. Or another, by a branch-line of the Trans-Siberian, crossing the great golden sandy wastes of Asia, where only the eagles circled overhead, and the legends of Jenghis Khan still saturated the land. Or those journeys his grandmother's generation had known, travelling by carriage, with style, in a *dormeuse*, four horses abreast, with two more added over the worst roads. Every comfort was included, every eventuality foreseen: backgammon boards and a small but choice library to while away the tedium; goose-feather cushions, bed-linen and ikons, to ameliorate wayside lodgings. The cook usually preceded the *dormeuse* in a *tarantass*, rattling his bones and the pots and pans and plate as he raced ahead to have dinner awaiting his master and mistress.

The Traveller's grandmother, who was as vain as she was fecund (she had fourteen children), was generally followed by another vehicle, carrying her hairdresser and the midwife. These precautionary measures had arisen after a journey when, attending a ball of the provincial nobility, she had been unable to have her hair dressed suitably by the local *coiffeur* and had been so chagrined that she had left the ball in the middle of a quadrille and, a quarter of an hour later, had given birth to her second son, the Traveller's father, attended only by a panic-stricken *femme-de-chambre*.

A character the Traveller had known by hearsay was the object of my especial envy: he always referred to her ceremoniously as *La Voyageuse de la Volga*. His father remembered her as a fabulously rich old widow, an eccentric, possessing vast estates in the region of Saratoff. She was convinced that her relatives planned to assassinate her, for a family feud had raged, even during her husband's lifetime. After his death, she had abandoned her house and, for thirty years, spent her summers going up and down the Volga on one of the steamers which plied the lovely reaches between Saratoff and Astrakhan. Her winters were passed on the Saratoff-Moscow railway, shuttling backwards and forwards. She was revered by the personnel of both boat and train and, since she knew all the people of distinction living along both routes, she was treated like a Queen. Wherever she stopped en route her friends, expecting her arrival, would drive to the landing stage or the station where she held court. She never left her compartment, or the deck (for she took no chances of some particularly venomous relative coming too close) but, standing at the window or leaning over the rail, she held court, received *le beau monde* and their compliments, exchanged gossip, extended her hand to be kissed or made the sign of the Cross over them; but withdrawing before they began to bore her. She had arranged her cabin with her own comforts; a gold-plated samovar, her books, and embroidered bed hangings, while her compartment on the train was said to be plastered with ikons and made fragrant by pots of sweet-scented green plants at the windows. This has always seemed to me a perfect way of life; yet she was considered mad for adopting it.

While the Countess puffed voluptuously at the *tchibouk*, her eyes half closed, an expression of exalted grief on her face, the rest of us worked steadily through what Hondof had left of the picnic, to the accompaniment of innumerable glasses of tea provided by the now restored samovar, which the Traveller managed skilfully.

Apart from myself, no one seemed to have thought of bringing anything to read on the journey, but all of them eyed me with a certain envy when I opened *The Mystery of Edwin Drood*. However the Traveller soon settled matters by snatching the book out of my hands and slicing it into five sections which he now distributed among us, regardless of sequence. Thus, Sergei found himself with the last chapter, while a middle section fell to my lot, leaving equally incomprehensible chunks of text to be puzzled out by the others.

'What's the matter? Now you've all got something to read, haven't you?' demanded the Traveller, who appeared to feel he had acted with both ingenuity and impartiality, although I noticed he had kept the opening chapter for himself. For the rest of the journey one or other of the Traveller's sons was ordered off to sit with Hondof in the luggage van, while all dietetic principles were cast to the winds and I was repeatedly sent the length of the train with delicacies for the dog rather than its human companion.

As the last pale after-glow lit the vineyards before Marseilles, we had come to the end of the pâté, the lobster and the strawberry tartlets and were falling back on the cucumber sandwiches.

'Pastries and vegetables are no good for dogs,' said the Traveller, 'but all the same, go along and see if Hondof fancies something.' There was no mention of the banished son.

I was selected for this mission rather than which ever of his sons was with us, for, as he explained, only the English really knew and felt for dogs. I bumped and lurched down the length of the train, stepping over nuns' cardboard suitcases and the kit bags of French sailors regaining their ships. The lights were pricking through the fast-gathering darkness when I reached the luggage van, where Kamran, the elder of the two sons, was sleeping on a mail sack, his dark head on the Komondor's woolly flank. Both gobbled at the delicacies. While Hondof crashed a great hoof-like paw on to my lap, loving and pleading, the Traveller's son eyed me with that same sly, sidelong glance as his father: and something of Hondof's pleading, too.

'So you and Papasha will to marry?' he asked, and smiled, a diffident, almost surly grin, which lit his sallow face and revealed the strong, square, very square white teeth of some Asiatic races. Kamran, I perceived, had nothing of Europe about him, and I liked him the better for that.

'Where you live?' he continued, 'I hope it being Paris, and I may come there also.' He spoke English in a basic manner, but was far more at home in French, to which he usually reverted, as now.

'I have never had a home,' he went on. 'I should like one... should like to know my father better. I believe that you are more acquainted with him than either Sergei or myself.' He sighed, and a forlorn look came over his flat-planed, youthful face. Suddenly I saw the Traveller as a young man, and I felt my heart turn in my side.

'Will you bring Hondof too?' I asked, to hide my confusion.

'If Papasha permits it,' he said, and again I noticed the almost slavish deference which both sons displayed towards the Traveller. To them, as to me, his word was law.

CHAPTER EIGHT

C orsica was quite unspoiled at that time. Like Russia, it had not yet become chic for tourists. There were few hotels, and fewer tourists. Boats put out from Nice twice a week, laden with food-stuffs and cattle. A little railway chugged through the cactus-studded hills at erratic intervals. There were some cars on the island, for the most part grotesque-looking taxis, perhaps retired there after their hour of glory on the Marne. The country, so precipitous and dramatic, was said to resemble the Caucasus by the handful of Russian émigrés who now found themselves at Bastia or Ile Rousse, which took its name from the red rock scarps, though I preferred to think of it as Ile *Russe* – a proper setting for our party. At Calvi, Prince Yussoupov and his wife, the Grand Duchess Irina, had an unpretentious little villa, round which clots of émigrés still discussed every detail of Rasputin's murder. The Yussoupovs had got out of Russia leaving behind almost their entire fortune and possessions – an amalgam of fabulous jewels, estates and palaces which exceeded that of the Romanovs and all the rest of the nobles. Like most of their kind, they had not the slightest idea of the value of money. Although they had managed to take with them two Rembrandts, a stupendous black pearl and an amount of money which might be thought enough to provide a comfortable if not spectacular way of life, Russian improvidence took no count of economics: and then, the Yussoupovs were generous to a fault, being surrounded by a retinue of dependent friends and unnecessary servants, while supporting various relief organizations, which were run in a rather chaotic fashion. Presently their assets had melted away, a situation they accepted with a mixture of fatalism and childish amazement. A short distance from our hotel, there was a small bar run by a Tcherkess colonel – a dashing type, one of the survivors of the celebrated *Dikiya Divizia* – 'The Wild Brigade' which had resisted the Bolsheviki so furiously on the Caucasian and Crimean fronts. Corsican mountains, they all agreed, were scaled-down versions of the Caucasus.

'Beshtau in miniature,' said the Tcherkess colonel indicating a rugged peak rising above the forest, and swirled with heavy clouds.

Every evening, in the stuffy little bar decorated with swords and daggers (Caucasian *shashkas* and *kindjali*, as I knew by my reading), I would listen to the talking and the singing that I loved. Sometimes a greenish-pale, silent man whose history no one knew, emerged from the corner where he usually sat over one small vodka throughout the long evening, and sang the old peasant songs of Russia. He would hurl them out on a note of such longing that it was as if he tried to reach across the Mediterranean, across France, north, far north, across the Hungarian *puszta* and the steppes which lay between him and some remote corner of his homeland, where the last echoes of his cry could sink to rest. A silence fell over the bar as each of the exiles returned in his heart to his home.

With the same sense of longing, I was peering through the darkness outside, to where the stars were scattered, projecting myself to an imagined landscape – the Caucasus. Away beyond that hill lies the *aôul* of Ghimri, I would tell myself... and Hadji Mourad and his Murids will gallop down from the mountains by that very path, to ford the Terek – the River of Death (I had been reading Lermontov again), and the great Imam Shamyl will make a last stand on that rock, for it is Gounib, no less.

The Montenegrin aunt never came to the bar: indeed, we seldom saw her. She spent her mornings on the hotel balcony, consulting the cards. Punctually at nine o'clock she would start laying them out for the day's prognostications, rather as, today, people tune-in to the morning news. Her headline résumés were always gloomy. When the sudden gusts of wind peculiar to the island scattered the pack, she sent me to collect a bag of pebbles from the beach, to serve as paperweights.

'Try to find cornelian, or agate,' she said, 'they are always washed up after a storm.'

When the Traveller pointed out that the season had been exceptionally fine, and we were obliged to return with ordinary grey pebbles, she was very much put out.

'It is those Yussoupovs,' she said. 'As if they didn't have enough precious stones already, without beach-combing... Why, in Moscow, I remember hearing that at the Coronation ball his mother wore a *parure* of rubies that were larger than strawberries... And yet they have to come here and grab all the cornelians.'

At which the Traveller remarked that Tartars were extravagant by nature. And with that curious faculty he possessed for linking a remote past with present life, he told how Tamerlaine's daughter-in-law was in the habit of throwing pearls to her goldfish, beating Cleopatra hands down for she, after all, only squandered one pearl on one man.

~

While Corsican beaches did not yield the treasures Aunt Eudoxia desired, the whole island seemed, I thought, to retain a certain hostility to visitors. It was alternately fiery in its heat and drought, its baked rock paths, lizard-infested, winding giddily upwards, or else a prey to sudden gale, with overcast skies, which brought hail whipping down from the mountains, turning a picnic into a trial by exposure.

I ventured to ask the Traveller why he had selected Corsica for our holiday, if, although recalling the Caucasus, it was so often uncomfortably hot or cold; to which he replied:

'Because I'm a spy, Miss. Well, that's what people say, don't they? You must have heard that often enough. It's easy to carry on stealthy business here. Look how smuggling flourishes. A wild coast, remote villages and those dense thickets of the *maquis* for cover. Perfect terrain. Don't you believe me?'

And perhaps I did. It was all in keeping with his climate of mystery, and it made no difference to my feelings. I wondered if there was anything he could have done, or been, that would have destroyed my love. A bull-fighter, or big-game hunter, now... Could I have felt the same towards him? Fortunately this acid test was not applied and I loved on, without reserve.

The Traveller hated Nature, which he always referred to in capitals. He also abhorred the British ritual of a daily walk, and only accompanied me under pressure.

'All those British walks and washes – they are dangerous, habit-forming drugs,' he would say, as I began to stir after the siesta. The rituals of my childhood still held. A day without a walk was, somehow, not right, just as reading novels in the morning had seemed, to Nanny, too indulgent, even in our bookish household. Non-fiction – essays, biographies, travels – these could be read at any time; they had the sanction of study; but novels, however classic, were only for the afternoon – from tea-time onwards. Such Anglo-Saxon disciplines were alien to the Traveller, who often spent a whole morning monopolizing either the bathroom or lavatory, reading current fiction, impervious to the inconvenience this caused others. If a book particularly displeased him, he was apt to stuff it down the lavatory, as proof of his scorn. After which, there was inevitably trouble with the drains.

'I am not surprised,' he would say when we remonstrated with him. 'Such rubbish is enough to choke up any sewer.'

~

While Aunt Eudoxia brooded over the sinister implications of her Tarot cards, hanged men, swords and bleeding hearts turning up regularly, Kamran and Sergei spent their time with the Tcherkess colonel, practising revolver shooting and learning to mix the most imaginative cocktails at the bar.

'As long as they don't mix their own drinks,' said their father coldly. He himself drank only vodka and kept me, very properly, to local red wines.

The character of these two young men differed greatly. Sergei, the eldest, was active, sociable, and clearly with an eye on the main chance, inherited, said the Traveller, from his mother, the Georgian beauty.

'All Georgians are opportunists, supple and astute. That boy will use his looks and his charm, and always fall on his feet,' said his father eyeing him approvingly, as Sergei set off for the beach, carrying the towels and sun umbrella of a trim-looking Frenchwoman who owned a villa near-by and sometimes danced with him at the bar, teaching him the tango, for which he showed great aptitude. I thought her the quintessence of chic, which indeed she was, with an extra, lacquered finish; but both Aunt Eudoxia and the Traveller agreed she lacked style.

'I know her kind – dressed-up for lunch, undressed for tea,' he said acidly, and the Countess, puffing at her tchibouk, shook her head in agreement. She had never lost that Balkanic, near-Eastern habit of shaking the head to signify Yes and nodding it to signify No; something which was to bewilder and amuse me all over again when, many years later, I lived in Bulgaria.

The Frenchwoman's yellow parasol could be seen bobbing along between the hedges of Barbary figs that led to the sea: as it turned a bend in the path I saw it waver, no doubt knocked sideways by the ardour of Sergei's advances.

Somehow, I could never associate him with his father. He bore a superficial resemblance, but there was something about him that was too assured, too pleasing, too regularly handsome, I thought. Except for his slanted dark eyes, there was not much of the Asiatic in his face. He could have passed for a Latin. Kamran was different – was his father's double, was all Asia.

'You spoil those boys – I always knew you would; but Kamran is your favourite, that's plain to see. Don't make Sergei jealous. Don't make *me* jealous either. Don't make me jealous of my own son!' He laughed: 'I don't suppose you know the legend of Akbar's favourite? She was buried alive, on his orders, because he saw her smile at his son.' He paused dramatically for the impact of this warning to sink in, and then, resuming his usual tone, pronounced that Kamran would always be a problem. 'He's a drifter. There used to be a whole population of his kind in Russia, living from day to day, content with little or nothing. No curiosity, no desires. I don't know where he gets it from. Not from me, anyhow. I don't see any Turki or Kirghiz in him either. He'd never ride fifteen hours in the saddle hunting his food with a falcon. He'd be mooning around the *yurt*, like Oblomov in the parlour. I can't imagine what he'll do for a living here in Europe. I suppose he'll just wait for life to pass.'

'I think he'd like to come and live with us, in Paris,' I said diffidently, for I did not want, once again, to be accused of favouritism. 'Perhaps you could find something for him where he could use his languages? After all, he speaks five if you count Turki – and he could easily polish up his English. I'd help him. He ought to find something where he can travel about... Like you,' I added, greatly daring, for having never discovered the exact nature of the Traveller's comings and goings I was always wondering if, at last, the moment of revelation was at hand.

The Traveller's eyes slid sideways to consider the sprawling figure of his son, as immobile in the sunlight as in the chill squalls which broke over the island so often.

'Look at him! He'll never travel – he couldn't even be a commercial traveller,' said his father. 'Travelling requires an energetic mind as well as an energetic body. Curiosity is a form of energy. He has none. He seems content just to exist – to be.'

'Content to *be* rather than to *have*, d'you mean? I think that's rather nice,' I pronounced, and received a withering look.

'You'd better not start thinking that way, Miss, or you'll never get to Siberia,' he snapped and returned to his attack on Kamran. 'He's been hanging round the veranda all the morning. Just the way the beggars used to hang round the church-doors in Moscow – great strong hulks as well as decrepit old creatures, the blind and the lame and the lazy – a pestilential lot. That's where he belongs – unless it's back in an *aôul*.'

'I think you are being rather hard – after all, he's not bothering anyone,' I ventured. Something in Kamran's forlorn air, his lonely figure, touched me. And his stillness seemed, at times, positively desirable after the climate of drama in which I now simmered.

'Hard? No. Just prophetic. He'll rot his life away – you'll see.'

I looked again at the still figure on the steps below us. I had often remarked this particular quality of stillness among Russians. It has nothing to do with Oblomov's inertia, however much the Traveller might cite him. Rilke, writing of Dostoievsky's *House of the Dead*, found it an exaltation of Slav passivity.

'There exists in the Slav soul,' he wrote, 'a degree of submission, even when harassed by the most urgent pressures, and the soul withdraws to the secret place it has created, a kind of further dimension of living, where absolute freedom is found, however painful outward circumstances may be.'

It is perhaps this quality which has enabled them, as a race, to endure so stoically the many hardships imposed on them, over the centuries, by successive rulers.

The fact that the Traveller had made no efforts to settle his sons in a more regular or remunerative way of life was something he refused to admit when Aunt Eudoxia boldly broached the subject.

The boys had, she said, no background, no money, no chances, no country even. What was the good of suddenly irrupting into their lives, treating them to a series of rich meals, a holiday, as now, and then forgetting them entirely, or resenting it if they expected help or advice? 'Why, you haven't even bothered to get them proper papers,' she added scornfully, and went on to disparage the Nansen passport which she herself had at last obtained. 'It's better than nothing, of course, and for me, it really doesn't matter now – but they are only just beginning their lives – they are living in France where papers matter so much. You really might do better for them. You of all people,' she added, alluding to the Traveller's self-proclaimed ability to obtain generally unobtainable permits. The Traveller shrugged and opened his mouth to reply, but she cut in angrily, warming to her theme.

They might just as well have been left behind in Russia, she continued, to become part of those packs of wolfish children who roamed, plundered, and lived lawlessly – the *bezprizorni* – without foyer – rootless, abandoned, children of the Revolution who defied all authority and were the terror of any person or community upon whom they descended.

'At least among the *bezprizorni* they would have belonged.' She glared at the Traveller and then, following up her attack, continued, tank-like: 'And what are you doing about the sort of women they pick up? I suppose they do?'

The Traveller shrugged again. 'What can I do? My dear Eudoxia, I haven't got a household – there's no *nianya* to arrange things any more.'

At my inquiring look, he enlarged on this intriguing statement. 'You see, in the old days everything of that sort was so well organized – none of your English hypocrisy and cold baths. And contrary to what you might imagine from reading rubbishy novelettes, our youngsters were not always toasting their mistresses in pink champagne. We started young, but not in the bordellos: it was all very natural. It was always the old family *nianyas* who arranged matters. I remember in our home, *nianya* watched over all of us boys: as soon as she thought it the right moment she'd go to my mother and say: "*Barinya*, we must think about getting a new house-maid. Master Dimitri's sixteen... it's time for him to find out for himself." And Mama would choose some healthy peasant girl, and that was that.'

'It was a delightful arrangement. The girls were always so proud to be chosen for the young master. They liked our uniform; we looked quite dashing – schoolboys or not. Everyone wore a uniform of some sort, then. At my Lycée ours was dark red, with silver braid... But I remember, it was only after we passed our final exams that the mathematics Professor took us all to a brothel to celebrate. Things were really very well arranged then.'

He looked across the terrace to where Kamran was now asleep under a narrow margin of shade provided by some cacti.

'Lazy young fool. He can't even arrange his siesta comfortably. Well, if he can't look after himself that much, I certainly can't be responsible for his papers, let alone his sex-life,' said his father, shrugging Kamran out of his line of vision.

～

We had discovered an old piano in the hotel. It was curiously shaped, elongated and graceful and looked as if it might have served Chopin in Majorca. A family of mice had settled inside and were flourishing on the felt-covered hammers. They used to scuttle off at our approach, their tiny paws making a scampering *glissando* as they raced across the strings.

In the hot Corsican noonday, we would take refuge in the empty, dim salon, and seated side by side, thump out the Polonaise from *Eugène Onegin*. The Traveller was unrestrainedly emotional over almost any music, and, as he picked out a haunting air – Alabiev's *Nightingale* – tears glistened on the high yellow cheek bones, while he told me how that lyrical and soaring melody had sprung from a musician who had been exiled to Siberia for some minor offence. Next, he was trying to re-create the whole of Rimsky-Korsakoff's opera *Kitej*. Humming, twiddling and banging, he scarcely did justice to the divinely lovely, melancholy music, but I was transported by his re-telling of the legend, sobbing with him, as he conjured the lost, loved city sunk below the lake in glassy calm.

Fumbling for a handkerchief he shut the piano lid carefully to avoid jarring the mice who, we had discovered, removed themselves to the farthest end of the piano during our duets. We never found out if, or how, they left or regained their resonant dwelling, for the lid was seldom raised; we came to the conclusion they led stay-at-home lives.

~

The Traveller, who had known so many of the world's capitals and their diversions, liked nothing better than small distractions – the local open-air cinema (seated on backless benches) or an outing to the *Place* – where we would dawdle over a *coup de blanc* and read the week-old newspapers pasted on the walls of the Mairie. Sometimes I would try to lure him to accompany me on my ritualistic walk.

'We could go down to the jetty and see if the mail-boat has come in yet.'

'Sly-boots – all you want is your walkies, like Hondi. And don't try to exercise *me*. Let me tell you – if ever you'd walked across the Gobi desert, as I have done, you would have had enough of *le footing* to last you a life-time. That was one particularly good thing about both the Kirghiz and the Kalmucks, they never walked a step. They'd jump on their little horses to trot from one tent to another... never put a foot to the ground if they could help it... like Americans in their automobiles.'

'Then let's ride,' I suggested.

'On mules? I haven't seen a decent mount since I left Russia,' he grumbled, and was off, describing pure-bred Karabakhs, Orloff blacks, and the racing camels of Outer Mongolia. He sat down, firmly, under a eucalyptus tree in the hotel garden, knowing that by his tales he would distract me from my exercise.

'You should have seen Ungern Sternberg's white beast,' he began. 'A magnificent creature. Its bridle was decorated with two of the blackest sables you ever saw.'

'*Black* sables?' I was barely familiar with the brown pelts which, in the West, we associated with luxury.

'Bargouzin sables – black as your hat,' he replied colloquially. He was given to these excursions into the vernacular, and occasionally they proved too much for him. Having heard Nanny address me, in moments of softness, as 'poor little mite' he later rendered this as 'poor little termite', while chilblains, ever a subject of conversation in English nurseries (although apparently unknown in Russia, where it was frost-bite or nothing), he called chillyblains. For all his languages he could never learn to correct such lapses. Argue was pronounced arg.

'*Pussinka!* Don't arg!' he would yell, nettled. 'Your English pronunciation is without any rules. Besides, arg sounds much more definite,' was his invariable defence.

I recall a cloud falling over the luncheon table at home when he announced that he and my father were going to Richmond Park that afternoon.

'And on the way home, I'm hoping to have some honourable virgins,' he said genially. My mother stiffened slightly and left us before coffee, murmuring something about Harrods.

What the sweet-toothed Traveller had in mind was an innocent plateful of little cakes, the famous Richmond Maids-of-Honour. When everything was explained, he kissed my mother's hand in his own way, in the palm, rather than on the back of the hand.

'You English women are angels,' he said. 'But do angels have appetites?' At which she gave him a curious look, a look I had seen on her face several times, when he teased her, or spoiled me too lavishly.

~

On the terrace at Calvi, a chill wind began to rustle a puny clump of banana trees, a dry, scaly sound, as if this tropic vegetation resented being transplanted to so harsh a setting. But the sinking sun was still brilliant, slanting over the roof-tops. In the gathering shadows the

Traveller was warming me at the fires of his memory and imagination; telling of Siberian tigers, the largest, most ferocious of the species, that are still found in the reedy shores of Baikal, their fur cream-coloured rather than tawny: telling of a breed of wild horse, native to Siberia, and named after Prjevalsky, the naturalist who first classified them: telling, too of the legendary *huluk*, a charger of preternatural strength: Jenghis Khan called his chargers his chosen marshals, worthy of leading his armies. The *huluk* is said by the Mongols to possess ribs which are formed in one single sheet of bone, like iron-clad plating; once this is hardened to maturity, the *huluk* can resist attack by wolves... Knowing this, wolves never attack a grown *huluk*, going only for young ones; or so the Traveller said.

Such were the curious pieces of information he enlarged upon: and sometimes, becoming more factual, he told of life among the Kirghiz, as they moved about the wastes with their flocks. This was something he knew well enough, since he had spent a whole summer's migration in the upland pastures with them when courting Kamran's mother. They lived much as their ancestors of the Hordes had done, he said. 'Which did not stop your mother spending an alarming amount of money at the dress-makers and hairdressers, as soon as I took her back to St. Petersburg,' he continued, fixing Kamran with a baleful stare. Kamran moved off, with a hang-dog air, Hondof slinking sympathetically after him.

Having disposed of Kamran, his father settled himself comfortably and resumed his story-telling, his mind seeming to hover and dart dragon-fly-like, about so many different scenes and settings, telling of Kazan, where mighty Potemkin's library, 80,000 volumes, had come to rest on the shelves of the city library. Of how the first roses were brought to Russia from Isfahan by way of Constantinople, being floated up the Don and the Volga in barges, destined for the Empress Sophia, the Paleologi Princess married to the Tzar Ivan III in 1472. Telling how *good* brandy smells of bugs – he emphasized the adjective. How Mongolian men's prowess – as stallions – was celebrated in Eastern Siberia, but that they were as nothing beside the Chinese, who were the dread of all women captured by them, being insatiable, and constructed – here Aunt Eudoxia interrupted him, firmly changing the subject, being no doubt belatedly aware of her responsibilities as chaperone.

Now the Traveller was recounting Asiatic plenty on other terms; of magnificence, and how the Baron von Ungern Sternberg knew that to be respected and obeyed he must be envied as well as feared and display a conqueror's glory. Like terror, splendour has power throughout Asia.

'Was he a friend of yours?' I was longing to learn more about this legendary figure.

'That *monster?* No, but I knew him well enough when his regiment was in St. Petersburg – he was in the Nerchinsk Cossacks. His family were Baltic barons. *Balts'* – he spat out the word rather as some French hiss the word *Belges!* – a mortal insult. 'As I was saying,' he continued, 'splendour is respected in Asia. There, furs and precious stones are coinage. In Siberia they are truly understood. Why, with all those mines of ours, my brother used to give the housemaids emeralds for Christmas. Jenghis Khan's tent was made entirely of leopard skins,' he went on, 'leopard, lined with sable. The sort of furs most western women wear would not be used as bath-mats by Asiatics.'

At which Aunt Eudoxia snorted:

'Oh yes, we all know you used to pave the floors with sapphires and sweep them with sables in Siberia. All the same, it was a very provincial sort of life... So far from everything...'

'And what about Montenegro?' muttered Kamran, who having been born in Tobolsk (which made him, in my eyes, a Siberian), shared the general Russian view that Balkan countries were very small fry. The Traveller waved aside the matter as unworthy of further consideration. Towards his own family as to mine, he maintained an unmistakable air of arrogance – an overlord, relegating the rest of the world to their proper place – serfdom. He shared Dumas' view that woman was merely *la femelle de l'homme.*

Indeed, his whole conception of the relationship between man and woman retained something medieval. It was easy to imagine him living in the manner of the old Russian landowner, Kachkarov, *barin,* or absolute master of his domain. There, in 1820, he maintained, like so many of the neighbouring squires, a whole harem of comely serf-girls, twenty or more, whose lives and bodies were at the disposal of their master. They did not consider themselves ill-used. The girls, having passed by the master's bed, were married off among the men servants, usually according to the whim of their master, who saw to it that they were well-dowered. Such Russian pashas lived in a curious mixture of indolence and energy, squalor and wealth. After a morning spent rigorously controlling the administration of his vast estates, Kachkarov would go hunting, and return to a dinner table set for thirty or more, for he had a large family and numberless guests. He himself ate with gargantuan appetite at a separate table, growling his criticisms of the suckling pig, stuffed carp, or other delicacies, while his serf choir sang traditional songs, or danced for him. After a game of whist, he would bid his meek wife and children good night and repair to his own quarters, one of the serf-girls having preceded him with a lighted candle, announcing, 'The *barin* deigns to retire.' At which the rest of his harem would follow, spreading their mattresses and quilts on the floor around his bed, for that was where he elected they should sleep. The chosen favourite for the night was expected to help the *barin* undress and then, drawing the curtains round the bed, tickle the soles of his feet (once a traditional method of wooing sleep among the Russians) until he snored. After which she must spend the night awake beside him, alert for his commands, to be cuffed, or caressed, to lull him with fairy tales, or just to keep the flies at bay.

'Very proper,' said the Traveller, smacking his lips as he recounted such goings-on, and fancying himself in the leading role.

'I remember our feet were still being tickled with goose-feathers when I first married and went to Kazan,' said the Countess dreamily, 'it was delicious... You should try it, if you can't sleep,' she said turning her blank stare on me.

'But who would tickle the soles of my feet?' I asked, with visions of some outraged daily being asked to stay overtime.

'Me, I would. Mamasha,' said Kamran suddenly. He seldom spoke, so that I looked at him in surprise. He was sprawling on the ground, beside my chair, and looked sullen, as if the offer was wrung from him against his will. His hair needed cutting and fell over his face in a dark wing of plumage. He was a handsome creature.

'Ridiculous! Mamasha sleeps like a log,' said the Traveller. 'A bastinado wouldn't wake her.' I thought his voice sounded unusually harsh. He led the way into the dining-room: the *barin*, deigning to eat.

He had certain dictums about women, whom he saw at once sentimentally and cynically. Like Pushkin (who contradicted himself in his portrait of Tatiana), he held they should not have character: only passions, when young. When not young...? Then no doubt they ceased to exist as women, a point of view loosely described as Oriental, but which in fact is not so, for in the East older women continue to wield enormous power, both in the home and outside it; but always with discretion, behind that veil which progress now wishes them to discard.

'Pretty women,' pronounced the Traveller, 'should always wear pink,' and he would shrug disparagingly if I wore another colour, thus nullifying the implied compliment. Or, 'all women should be able to play the piano – it suits them to play Schumann or Chopin; especially on summer evenings in the country... As long as they're playing, their husbands know they're not up to mischief... or watching them too closely.'

He would smile sardonically, and then sigh and fall silent. I think he was recalling his childhood, his domineering father and his frivolous mother. Recalling her in the long white nights of Russia, seeing again their country house set on a hill above the river, seeing again the greenish dusk of the garden paths and the lamplight falling on the wide veranda; the smell of lilac and the sound of an accordion floating up from the village, overcoming the limpid notes of the piano, as his mother, so graceful in her pink chiffon tea-gown tackled a *valse brillante*, not very well perhaps, but well enough... Well enough for her little son to stop spinning his top and listen and her husband to light his cigar and smile, reassured, as he followed her maid upstairs: another *barin*, indulging himself.

CHAPTER NINE

Although the Traveller had not brought anything to read on the train, he usually carried a few favourite books about with him, so that one or more could accompany him on even the shortest journeys. Or the longest evenings, he might have added, for he was ruthless when bored, making no attempt at civility, and would show his dissatisfaction with the assembled company by retreating to a corner, producing a book, and burying himself in it, to the chagrin of the hostess. Over the years, this ambulant library did not change; it represented, I supposed, his abiding favourites, to which he could return perpetually. Among them was Gogol's *Government Inspector*, in a battered edition acquired during his schooldays. Sometimes, from a vertiginous hill-side above the port, where I had succeeded in dragging him for the ritual walk, he would read to me from which ever book happened to be in his pocket that day. If it was in Russian or German he went straight on, seldom stopping to translate.

'You don't follow? Too bad. Then listen to the language.' And he would plunge into an exchange between Dobchinsky and Bobchinsky, laughing uproariously at Gogol's sardonic scenes.

Once, producing Landor's *Imaginary Conversations*, he remained silent a long while, turning the pages, and pausing to look down the rocky slopes to where, far below, pygmy figures darted about the Place du Marché and the carts began threading their way out of the town, towards the country. From a great distance I heard the noonday bells ringing, a gnat-like humming, and my built-in Anglo-Saxon sense of punctuality began to assert itself.

'It must be after twelve. We shall be late for lunch unless we start down now.'

'Listen!' he said, and read me Aesop's words to Rhodopé.

'If, turning back I could overpass the vale of years and could stand on the mountain top and could look again far before me at the bright ascending morn, we would enjoy the prospect together, and we would walk along the summit hand in hand O Rhodopé! and we would only sigh at last, when we found ourselves below with others.'

He shut the book and took me in his arms.

'Now you see, my Rhodopé, why the name fits you so well, quite apart from all that sugar-icing pink and whiteness of yours.'

'Well, I shan't call you Aesop, however appropriate – it's a hairy Old Testament sort of name – not you at all, even if Aesop was twice Rhodopé's age.'

The conversation now took a yet more personal turn, and we missed lunch altogether.

~

Occasionally the Traveller was persuaded to go on an expedition – to cross the mountain passes, or to explore little towns like Cargese or Ajaccio, an overnight outing in a hysterically- behaved hired car.

'You really love *mileage* – distance for distance sake,' he would grumble as I watched the country unfold before us at each turn of the road.

'Yes, you do,' he continued. 'Just going – moving into space satisfies you. Not for nothing were you born a Gemini. They're always fidgeting. But with that passion in your blood, Corsica's too small, like England – like Europe, indeed. You'll soon fall off the edge. Only Asia will be limitless enough for you. I suppose, subconsciously, that's why you crave Siberia.'

~

Some of the Traveller's tales assumed, over the years, a legendary quality. Their telling and re-telling became a ritual, where each fresh embellishment was savoured, discarded, or integrated. But where truth ended and embellishment began was a delicate point.

'I don't remember that bit about the fugitive hiding in the Chinese quarter at Nijni-Novgorod – but do go on...'

A sharp look. 'That's because I never told you that I was the man they were after... That was when I first shaved my head...'

I liked to think that every treasured word, every fabled landscape was exact. However high-flying, given that faraway setting of white nights and limitless distances, I felt anything could be. However extravagant the episodes, I always preferred those of an allegedly autobiographical nature, for they pierced, even fragmentarily, that screen which the Traveller had chosen to set up between himself and the rest of the world – myself included.

Sometimes I would try to trap him into some further proofs of personal involvement, but he would parry, side-tracking me with a gaudy detail, or making one off his strategic withdrawals into a limbo-land of concentration, where he knew I could not follow, lurking behind that façade which tormented me with its mystery. Or he would toss me an autobiographical crumb which I would hoard, trying to fit it into the mosaic of circumstances I already possessed. Direct questions were not encouraged, often being met with silence rather than evasion. Nevertheless, he himself would interrogate ruthlessly, and when he fixed his victim with that unblinking stare he was always answered.

It might be supposed that some of the Traveller's friends, his aunt or his sons, whose respective mothers had, after all, shared some part of his life, could have told something more of that background lying behind the façade of baroque ornament he vouchsafed. I longed with a bourgeois craving for some sort of *curriculum vitae*. Birthplace, parentage, education, career, hobbies – clubs? At least some basic structure upon which to place the flourishes. Yet no one was able to tell me much more than I knew. It was not that they withheld anything, but rather that they were passive. Perhaps, being Russians, or Asiatics, and sharing fundamental characteristics of nomadism, roots were of no account. They took things for granted, including gaps in time, for, like animals, I noticed that a week, a month or a year was to them of no specific importance. They themselves existed. They had been, they were, and one day, they would be no more. Where, when, did not trouble them over-much.

'When I was little... over there,' Kamran would say, jerking his head towards Asia. But he did not recall his father being there too. He thought he remembered a big herd of horses... an encampment in the mountains... gun-fire... a falcon that had shared the saddle-bag in which he travelled to some city... strange songs he could still recall... Songs of the Ktché Dj, I thought longingly.

'Sing some!' I commanded, waiting for the reedy cadences of Asia. But while he was frowning in concentration, his father appeared suddenly, silently, almost stealthily, as was his habit, stepping cat-like, in his soft Torghut boots.

He eyed us enigmatically. 'Where the apple reddens never pry, lest we lose our Eden, Eve and I,' he remarked, displaying, once again, his curious faculty for quoting appropriate lines in a number of languages.

But I was not to be put of, Browning or no. When he was safely in the bath, I would sidle up to Aunt Eudoxia's balcony, where she was ritualistically laying out the Tarot cards for the morning's disasters. If a particularly sinister conjunction appeared, and her sense of drama was appeased, she was more inclined to be communicative. She was, it transpired, only a few years older than the Traveller, and perfectly sane. (So much for the appellation 'old, mad'), but her second husband, the Traveller's uncle, had stemmed from one of the ancient Tartar families of Kazan. She told me she had seen her nephew-in-law for the first time in that city, when he was twenty, and on manoeuvres with his regiment.

'Which one?' I asked breathlessly. Now, at last, some facts. But my question was not to be answered.

'I don't remember... he wore a shako... No, that was my first husband the Bulgarian – anyhow, it's of no importance now,' she said, shuffling the pack, poring intently over Justice, Misero, the Fool, and the Crumbling Castle.

'I was only his aunt by marriage, after all,' she continued. 'He was moving about a lot just then, and seldom saw the rest of the family. His father was descended from one of the Hordes I believe, but his mother was from the Caucasus – a remarkably beautiful woman. So sad she had such an ugly-looking boy.' (Ugly? was it conceivable that anyone found that darling Asiatic face *ugly*?)

The Traveller seldom spoke of his father, but all these intriguing statements of Aunt Eudoxia's were, I hoped, to be expanded at voluptuous length. 'He left the army after some scandal: a duel' (a duel to the death, I wondered?) 'He always was impetuous, a real *scandalist!*' continued Aunt Eudoxia, 'I believe he went and joined a scientific expedition to the Gobi, and got himself involved with some Kirghiz tribe... Kamran's mother was one of them – or was she a Bashkir? Something savage, I remember. Anyhow,' she continued, dismissing the Hordes with the wave of a plump hand, 'he spent years on and off in Siberia – crossed in love, his mother always said, though I never thought he cared that much about anyone. Siberia! and after the family had settled in that charming house in Moscow, too. But then he never did anything one expected.'

It seemed there was a good-for-nothing elder brother who lived in Irkutsk – something to do with gold mines thereabouts, belonging to the family. Aunt Eudoxia couldn't recall exactly where. 'What difference does it make now? They must have been nationalized long ago, and he must have been killed.'

Once when she was in Switzerland the Traveller had written asking her to engage a French-speaking governess for the wives of some Turcoman Khan whom he had encountered doing the cure at Vichy.

'I remember he wrote that the Khan had seven hundred wives – not all with him, of course. I don't know why, but it made an impression on me, at the time,' she said. 'I lost touch with him for years after that, and only ran across him again by chance, after we got out through Constantinople... He'd had a bad time, and was given up for dead with cholera. The wounded were packed into cattle trucks – it was that, or leaving them behind at Batoum. They put the dying ones in last, so they could be thrown out as soon as they died, without disturbing the others. One of his friends told me it hadn't seemed worth transporting him, he was so obviously done for. But there you are – Destiny willed it otherwise. He didn't die, though he was in a Turkish hospital for months. As soon as he was about again he got himself into heavy trouble over some business beyond Erzerum. Something to do with the turquoise mines, he said. But it was much too near the Russian frontier, to my way of thinking.'

Her face clouded over. 'I've never discovered what he was up to there... but then I've never understood – at times I begin to think...' She checked herself abruptly, and I watched a brooding darkness settle on the carefully painted plump face.

As the morning sun rounded the hill-top, its rays poured on to the balcony, gilding the Tarot cards, and turning the Countess's painted cheeks to over-ripe plums. Sadness sat badly on such a countenance, for it was accustomed to more violent emotions – fury, gaiety, or anguish. Yet sorrow, a sort of passive melancholy, always possessed her when she consulted the cards concerning the Traveller. They told her nothing good, and she would call on Heaven to witness her despair.

'Mother of God! I don't like it. I often do the cards for him,' she said. 'He believes in them implicitly, as you know.' (I didn't.) 'I think Ungern Sternberg's fate influenced him.' It seemed that this sinister and complex figure allowed himself to be guided by a Chinese necromancer, and that his campaigns in Outer Mongolia (against the Bolshevik army) and his own end had all been foretold to him exactly.

'Every hideous twist,' continued Aunt Eudoxia, muttering of Japanese designs in Manchuria, of Allied treachery. Kolchak's betrayal and 'those *moujiks*', as she always described the Red Army. What, if any, was the Traveller's part in all this, she did not reveal. But anticipating some supreme moment of truth, I was making furious efforts to keep up with her, to memorize the names and implications.

Her plump ringed hands swept the cards together as she talked, shuffling them and dealing afresh. I watched their symbolism unfold. The Hanging Man, the Wheel of Fortune, the Fool, and the Lovers. 'There you are – you always turn up near him now,' she said, tapping the designated card with a padded white finger. 'But it's dark... darkness, always darkness... No good will come of it. I've tried telling him, though of course he won't listen to me. He enjoys drama. It's become part of his life.'

'*Bojhe moyi!* I don't like it... Such darkness round him. I don't like it at all. Although he's only my nephew by marriage, I'm very much attached to him, even after that business about the box buried under the bath-house in Kazan. Oh, don't you know about that? Well, remind me some other time... I must work out his cards now.'

She gave me a beady look.

'Don't try to understand him. Men hate being understood. And he was always like that – always mysterious,' she added. But I could have told her that. Once more the moment of revelation had eluded me.

~

Our Corsican evenings were often enlivened by the Tarot cards. When in the mood, the Countess told the fortune of anyone within sight – the other visitors, the chef, fetched in from the kitchen, or once again, our own family circle. She would hold forth on the cards' mystic origin. They derived, she claimed, from Egyptian occultism, first brought from India by wandering Gypsies, who introduced them to Europe. Then the Traveller, who rarely accepted other people's theories unchallenged, particularly those of women, would remind her the Gypsies were not known in Europe in any number before the fifteenth century, whereas the Tarot cards were in use as early as 1350. An uproar would ensue regularly, both of them behaving in a manner the English nannies of their Slavic childhood would not have tolerated for a moment. One particularly violent argument had arisen after Aunt Eudoxia had found an interesting old pack of Italian playing cards on a book-stall in Ajaccio, and had been laying them out before dinner in the manner of a mystical apéritif. She had, on this occasion, designated the Traveller as the Knave of Spades, when of course he saw himself as the King of Hearts.

'*Le Valet Moi? Le Valet de Pique?* You must be mad! Your own husband always said you were!' Typhoons of ill-temper now rose round us, till the Traveller, stamping his denials, kicked over the ever-present *tchibouk*. At which Aunt Eudoxia, livid beneath her rouge, for the thrust about her husband had pierced deep, flung the cards in his face and announced she was leaving in the morning.

'And I shall take her with me,' she hissed, stabbing in my direction. This threat was not to be taken lightly for, without her presence on the island, she knew my parents would not sanction my staying on.

In reply, the Traveller seized the menu (the only one provided by the hotel) and tearing it to shreds, flung the particles after her, and hurled a tray of *hors d'oeuvres variés* to the ground. Aunt Eudoxia rushed to the reception desk, taking refuge behind the hall-porter and demanding the boat time-table. The knock-about nature of this scene was not apparent to Kamran or Sergei, who fled to the Tcherkess bar, while Hondof crouched shivering beneath the table.

'Really! What a fuss about nothing! You ought to be ashamed of yourselves!' I heard my voice echoing generations of English nannies. Oddly it seemed to calm the furious Slavs for Aunt Eudoxia emerged from behind the reception desk and swept up to her room, making an exit worthy of Duse at her most tragic, while the Traveller sank into a basket-chair on the terrace, relaxed and purged, wearing a seraphic smile. Suddenly, this sophisticated pair appeared to me as the over-excited, undisciplined children they must once have been. I saw them in a Moscow nursery, fighting over their toys, slavishly indulged by the old Russian *nianya* and sharply disciplined by their English nanny. 'My little pigeons,' sighs Matriona fondly, as the baby Traveller (at this age, his head is covered in dark curls) hits the pinafored Eudoxia over the nose with a piece of fire-wood lying beside the high white porcelain stove. Eudoxia yells, and takes a bite out of his neck (which emerges from a peasant-embroidered *roubashka*). The children have been fighting for possession of a carved wooden sleigh – it is the one which I now treasure – and soon, kicking and hitting, both are rolling on the floor, entangling themselves with the fringe of a crimson chenille tablecloth, so that Matriona's sewing basket and a samovar (fortunately not lit) are brought down on top of them. At which Nanny Smithson (six years as under-nursemaid at Chatsworth and later head nurse in a Grand Ducal household) comes briskly into the room, a Mrs. Noah figure of starch and whalebone.

'Goodness me! What's all this about? What a to-do! You ought to be ashamed of yourselves,' she says, and with no more ado the struggling brats are separated, stuck into their high chairs and told not to be so silly.

So now, in a Corsican hotel, the pattern was being repeated, the uproar quashed by my brisk nursery phrases. When, an hour or two later, harmony was restored, the Traveller and Aunt Eudoxia having apparently forgotten their differences in a common desire for dinner, it was found that dinner was off. The waiter, having spooned up the *hors d'oeuvres variés* from the floor, was now removing the cloths and salt cellars with an air of satisfaction, before vanishing.

'Grandmama was right. It was the beginning of the end when the serfs were emancipated,' sighed the Traveller, and the Countess agreed.

~

Kamran had disgraced himself, falling dead drunk across the tables at the Tcherkess bar where he had been fêting my eighteenth birthday in a traditional Russian manner. It was an old custom for an admirer to drink the lady's health by downing the number of glasses of vodka which corresponded with the number of letters in her name Thus 'Ann' demanded only three glasses, but 'Grushenka', nine, and so on. The unfortunate Kamran had struggled gallantly through five of the six glasses my name required before succumbing. The Tcherkess colonel laughed uproariously for he had substituted extra large glasses for this celebration, which I thought most unfair, but Kamran had accepted the challenge and downed the first two at a gulp.

It was a touching tribute, being so plainly designed to create the Russian ambiance he knew I loved. I was entranced, but anxious. Such violence was nothing if not Russian. Sergei watched with a certain sulkiness; it would, he said, have been just the thing to gain the favours of Madame Pelletier – the Frenchwoman with whom he now spent most of his time.

We had just succeeded in lugging Kamran back to the hotel when we encountered the Traveller, who was setting out to join us at the bar. For a Russian, he was always unsympathetic to hard drinking, but now he seemed unreasonably angry. I pleaded indulgence, but was met with a scowl.

'It's lucky for him you're not called Elizaveta-Anastasia-Alexandra, like one of my mistresses when I was his age. I played the same fool's game right to the end – twenty-seven glasses of vodka! The real stuff we used to have then, mind you, not the wish-wash you get here... But Kamran's useless – he can't even hold six glasses!'

Seizing his unresisting son by the scruff of the neck he dragged him away. Kamran was not seen again that night, and when next day I went to his room to find out how he felt, the Traveller was impatient of my solicitude.

'Let him alone. That will teach him.'

'Teach him what?'

'Not to be so Russian. Now stop fussing over him, Miss.'

~

In Corsica we contrived to live becalmed: no letters and few newspapers reached us – nor was there, at that time, the intrusion of news-broadcasts. On the rare occasions when the Traveller came across newspapers he would dump them straight into the wastepaper basket.

'As pointers to what we may expect from the future, I find them unnerving. I'd rather crystal-gaze, and see what I want to see... Or look back...' His eyes narrowed to that stare which meant he was thinking Russia. This was my cue; soon we would be faraway together, safe in our own Slav limbo-land, playing the Run-Away Game, Magic of Magics...

'Païdium! Let's go!' I pronounced the old formula.

'...lonely no more,' sighed the Traveller, recalling the old Siberian song. He held out his arms and I rushed into them.

~

Although our golden-crowned wedding was imperceptibly assuming a remote and legendary quality, becoming a shared future as distant yet believable as that past in which we liked to dwell, we often spoke of it when alone together, and to my joyous surprise the Traveller announced he was plucking up courage to approach my parents on the subject.

'Though I know what they'll say.' He stared gloomily out to sea, northwards, towards London, towards reality.

'I expect they'll say we must wait till I'm twenty-one.'

'They'll say a lot more than that.'

~

Kamran and Sergei continued to address me as Mamasha and seemed to have no doubt as to my place in their life; as their father's future wife I was treated with a deference I found unexpected and pleasing, for it seemed to set the seal on my adult status – something which I still thought both improbable and desirable at that time. But Aunt Eudoxia, not unnaturally, saw the whole thing as a familiar joke.

'Your father is not the marrying kind – *you* ought to know that by now,' she said sharply, when Kamran sprang to my defence and said everything was settled and he was coming to live with us when we set up house in Paris.

'The candles carried at the wedding ceremony must be kept to light the first night of the first-born,' I told the Traveller, for I had been reading an anthology of Slav folklore, and was, moreover, now ensnared by a maternal urge, fancying I would enjoy a little Slav of my own.

'Mumbo-jumbo,' was the only reply I got from the Traveller but he did not seem displeased. All that day he had been morose, 'thinking Russia'. Together he and Aunt Eudoxia had been recalling old times, telling of exotic characters they remembered from their Russian life: Tiflis, it seemed, had been peopled with the most furious and seductive types.

'D'you remember how they used to dance?'

Aunt Eudoxia sighed, recalling, no doubt, some romantic interlude.

'The Dance of the Eagles...' Now the Traveller was launched, describing to me the feudal Georgian Court dances, stately or fiery, a living tradition there.

He possessed that curious magnetic power found in the street story-tellers of the East, crouched among their rags, holding a circle of listeners spellbound, becoming, by some sorcery of their own, each character in turn, conjuring, with a flick of a tattered sleeve, brigands, Caliphs or all the peris of Paradise. It did not matter that the Traveller was a man, in European clothes: with a turn of the shoulder, a movement of his hands – the supple hands of a magician – he could conjure up the gliding grace of the Lezghinka, evoking the Georgian noblewomen as they advanced or retreated, promising, denying, each step a stately ritual. Or, with another change of pace, or magic, crashing his foot down with that fury only Slavs and Spaniards know, he would summon up the dark fur-capped warriors of Elbruz leaping across steel in the dagger dance, or performing other strange, almost imperceptible steps, vibrations of passion.

Many years later, in the shadow of Elbruz, I was to watch these same fiery dances, the Dance of the Eagles or of the Partisans, and knew that I was seeing them for the second time; for their reality was in no way sharper, more true, than his sorcery.

Now Aunt Eudoxia was describing the manner in which the Georgian women seemed to float, gliding swan-like, infinitely remote, deified creatures of mystery.

'Your mother caught me that way,' remarked the Traveller, whacking Sergei hard over the head with a fly-swatter; but this seemed a gesture of affection rather than malice. 'She was one of the youngest beauties at the ball,' he continued. 'They all wore white... trailing skirts, scarves, veils, shawls... that's how women should be – like well-wrapped parcels – to be undone.'

'And the men! O! those Georgian men!' sighed Aunt Eudoxia, telling of the soft leather boots they wore, and how they rose *sur les pointes* like ballerinas. And then, how they seemed to stab the ground with violent steps, circling round the woman, stamping furiously, like... She came to a full stop, searching for words to describe this *contredanse* of desire.

'Like rutting animals – after all, it was a pantomime of conquest,' the Traveller reminded her. "But *chevaleresque*, too. Don't forget that all the while, as they circled, the man's tunic must not even brush the skirt of his partner. It was a tradition. She was his goddess, his *Princesse Lointaine*... But she wore a dagger, and knew how to use it, too. Those women knew about hating, as well as loving... D'you remember Anyia's mother – the Princess who ran up all those debts in Tiflis?'

Aunt Eudoxia nodded, and the Traveller went on to relate how the lady, who had been a famous beauty, had cornered the Tzar at a State ball and asked him to silence the Jewish money-lender who pressed her the hardest.

'But my dear Princess, what can I do? I can't murder him,' said the monarch.

'And you call yourself a Tzar!' she spat.

No, she had not been sent to Siberia for such daring. But then she was a great beauty. Aunt Eudoxia sighed again, her plump painted face folding into lines of envy and resignation.

'And it was the Caucasus,' the Traveller reminded her. 'Everything was more emphatic there. The Georgians were a fiery race, and the Russians always forgave them. I remember a story another old Princess used to tell. She was still a splendid ruin when I knew her. She wore the traditional velvet dress, the *katiba*, and the little flat cap, with two long curls each side of her face... But she still had a look about her... she was still very much a woman... Well, anyhow, I used to like visiting her. One afternoon we were sitting under the vines of her estates outside Tiflis: she used to have the samovar and her needlework brought out there on summer evenings, and once, she started talking about her marriage. Her husband had been an exceedingly jealous man, but she loved him.

'"I was only unfaithful to him once," she told me, "and then only in my mind... though that's the same thing really... It was when I was very young. I caught sight of a tribesman from the mountains – one of those barbaric creatures that were still skirmishing with our troops. What a troublesome lot they were. They simply *refused* to be subdued! I saw this man riding through the woods. He had his *bashlyk* drawn over his head, so I only caught a glimpse of him, but he had the bluest eye you ever saw..."

"'Only one?'"

"'I only saw the one, for his hood hid the other. But that was enough. He looked at me... a long look... and I was unfaithful to my husband – in my mind. I couldn't forget that blue gaze. I was a silly girl. I told my husband about him. Blue eyes are rare among the tribes. My husband tracked him down easily enough. A week or so later he brought me his head. One eye had a dagger through it. The other was wide open, staring... staring at *me*!"

"'There's your blue eye for you,' said my husband.'"

'So much for jealousy, Caucasian style,' said Aunt Eudoxia, and breaking the spell she began to talk about unobtainable Russian delicacies – *koumiss* – and a special kind of jam made from *black* radishes 'the kind Praskovia used to make.'

'Yes, Proust was right,' sighed the Traveller. 'The only real Paradise is the one we have lost.' The Traveller might sigh, but I, having not yet reached the watershed of time, still looked forward rather than back. At that time, I was entirely happy.

~

Below the terrace an enormous concourse of late-mating frogs croaked their bliss. The sun dipped below the mountain abruptly, and the valleys turned sharply violet. The Traveller was manoeuvring to attract my attention behind the Countess's back. He started pulling his ear, a signal, meaning: let's get away together. In the wild Corsican countryside we had discovered mountain slopes covered with that dense and aromatic vegetation known as the *macchia*. It was sometimes shoulder high, and sheltered us even more completely than the bracken on the Clovelly cliffs where once we had dallied innocently in the green shade of Gallantry Bower. But this *macchia* had a strange atmosphere of drama, something overpowering, like its perfume. It knew so many secrets: it had hidden bandits and lovers and fugitives. Violent crimes and joys and fears were woven into its twisted branches, communicating something of their fury to our bodies. Beneath the intertwining leaves the ground was dry and powdery, smelling of herbs and honey. The Traveller's polished Chinese head lay beside mine, pillowed on tiny mauvish flowers.

'No, I do not know their name, nor do I know if they grow in Siberia, if you thought of asking,' he said in those smoky, wooing tones which could turn the most dispassionate sentence into a declaration of love.

The first stars glimmered through the lattice of the macchia.

'We must make a wish,' I said, and began the old nursery doggerel -

'Starlight, star bright, first star I've seen tonight

Would we could, would that we might....

TRAVEL ON THE TRANS-SIBERIAN!'

The Traveller leant over me, staring down with that expressionless mask from which the narrowed eyes told so much.

'*Pussinka!* Stop thinking about Siberia. Kiss me -' his voice was rough, like his hands. Then he laughed. 'I tell you, I won't have half Asia for a rival... or a railway train either! Still, if that's what makes you feel more loving... Come closer – come and be loved in a Mongol *yurt*, like you were in Dijon... *Doucinka moiya*... this is our tent beside the Amur... *Now* kiss me properly...'

Presently he resumed his teasing tone: 'You're such a romantic creature – I wonder, would you have followed me to Siberia in the classic manner, like Raskolnikov's Sonia, and Albina Megouria and all the rest of them? Russian women... how strange, how sweet they are...' He was thinking aloud now, staring his inward, Russian-turning stare. He held me in his arms but he no longer saw me... 'The wives of the Dekabrists... what passion, what softness, what abnegation... so *Russian*.' His voice sounded a curious, ardent note I had never heard before, as if he were in love with an abstraction – a Russian characteristic. This softness, or tenderness – I do not call it sentimentality – is the reverse side of the coin to brutality and often found in the Russian, but never, I think, alongside the methodical cruelty of the German, or Austrian, who is certainly sentimental. Over the years I have come to recognize it is an inherent Russian trait.

'We were always told to give something to the prisoners we used to see being marched off,' one Russian woman told me, recalling her childhood in Tobolsk. 'Our *nianya* used to say "Give to the *nestchalnie* – the unhappy ones – give to the poor little prisoners," she'd say with tears in her eyes as the criminals passed by. She'd find a kopek or two in her pocket, and we'd run after them, distributing our coppers, or the cakes and *bublitchki* we'd bought for ourselves. And they'd call down all the Saints of the Calendar to bless us.'

Thus the nursery; and a like compassion was sometimes reflected in a harsher world. In 1905 the abhorred Grand Duke Sergei Alexandrovitch, governor general of Moscow, was marked down by the terrorists to be blown to pieces as he drove out from the Kremlin. The whole thing was timed to the second. But Kaliayev, the would-be assassin, clutching the bomb in readiness, was disarmed by the sight of two motherless children, the Grand Duchess Marie Pavlovna and her brother, the Grand Duke Dimitri, sitting beside their uncle in the Imperial carriage. Such innocence! Kaliayev stayed his hand. But two days later the Grand Duke drove alone, and so was blown to pieces after all.

Such inconsistencies run like an undulating line through centuries of Russian life, and lie as a haze, obscuring the clear-cut horizons of history; simplicity beside cunning, cruelty and compassion; all are deep in the Russian character. This stratum of cruelty the Traveller attributed to the fact that Tartar blood conflicts with the Slav *bon enfant*. Even when no Tartar strain is traced it must be remembered that the Khans ruled for centuries, dominating as much by craftiness as terror. At last the elliptical approach, so essentially Asiatic, so alien to the basically guileless Slav has become an integrated characteristic. In every field there are examples of this inconsistency.

In the gathering darkness of the Corsican evening the Traveller was quoting Nekrassov, translating his beautiful verses on Russian women, evoking the sublime spirit of sacrificial love shown by the Princesses Volkonskaya and Troubetskaya, Countess Mouravieva and the rest of those heroic wives who shared their husbands' bitter years of Siberian exile.

'There was a Frenchwoman too,' I reminded him.

'Ah. You know about her? Pauline Guèble.' He seemed annoyed – 'but her motives were not so pure. She had something to gain (she was *French* don't forget). Just a little *couturière*, who became mistress of the Chevalier Garde Count Annenkov. She didn't have so much to lose as the

125

others, either – no roots, no traditions, titles or estates to abandon.' (Her baby, whom she left and was never to see again, he ignored.) 'She had never known the luxury and privilege to which the others had all been accustomed. Moreover, when she reached Siberia, Annenkov was obliged to marry her, so she became a Countess after all. No; she was quite a different case,' he said, dismissing the Frenchwoman with a shrug; and for a moment I hated him for his cynicism, even for his national prejudice. He seldom passed up a chance to denigrate the French, and I wondered what event or person had brought about this profound hostility.

Abruptly, he turned to me: 'But you're so *nearly* Russian, my darling, so sentimental and *têtue*, so sublimely silly, I do believe you would do what the Dekabrist wives did... Would you? But then –' his mood was suddenly teasing – 'But then, wouldn't that be because you were really in love with the *land* rather than the man? I always said you were more in love with the train than me. O *Pussinka*! You'll never love me in the way I love you... Never mind. Don't start denials and explications! Never mind about the Irtysh and the Angara and all the rest of Siberia. To hell with Siberia. Let's get on with the loving...' As he leaned closer he blotted out the starlight and for a while even Siberia was forgotten.

Slithering down the rocky paths, brushing pine-needles and ants from our crumpled clothes, we could see, far below, light streaming from the hotel windows, lighthouse beams alerting us to the conventions, explications and obligations of everyday life; rocks, waiting for us to founder on them.

'Are you hungry?' I asked, half-hoping we could turn back.

'Yes. As I always tell you, emotions need feeding.'

'But imagine, now, if we'd been on our train.' I was harking back to my sigh-away, die-away dream, 'Imagine, just us, shut in together, for a week, and all Siberia outside... and when we pulled up the blind we'd see that snowy emptiness rolling past, and the little villages hunched under the weight of the snow, day after day, night after night... We should be so cosy in our red velvet compartment... we shouldn't have to walk down the mountain-side, or even go to the Hôtel de la Gare at the next stop. We'd light the lamp, with its green shade, and order caviare and champagne to be brought to us there.'

'Yes, it's an erotic image. By the way, I prefer tea with my caviare.'

'Tea then; and then -' I stopped. The image was overwhelming. The place and the loved one. '*That* would be Gallantry Bower,' I finished lamely.

We had reached the courtyard behind the hotel. The Run-Away Game was over. The Traveller drew me into the shadows of the outhouses.

'*Pussinka dousha*, don't you know yet, that Gallantry Bower is wherever we are together. Don't always look for it the other side of the world, it's here and now, whenever we kiss.'

CHAPTER TEN

And so it was, for the rest of that loving summer. When an unexpectedly early autumn lashed Corsica with its gales and rains, and snow powdered the mountains, the unheated, stone-walled hotel ran with rivulets of moisture where snails collected. 'Now it's really like life in a Caucasian *aôul* – village to you,' said the Traveller, relishing my discomfort. In this dank setting we shivered, munched hot chestnuts and at last decided to seek the remains of summer on the mainland, towards the Italian border.

Aunt Eudoxia was becoming restive. She was urban by inclination and spoke of returning to Paris with longing, but Kamran and Sergei, their father's double-shadow, seemed content to linger in the south.

It was a rough crossing. At Marseilles we hired a car and made our way slowly along the banal stretches of coast studded with self-conscious playgrounds. Antibes, Cannes, Nice, Villefranche, Monte Carlo, all of them were made acceptable to me by their Russian associations; but in my heart I was not captivated, and wished, in secret, that we could have been making for some more thrilling scene, the Albanian mountains, at least.

Yet countless Russians had been drawn to the Riviera, finding it beautiful and romantic. Perhaps I could do the same. The lavish villas of the former Grand Dukes or their mistresses abounded round Cannes, set back from the vulgar gaze and deep in lush vegetation. Few if any of them had the swimming pool which today is as usual as a garage; but quite a number had small chapels in the medieval Russian style, onion domes and Orthodox crosses set down incongruously, beneath the palm trees. Ersatz as they were, they warmed my heart. At Nice, the Russian Orthodox Cathedral rose from behind the railway goods yard, an exuberant memorial to the frail young Tzarevitch who had wasted away in an Imperial villa on the same spot.

On the Promenade des Anglais, Marie Bashkirtseff, as an *enfant terrible* of fourteen, corseted and draped in *écru batiste*, sat on the balcony of her mother's villa, seething with passion for an English Duke who would shortly drive past, all unaware. 'O God! Give me the Duke of H!' she writes in her celebrated journal. A great compatriot, with nobler aspirations, Alexander Herzen, also lived and suffered and is buried in Nice. His statue is to be seen in the cemetery, above the old town. At Monte Carlo, beside the Hôtel de Russie, one jeweller and pawnbroker's establishment carried, until lately the sign 'Lombard' in big gilt Kyrillic lettering. The word *Lombard* was the Russian name for a pawnshop. No doubt the Principality decided it was as well to offer immediate, easily recognized aid to those despairing and impetuous Slavs who rushed ruined from the Casino prepared to leap from the suicides' bridge.

At one elegant hotel there was a very old wine-waiter, whose monkey-like features used to crease into a joyous, toothless grin whenever he saw the Traveller. It was difficult to believe that once he had been a Tzigane fiddler from Odessa, whose music had delighted some capricious Russian nobleman. He had been engaged to accompany the Prince on his travels. One fateful summer the Prince's yacht had put into Monte Carlo harbour, where it had moored, lit from stem to stem each night, while the Prince gambled away his estates, his mistresses, his wife's dowry, everything, except his Tzigane fiddler, though a number of his admirers offered a high price for him. When the last card had been played, and the last roulette wheel spun against him, the Prince blew out his brains. The yacht was impounded and the crew repatriated. But the Tzigane fiddler stayed on at the hotel, going from table to table in the restaurant, his violin sobbing out its intimacies to enchanted or self-conscious diners. At last arthritis had put a stop to all that; but the old man remained to shuffle about with the wine-list. He was a favourite with successive *maîtres d'hôtel*, the Traveller explained; something about shady connections... Gypsy women were most efficient at procuring abortions. 'Always handy to have people like that around in a big hotel,' said the Traveller, patting the old man's gnarled paw affectionately. They had, it seemed, known each other for many years.

~

The holiday was almost over, and summer done. Yet we lingered. I think all of us, in our different ways, sensed that never again should we have this moment of timeless well-being, becalmed between the past and the future. For the Traveller and myself this was an ideal state, as we drifted from a reality which seemed as unreal as that Russian limbo-land into which we sank with such nostalgic abandon. I have often thought, since, that Aunt Eudoxia must have been either a very unworldly woman or a very, very worldly one. Our preoccupation with each other appeared to have escaped her, although she was for ever urging Kamran and Sergei to go off and find their own amusements.

'Boys of that age should be having affairs,' she said firmly.

'People of all ages,' replied the Traveller with equal conviction.

Sometimes the Traveller and I contrived to spend the day alone together, crossing into Italy for lunch at Ventimiglia or San Remo. It was only a day-excursion yet, to me, crossing the frontier seemed to invest it with the quality of a romantic evasion. The Traveller fostered this mood. At the Italian frontier, when sallow Romeo-like *gendarmes* requested our passports, he proffered his, a rather irregular-looking fold of paper which I had never been allowed to see, muttering, 'and if they don't like that one, I've others,' a cloak-and-dagger remark I appreciated.

Thus, in an atmosphere of high adventure and exploration, he, the blasé world traveller, and I, the apprentice, would climb the steep tunnelled streets of old San Remo searching for an ancient creature who remembered seeing Garibaldi or a place where they cooked seaweed patties... And the Traveller would give me advice by which I have profited, ever since.

'Always explore a new town on an empty stomach,' he would say. 'It sharpens the vision.' 'Leave the main thoroughfare immediately.' 'Spend your time dawdling, or just sitting. Let the town come to you.' 'Forget monuments. Look at daily life first... it was this which made the men and events which the monuments commemorate.'

San Remo's Russian church, with its fish-scale, starred and

coloured domes emerging from the surrounding palms, made the Traveller shudder, but to me it was all beauty, and I would drag him for a last lingering look, before we caught the train back to Menton.

'Cheap and artificial,' was his judgement. 'Wait till you see Yaroslavl, or the churches of Novgorod, or Sveti Ivana Voiina – St. Ivan the Warrior – near our old house in Moscow... Then you'll see why all this sets my teeth on edge. *C'est faux! Faux!* like all that rich *déraciné* lot who made the Riviera their second home. Now they are émigrés in earnest. Serve them right. They used to snub Russia, never spoke Russian, spent as little time there as possible and cared nothing for its history, architecture and resources. For them, it was just a banking background – estates where their fortunes came from. Sickening lot, trading on their titles and their charm. And then, cashing-in on nice little soul-saving chapels, like this one, where they could corner their patron saints and buy forgiveness for gambling away their birthright.'

~

Along the cypress-bordered paths that wind through the old cemetery, high above the frontier bay of Garavan, the Traveller and I would clear away the brambles, bitter-smelling lentisque and rosemary which choked the tombs gathered round the little blue-domed, gold-starred Russian chapel where so many Russians are buried, so far from home. 'Here lies...' 'Until the Day Breaks...' I would spell out the Kyrillic inscriptions laboriously. At which the Traveller would become impatient:

'Hurry up! Talk about the quick and the dead! Can't you be quicker than that after all this time? If you want to be married in a Russian church you'll have to get all the responses pat. In fact, you'll have to be converted to Orthodoxy. I don't believe you've made any progress since I first taught you our alphabet. You were seven. You had measles at the time, don't you remember?'

'Of course I do. Those soft L's and hard L's and signs at the end of a word, and your D being our G and our H your N, besides all those totally different letters. It was much easier learning to count in Yakute.'

He pulled me close. 'What a lot of odd things I've taught you.' Now he was pushing me down across a stone slab, lichen-spotted and overgrown with feathery creepers. Above my head the gold-starred blue cupola shimmered in the heat haze.

'You can't! Not here!' I was scandalized.

'Why not? D'you find it uncomfortable or immoral – or both? I see I haven't taught you to be free of all those idiotic conventions yet. You don't suppose the dead care? Unless they envy us.'

'But we might be seen...'

'Up here, in the heat of the day? The French don't sight-see or mourn at lunch time – they've other things to do. They're all eating or rolling about on comfortable beds or sofas, behind closed shutters just now. They don't care for *le pique-nique* – not this sort, anyhow.'

When, later we returned to the old town, we generally found Aunt Eudoxia installed in the depths of a café reading Tauchnitz editions of Robert Hitchen's novels – 'so good for my English' – and puffing at her *tchibouk* (which she carried about with her in a kind of nose-bag made of Roumanian peasant embroidery), quite impervious to the gaping locals. Then the Traveller played chess with his sons, while I sipped apricot brandy. This was considered harmless, because of its excessive sweetness. Besides, Hondof liked it, licking his chops as his lolling pink tongue explored the glass which the Traveller snatched from me to indulge the dog.

In those days the little restaurants and cafés centred round the more unfashionable Mediterranean ports were not yet given over to plastic and strip lighting – worse still, to photographic murals. They still had their own distinctive idiom of decoration; marble-topped tables, mirrors and frescoed walls in an Italianate idiom depicting some blue gulf ornamented with a toy-like yellow port, where red-capped Neapolitans crowded the jetty dancing the *tarantella* or playing the guitar, or congregated under vine-wreathed arbours – the whole mellowed to a sticky amber tone by the fumes of a thousand *tables d'hôtes*.

Here, the diner could round off his meal by calling for a *café cognac* and the newspapers, which used to be presented furled on to cane batons, a practical arrangement, now obsolete, for today we are fed the news by loud-mouthed radio bulletins or flickering television screens.

Sitting beside the Traveller in such cafés, the evening calm broken only by the rattle of dominoes and the Damier goblets or the hoarse voices of the habitués, playing *belotte*, I would trace the halcyon landscapes that adorned the walls. Charming scenes; but why were there never any restaurants with murals depicting the frozen north at its most picturesque? Russian *boîtes de nuit* in Paris, said the Traveller, would disappoint me. They relied solely on the costumes of the waiters, embroidered *roubashkas* and the like. I recalled my one excursion into this world of nocturnal festivity. Certainly the setting for the Tziganes in Passy had been without any concessions to the picturesque. I longed to see the same innocent technique of wall-painting which flourished in the south applied to a Northern scene; golden domes sparkling through a snow-storm, princes winging along in troikas, peasants and bears dancing a *gopak*.

~

'Too many Russians here – the wrong sort,' said the Traveller, casting a jaundiced eye over the coquettishly pretty little bay where we had at last come to a standstill in an old fashioned hotel and were now lunching. By the wrong sort, he meant the kind which bored him, those who talked incessantly about returning to liberate Russia from the wicked Red clutches. Our polyglot party – of Russian, Montenegrin, Kirghiz, Georgian and English origins – aroused the liveliest curiosity among other visitors along the coast. The French, as usual displayed no curiosity; we were merely *les étrangers*. They shrugged us off; but we enjoyed listening to the speculations of others as to our racial origins and relationship. Sergei upset both the management of the hotel and a number of guests by telling some pressing Belgians that we were a circus troupe from the U.S.S.R. and kept our performing boa constrictors upstairs. 'We do not bring them to the dining-room, but if you would like to see them...?' The Belgians left that night, and there was a good deal of uneasiness among the rest of the visitors, who appeared to find both of Sergei's statements equally alarming, so that the Manager coldly suggested we might prefer to move elsewhere. But the Traveller calmed him down and we stayed on.

'Because it reminds me of the Krim,' he said with finality, and Aunt Eudoxia agreed. 'Although our Montenegrin coast below Cattaro was really lovelier, and far more wild, which seems to be what you like best,' she said, turning an unsympathetic eye in my direction. She herself craved cities, chic night life, all the things our holiday did not provide. She had travelled little, beyond her own Balkanic and Russian perimeter and only once visited London, which had disappointed her, particularly the Crystal Palace – still a landmark of Southern London at that time – 'but not a patch on the Winter Palace, one must admit,' she said, turning to the Traveller for corroboration, and deaf to my explanations that the Crystal Palace housed dog-shows or agricultural exhibits, rather than Royalty. It was a Palace and, to her, a sub-standard one.

'Thinking Krim,' I would float off-shore in the turquoise shallows, then uncorrupted by those 'attractions' later to be imposed. No floats, snack-bars, or *pédalos* affronted the eye at that time; no roar of an outboard motor-boat towing shrieking water-skiers shattered the ear. I would look landward at the steep encircling hills silvered with olive groves (undefiled by blocks of cement and steel apartment houses), rising to the crags of the passes above the Italian frontier, where the smugglers did a brisk trade above, rather than under, the noses of the *gendarmerie*. Little pink and yellow villas were dotted about the lower slopes, embedded in luscious foliage, feathery palms, plumbago, trumpet vines and the heavy-belled datura. The old town climbed the hill-side and was topped by the blue cupola of the tiny Russian chapel, its gold stars and crosses glinting through the dark spears of the cyprus trees. The whole panorama had precisely that Southern felicity which enraptured Schredin, the nineteenth-century Russian landscape painter, on his Mediterranean excursions; his paintings are romantic, meticulous, and quite unfashionable; but, fortunately, still prized in the U.S.S.R.

Yet however charming this scene spread out before me, it was not, and could never be, the landscape of my heart's desire. It was useless to count my blessings, to compare it favourably with the wind-swept beaches and bracing dips of my homeland. Nor to reflect that in this halcyon bay I should be spared an encounter with those terrifying water-snakes, five or six feet in length, knotted together hideously, floating on the surface, sunning and hissing, as the Traveller had seen them along the shores of the Caspian. Black Sea or Caspian or even the hostile Sea of Aral, I thought, would have meant more to me than these pellucid waters. Yet here the sun was as strong, the water as blue, brighter, even, and the mountains and valleys almost identical with so much of the Crimea... *His* Krim! Would it ever be *ours*? Overcome with longing I would plunge my head underwater and then, with bursting lungs and choking emotion, surface to tread water furiously, telling myself it *is* the Krim. It *is*! Magic of magics! I am there! But my magic was not strong enough to overcome the shrill *badinage* of French bathers kissing self-consciously as they swam past. And thinking how a few fur-capped Tartar fishermen chanting their minor melodies, and a mosque or two would have improved the day, I paddled ashore, as usual losing present sunlight for shadowy illusions.

~

The mistral had raged for a week, as if trying to drive us away. All night the waves surged against the rocks uneasily, and the October moon came and went behind scudding clouds. We were beginning to pack. Kamran and Sergei were as overcast as the skies. Hondof was to be left behind. Paris could not provide the sort of freedom he needed. A happy home had been found for him with an old Russian couple – he had been a general in the Caucasus, and she now served teas from their little cabin perched on the side of the steep track up to the Annonciade Monastery, set high in the hills behind Menton. We knew Hondof would have loving care with them and all the hills and valleys to roam. Already, the General's wife was setting aside the best of her home-made cakes for him rather than reserving them for the rare customers. Still, all of us dreaded the parting.

Kamran was to continue his architectural studies at Grenoble, while Sergei was to rejoin his mother in Brussels. Both these programmes appeared repugnant to them. Even Aunt Eudoxia, who had fretted for city life, now complained she would have nothing to wear and must look for a job.

'Or a husband?' suggested the Traveller, at which she sighed tragically.

'At my age? Don't be ridiculous. Why, I remember in Montenegro a woman of thirty was of no more account.'

The Traveller smiled slyly. 'Let me remind you that it was Lenin who said the greatest crime for anyone was to be over fifty-five. Perhaps you'll agree with him, for once?'

Although the Traveller remained non-committal as ever over his own plans, my happiness was replaced by vague forebodings. Partings were in the air. Partings and renunciations. The Traveller had not told me, but he had at last concocted a letter to my parents breaking it to them that we contemplated marriage. Their reply came in the form of a telegram. I was to return immediately.

'And not talk such nonsense – I can hear them saying it. I can't bear it, after all this.'

'Darling, you must, for a while. We jumped our fences. It wasn't difficult to become your lover but it would be very difficult to become your husband, at present. Don't you see, you're under age. They can do what they choose about you till you're twenty-one – you can't dispute their authority. They can even send you back to the convent. They could probably send me to prison for what I've done. It's wiser to wait a little while – just a few months more. Don't forget, this is Europe – and you live in an Anglo-Saxon world. I can't organize one of those steeple-chase abductions like the nomads of Central Asia, though no doubt that's what you'd enjoy. No Miss, my darling. I shan't change – I don't think you will either. But they will, once they get used to the idea that you are grown up. You must give them time. You must give me time, too... there are other difficulties...'

His face was sombre, but he did not expand on the nature of his problems, which, I sensed, would take him away from me once again.

'You'll go away – you always do.'

'Yes – but I'll come back – I always do.'

He tried to console me, talking Siberia, talking Russia, playing the old Run-Away Game.

'Shall we take a boat down the Volga? Shall we go and dine in one of the little Armenian restaurants overlooking the river, in Tiflis? I know! We're at Alupkha, where the Vorontzov palace hangs over the water; it's very like this... the same cyprus trees, the same sound of the sea... Yes, *Pussinka*, I know the French Riviera is without interest to you – to me, too – but let's pretend the Black Sea is out there (it can be terribly rough) and those lights bobbing about are the boats of Tartar fishermen. That's better! Tomorrow we'll go to one of their villages you always wanted to see. You remember,' he coaxed, 'the little bay where the Tartar beauties used to come down to bathe, wading in, wearing baggy pink trousers that ballooned up round them.'

'... and their dozens of black plaits floated on the water like strands of seaweed,' I finished.

It was one of my favourite images, but I was not to be consoled.

'Poor little termite,' said the Traveller, returning to nursery endearments, but kissing me passionately, in a sort of voluptuous counterpoint. Continuing our journey into the mind's eye he promised me Bakhtchi-Serai.

'The Khan's Palace?'

'If you like. Anywhere you like, tonight.'

'Pushkin's Fountain then...'

'The Fountain of Tears? Oh, *Pussinka*!'

He kissed me reproachfully.

The wind buffeted round, and the palms rattled against the shutters which banged fitfully. I went to close them, and felt a fine, driving rain on my hands. Suddenly it was the French Riviera again, shoddy and meaningless, as only it can be, when it no longer basks. I began to cry.

'I hate this place. I hate the Côte d'Azur. I don't care if it is like the Krim. I don't want that, either. I only want us to be together in a snow-storm... together in our Trans-Siberian train.'

PART FOUR
BRIDGE OF CLAY

The Thames goes under London Bridge,
This year, like last
The present turns to past.
It's day then night then day while I
Watch the Thames go by.

Lift your fingers and touch mine:
We make a bridge in air.
You and I stood here
This year, last year, and every day
Building a bridge of clay.

Building a bridge of silver and gold:
Love dissolves and is washed away.
Washed away like wood and clay.
London Bridge has fallen down
We thought we'd built in stone.

Silver and gold are stolen away;
London's dark and daylight's gone;
Our hands have fallen away.
With you and now without you I
Watch the years go by.

Laurence Lerner

CHAPTER ELEVEN

Next winter, I lost the Traveller, and so learned to look back, a practice which time perfects. No one knew what had become of my Asiatic love, neither his sons, nor Aunt Eudoxia, nor anyone who had known him, could give me news. He left me, as casually as ever, on one of those sudden departures which had become an accepted pattern. My parents had insisted there should be no further talk of marriage for at least a year. They had been less strict than I had anticipated, appearing to dismiss the question as some kind of childish make-believe: which perhaps it was, so that our project in no way disrupted their friendship with the Traveller; but then, of our expedition to Dijon they still remained in happy ignorance. My mother's attitude towards me seemed to have changed subtly; it was difficult to define precisely. I sometimes caught her eyeing me speculatively, but she did not ask for my confidences. Perhaps she knew she would not have them. Ours was a singularly detached family. I knew little of my parents' life, and nothing of their family background: they might almost have qualified for the state of born orphan-hood.

Lulled by this interim period, as I regarded it, I laid no particular stress on the Traveller's comings and goings. 'I'll come back, I always do.' He had said it so often that I came to believe it, as I believed in the rising and setting of the sun. Thus I do not recall the manner of our last farewell; for I did not, and perhaps he did not, recognize it as such. I had learned not to ask him where he was going, but I seem to remember asking if he would be gone long, to which he replied with the old convenient formula. 'It's all according...' Perhaps, like Byron, he believed all good-byes should be sudden ones.

And so, stepping cat-like-soft down the street in his Torghut boots, his overcoat flung over his shoulders, he went out of our lives. To all of us, he remained a creature of mystery, remote and fabulous, like his Asiatic background.

~

On a shining morning in May, a week or so before my twenty-first birthday, a packet was left at our door. 'For the young lady,' said the bearer, leaving no name. I was out at the time and none of my questionings ever obtained any further details from Mrs. Cork, the char, who had opened the door.

'Just one of them foreigners,' was all I could elicit.

The packet, done up in scrubby brown paper, revealed further wrapping of printed pink calico. Inside was a small and very beautiful prayer-rug from Samarkand. It was folded round an eighteenth-century silver-cased ikon. I recognized it as the one which had been the ikon of the house in the Traveller's Paris quarters. With these treasures was a shiny-covered black note-book, and a letter in the Traveller's longed-for handwriting. It bore no date and no address, and was written in pencil on a page torn from the note-book.

'I do not know if this will reach you in time for your twenty-first birthday – 21 – three times seven, Magic of Magics!' he wrote, 'or indeed if it will ever find you, *Pussinka Moiya*. What I send is to remind you of that Russia we shared. You will find other prayer rugs and ikons on your way. You love them and they will always come to you. I too love you, but I cannot come to you any more. Don't ask me to explain. Now you will have to play our Run-Away Game alone. We shall never make that journey on the Trans-Siberian which was your favourite day-dream. To want anything so much is unwise – it gives fate a chance to hurt you – a chance fate seldom misses. The train, as I knew it, is gone. There are new landmarks and new passengers all along the route. Sverdlovsk, Magnitogorsk, Asbestos – all tell of wonderful achievements and human endeavours, but the Traveller's Train you believed in is no more. The last time I made the journey in *your* way, the way *you* wanted it to be, was before you were born. Right up to the Revolution something of the legendary flavour remained. You believed in it. You had this *idée fixe*, and no doubt you were meant to make it then. But as I so often told you, there was an accident in time. The idea of my taking a child on such an expedition seemed too complicated. All that fuss about warm underwear, the right food and getting to bed early... After all, you were only about six or seven. But I was wrong. I should have hidden you in a valise and vanished! It is not the conventions which are too strong. It is we who are too weak. You knew best, my little Douraka. You should have made the journey then. It was the last moment to have tasted its full romantic flavour. And it might have led you where you were meant to go.

Subconsciously you must have felt that. The young have instincts which are far more sure than all our mature reasonings. Who knows what you were meant to find *en route*, or where it might have led *us*, later? Even at your age, it must have had some part to play in your life. Now it is too late. We have both missed sharing that particular moment of time and place.

'Soon, no one will ever make the journey any more or even recall how it was. Aeroplanes will take its place and fly over the disused tracks. Even if the train still runs, its character will have changed. Its passengers and its landmarks will be entirely new. I made the Trans-Sib journey so many times that it became part of my life. This note-book will speak especially to you. It contains some things that were to be part of a book I was always meaning to write. They were made at a time when each journey would have been, for you, a journey deeper into your heart's desire. For us, together, our Gallantry Bower achieved.

'*Ah! que nos désirs sont sans remède...* You always hated my quoting that. You never learned to accept fate. I don't think you ever will. Perhaps it might be better if the journey remained as a journey into your mind's eye. As someone or other said: granting our wish is one of Fate's saddest jokes. I am sad not to have made the journey with you, *moiya doushinka*, my Nursery Traveller, but like our marriage, it was not written. Remember Rhodopé, "there are *no* fields of amaranth on this side of the grave: there are *no* voices that are not soon mute, however tuneful. There is *no* name, with whatever emphasis of passionate love repeated, of which the echo is not faint at last." That's Landor. (But I quote from memory.) Now it is time for the Traveller and his Tales to go out of your life, and for you to begin your own journeys. The Turkish people say farewell beautifully, "*Guleyh*," they say – Go with a smile.'

There was a postscript:

'Be kind to Kamran and Sergei if ever they come back into your life.'

The warm sunlight that fell across the page faded; suddenly everything had turned cold and grey.

'No. No message – just the presents,' I told my parents, trying to appear casual. I could not share my letter, and I could not bear them to speak of him or know how much I mourned him.

'So we are no wiser,' said my father.

I never told of the note-book, either. But in secret, I used to take it from its hiding-place under my hats in the Russian-disguised dolls' house, to play the Run-Away Game, making over and over again that magic journey into my heart's desire – alone.

~

As time passed, and the certitude of my loneliness became apparent to me, I noticed that all which had seemed real in myself was lost, with him. With his disappearance, part of myself had vanished too. What was left did not belong to the setting in which it remained. I had been formed in a mould of his creation, and all my longings and instincts were now fixed on some remote and seemingly unobtainable world – his – which I was determined to reach.

With a blank face concealing my anguish, I would listen to my parents speculating on his probable fate... They had obstinately refused to take our projected marriage seriously, and now seemed equally obtuse concerning my emotions. Killed 'somewhere over there...' trapped, on some dangerous mission... Counter-espionage. Always, the whispered label: *agent provocateur*...? Somebody wildly suggested he could have been a *tsaiking*, or Taoist brother, at large in the world, and apparently of it, but in truth only there to accomplish some special mission, and one who must ultimately return to his monastery.

I saw him in another guise, father of all bandits, grown more Asiatic-looking, a wisp of grizzled beard on his parchment chin, the narrow eyes still narrower against the biting winds of Asia, for of course he was there – no Europe, or even a European grave, could have held him, I knew. I saw him riding out on a shaggy little Mongolian horse, wrapped in a padded caftan, leading some unexplained foray – for – against? He was always against authority, no matter what. Or was he simply becalmed in fatalism, following the pattern of his ancestry; waiting...? Waiting for life to pass? Yet his spirit seemed as ardent as ever, always beside me, luring me deeper into the horizons of my desire.

Somewhere there, he was; and I must find him. He would still be spinning his marvellous web, but telling, now, of a softer, western world which he had shared with me. I saw him telling of a window on the river at Richmond, of walks in Kensington Gardens, and of fire-light flickering on a nursery ceiling. Seen from Siberia these things would have assumed an inverted exoticism.

Just as once he used to tell me the names of the Hordes, the great

Asiatic dynasties, the Djaghataídes or Timourides and their territories – nectar to my imagination – so now he might be holding a circle of Asiatics spellbound as he reeled off the names of London's Underground stations – mighty-sounding names for vast, echoing subterranean ways where British hordes swept down and were carried far beneath the earth to emerge elsewhere: Hammersmith, Earl's Court, or Potter's Bar. No doubt even Metro-land sounded sonorous, from Siberia.

I imagined him there, somewhere near the Mongol frontiers, crouched in a Kirghiz *yurt*, pushing aside some yak-fat delicacy to tell of crumpet teas. Telling his niece, the now grown-up Sofka Andreievna (she who had aroused my envy by tales of her six-foot birthday sturgeon) of an English child's midsummer birthday-party under the elm trees, tables piled with jam-puffs, brandy-snaps and a pink-and-white-icing birthday-cake.

'Brandee snaps? *Shto eta takoe?*' asks Sofka Andreievna languidly. She is sitting on a bundle, beside the grass-grown tracks of the Trans-Siberian railway. She has become a bundle herself, for the child of Omsk has become a woman of thirty or more. She wears a sheepskin-lined overcoat buttoned awry, a handkerchief tied over her head, peasant-fashion, in the hopes it will conceal the fact she is not one; that she still has an *arshins'* length of fine pearls sewn into her corset. She has a long pale face, and the same slit eyes as her uncle, but hers are a pale green. Together, uncle and niece stare out across emptiness for that faint smudge of smoke which will tell of the great train's approach.

It no longer keeps any schedule. Would-be passengers camp beside the track, sleeping round their treasured samovar, patient in the hope of being able to climb aboard... one day... It goes so slowly, now, that this is easy; but it is always crowded to suffocation. Passengers even hang outside, clutching the door-handles, falling off, in winter, as their hands freeze. Their bodies lie there, frozen stiff as the huge birthday sturgeon, until spring suns come to thaw them, and rot them. People are sprouted all over the roof of the train and jammed in beside the engine-driver. Sometimes a band of nomad fighters gallop their little horses alongside the train in wonder, or in hatred, cutting down anyone they can reach, believing that all are enemies, all invaders of their territory, wicked Russian aristos or the latest Red oppressors.

'Mark my words. Those Bolshies have got him,' said Nanny, who had long since retired to run a babies' pension at Bognor, but still visited us, and took a keen interest in disaster.

'Got him? Possibly. But in what sense?' asked my father. Unlike Nanny he was aware of aspects of the Traveller's nature and beliefs, which made it quite as probable that he was alive, somewhere in Central Asia, and working towards that millenium in which, oddly, his cynical soul believed. Or had his cynicism only been a camouflage, something which concealed his true self from that Europe in which, at heart, he remained an alien? So while all the Russias, and his Siberia, were re-forming, moving towards their destiny, I would ask myself where my own pygmy, all-absorbing pattern was to be played out?

While St. Theresa of Avila pronounced that our desires are without remedy, Balzac described desire as a memory that hopes. All my youth, I desired and was groping nostalgically for a land and a people very far from my London roots. It was as if I felt myself to be moving forward into the past, approaching my own moment in time, which was remote from the present.

To me, it has always seemed that each individual has such a moment. It is a fixed point in eternity, varying with each person, which they reach, sooner or later, in their trajectory through time. It is this moment which most perfectly expresses them, and to which essentially they belong, in which they live most fully. Both before and after some awareness of this lies within them, so that in varying degrees of consciousness, they are seeking that moment in order to be fulfilled, or to find again in that fulfilment and setting, the persons who shared it with them.

Through the Traveller and his Tales I had glimpsed that moment which for me must be set in Russia, though in what conditions I cannot tell. Am I looking forward, or back? Perhaps it is yet to come, in some vast industrial centre of the Siberian steppes. Or it has already been, in the dark, low-ceilinged rooms of some medieval Moscow-merchant's house where the women sat all day at their spinning and outside the tiny windows the ravens strutted in the snow. Equally, it could be compassed by some peasant *izba*, reeking of tallow candles and fish soup. A lifetime or a moment is all the same; a whole cycle lived richly, or thinly, or one day. Each can prove to have been the meaning of a life. We cannot know, from where we stand. But if we seek, and are aware we have missed the moment we seek, our own absolute moment in time, then we live out our lives unfulfilled. In the words of an eastern proverb: we die with our eyes open – we cannot rest; even in death we are still looking for it.

CHAPTER TWELVE

A silence, absolute and tomb-like, had fallen round the Traveller's name. I could not speak of him and, soon, no one spoke of him to me. His sons and Aunt Eudoxia, they too had vanished; the few letters I sent them were returned to sender. Reluctantly I began to come to terms with life around me, pursuing the outwardly conformist Anglo-Saxon pattern of my life. But beneath the façade of conventional interests I was groping eastward, flinging myself towards all things Russian. My youthful passion had crystallized into an adult obsession. I was entirely possessed by a shade and his setting and I sought, wherever I was and with whoever I might be, to recapture something of that particular climate I had known, beside the Traveller.

'Every woman should marry three times' had been one of his dictums, which he often impressed on me. 'Marry first for love – get it out of your system – next for money – get that into your pocket and then marry for pleasure, which has nothing whatever to do with love or money.' At the time I thought this a puzzling statement, but in perspective, I see it contains much truth. An early marriage which I had recklessly contracted outside the charmed Slav circle was naturally doomed and soon perished unmourned. Henceforth, friends, lovers, all the emotional *va-et-vient* of my life remained centred round my national preoccupations.

But no one stood the test of comparison to the Traveller. Perhaps they might recall some of the same horizons, tell of some similar background even; speak with something of the same smoky tones, or possess the narrow, slanted eyes of the Tartar: but they came and went in my life leaving little or no mark. 'Things remain when people go,' the Traveller had said. Thus I set the scene scrupulously *à la Russe*, eating Russian food off the few pieces of Russian Empire porcelain I had collected. Beside me, on a charming old painted table representing the Kremlin at sunset, the little brass samovar the Traveller had given me on my fourteenth birthday hummed companionably, competing with recordings of exclusively Russian music.

Those few non-Russians who were admitted – admirers, perhaps, whose advances I favoured – were often severely tested by my versions of Russian cooking, pickled fish in sour cream, or rissoles which I called *bitky*, and *kasha*, which to them was porridge. I recall one suitor who carelessly reached up from the sofa and lit his cigarette at the lamp which burned before the ikon. It was the Traveller's Siberian ikon, now the Ikon of the House. Double sacrilege!

He had defiled the Sacred Image and also the memory of the Traveller. He was thrown out, never to return. Others, more mindful of my mania, were nevertheless compelled to shout their endearments above recordings of *Chastoushki* – the shrill peasant songs of provincial Russia, which are delivered with a particularly piercing exuberance. Or they would be required to listen with bated breath to entire operas, *Roussalka*, *A Life for the Tzar*, Shostakovitch's latest symphony, or any other national manifestation which only too plainly distracted me from themselves.

The men about my house – for so I was arrogant enough to regard most of them, rather than as the men in my life – were generally Slavs – Russians: although Serbs were sometimes admitted. Poles were, somehow, a world apart – not my world – and I resented the influence some of this nation had exercised over the Marquis de Custine, tingeing those astute yet prejudiced views he records in his *Voyage en Russie en 1839*.

Some of the Russians I knew – *collected* would perhaps be a more exact word to describe my enthusiasm – were very old, with marvellous memories to be harvested; memories stretching back to a Caucasus where even more aged figures had described to them seeing Lermontov cutting a dash among the *ton* at Kisslovodsk; or telling of a childhood in a family which enjoyed some Court appointment, and I would listen greedily as they told of now forgotten rituals they had glimpsed; of the black and orange uniforms, and plumed hats, worn by the Court runners, the *Skorohod*.

Their curious loping pace, and the manner in which they bowed, and delivered their message, was peculiar to themselves, traditionally preserved, like the turbaned splendours of the Court Negroes, Scheherazade figures, who had been in service at the Tzar's palaces for generations, their purpose, it was sometimes said, to perpetuate the dusky personality of Hannibal – the Arab of Peter the Great – the Tzar's Abyssinian protégé who rose to be a general, studied military science in Paris, married a Russian noblewoman and whose great-grandson was none other than the poet Alexander Pushkin...

Pushkin! To have known him, been loved by him, to have seen him from afar even, was a longing which possessed me entirely, which still sometimes clouds my spirit with a sense of failure, and I comfort myself with the thought that the young Elizabeth Browning was equally consumed by an equally unrealizable dream – to have been Lord Byron's page. My aspirations were more daring. The Traveller had been right. I should have liked to be Pushkin's mistress – one of his many, even. In this spirit of exaltation I wasted a great deal of time trying to produce a translation of his love-letters, an undertaking linked with a Russian friend living in New York, and therefore one which became too attenuated, and perished.

Pro- or anti-Pushkin: this was the yardstick by which I measured nineteenth-century Slav personalities in that nebulous world where so much of myself was centred. This one lent him money: that one patronized him: another set his poems to music... The fact that Karl Marx had learned Russian at the age of eighty in order to be able to read Pushkin in the original was, I thought, automatically enough to make one favourable to Marxist doctrines.

As to Ivan Turgeniev, he paled beside his kinsman, the less known A. I. Turgeniev, who rose to sublime heights in my estimation because of his devoted friendship with the poet: moreover, he had come to possess that legendary oriental ring, the Talisman, subject of one of the poet's autobiographic verses, a *gage d'amour* which Pushkin had treasured and always worn, being his last link with Princess Eliza Vorontzova who had been the love of his youth, of his life, it was said. Turgeniev had in turn treasured this ring, bequeathing it to a relative. But during the convulsions of the Revolution it vanished.

But then this is in the true tradition of Talismans. Such objects know how to vanish, how to cross frontiers and seas, going where they will, conferring their magic on whom they please. For many years after the Princess gave the Talisman ring to her young lover, whom she was never to see again, his life seemed charmed. His star shone brilliantly; his genius was acknowledged; he escaped, miraculously, a series of foolhardy duels; he won every woman he wanted, and, at last, married the acknowledged beauty of all Moscow: only then, did the magic seem to falter. Nathalie was very young and frivolous, soon becoming a worldly coquette whose extravagance exhausted Pushkin's nervous and financial resources. But he loved her to distraction. Could the spirit of the Talisman, still obedient to the will of its original donor, have begun to turn away? Eliza Vorontzova must have followed the trajectory of Pushkin's life from afar, first with longing and pride, but gradually with misgiving turning to despair. Perhaps even with jealousy; Pushkin's love for his tiresome young wife was all-consuming.

I have never been able to discover whether the poet was wearing the Talisman when he went to the duel at the Black Brook. Had he worn it that day, hoping by its aid to finish off his enemy, the worthless, taunting D'Anthès? I would rather believe that the Talisman knew Pushkin's life had now become unbearable: that instead of saving his life, preserving him for further humiliations, for more years of fret and fume, the venom of the Court, the pressure of debts, the *frasques* of Nathalie, and all the gathering shadows of the years, it chose to speed D'Anthès' bullet towards him, and so wing the poet to Parnassus.

Whether I kept company with some Slav who, seeing the lie of the land, quickly announced he had been brought up at Tzarskoe Selo, or others from a more documented background who made no such claims, all served to deepen the colours of my mirage. There I saw birches merge with belfries, snowstorms swirling round little wooden *izbas* and granite palaces; there, under the black skies of a painted Palekh box, gigantic brass samovars puffed like volcanoes, dwarfing the surrounding villages and their blue-domed churches in some topsy-turvy vision recalling an early painting by Chagall at Vitebsk.

At home I fled the present, and, quite transported, listening perhaps to recordings of an opera by Dargomyjsky or one of Borodin's divine melodies, undulating from minor to major key and back to the minor again in that manner peculiar to Russian music, I was intolerant of any distraction. Emerging from my limbo-land I would cut in on the soft speeches of my beaux, to pursue my own perspectives, where fantasy, fact, geography and music all merged intoxicatingly.

'Don't you *long* to have known Borodin?' Without waiting for a reply I would rattle on about his descent from the ancient kings of Imeretia; the disordered atmosphere in which he lived in Moscow, invaded by bodies of students seeking encouragement, by charity organizers seeking support, by friends and relatives from the provinces, all of them taken under Borodin's large wing: all of them consuming his time, sleeping anywhere, on all the chairs and sofas, asking advice and help, coming between the composer and his creation, more exigent and as indulged as the numbers of adored cats which swarmed about, climbing on the musician's knees as, all too rarely, he sat at the piano.

My mind's eye saw the grey skies and golden, snow-padded domes and rooftops of Moscow, and peered in at the double windows, glimpsing Borodin's bulky figure, Prince Vladimir's melting aria sounded in my inner ear. Or was it the record now being played in my own room? I scarcely noticed how restive my admirers were becoming as once again I left their arms for Russia.

But some Slavs, enjoying the double-strength doses of local colour I provided, capped my anecdotes with others: then all went swimmingly and I hung on their words. They had only to tell of family life as they recalled it in the province of Tver, or Ufa, or anywhere else within the enchanted sphere and I was lost. Listening to them, to that tongue which can sound majestic or earthy, barbaric or tender, but never trivial, they could have been reciting seed catalogues or ships' tonnage – I was in love. But as the candles paled the Traveller's shadow fell once more and the suitor, found wanting, was shown the door. After all, the Run-Away Game was best played alone.

So, wearing the padded *khalat* he had sent me from Bokhara, its long rainbow silk sleeves dabbling in the *kasha* and sour cream, and regretting that a bottle of Graves from the local grocer was not one of the Caucasian white wines (even though Gautier had described them as 'epileptic cocoa'), I re-read *Ammalat-Beg* for the twentieth time, or, surfacing from Caucasian romance, plunged again into *The Chronicles of Bagrovo*, returning rapturously to patriarchal Russian life on the estates at Ufa.

I yearned for it. I was up at dawn, wearing a red *sarafan*, preparing the samovar for the old landowner's tea, as he sat on the veranda, ruminating, and the morning sun rose golden over the rich black earth... Returning to my own earth, to my little eighteenth-century house on the river at Richmond, to pour myself another tumbler of tea and to watch the reflections from the water shimmering across the panelled walls as the barges chugged past, leaving their wake of glittering ripples lapping to the shores, I would agree with Pierre Loti: *'le bien être égoiste de chez soi'* he wrote, seated cross-legged on a divan in his little house at Eyüb, up the Corne d'Or (which was his version of Gallantry Bower) and where, no doubt, he watched similar shimmering reflections as the *caiques* glided below his windows. Here Loti projected himself into the Turkish ambiance of his choice with an ardour which I understood and emulated.

But Loti, playing his own variation of the Run-Away Game more than seventy years before, had contrived to surround himself with three ingredients necessary to the proper realization of his dream. First, a withdrawal or temporary cessation of daily life; next, a devoted servant; lastly, the possession of a person who was the embodiment of his national obsession. Aziyadé was only a little Circassian slave but she represented for Loti the Turkish land, people, and way of life which he craved for his own.

My limbo-land was less successful than Loti's, being constantly shattered by the telephone, the man who came to read the gas-meter, or the exigencies of the char. Then there was the question of earning one's living. 'Can we have your copy by the morning?' a harassed sub-editor would telephone and, regretfully, I would put aside Lermontov's *Hero of Our Time* – his times being, I felt, my own – to spin out a thousand words on petit-point at Eton, a visit of the Comédie Française, or any other manifestation of current culture.

As to the passionate companion of my reveries – this revenant, part Traveller, part Mongol rider from the steppes – where was he? While Marie Bashkirtseff, being Russian, saw romance in Anglo-Saxon terms, and invoked Heaven for an English nobleman, I aspired to some wilder image, something no right-minded Deity would have considered conferring. O God, send me Mamai the Tartar! I prayed. Grant me an Uzbeg lover! Let me wake beside the Loved-one in a *yurt* in Turkestan! Such were my desires; and it was with a sense of resignation I would abandon them, decking myself, perhaps, for some Anglo-Saxon revel, setting off to dine, if

I were lucky, where both the wine and talk was good, or to dance at some night-club where hard liquor took over and the band prevented any attempts at communication.

Country expeditions were also subjected to my ruling passion. Gravesend was a particularly tantalizing outing, as I combed the water-side pubs for traces of the young Rimsky-Korsakov. When a naval cadet, his ship had been stationed in the Estuary while he was composing part of his first symphony – without a piano. On landing he had rushed to try out his composition on the first piano he could find. We can imagine what sort of a rattle-trap, beer-warped instrument awaited him at any of the seamen's bars of those days. But I never found so much as a memorial plaque to mark his passing.

Then, the Portsmouth road took preference over others, because half-an-hour's drive brought one to Ripley, an inconspicuous little Surrey town made memorable in my eyes by an inn called *The Tartar*. After *The Jolly Wagoner*, *The Flower in Hand* and suchlike, *The Tartar* struck a mysterious and rather chilling note as if, once, the Kipchak Horde had come streaking across the Hog's Back, plundering Guildford and sacking Cheam. The pub itself was an uninteresting building and I never discovered the origin of its intriguing name.

In the matter of reading I was considered affected: my friends accused me of disloyalty when I maintained my preference for Gogol over Dickens. It was not that I denigrated my English heritage, the stature of Dickens, or made futile comparisons: I simply found a keener pleasure in Russian writers. But there was no denying I was swayed topographically. Scenes set beside the Don seemed more enthralling than those placed by the Medway. As a heroine, Bela, the captive Circassian girl dying in the arms of her lover, the splenetic Russian officer, seemed more moving than poor Tess of the D'Urbervilles.

And then, the manner in which the fallen women of Russian fiction so often expiated their sins by following their men and marching eastward – to Siberia – was more understandable, and far more interesting than the contrite but stationary end English authors usually allotted similar characters. As to any number of Dostoievsky's luminous repentants, I ached for the chance to emulate them, to show my mettle as the Traveller had once suggested I might: to express a great love in such a manner; above all, in such a landscape.

Thus, succumbing entirely to my passion, I was swept along on this irrational tide. Then, too, my inclinations were sharpened by a prejudice against so many French and German classics. Loathing anything German with inbred, indiscriminate hostility I was only able to enjoy the Romantics such as Hoffmann and Tieck because, although the setting might be nineteenth-century Germany, it was soon transposed into some phantasmagoric or horrific realm. French authors were admirable but alien. I found Proust fidgety, Racine monumental; there was no denying the genius of Flaubert, and it was, I knew, unreasonable prejudice to prefer Anna Karenina to Emma Bovary. But there it was: topography again.

Scenes of French provincial life inevitably paled beside those which conjured the high skies and still woods which Turgeniev evokes, or scenes peopled with his wan gentry, their pent-up emotions simmering like the great samovar round which the whole household congregated. Even the sordid and lustful Goloviev family which Saltikov-Schredin describes so mercilessly seemed more fascinating, as I imagined them in their painted wooden house, snug in the snows of a long country winter, than anything set in a more familiar zone. Thus the double-distilled clarity of French writers dazzled but did not command me. Their materialism, whether elegant or brutal, always overcame me with a sense of peculiar desolation, which I could not shake off, even in Stendhal's brilliant company.

There was, I perceived, a marked kinship between English and Russian writers: an affinity to be traced in both their humorous and tragic vein. *Dead Souls* can be appreciated by the English reader, just as *Alice in Wonderland* is treasured by the Russian: yet neither of these wild masterpieces translates well, or is, in general, truly savoured by the logical French. How many of Trollope's clergy are to be found, transposed, in Leskov's provinces! Turgeniev's lyricism, Tolstoy's profundities – together with his innocence, his grandeur and simplicity – are better perceived I think, by the English reader. Similarly the Russian and English languages inter-translate more justly than either can do when rendered into French. For then, it seems, the key is transposed from minor to major and the basses become tenors. The abiding French preoccupation with form, expressed in their architecture, cuisine, and the social structure of their lives, produces formality, and structures are apt to become strictures. Or so it seems to me.

Thus, it is with a sense of both adventure and escape that I plunge for the twentieth time into Aksakov's *Chronicles of Bagrovo*. Shivering, for I feel a breath of black frost rise from the page, I read: 'In the middle of winter in the year 1799 when I was eight years we travelled to Kazan. The cold was terrible...'

Kazan! The fabulous Tartar stronghold on the Volga... Now I too am in the sleigh, crouched down among the bear-skins, my eyelashes freezing together. The plumes of snow fly past and the coachman's great padded bulk rocks dangerously as we hurtle onwards, under a livid sky.

It is very quiet in my room overlooking the river. 'Sweet Thames! run softly...' The swans are drifting past, going with the green tide. The sweet damp smell of the riverside rises to the window where the wistaria twines round the rickety little iron balconies and my adored cats and dogs sprawl together in the sun. But my thoughts are elsewhere, at Bagrovo in the Bashkir steppes. Harvest-time, saint's day dances, the serfs, or 'souls' are pickling, bottling, scything, spinning... it is the same immemorial scene, all Russia, all escape, all my heart.

I open the *Chronicles* at random, at the chapter telling of the author's mother, Sofia Nikolaievna, arriving at Bagrovo as a bride. It is an early summer. The linden trees are reflected in the stream, the Nasjagai, or Swift Pursuer, as it is known to the Tartars and Kchouvass people thereabouts; the black earth of Bagrovo yields splendid crops, oats, barley, wheat: the cattle are sleek, the nightingales sound above the songs of the villagers. The bride's father-in-law, the old tyrant Stepan Milkhailovitch, has laid open his granaries to his 'souls'. 'Accept it as a gift in God's name,' he says, majestically happy at his son's marriage. The simple wooden house overflows with family guests and serfs, and I am there.

I have become Sofia Nikolaievna herself! I am welcomed to my new home by my mother-in-law Arina Vassilievna, in her fur-edged velvet jacket, her head bound in a gold-embroidered silk kerchief. She is a plump and comely figure, padded by her clothes and her flesh, resembling one of those *matrioshka* wooden dolls of old Russia. With a rolling gait, she waddles forward and offers me the bread and salt of tradition. Beside her, my father-in-law holds the Blessed Virgin, the Ikon of the House, on high. Behind them stands Father Vassilii, chanting in loud tones. 'Blessed be our God! Who Is, and Was, and Is to be...' I turn to find my husband, but his face is shadowy... 'Blessed be our Russia! Which Is and Was, and Is to be!'

I have reached home.

CHAPTER THIRTEEN

E verything I saw, or read, ate or thought was tinctured by my infatuation. As once at school, history was still seen through this prism of passion. When I dawdled along the Richmond towpath with my dogs, letting myself out by the blue gate under the fig tree where the wild ducks waited to be fed (for I too have lived in Paradise, only, as is the habit of mankind, I did not know it at the time), I would stop before Cholmondeley House which was, I believe, that which Alexander Herzen had occupied soon after his arrival in England in 1852; and thus, in my eyes, sanctified ground. I would look at the little side window giving on to the brick-walled lane, and think: this is where the cabs must have stopped, when that never-ending stream of Revolutionaries arrived, eager for inflammatory talk, sustaining food and hard cash, all of which Herzen could be trusted to provide. What scenes, what talk Cholmondeley House must have known. And now, nearly a century too late, I stood beneath its walls – another exile.

~

The Russia which drew me especially, above the high drama and bright colours of more general images, was that patriarchal pattern which eschewed the Frenchified ways of the capital and was divided between country estates and old houses in Moscow. There was something generous, large and simple here, like the Russian land, having nothing of the corruption of life in the capital: or so it seemed to me, reading descriptions of it in the memoirs and novels of the period.

In spite of the monstrous injustices of serfdom there were still a few contented peasants: all depended on the character of their owner. The principle was wrong: but in practice (such as on the estates of Princess Dashkov, a benign despot) it sometimes worked well enough. This patriarchal tempo possessed an ample concept of time and space. Hurry, that nagging misery, was unknown, both to the age and the nation. The big houses were closely allied to, and dependent on, the land. They were enclosed, self-dependent units. Their carpenters made beautiful furniture from timber grown and seasoned on the estates. Their pastry-cooks made delicacies using flour milled from their own wheat; they had their own

154

plough-men, blacksmiths, horse-doctors and piano tuners, even; their innumerable maidservants and seamstresses worked over linen spun in the long winter evenings, from their own crops of flax. Grooms and coachmen were by the dozen: forty lackeys were not considered an extravagance, some of them doubling as musicians, fiddling far into the night when the *Barin* wished, for they were unquestioningly at his command – all of them his serfs.

'No wonder you long for that sort of life – for of course you see yourself as the *Barinya*,' the Traveller had once remarked, when I sulked as domestic shortages were already beginning to overshadow English households.

I had been detailed to wash up for the third day in succession, since the daily help had once again failed to appear. ('It's me legs, Doctor says. I come over ever so queer Sunday. I couldn't say when I'll be back,' she had said when cornered, queueing outside the Majestic, to see *The Loves of Dracula*.) Thus I sloshed tepid water over the crockery and thought of those Russian households where the absence of one, or even ten, domestics would have caused no inconvenience. Such abundance, however much organization it demanded – and there was this, even in the feckless Russian way – must have spelled an unimaginable degree of comfort. Besides domestics, almost all requirements were to hand; the coiffeur to curl one's hair, the priest to save one's soul, a *lectrice* to save one's eyes, and French and German tutors to strike a note of European culture. There were, besides a *dame de compagnie*, the bailiff and the steward, and that curious being, indispensable adjunct to all Russian households of standing – the *prejivalka*.

The place of the *prejivalka* (its exact meaning is parasite) was peculiar to old Russia. She was a kind of self-effacing busy-body, confidante, and sometimes spy. By origin, she was perhaps an impoverished gentlewoman grown old in the family service, who knew all its secrets, and was at the beck and call of everyone, patronized by the masters and despised by the domestics. Her status was never as clearly defined as that of the *nianya* , nor was she so loved and privileged. She had to show considerable *souplesse*, for she might be called on to act as go-between, carrying *billets-doux* from her mistress to the French tutor, or the son of the house to the young governess; or to clean out the old Barinya's bird-cages; to scold the children for playing too noisily; to check

the cook's accounts or smuggle out a baby born in the housemaids' attics...
She was a buffer between all this concentration of people. It was a
thankless life: yet she *belonged*. She, the arid old maid, had a place, however
small, in the surging pattern of family life. She had her arm-chair, usually
in the wide, warm hall, from where she was aware of all that was going
on, for good or ill. She was part of the pattern. It was not the pinched,
lonely end compassed by a bed-sitter, which would be the lot of her
counterpart in Western Europe today. Or, for that matter, as a unit in a
State-run old people's home, Russia's present solution to the problem.

The spacious life of these Moscow landowners has been described
by many Russian writers. In his *Memoirs* Prince Kropotkin tells of the
bi-annual exodus of such households; in the spring, from Moscow to the
country: in the autumn, returning to winter in the city. Such moves
required elaborate planning. The steward left well ahead with a skeleton
staff and a number of carts laden with stores; the family following later, in
their lumbering coach, stocked with provisions for the route. Returning
from the estates, in autumn, they would bring sacks of flour, honey, sides
of home-cured bacon, a bear's ham, fiery home-brewed liqueurs, pickles
and jams. And in the spring, when the ice had melted, the whole caravan
set off once more, crowding the courtyard before the town house and, at
last, winding down the narrow Moscow streets as, one by one, the big
houses emptied, making across the steppe country and the forests, to set
up all over again in some remote province. It was a rhythm which stilled
some of that nomadic craving, inbred in the Slav.

There was nothing especially beautiful or luxurious in most of
these country houses, but there was taste. To every one of splendour, such
as Archangelskoye, the Yussoupov palace, or that Voronince which
encompassed Liszt for so many years, there were a hundred simple places,
long, low, welcoming houses, with their classic pillared portico and wide
veranda overlooking gardens sheltered by alleys of sweet-smelling lime
trees, acacia and lilac. The land usually sloped to a river, for in the *ennui* of
these seldom-visited provinces, a water-way was as likely to provide
distraction as a highway. All around lay woods merging with profound
forests, the horizon broken only by the belfry of the village church.
Halcyon scenes and innocent pleasures were here: mushroom picking, carp
fishing, or picnics in the woods to visit some renowned hermit, or an
immeasurably old bee-keeper who shared his life with an amiable bear...

home-made music or a game of *Preference* by candlelight, this was the tenor of such a life.

Yet the menacing shadow of Nicholas I fell even here, disrupting the quiet, blighting the defenceless villagers. When his military levies descended demanding a number of men for enlistment there was no redress. Not even the most protective landowner dared defy them. Twenty-five years was the term of service then, and knowing what that implied – floggings for the slightest misdemeanour, or on the whim of their commanding officer, and the appalling living conditions in the army, some peasants killed themselves sooner than be taken. Once conscripted, they were clapped in irons to avoid escapes, while the lamentations and wailings around them were of a community grieving for those whom they would most likely never see again. On the rare occasions of a serfs' revolt, the Emperor Nicholas knew how to deal with it. His generals flogged to death every fifth or tenth man and laid waste to the village, so that those who remained were forced to go begging for bread in neighbouring provinces.

Was this the Russia for which I hankered? Only because, as the Traveller reminded me, I saw it from the Barinya's position of privilege. But had I been a serf? 'As to the poverty I saw in certain villages, especially those belonging to the Imperial family, no words would be adequate to describe the misery,' wrote Prince Kropotkin, an emotional observer, but a man who came, very early, to understand and appreciate not only the Russian peasants' goodness, but his abilities and potentials. He had been cared for by his peasant *nianya* Vassilisa, poorest of the poor, who loved the neglected motherless little boy like her own. He was to repay her affection by a whole life devoted to bettering the peasants' lot. 'Few know what treasures of goodness are found in the hearts of Russian peasants, even after centuries of the most cruel oppression which might well have embittered them,' he wrote.

~

Although with the years my love and knowledge of all things Russian deepened, I could never acquire ease in the language. I understood most of what was said to me, but reading remained a fearful effort. I could write the Kyrillic characters quite quickly and rather incorrectly. A good pronunciation and absolutely no grammar was, and remains, my condition. Thus, on the journeys I at last began to make to Russia and the researches into which I plunged, many years later, preparing my biography of the Imam Shamyl, it was not enough to scrape along in *petit nègre*. The nuances always eluded me or had to be distilled, phrase by phrase, through an interpreter, so that when working I was in a permanent state of frustration.

Even though I have never been able to tear down these barriers of language, I felt, and feel, assimilated, and I am gratified when, as so often, my most exasperated Russian friends (to whom the acquisition of a new language never requires more than two or three months' application), concede that they regard me as one of themselves. *Ona Russkaya dousha*, they say – she is a Russian soul; no compliment could be dearer to me. Sometimes they twit me for my excessive longings, as the Traveller used to do, and I remember how he would call me 'Charlotte Russe'.

There is a picture by Koustodiev of which I am particularly fond, for it represents a way of life, of vanished Russian provincial life which remains, for me, wholly desirable.

A quality of lyric materialism pervades this picture. It is a dream world given over to the senses – to the appetites; a world of flesh embedded in comforts; an ample world. It is a summer's evening in some provincial town. The day's work is done. The setting sun strikes low over the blue belfries and cupolas. A balcony occupies the foreground, and this balcony, shaded by heavy-leaved trees, appears to be entirely occupied by one spreading figure, that of a young woman. Let us call her Praskovia Stepanovna. She is seated at a loaded tea-table, a massive, well-shaped arm propped on the table, a plump hand balancing a saucer of tea. She is the vast, cushioned archetypal woman of Russia – or rather, the Russia of the nineteenth-century merchants.

She is the wife of some such well-to-do man, and taking her ease. Her large, rather pudding-face expresses a bovine beatitude. Praskovia Stepanovna wants for nothing. She lives well; her household duties are not heavy; there are young girls and old women to pickle the cucumber, salt the fish, stone the cherries for jam, wash the linen and wax the floors. Praskovia Stepanovna commands them all with easy-going authority. She does not nag, nor rack herself with emotions; she does not even think. Thus she is never nervous or tired. Angst is unknown to her. Basically, she remains a supine Asiatic woman. Everything is God's will. He has ordained this good table at which she feasts. It is His bounty. Dominating the table, as massive as she, stands the samovar. The *bublitchki*, the raspberry preserves, and the sumptuous melon, its rosy flesh as inviting as her own vast and melting bosom, so generously displayed, are all His work. It is the feast of life. Praskovia Stepanovna simmers in content. She will sit there munching and sipping till late, till her husband or her lover joins her, till the summer night darkens at last and it is time to cross herself before the ikon of the house and go to bed. *'S'Bogom!'* – with God! In this latitude of the senses of an old picture, of an imagined, vanished world, I long to be.

~

I think it was Nietzsche, seeing Russia through the eyes of Dostoievsky, who described the race as 'volcanoes, either extinct, quiescent or in a state of eruption'. And so they seemed to my English friends. They simply could not comprehend the degrees of emotion, the depths of gloom, the elation and the apathy which successively gripped both the characters of Russian fiction and the Russians they came to know personally, whether of the Dispersal or more rarely those few who arrived in London as members of the *Corps Diplomatique* or governmental missions. At that time the latter were rarely encountered save in the watchful confines of officialdom; but already, in the comparatively short time Soviet dictums had prevailed, a change was apparent; a curious note of moderation, of discipline had sounded. The more chaotic life led by the earlier émigrés was closer to preconceived English notions of Slav turbulence and, also, to the characters of Russian fiction which they often condemned. In his memoirs, Sir Osbert Sitwell quotes a fellow-countryman as having returned a copy of some Russian classic, remarking that none of it would have happened if the characters had been to an English public school.

In all the Russians I encountered I sensed something dynamic rather than nervous, revitalizing rather than devitalizing; their uproars did not exhaust me, perhaps because I was never bored by them; although it must be admitted that, among them, I lived far beyond my emotional means. It was as if I had found, in them, a *force de la nature*, an affinity with the earth and its fundamentals (apparent even in a wan group of basement dwellers) which my own urbanized and generally over-sophisticated race had lost. It was a quality which my system craved with a drug addict's intensity.

I was, in short, a renegade, biologically as well as intellectually and emotionally.

~

Among those whom I had first encountered in Paris so long ago, in the Traveller's circle, and whose friendship I was to treasure till his death, was the theatrical director Feodor Komisarjevsky. There were many ways in which he recalled the Traveller. The same egg-bald, Asiatic skull, the same profound knowledge of the arts and, beneath the façade of a blasé international rake, the same sense of desolation, of the expatriate patriot. Neither of these men should ever have left Russia for, fundamentally, whatever they achieved outside it was to them unreal. With Komisarjevsky I could 'talk Russia'; with him, had I not felt it disloyal, I could have re-created the Run-Away Game. He too loved the *genre* paintings of Venezianov or Fedotov; portraits by Kiprensky, as well as prints in the idiom of *Images d'Epinal*. Here haloed Orthodox saints opposed lively devils, or fleshy beauties surged out of their chemises, lolling on sofas, tickling the paws of sleek cats, while serf-girls in turn tickled their feet – bliss, in the idiom of the peasant – such naïve aspects of old Russia Komisarjevsky savoured particularly. We shared a passion for Ostrovsky's provincial dramas and the long-vanished way of life they represented, and together we looked backwards.

His father, an opera singer, had gone to fight for Garibaldi and died in Rome, and so, by way of the many legends of Russian émigrés in the Eternal City, there was Gogol's tormented life there as a further point of interest, thus, a circuitous return to Russia. We had many friends in common among the exiles in Paris and when, one day, he carelessly produced two young sons, although younger than Sergei or Kamran, and appeared as vaguely disposed towards them as the Traveller had been to his own, I had the impression my life had gone into reverse, towards the Corsican idyll. A new one now began. Komisarjevsky was a past-master in the art of pleasing. 'You must be the only woman in England to read Bestoujef-Marlinksy's tales' he would say, and no wooing phrases could have sounded softer to my ears. 'All the same, you really are far too Slav for me,' he would add, watching me leave for my ritualistic outing to the Russian mass on Saturday evenings. Too Slav? In a mood of content I went on my way.

Even my devotions, never a matter of profound conviction, continued *à la Russe*. But then I remained primarily influenced by aesthetic considerations. After the Church of England worship I had barely glimpsed in my childhood, Russian church rituals continued to lure me, appearing as splendidly dramatic as their setting. I coquetted with Orthodox dogma, falling back before more specialized theological intricacies, believing I preferred Orthodoxy to all other creeds. But what I really liked was its visual or, perhaps, its sensual appeal. The gold-crowned priests appearing from and disappearing behind the gilded iconostas, were to me so many theatrical figures making their exits and entrances. There was, too, something dramatic, sinister even, and infinitely alluring in the darkness, lit by a sudden blaze of candlelight glittering over the jewelled ikons. Their brooding narrowed eyes seemed to follow my restless, secular progress with something of the Traveller's same sidelong ironic glance. I trespassed there, and they knew it.

Yet something, among all these Byzantine splendours, spoke to me as no Gothic cathedral could do. Just as in London, the Russian Church in Victoria, a disaffected chapel I believe, or the more intimate atmosphere of the little Russian chapel at Baron's Court, was poor substitute for the Cathedral in the Rue Daru (and this, in its turn, was as nothing compared to the Russian churches I came to know, elsewhere, in the Balkans and Russia itself), I never crossed the threshold of that pallid chapel reconsecrated to Orthodoxy, without the same heady waft of incense catching me by the throat, and transporting me to some visionary realm peopled with the crow-like figures of Leskov's clergy, or black-wimpled nuns and bearded boyars, massed, as in the Coronation scene from Boris Goudenov, pure theatre, while the rolling deep voices of the choir chanted their traditional responses, humble and despairing. '*Gospodi pomiloe, Gospodi pomiloe...*' Lord have mercy... O Lord have mercy...

Komisarjevsky understood how my taste for dramatic effects, for the theatre of stylization such as he knew so marvellously how to create, was gratified by the settings and rituals of the Orthodox Church.

'Full house?' he would ask slyly when we met later for dinner.

PART FIVE

THE JOURNEY BEGUN

. . . travelling, everywhere intent upon
following, as though it were a strain of
fugitive music, the perpetual tradition
of the past.

Edmund Gosse

CHAPTER FOURTEEN

I t was inevitable that, sooner or later, I would reach Russia, and in the early thirties I did so, owing to the generosity of an English admirer who, finding bouquets and soft speeches had not won me and hoping, perhaps, to lay the Slav ghost by realities, offered a return ticket to the U.S.S.R. while tactfully declining to accompany me on this emotional pilgrimage. The manner of my first visit to Russia was not strictly in accordance with my secret longings for it was a controlled programme, beginning with Leningrad, rather than Moscow, or Novgorod.

'St. Petersburg is Russian – but it is not Russia,' the Traveller had said. But it was the first step. Such a journey was not then fashionable, being only undertaken by the daring few. If I remember rightly, we embarked on a Soviet cargo-boat at Tower Bridge and made for the Baltic by way of Kiel, coasting Sweden and the former Hanseatic ports. We were abjured (by those who had not made the trip), to take bath plugs, insecticides and every kind of patent medicine, all of which I was fortunate enough to find unnecessary. Every evening the crew played chess, listening to Russian folk music on an old gramophone planted in the place of honour below the portraits of Lenin and Felix Dzerjinsky which graced Red Corner in their mess. The bunks were hard, the food indifferent, and none of the lavatory doors closed properly, but it was a lovely voyage made sweet by the smiling personnel, made intoxicating by the air which blew from the north, smelling of snow and ice and dark forests – Russia.

We had reached the Gulf of Finland and suddenly the island fortress of Kronstadt rose out of a pearly haze, nebulous, its silhouette veiled in mist, and I remembered how those few of my old Russian friends who took milk in their tea always asked for it 'Kronstadtski' – with the merest dash of milk, only enough to cloud the clear tea, as now, a haze clouded the transparent northern air.

Soon our ship was edging past timber yards, stacked high, where huge rafts of lashed tree trunks were being poled along by young men wearing the picturesque red *roubashka* of tradition. Here in the U.S.S.R., were the Selifan and Grishka of my reading! That they were members of some Collective Timbermen's Union, that their wives and sweethearts were Shock Brigade workers, did not affect their superficial likeness to the eternal Russian peasant of my mind's eye, a character that I enjoyed on aesthetic grounds. This was something I could never explain to the new generation of Russians I now encountered. They suspected me of patronage, or some profound admiration for a Tzarist past, based on its political rather than picturesque aspects. So purely superficial a point of view as mine they could not, of course, comprehend, much less condone. At that time, they saw all literary or historic associations politically – or subjectively – as subjectively as I saw their country.

Hanging over the ship's rail, indulging in my customary nostalgic flights, I had not noticed how the silhouette of Leningrad had emerged from the milky haze to spread across the wide horizon in all its splendour. There was the great bronze dome of the St. Isaak cathedral, there the spires of the Peter and Paul fortress and the Admiralty. The Bronze Horseman, the Winter Palace, the Nevsky Prospekt, Pushkin's city, Dostoievsky's city, the city of Peter the Great... Was I at last stepping into this passionately desired scene? This was a journey into my heart's desire as well as my mind's eye, the consummation of a double-visioned longing – my own and that of the Traveller. I looked down over the ship's rail, at the prosaic Customs shed and across to the distant city, and knew that each thing I saw would recall him to me, as he had so often recalled them for me.

In this mood of exaltation it was unfortunate that my first sacramental-seeming step on Russian earth was taken unperceived (not that I should have gone to the lengths of those fervent souls who, we are told, landing in America, so often fling themselves down to embrace the sod). Nevertheless it was, for me, a solemn moment which should have been charged with emotion had I not been searching at the bottom of my handbag for my keys while holding my passport in my teeth. Nor do I recall much of the long drive into the city, nor of the hotel, nor of my vast bedroom crowded with frowzy *fin de siècle* comfort, a darkly canopied bed and even a grand piano (locked). I have a vague recollection of a particularly sustaining breakfast-tray – tea, horse-meat and caviare, which stood me in good stead on my long lunchless excursions.

I had soon discovered that to return to the hotel for lunch was to spend most of the afternoon in the dining-room, 'in alternate uproar and sad peace', for the food was good but the service had that timelessness associated with the East. No complaints, no pleading affected the beaming gold-toothed Tartar waiters: '*Sichass! Sichass!*' they promised; At once! and disappeared, so that I was able to sharpen my appetite between the *borshch* and the *golubtsi* of dinner by a walk; in Moscow, to the Kremlin's crimson walls, but first, in Leningrad, to the Winter Palace, with ample time to indulge my mind's eye by standing before its sullen bulk, shuttered and still, as I romanticized what has remained to me one of the most dramatic images of the Tzar's city. Every night from sunset to sunrise, I had read somewhere, squadrons of mounted Cossack guards used to defile 'like moonlight spectres', circling the palace, hour after hour, the tramp of their horses' hooves muffled by deep snow as this ghostly patrol ringed the building where, nevertheless, bombs were sometimes planted (under the Imperial dinner-table on one occasion) and an atmosphere of tension always prevailed. Although it was now a museum, impersonal and mute, and the vast square before it deserted but for a lone pedestrian plodding homeward across its immensity, some sinister spell remained, some aura of tension, of brooding malevolence still prevailed. It had never been a particularly happy or fortunate place and the last two Tzars had preferred to live elsewhere.

~

While outwardly coming and going among the few other tourist groups, I was at the same time keeping company with a shade, now playing a more positive version of the Run-Away Game, stepping into the very scenes I had known by heart for so many years, willing myself there. Thus nothing appeared unfamiliar to me, whether in the quarters of former splendour or those sad, straggling outskirts beyond the Moscow Gate, among the asylums, the cattle markets and the railway yards. Empty streets and overcrowded houses were everywhere apparent; tufts of grass and weeds sprouted along many of the finest thoroughfares, and peering in at the windows of the more splendid houses of Millionaya, I could see the lofty rooms divided up among several families, their washing strung between the unlit crystal chandeliers. Yet my sense of home-coming was not diminished. The present was a Kronstadtski haze, barely veiling that glowing past I sought to recapture.

As my nostalgia gathered momentum, I was sometimes aware of unspoken criticism among the officials of tourist organizations. They appreciated my enthusiasm (and stamina), and recognized that my awareness of so much of their past was uncommon for a foreigner but, they inferred, I must surely want to see more examples of progress? In vain they would offer me factory tours, suggest outings to collective farms and other splendid achievements. I admired their efforts and long-term plans whole-heartedly – but how to explain to them that I could not concentrate on the present or the future with such a past around me – and such a revenant beside me? Theoretically, ideologically, I looked forward. Aesthetically, emotionally, I looked back. It was due to no promptings on the part of my accompanying shadow that I cherished those illusions de Custine despised. My tastes and knowledge had already crystallized into a specialized mould – Russia of the nineteenth century – which remained my first interest and which, many years later, led me to write the life and times of the Imam Shamyl.

Thus, going between the museums of Leningrad and Moscow, I sought out all I could of this particular era, setting it above larger sweeps of history or more celebrated tourist shrines. The Gallery of Field Marshals in the Winter Palace claimed me before the Rembrandts in the Hermitage. Rembrandt could be seen in other countries; only here could I find the likeness of Field Marshal Prince Bariatinsky, who received Shamyl's sword of submission at Gounib; only here find Kutuzov, Yermolov or Bagration, whom I felt I knew personally, as well as I knew Natasha or Prince Andrei, from reading *War and Peace*.

Only here could I find Brullov's dashing portraits or Alexiev's meticulous perspectives, for which he was dubbed the Canaletto of the North. Only here find Nesterov's Holy Russia, or so many charming *genre* paintings so little known outside Russia – Venezianov's peasants; a street scene by Schredovsky, where impudent young workmen jostle self-important merchants. Narrative painting, theatre, rather than art, but telling a tale which fascinated me. Scenes of bourgeois life, full of archness or bathos; old maids coquetting with pot-bellied majors, spied on by tittering families; a young widow mourning by an ikon-lit empty bed. (Their contemporaries, in England, were such canvases as *The Last Day in the Old Home*, *The Awakened Conscience*, or *Too Late*.) But even Fedotov's scenes of swarming family life set in Beidermeyer interiors reflected some essentially *national* quality – the Russia of their moment. An extreme note was apparent: there was some overwhelming theatricality, something grotesque, or even sinister, compared to the calm of similar scenes rendered by German Romantic painters.

Only a frontier away, domesticity was presented very differently. In Dresden or Munich we see Caspar David Friedrich's quiet maidens at their embroidery; or Runge's solitary figures playing Schumann on the flute in prim attics, while contented women sit at flower-stocked windows peeling vegetables... *Der Stille Garten*... Not so in Russia: a feckless, reckless mood invades each interior, however stuffy. I found it infinitely revealing: it was as if the painters shared something of Gogol's bitter and chaotic inspiration.

The works of these Russian artists were generally neglected – even by the Russian public. Whole rooms of these treasures remained unvisited, snubbed by them, and certainly snubbed by the tourists who appeared magnetized by the great collections of French Impressionists.

In Moscow, on my first visit, one of the many beautiful old houses was then arranged as a military museum, with archives and pictorial documentation set out to show nineteenth-century Russian campaigns. Here the romantic figure of the exiled poet Lermontov was seen in a purely military context as the daring young Lieutenant mentioned in dispatches; here Tolstoy was a dandified young officer off to the Crimean wars (but having received his baptism of fire earlier, in the Caucasian wars). Here was Griboyedov, not presented as the author of *Woe Through Wit*, but seen as the diplomat who negotiated the treaty of Turkmentchai with the Persians, who were later to run him to death in the Russian Legation at Teheran. And here was Pushkin's self-portrait at the storming of Kars, a monkey-like, tall-hatted figure enveloped in a *bourka* and riding a bony nag. Among the warriors, so many men of letters.

But then this side-stepping had always prevailed in Russia and derived from the rigid caste system of *tchin*, which enclosed each man in his special grade and uniform, as a *tchinovnik*, or civil servant. The hierarchy of the *tchin* was as strict as the gold-laced uniforms, in mounting degrees of splendour, from the modest Registrar of College to Titular Counsellor (recalling Gogol's play, *Revizor, The Government Inspector*), to Counsellor of College, Court, State; and then – pure Gogol this – True Counsellor of College, as if all the former ranks were so many puffed-up inventions. The system had been founded by Peter the Great and was taken from a method of Swedish administration where each Ministry or Department of State was designated a College. The *tchin* reached its apogee during the reign of Nicholas I, who particularly rejoiced in its exactitude; it remained, in slightly decreasing force, until the Revolution; thus we see the anomaly of so many writers and musicians being officially nominated otherwise. Borodin the chemist; Moussorgsky an officer in the Preobajensky regiment. Gogol and Griboyedov sharpening their quill pens in Government Ministries. Pushkin appointed Gentleman-in-Waiting (chiefly to insure his beautiful wife's presence at Court) and, in the mind of the Emperor, no doubt, to classify him within the limits of his grade, rather than in the limitless glory of his poetic reputation. It was, said Authority, absolutely essential to belong to some definite category – thus Anton Rubinstein, applying for a passport and describing himself as 'musician' was sharply told that this was not listed as a profession. Since Rubinstein had somehow avoided any other occupation, Authority was at last compelled to describe him as 'son of merchant of Second Guild'.

I had hoped to visit Mikhailovskoye, Pushkin's estate where he spent a lonely winter exiled from the capital and his friends, snowed-up, in the company of his old *nianya*, Arina Rodianovna, with whom he had found inspiration for some of his loveliest work. But this expedition seemed unaccountably difficult and I had to content myself with an excursion, undertaken in a mood of gloomy reverence, to the Black Brook, where D'Anthès bullet had awaited the poet. Nearer at hand, his little house on the Moika canal, with its sombre library facing inwards on to an equally sombre courtyard, was much as it had been the day he died there, being meticulously preserved as a national shrine.

'Good-bye my friends,' breathed the poet, his eyes fixed on his beloved books... 'Life is over' were his last words. Had I read Zhukhovsky's poignant description of that scene, or was it the Traveller's voice that told me, once again, as I hung over the bronze death-mask? There was no trace on those calm features of the sufferings that had racked Pushkin's last hours and it was very quiet in the little house, yet it seemed to vibrate with the agonized cries that were wrung from the poet during his thirty-six hours of dying. The afternoon was overcast and the room felt very cold. Outside the window, the courtyard was already stacked high with firewood for the winter stoves – those tall white porcelain stoves which, in varying degrees of elegance or functionalism, have always been an integral part of the Russian interior. Beside the firewood a solitary crow was pecking abstractedly at a tattered cabbage leaf.

'Come away, *Pussinka*,' I seemed to hear the Traveller say, and as I went out I was crying – for a poet I would never know and a man I had lost.

~

So he led me, by way of memories and monuments, great occasions and mean streets, through the history of his country. 'History is the people's memory – but to remember one has to know,' wrote S. S. Smirnov. Together the Traveller and I would linger in the Senate Square, honouring the Dekabrist cause, recalling with our double vision the heart-breaking events of that icy grey December day in 1825.

In lighter mood we took ourselves off to the convent of Smolny, glutting ourselves on its sumptuous blue and gold beauty – Rastrelli's legacy; and I would imagine myself one of the Noble Young Ladies cribbed there in such incongruously Spartan simplicity. Russian excess and counterpoint again: the pupils emerged from this strict convent-like atmosphere, to be plunged almost overnight into the glittering intrigues of the Court, or the extravagant life lived by the *beau monde* of St. Petersburg. Then the Traveller recalled me to larger issues again. Lenin had made Smolny his headquarters during the first decisive weeks of the Revolution. From here he had issued his famous call to battle. Where once the demoiselles had practised court curtsies and perfected their French, he sat in lonely responsibility issuing manifestos, drawing up his strategic plans for the 1917 *coup d'état*.

The city assumed varying aspects, according to the mood of my unseen companion. At times it seemed to be St. Petersburg, at others Leningrad and, at moments, Petrograd, as perhaps it had been the last time he was there, I imagined. When I walked along the Court Quay, a pygmy figure below the stupendous façade of the Winter Palace (where a staff of eleven thousand persons was once employed) I saw it as St. Petersburg, with the Palace of the Tzars as a setting for unimaginable splendours, Court rituals and an implacable protocol, which nevertheless remained unshaken by the frequent detonation of terrorists' bombs. Or I would wonder from which balcony that hopeful, exploited mass of simple people led, or misled, by Father Gapon, had expected the Tzar, their little Father, to emerge and listen to their wrongs, before the Cossacks shot them down and the Tzar, unknowing it seems, spent one of his pleasant family evenings at Tzarskoe Selo.

171

I turned towards more sugared images of the Palace. To my inner-eye, the stairways were always lined with the Empress's Negro pages, traditional reminders of Hannibal, Peter the Great's Abyssinian protégé. Marbles glowed and crystals shimmered perpetually. Ladies-in-waiting were always trailing five-yard crimson velvet and ermine trains, their veils flowing from high, jewelled *kokoshniki*; while another Emperor, my favourite, Alexander II, 'Liberator of the Serfs', in a white and gold Hussar uniform trimmed with sable, was followed by his suite, also in the white and gold of the Chevalier Gardes, perpetually pacing through the stately measures of the Polonaise, for ever opening a Court Ball to the strains of Glinka's *A Life for the Tzar*.

More factually, I also saw the city as Leningrad; no more pomp but much glory as a triumphant anchorage for the Cruiser Aurora, riding there on the grey choppy waters, at once menacing and reassuring, lying symbolically between Palace and Fortress, and dominating both. And then I understood the surge of pride which infused the revolutionaries when the city fell to them – at last!

Sitting in a pale-blue hung box at the Mariinsky Theatre among an outing of Collective Truck Drivers of the Ukraine, listening to Shostakovitch's opera based on Leskov's *Lady Macbeth of Mtsensk*, hearing Katerina Ismailovna singing her last, blood-curdling aria among the Siberian prisoners, as she leaps to her death dragging her rival with her, I remembered the Traveller's accounts of the branded *brodyagas*, vagrants and prisoners he had known in his youth, in the villages and settlements around Baikal. I was no longer aware of operatic values, for I was deep in Siberia, but as Shostakovitch's music took on even more intensity, I felt the Traveller's presence as something tangible. I knew how he felt about Leskov's terrible tale – but how was he liking this production, this music? (Some years later Stalin and Molotov were, mysteriously, to condemn it as derogatory to Soviet prestige.) I had only to turn my head to see the Traveller seated at the back of the box, half-hidden, his Chinese bald pate light against the shadows. So strong was this impression that I did not turn – there would be time to talk when it was over. This was a new opera – new to both of us – there would be much to discuss. But when the curtain fell, he was no longer there. Only the echoes of his voice remained, telling of the Siberian prisoners such as he himself had known.

And so it was, on this, my first visit to the U.S.S.R. and others I was to make later, where, in the cities or the country, along the gorges of the Georgian Military Highway, at an Uzbek market in Samarkand, in the foothills of the Pamirs, beside the silky rivers, or in the deep forests, all spoke to me of him, as he had so often spoken of them to me.

Only Siberia eluded me – eluded us, rather. Was the Traveller's desire not strong enough to will us there? Or had he known it too well – under some particular stress? Siberia remained unobtainable. No train ran just then, I was told. No permits were being issued... The climate was bad. There was no suitable accommodation at present, said the Authorities. And just why did I want to go there, they pressed, having as yet little experience of people wishing to go to Siberia for pleasure.

~

Along the Nevsky Prospekt a few decrepit *droshkies* still plied for hire, the hoary *izvostchik*, or coachman, still wearing the grotesquely padded full-skirted coat of tradition. In the greying contemporary scene this note of local colour stood out like an exclamation mark emphasizing the passing of the picturesque.

Riding in one of these *droshkies*, watching the façade of some recognized building loom up suddenly from behind the coachman's spreading bulk, was as I had imagined it (although my mind's eye saw him wearing the *yamstchik's* traditional velvet coat and peacock-feather cap). Tram rides were not at all the same thing for, apart from suffocating loads and my uncertainty over tickets and destinations, trams had not been the Traveller's means of moving about the city and it seemed his shade hung back from this experiment in collective transport. He had used *traineaux*, *droshkies* or troikas; which latter I should have preferred, but there were no troikas left in the city. There never had been many; they were for the countryside, or driving to the Islands. When I came on the place by the Fontanka canal where I knew they used to stand for hire, there was nothing but a street-vendor's stall offering little glasses of *sbiten*, a sickly drink.

Very well then, a *droshky* will have to do. Now I am *living* the Run-Away Game. Settling myself on the cracked leather seats of a rattle-trap vehicle I move over to make room for the Traveller, for of course he is beside me. I know this route well, by the map and by my heart too. Across the city is the station from which trains run to Western Europe.

This is the route the Traveller used to take when he came to see us in London. But now things have gone into reverse. Now he is leaving St. Petersburg for London, but I am no longer pleading to accompany him, for I am here, in the latitude and longitude of my heart. I shall wave good-bye without that anguished longing and sense of frustration I used to experience when he left England for Siberia. I shall wait for him quite contentedly; nor shall I be tracing his imagined journey in my atlas.

When he returns he will be bringing me presents, souvenirs of his travels, as he always did. Only now, the caviare, the Bokharan *khalat* or the three-tailed standard of a Mongol chief will be transposed into other terms – a Stilton cheese instead of caviare, a Jaeger dressing-gown for the Bokharan *khalat* and a Briggs umbrella in place of the Mongol chieftain's standard. No doubt a fair exchange if I can see them through Russian eyes.

So, as the *droshky* rattles along, my inner ear listens to the old song of the coachmen, 'Down Peterskaya Street'.

'Drive on! Drive anywhere!' I tell the *izvostchik* wildly. He turns round and gives me a soft look. In old Russia fools were always indulged, were 'holy fools' when he was young. Now I, the Traveller's companion – mistress – wife – my status is never quite clear – am driving into the heart of the Run-Away Game once more. We are away! There is no telling where, for all Petersburg lies before us and now I am heading towards those places which once I could only reach through a picture frame.

'Remember,' the Traveller admonishes me once more, 'St. Petersburg is Russian – but it is not Russia.' No matter. The sun shines. To Oranienbaum, along the wide tree-shaded road once lined with coquettish little datchas and fine houses, to the palace built by Menshikov, the high-flying pie-seller who rose to become Prime Minister, the all-powerful lover of Peter the Great's widow, the first Empress Catherine, before he fell from glory to suffer Siberian exile. Now the fine houses are boarded up, the datchas deserted. But I do not notice the present. I am in another moment of time. We have brought a picnic, *rastegai*, fish patties, *Pojarsky cotletki*, *syr*, a white cheese, and a bottle of the celebrated greenish-coloured wine from Georgia. We do not know famine in my dream-Russia and, in this haze of well-being, we shall explore the little Chinese house and Catherine the Great's pavilion, the *Damski Domik*.

Now it is night – a winter's night of absolute, snow-bound silence. How quiet these streets, crowded yet muffled in hard snow, the *traineaux* brushing noiselessly, smoothly across the whiteness. We are in a troika, off to the Islands, racing over the ice, for the Neva is frozen solid and the floating boat-bridges have been removed, as they are each winter. We are huddled against the wind which bears down on us from the Arctic. The yamstchik calls to his horses. *'Gaida troika! Gaida troika!'* the old song comes back to me as we race into the darkness, bells jingling. Seized by this intoxication of speed, *le vertige de la vitesse* which grips every Russian, I am still remembering the niceties of Russian as propounded by the Traveller: 'remember, a *droshky* driver is an *izvostchik*, a troika is driven by a *yamstchik.' Gaida troika*! We are racing through the birch woods to a little restaurant where, much later, the Tziganes will sing for us until morning. And in memory of a night in Passy I shall ask for *The Black Shawl*.

Now we are wandering through the warren of booths that make up the Gostinny Dvor, the huge covered bazaar behind the Nevsky Prospekt where, it seems, anything in the world can be bought, and one whole section is devoted to the sale of ikons, jewelled ones, peasant ones, old, new... glittering, fusty, naive, haunting... God in our Midst. I want only Russian goods; embroidered leather slippers from Torjok, amethysts from the Urals, little carved wooden toys, or rainbow silks woven by the Uzbeks. Perhaps we shall decide on more domestic purchases, and go to the street markets behind the Haymarket, where Dostoievsky sets the scene for *Crime and Punishment* and where the best sturgeon is to be had. For now I have become a prideful housewife, making a *koulibiak* as good, or better, than at Palkin's *traktir* (or so the Traveller says). We both prefer the real Russian dishes of these modest *traktirs* to the international cuisine of more sophisticated restaurants. But best of all we like to dine at home, in our apartment overlooking the Fontanka which, I am so often told, recalls the canals of Venice.

But I am content that it is Petersburg, in all its strange, sad, northern beauty. Across the rooftops I can see the immense bronze dome of the Kazan Cathedral and part of the sweep of its gigantic colonnade. Everything about the Kazan Cathedral is heroic, gargantuan – a place of worship for giants, for the legendary *Bogatyri*, no less, so that the merely human trophies, banners won in battle by Kutuzov and his regiments in 1812, seem dolls' delights, no more. By their immensity, both the Isaak and the Kazan Cathedrals remind us that this people's lusty physical appetites were matched by the fervour of their mystical piety. Today, these buildings look like colossal paper-weights pinning down the long vistas of this sprawling city.

Yet sometimes, in some lights, the city's monumental masonry appeared as insubstantial as so many soap bubbles. Vaporous wisps of cloud merged with the mists that rose from the canals or drifted in from the open expanses of the Neva, so that the massive façade of the Admiralty, like the towering Alexander column or the scattered palaces, emerged and retreated through the mists, phantoms of glory.

This northern capital, St. Petersburg – Petrograd – Leningrad, call it what you will, had none of the stocky materialism of Moscow, so deep-rooted in the earth. St. Petersburg rose from a miasmic swamp, commanded by the will of one man, 'built on a territory destined by nature to be the patrimony of wolves and bears'; but for all its violently-willed beauty and immensity I had the impression that the city about which I walked could dissolve into its mists, or sink into the waters from which it had risen, without the earth in which Moscow was rooted recording the least tremor nor the country as a whole being even aware of its passing.

Only in its gigantic conception did Leningrad proclaim its Russian origin, for it was scaled to those infinite Asiatic horizons over which the country spread. 'Nothing is little, or moderate in Russia. If the land is not one of miracles it is today a land of giants.' De Custine, again; but not having the last word. Let a Russian, Prince Volkonsky, his contemporary, have that: 'Russia,' he wrote, 'is an immense edifice appearing European, ornamented by a European façade: but inside furnished and administered in an Asiatic fashion. The great majority of Russian administrators are disguised as Europeans, but proceed in the exercise of their functions *en Tartare*.'

How much that verdict applies today would be difficult to say. As I write, contemporary U.S.S.R. must surely appear a land of miraculous achievement, especially when we consider its past, and the devastations of World War Two. But I fancy many fundamental Slavic, or Asiatic characteristics remained unchanged by even the most determined applications of progress. And the people are not depleted by the multiplying superficialities of our civilization.

~

Sometimes, in my wanderings about Leningrad or Moscow – and later in other Russian cities too – I felt myself impelled towards a certain quarter or street, without knowing why and, equally without any specific reason, would find myself peering in at a window or a courtyard, searching it seemed, for some person or episode which eluded me, as if the shade of that other self that had, I believed, been Russian (or was it the Traveller operating through me?) was now able to revisit through my present self some place which had once been of significance to one of us. Thus, between my own desires and these other promptings, I covered a great deal of ground, generally outside the tourist orbit.

There were certain lodestar points to which I always returned. The railway station ranked very high among these. In Moscow I would sometimes hire a taxi and with voluptuous deliberation pronounce the magic formula: '*Na Yaroslavski Voxal!*' To the Siberian Station! There, like a Peri at the Gates of Paradise, I would stand disconsolate before the florid Kurhaus façade – portal of bliss – through which scurrying crowds surged, dragging their bundles, their children, samovars and lumpy sacks of provisions, for that long, long journey it seemed I could not make. Puffs of steam and the wail of the engines eager to be off merged with the pandemonium of the main hall. Away beyond the barriers I could see the high, curiously shaped funnel typical of Russian engines. Then, as I gazed, they shunted majestically out of sight while I strained my eyes, lover-like, for a last glimpse. At the ticket-office endless queues were inching up; but each person presented a pass which alone entitled them to a ticket, to the right to travel eastwards into that mysterious, withheld land of my desires.

The Tzar Nicholas I had distrusted innovations such as railways, holding they were likely to foster unrest (a view shared by his contemporary, the Duke of Wellington, who held they would only encourage the working classes to move about needlessly). Perhaps this view was still shared by the Soviet authorities, for it seemed *déplacements* were generally discouraged.

Since I had no pass I would sadly turn back to my waiting taxi. The chauffeur was usually dozing across the passenger seats, surrounded by husks of *semitchki* – those dried sun-flower seeds which the Slav peoples nibble in such untidy quantities. He would spring awake, smile widely, a disarming, and usually silver-capped smile, and thrust a twist of paper containing the remaining *semitchki* at me. Nibbling and spitting out the husks (an occupation traditionally known as 'Siberian conversation'), we would drive back to the hotel companionably. But in the cracked mirror above his head I would see him eyeing me with a puzzled expression. Foreign ladies going all across town to the Siberian Station just to stand there and stare were to be humoured – but returned quickly to the Intourist Bureau.

~

If I had felt myself entirely at home in Leningrad, because I seemed to know St. Petersburg so well, my first impression of Moscow was of violent impact – a feeling so intense that, seeing the Kremlin for the first time, I wanted to swallow it in one great gulp. This was the real blood and bones of Russia – of Muscovy, of Pushkin's Golden-Headed Moscow: 'In Moscow', wrote A. Ostrovsky 'all that is the true Russia becomes more understandable, more valued.'

The Kremlin! What words can conjure up this fabulous conglomeration of palaces, churches, prisons, treasure-houses, belfries, gilded cupolas, pinnacles and crimson walls? Its terror, its legends, its loveliness are like nothing else in all the world. No life, I felt, would be long enough to know it in all its aspects. Seeing it rising, sumptuous and barbaric, archetypal Russia, shimmering above the grey waters of the Moskva river, my degree of possessive, lovers' greed was such that my mouth watered.

Over the years the Kremlin's beauty has never staled for me. No other building or site compares and, for me, it remains the eighth wonder of the world. In snow, in sun, by dawn or twilight, it is incomparably lovely; most proudly beautiful, as I recall it through a snow-storm, from a window across the river; most heart-breakingly lovely at dusk, on an autumn evening, from within its walls.

On later visits I often went there expressly to savour that last quiet hour when the sight-seeing crowds had left, and settling myself on the steps of the Ivan Velikii bell tower, I could watch the drama of a long northern afterglow fading slowly, lemon against the golden domes, fading, greenish and luminous, behind the covey of little cupolas above the diminutive Cathedral of the Redeemer Behind the Golden Railing. These cupolas are long-necked and graceful in form, like strange birds come to rest on the roof, and in the stillness of twilight, as I turned to go, I fancied I might hear them scuffling, bird-like, settling themselves for the night, perched there, among the giant Byzantine eagles of history.

Thus, returning to my hotel from a concert or a theatre, although marvelling at the spectacle of Shock Brigades toiling under arc lamps, strong square figures of the future moving purposefully among the cement mixers, swarming about the scaffolding of the huge building then under construction, I always tended to double back from my place in the admiring crowd for a last midnight glimpse of the Kremlin's crimson walls and turrets.

A splendid disregard for scale or generally accepted proportion prevails in much of old Russian architecture. Stumpy pillars, squat arches, chunky, dwarf-sized doors, give a violently national flavour; yet the whole remains harmonious. Perhaps there is some affinity with the square, rather short-legged *moujik* types of the past, and the race, as a whole who, however well built, do not have the attenuation of some others. This same thickness, this solidity and sense of being rooted in the earth, is found in their most grandiose monuments. It even affects the Italianate compositions of imported architects: for the better, to my way of thinking, for it imparts strength to what might otherwise become merely ornate. At Peterhof for example in the 'Coat of Arms' wing, the domed roof is disproportionately large above the Dutch-flavoured palace: the gilded cupola tops it like a monstrous salt-cellar; it is a toy, with something of a toy's clumsy charm.

In Moscow, the domes and pinnacles of the Kremlin used, until the advent of sky-scraper buildings, to tower over the city. But like the pineapple and onion domes of the neighbouring Vassilii Blajennii Cathedral ('La Mosquée', to Napoleon, aware of Russia's Asiatic undertones), they rise stockily, from hugely planted bases, so square, so squatly arched that they belie the height above.

Curiously, this same essential chunkiness is expressed triumphantly in one of their newest buildings, the Palace of Congress, within the Kremlin complex, where the seemingly low, thick pillars of the foyer delude the eye by their actual height. The whole effect is of the utmost felicity, uniting an entirely contemporary idiom with the traditional, purely *national* sense of four-square strength.

I love the sense of intimacy which this obtains: I find it at once

179

reassuring and comprehensible. Cosy, is perhaps the exact word, the one which comes to my mind when I recall Kolomenskoye, or the Zagorsk Monastery, or the old churches along the Don. To me, they speak of 'God in our Midst', like the Ikon of the House; something at once mystic and personal, as in mosques, unlike Gothic or Romanesque cathedrals, which remain remote, being essays in logical piety, while Baroque and Rococo are worldly variations on the same theme.

~

Beneath its majesty, its contradictory air of intimacy, the Kremlin also strikes a sinister note, recalling many terrors. The Tartar invaders first planted their horse-tail standards there in 1382 (kremel is the Tartar word for fortress). In the nineteenth century alone, five unhappy Tzars were crowned within its walls. Of those five, one died, or vanished under mysterious circumstances; one was believed to have taken poison, to end the miseries of defeat in battle; one was blown to pieces by terrorists; the last was shot down in a Siberian cellar. Later, the Kremlin Trials continued the darkness of legend and fact.

Yet the Kremlin could reveal a softer side. It was here that Tolstoy came with beating heart to woo the young Sonia Behrs. Her father was installed there as a doctor attached to the administration. His large, gay, carefree family was crammed into pinched quarters dominated by the splendours of medieval Russia massed around them. It has always seemed to me particularly fitting that Tolstoy, the supreme Russian genius, should have found the embodiment of all his happiness, and later, all his bitterness, within the Kremlin, in the heart of Moscow, at the heart of all Russia.

~

When I made my first rapturous steps in the U.S.S.R. an agreeable lack of regimentation prevailed among the Intourist organizations. By that I do not mean that they were inefficient, but they were less prepared to organize pre-digested tours. Tourists were something new. Very few had fixed notions of what they wished to see or ought to see. Thus personal preferences, for those who had them such as myself, were studied, though not always encouraged. And no one else, they assured me, asked to go to Siberia.

I recall travelling back from Moscow for a second spell in Leningrad, an all-night journey, without a ticket, something absolutely unimaginable at that time, for the ticket was part of a strip of vouchers which included hotel bookings, and food tickets too. In my prevailing state of exaltation I had lost the lot. My alarm was such, for I feared my stay might be curtailed, that I contrived, by looking both outraged and business-like in a briskly Anglo-Saxon way, to infer it must be the Tourist Bureau themselves who had mislaid the vouchers. Their goodwill being only equalled by their doubts as to their own efficiency, they accepted the charge without protest and reissued the vital papers. Such *laissez-aller* would not be so likely today, although generous impulses are just as apparent. So whole-heartedly did the authorities blame themselves in this instance that, when I was back home in London and the original ticket was revealed in the lining of my suitcase, I became a prey to remorse, to that voluptuous longing to confess which is one of the most deep-seated impulses of the Slav nature.

It was as if, at last, something profoundly Slav had taken root in me, and was no longer a deliberately acquired attribute. But perhaps after all, it was just another example of the Traveller imposing his faculty of remote control.

Occasionally I had the curious impression that not only was I guided by him, seeing all through his eyes, but that he chose, unexpectedly, to speak through me too. His old flippant tone sounded, replying to the earnest officials of the Intourist Bureau. In Moscow I had been visiting some new experimental nursery schools and the delightful Children's Theatre. Perhaps this had bored the Traveller. He had seemed withdrawn for the last few days, as he seemed when I made half-hearted efforts to visit other progressive ventures. Now it was suggested that I should be shown yet another experiment in social welfare – a home of rest for prostitutes (described as being the last victims of Tzarist corruption). Their newly inaugurated rest-home was part of a programme for their rehabilitation and reintegration into a more wholesome way of life.

'But I'd much rather see them at work,' I heard myself reply, and behind my flippancy, the Traveller's cynical tones sounded unmistakably. I was aghast. He had blotted my copy-book.

Sternly putting the Traveller, like Satan, behind me, I made what amends I could by evincing the keenest interest in one particular day-nursery, chiefly because I had discovered it was installed in the former Kropotkin house, once the childhood home of Prince Peter, 'the Anarchist Prince'. Everything about him intrigued me; I admired his idealism and envied his Siberian experiences. Through his *Memoirs* these had long been familiar to me, like his descriptions of life in the aristocratic, patriarchal Moscow of the 1840's. Now I wanted to see this setting of his youth.

The sober elegance of the Old Equerries' Quarter behind the Manège was typical of late eighteenth and early nineteenth-century Moscow architecture. It was less grandiloquent than St. Petersburg and its classic nobility retained a feeling of the land – of country-house life. The yellow walls and white plaster work decorations were austere beside much of St. Petersburg's splendour, but these old Moscow houses were dwellings for the aristocratic families such as Tolstoy describes in *War and Peace*, large in their concept of living, with style, with grandeur even, though very far from the febrile pulse of the northern city. Even in the Moscow I first knew, one still felt the nearness of fields, of cabbage-patches and stables.

In the lofty, beautifully proportioned rooms of the *piano nobile*, the gurgling and indulged infants were sliding about the fine marquetry floors, and I tried to imagine the young Prince Peter here, in this setting he had at last repudiated. Was it this very room, I wondered, that had witnessed his resolve to break with the abuses which prevailed in his aristocratic milieu? The manner in which his father treated his serfs, the emptiness and stagnation of life at Court, these things soon became intolerable to Kropotkin. The trajectory of his life and thought can be traced by the physical transition we see in his portraits. First, the handsome boy in Corps des Pages uniform; then the young man, already the light of idealism in his eyes, seeing far beyond the horizons of Siberia where he elected to work, seeing a world which he returned to achieve. At last, the white-haired visionary, gazing out through professorial steel-rimmed spectacles, seeing a new Russia forming, a Russia for which he had spent his whole life and fortune.

Kropotkin's *Memoirs* cover a vast span of nineteenth-century Russian life, and years of convulsive change. As a page at Court, he had stood guard over the catafalque of the Emperor Nicholas I, Catherine the Great's grandson. Sickened by the pomposity of Court and the swagger of the Guards regiments, he had joined the Amur Cossacks (social suicide to chic St. Petersburg) and been posted to eastern Siberia. There, administrative reforms and scientific research as geologist and botanist filled his life, until at last he returned to become known as the Anarchist Prince, living and having his being among the revolutionaries. Banished from Russia he had joined the ranks of political exiles in Switzerland, at last settling in London.

But as an old man, impoverished by his own idealism and by-passed by the surge of the Revolution, his untarnished beliefs had brought him back to Russia where, although Lenin was solicitous in sending the best doctors, he died, rather disillusioned and neglected, in 1921. He was accorded a national funeral; but the ironic aspects of this ceremony are worthy of recall. Some of the 'Anarchist Prince's' anarchist friends, now incarcerated in the dread Boutirky prison (immortalized by Tolstoy in *Resurrection*) were, surprisingly, allowed out on parole, to follow the coffin of their leader: others, being listed to attend, were mysteriously declared unavailable by the Tcheka. The International was not played, since Kropotkin had particularly disliked it, so his mourners marched to Tchaikovsky's *Symphonie Pathétique*, on the whole a good choice, for it was the last time banners proclaiming such dangerous sentiments as 'Where there is Authority there is no Liberty', or 'We the Anarchists demand to be freed from the prison of Socialism' were seen in the new Russia – that Russia for which Kropotkin had laboured. It was, said one eye-witness, the last large-scale public manifestation against Bolshevism. It was also a wholly old-style Russian episode; as Russian as the Dekabrist débâcle, muddle-headed and ennobled by idealistic courage; as comically tragic as anything by Gogol in his most grotesque vein.

Gradually, I began to feel the Traveller was exercising too strong a personal influence over my choice of wanderings; I had become the instrument or means by which he revisited the scenes of a former life – these scenes being, as my governess remarked of those postcards he had sometimes sent me, 'not always in the best of taste'.

'*Cubat* – what is that?' asked the guide, an earnest young person who knew nothing of the raffish ghost prompting my expedition. She could not tell me where this celebrated restaurant had stood nor if another, *Ourouss*, The Bear, was still standing.

'You wish for a restaurant, for eating? We have. Where is book of food tickets?' She smiled her wide, sweet smile, that expression of luminous softness which is so typical of Russian women, a softness upon which the Traveller liked to dwell. It is womanly rather than feminine, and triumphs over indifferent figures and unbecoming clothes. It is a quality that becomes increasingly rare among the more sophisticated women of other Western nations; a look which no régime has altered, which neither good times nor bad times change. I fancy it was also on the face of some of the most determined Nihilists and those terrorists who, hurling their infernal machines (so often home-made by faulty recipes, and not always reliable), were still doing it all for love – for love of an ideal, for universal brotherhood; only to be achieved by such means, or so it seemed to them. And thus they smiled softly – at their fellow-anarchists, their lovers, their frantic families and their victims too, in all probability; certainly at their judges and executioners, for they were *exaltées* and mystically sustained.

I had so often heard the Traveller enlarging on the particular qualities of Russian women: but Russian men? Now I had begun to formulate my views on them, too. They were entirely unlike any others, by some unspoken, unmistakable quality apparent in their relation to women. It was not necessarily that they wooed them or won them in that slick fashion held to be the hall-mark of Latin lovers. Or that they possessed that animal, or hawk-like attraction of the desert Arab, quite another kind of conqueror. Was it that they retained some touchingly romantic quality? That for them, women were still a mysterious citadel – to be stormed, but to be loved, in every sense of the word? This could compass violence and cruelty too. At this time I was young and, I believe, pretty, and I had travelled considerably. I had many occasions to weigh up men of different races. Always I came back to the Slavs. When they looked at you, it was not with the rapid professionalism of the Latin nor the all-possessive glance of the East; they looked into one's eyes, and beyond, as if to know the woman behind the façade. In short, to understand the creature before them, with all her charms or frailties. Men do not like to be understood, Aunt Eudoxia had said; with women it is otherwise.

~

'Cubat's?' persists my guide, anxious to offer me all her country. But I am unable to explain the depths of my triviality. How to explain that I am recalling the Traveller's accounts of uproarious nights spent there in the most extravagant company; the *jeunesse dorée*, army officers and such of the high-living merchant patrons as were suffered there, for even the depravities of the capital were not to be enjoyed in too mixed a society. The Traveller had been in one such establishment on that short, darkening afternoon in November 1917. A historic moment. We had been in Corsica I remembered, when I asked him how he had spent that fateful day.

He had laughed. 'You see, history has a way of taking one unawares.' To him, as to many others, it had seemed just another day. For him, it promised a rendezvous, one he had expected to enjoy particularly, in an upstairs room the restaurant reserved for such purposes.

He had lately encountered a ravishing creature whose temperament was only equalled in its intensity by the jealousy of her husband. But it was worth all the risks; the Traveller could think of nothing but her charms.

'What a woman! What temperament! When I took her in my arms she fainted!' So, hurrying along the strangely deserted streets, intent on rejoining this paragon of passion, he had not attached much importance to the sullen air which hung over the waiting city. Those were uneasy times. It was four o'clock and already the day was darkening to an icy, early twilight. But once within the glowing embrace of his *inamorata* all else was forgotten – even the indifferent service of a few scuttling waiters who seemed curiously absent-minded. Only after repeated ringings had they answered the bell. The champagne had not been properly iced and the caviare was not the kind they had ordered. A curious state of affairs... Many hours later the lovers had called for the Gypsies, whose music, they thought, would round out the night suitably; but no one answered the bell they tugged with increasing fury.

A most unaccustomed hush prevailed in the restaurant below, and, when the Traveller went to investigate, he found it empty. The tables were only half-laid and no staff were to be seen beyond the darkened dining-room. One chandelier blazed with bizarre brilliance in the foyer, illuminating a snoring figure that lay across the threshold muffled in his bear-skin *pelisse*. It was the doorman. The Traveller kicked him awake. He seemed surprised. He had not expected anyone to have remained, he said. Clutching an empty bottle of vodka he staggered to his feet.

'Doesn't the *Barin* know? The Revolution has begun! Didn't the *Barin* hear gun-fire? No, perhaps not...' He winked roguishly. 'They've been shelling the Winter Palace,' he went on, 'but I reckon we're safe enough here – they've other things to think about... and so have we... there is plenty to eat and drink'. He smacked his lips. 'I've locked all the doors and thrown away the keys. No one is going to get in here,' he said proudly.

Or get out, it seemed, for the heavily barred, iron-shuttered windows discouraged any exit. Only a meat cleaver could hack such bars apart. Clearly it was wisest to make the best of things. The doorman, belching contentedly and hugging a bottle of vodka, rolled himself up in his *shuba* and was instantly asleep. The Traveller having helped himself in the kitchens and cellar went back upstairs to rejoin his *inamorata*. Among other things, the Revolution was going to provide a marvellous silencer to any awkward questions irate husbands might pose.

Not a very edifying anecdote for such a moment of high destiny; yet it had stuck in my mind, and I heard the Traveller laugh, saw again his malicious smile as he told me the tale. Now he was willing me to the place, doubly amused to be rousing my jealousy by even the echoes of a ghostly rendezvous; and also to affront the sterner moral code of a younger generation of Russians.

~

I had not been disappointed by my first sight of Russia: nothing was different to what I had imagined, for I had stayed within the horizons of my desires. Once, in the schoolroom, as I longed loudly for Russia, the Traveller had said: 'You will always be a happy traveller; you have so steeped yourself in fantasies and past scenes that they have become part of yourself, more real than what is round you. Lucky *Doucinka*! Your journeys will always carry you back into this magic world of your own desires.' And so it proved to be. Even taking a symbolic turn at the building of the grandiose Moscow subway, wielding a shovel among the ardent citizens as a gesture of solidarity, did not impinge on those remote inner visions I cherished, where subways were unknown, and it was troikas, troikas all the way.

I left Leningrad on the last boat before winter clamped down. Already there were early snows and ice-floes drifting south to harass the shipping. I felt no anguish at leaving, for I knew I should return. Siberia was still an hallucinatory dream, but that too would materialize, one day. The first step eastward had been made – the journey begun.

CHAPTER FIFTEEN

U pon my return, a yet greater fervour for all things Russian caused even my most sympathetic friends some uneasiness. The political scene had long crystallized, with Russia emerging triumphantly as the U.S.S.R., but I still held to my subjective conception of the country, seeing it neither as Holy or Unholy Russia, but only as it had seemed to the Traveller when he recalled it for my delight. How much of that was truly his remembrance and how much of it his especial vision – a Russia which was remote from him too, but *created* rather than recreated, for the romantic illusions we both cherished – I never discovered.

Meanwhile, both Russians and English attributed to me some mischievous designs I did not have. While the few Soviet citizens I encountered found my interest in them curious for one so obviously engaged in a bourgeois way of life, White Russians, particularly those of the Nansen passport generation, regarded this interest as a dangerous aberration, for they had thought my first visit to the U.S.S.R. would disillusion me. I now found myself excluded from several agreeable dinner-tables because both host and hostess were unsympathetic to my views, so loudly expressed, and, oh! fatal error, in front of the servants. 'I *do* wish she wouldn't... it only puts ideas into their heads,' was the complaint of those who, knowing servants to have become a vanishing species, to be preserved like wildlife, or placated like household gods, had not yet realized that in the heads of those same domestic workers, as they now preferred to be called, 'ideas' had been replaced by ultimatums.

But I had, I felt, crossed the Irtysh, as the Russian saying goes (the Irtysh was a river which all political exiles to Siberia must cross on their way East: once across there was no turning back). In proffering even the most superficial acceptance of the new Russia I must also accept being eyed askance, cut even, as if I had unfurled the Red Flag outside the Junior Carlton Club.

When, a few years later, I planned another visit to the U S.S.R. I was rebuffed in my attempts to obtain a visa for the Caucasus; something which discouraged me sadly, for I felt my enthusiasm and purpose merited Soviet sympathy. I had fixed my sights high, planning a book on the Caucasian wars, but it was to be another twenty years before I was able to write it. Meanwhile, my rebuff had quite illogically enraged an old friend, born in Russia but who, brought up in England, expressed himself in the vernacular.

'Refused you a visa to the Caucasus? Well of all the bloody cheek! Who the hell do they think they are?' he said, scowling in the direction of the Soviet Embassy. 'But serve you right for wanting to go to such an outlandish place,' he added, revealing by this remark how deeply he had assimilated the English spirit.

~

In the London of the thirties there was a very marked prejudice against all things Russian, even cultural, unless it were, as I have recounted, those *entrechâts* and other steps performed by strictly white feet. To like Russia had not yet become chic. But in 1934, Colonel de Basil's ballet company exploded on London and, overnight, the mystique of ballet and balletomania came into being. The dancers came from performances in Paris and Monte Carlo; most of them were very young, being second generation Russian émigrés, but among them were a few who had been trained in Russia. Some had belonged to Diaghilev's company: technicians, stage managers, designers, musicians, all of them Russians, a world of their own, turbulent and magnetic, glittering Harlequin figures for whose public and private lives the British public was soon avid. During their first unpampered seasons they lived in small dingy hotels round the British Museum, their narrow bedrooms stacked with steamer trunks. Massine was at the Savoy, but the rest were more modest. Their mothers (for they moved in family units) darned tights and fought among themselves for the supremacy of their children: some spoke nothing but Russian, and would stand in the wings throughout the performances, hissing encouragement, over-boiling like kettles at some fancied slight to their progeny. All of them had splendid tales to recount; tales of adventure, of *accouchements* in railway trucks, of abandonment in the steppes; of their own highly-coloured youth gilded by the attentions of some Grand Duke, perhaps. The fathers, for there were some among the matriarchy, were less apparent. Indeed, ballet fathers are seldom seen; it is ballet mothers who dominate, so that I have often wondered if the ballerina is not perhaps the flower of some immaculate conception.

When at the end of the season the company vanished for the more refulgent ambiance of Monte Carlo a certain bleakness descended on my spirits. I was then living in Albany, working on a glossy magazine and encouraged by the management to pursue what they called 'Gracious Living' both in my work and *train de vie*. This state of 'gracious living' I preferred to label *good-gracious* living, and I always sought ways of escape. The Ballet, not yet having become entirely absorbed by the arch-exponents of such living, was one of my principal means. Alas! with its departure, I could no longer steal away from 'gracious' gatherings to find bliss among the steamer-trunks and squalors of the Bloomsbury lodgings. Love and *entrechâts* had to be replaced by more sober expressions of my Russophilia.

Happily these were not lacking. No distance across London in an overcrowded bus seemed too arduous after my day's work if, at the end, I found a roomful of Russian intellectuals thrashing out some remote subject. As the bus ground its way north or south (for they were generally centred in these two unfashionable zones, in considerable discomfort, it must be said), my heart would lighten, for I knew that soon I should hear the sort of talk, on the sort of subjects, I craved. Merejkovsky's strange book on Gogol and the Devil; Belinski's effect on his contemporaries; the poems of Anna Akhmatova; or those of Blok or Yesenin – for in the matter of poetry, no political prejudice existed.

With every jerk of the bus I drew nearer to this elusive realm. We passed the bright-lit streets, the crowds surging up Shaftesbury Avenue, bent on their pleasure, the shop-windows full of black lace underwear and pornographic merchandise; and the strident glare of the theatres faded as we took a more sombre route through Seven Dials towards St. Pancras, Islington or Hoxton. This was the London immortalized by Cruikshank in his illustrations to Dickens or the Comic Almanack – a scene at once seedy and sinister. Now only an occasional greenish glow from an antiquated gas-bracket shone through a fan-light over a once elegant door, while lonely cats sidled round area railings. There were few people in the silent streets and crescents: it was London City's urban suburbs, a submerged area, becalmed in the stillness which fell, each evening, as the workers left their offices and headed for the outer suburbs and the green belt. Housing shortages had not yet predisposed the more eclectic Londoners to abandon 'their' London (which in the thirties generally meant a mews flat in Mayfair, or S.W.7), for some artfully restored Regency or very early

Victorian house in the areas of which I write. No sugar-pink or lime-green doors or window-boxes broke the frowzy façades. Here many of the exiles had gone to earth, shuttling backwards and forwards to the British Museum Reading Room, where their sporadic work on translations or research kept them long hours, poring over the stacks, a stale bun stuffed among their note-books to sustain them on the long walk home at twilight.

None of my Russian friends owned cars; some could not afford even a bus or underground ticket. They walked everywhere. Taxis simply did not come into their sphere of comprehension or else were regarded as Babylonian luxury, a point of view my own financial state led me to share. Taxis were to me something to be used with extreme caution – in a crisis or for a dressed-up outing, which these Islington evenings most certainly were not. But no doubt had I started on the downward path of taxi-addiction early, my reading would have suffered. So many hours were spent profitably, on long bus rides, plunged into pocket editions of the classics. The memoirs of Alexander Herzen, *My Past and Thoughts*, six volumes, each conveniently scaled for carrying in the handbag, were my most regular accompaniment.

Wonderful, illuminating Herzen! Would I have loved and known him so well, except for the London transport system? Lurching and strap-hanging in the Underground's rush hour he kept me company. I was beside him in his Moscow, listening to the old Princess's tales or Belinski's outbursts. I was in Nice when Ogaryov betrayed him. I was his confidante, sharing his lonely exile in Viatka... As the No 27 bus ground its way out to Richmond, it was always taking me to Cholmondeley House, where Herzen and his young son are passionately vowing themselves, at midnight, to the cause of Freedom. The heights of Hampstead become the Sparrow Hills where, looking down on Moscow, the young Herzen is again invoking Freedom and vowing to avenge the Dekabrists. Herzen would have found many to help him among the exiles I knew – exiled by that very Revolution he had desired so ardently, and for which his journal, *The Bell*, fought so vigorously.

Herzen has always seemed as real to me as any of my Russian friends and it would have been no surprise had I found him among those I visited so regularly, the bearded Titan dominating some basement flat, talking, talking, far into the night.

It was then, with a mounting sense of excitement such as I never knew on more elegant occasions, that I would at last reach some dilapidated doorstep and, peering down the area into the basement (the cheapest, and therefore the part generally occupied by the exiles), glimpse, through the carelessly drawn curtains, this pale agitated circle, all arguing vehemently, their gestures and voices in such robust contrast to their drawn faces. As I stood there on the threshold of bliss, snatches of their talk would resound up the damp-streaked stone steps, tantalizing snatches, so that the steps, the doorway and the whole dingy street seemed suddenly suffused with a golden blaze – the light of knowledge and desire.

In this forcing-house my appreciation of Russian literature and music bloomed with tropical exuberance, and presently I joined a Society for Cultural Relations between the U.S.S.R. and Britain, an organization which fostered lectures, art exhibitions and the exchange of films. It was, I believe, an earnest and innocent venture. In the matter of films, at that time, the cultural scales were heavily weighted on the Russian side; the players in *The Childhood of Gorky*, or Tcherkassov as Ivan the Terrible tipping them heavily against Anna Neagle as Nell Gwynn, or even Laurence Olivier as Nelson. But these latter performances were more generally appreciated, and my puny efforts to widen the pioneering work of the Academy Cinema programmes (then, except for the Film Society programmes and the Workers' Film Society, London's only means of seeing Russian films) were foredoomed. Letters I sent out urging my friends and acquaintances to join me in various excursions into the Slav cinema met with little or chilling response. Perhaps it had been a mistake to use the Cultural Society's writing paper. The scarlet embossed hammer and sickle were generally *mal vu*.

Many years later (in the fifties), I found a left-over packet of this invidious writing paper among my affairs which had followed me out to America, where my husband and I were then *en poste*. I remember how much I enjoyed using it up, the heading struck through with an apparently careless stroke, when I had occasion to write to those few of my American acquaintances whom I knew to be admirers of the all-puissant Senator Joe McCarthy. But this was not in the best tradition of diplomacy, and the writing paper had to be consigned to the dustbin. I hope it caused no embarrassment to the dustman.

CHAPTER SIXTEEN

I had never altogether given up hope of finding the Traveller again, or at least coming on traces of him or his sons. Sergei might have gone to America, seeking the proverbial pot of gold, but not Kamran. And their father was of quite other clay. Since he had always seemed surrounded by mystery and drama, I believed him to be somewhere in Russia – in Siberia, or in the Mongolian wastes, and now unable to communicate or leave. How otherwise could he not have come back to me? (This theory I found far more acceptable than any possibility of rejection, something I could not even consider.)

So, since for the present further journeys to the U.S.S.R. were too expensive, too difficult to achieve, I learned to content myself with more conventional travels, the picture-postcard Europe that I did not want, that I was always comparing unfavourably with the Asia for which I lusted. And near at hand, there was Paris, where so many of my old Russian friends now lived and where I always hoped there would be, one day, someone who would throw some light on the Traveller's disappearance. But they seemed unwilling to cooperate or to discuss him even, and I met with blank stares or a non-committal shrug. Fearful of some revelation which, nevertheless, I sought, I never pressed them, but was for ever moving among them as it were on tip-toe, my ear to an invisible key-hole, eager for some passing allusion. But it was clear they avoided discussing him, with me as among themselves.

'Where the apple reddens never pry, lest we lose our Eden, Eve and I.' Browning's lines, spoken in the Traveller's smoky voice, came back to me. Although my Eden was lost with him it was wiser to leave him unsought, where he had vanished, in that half-formed world of my desires. There sometimes we still seemed to meet, to steal away together, through a picture-frame or by means of a magic pass-word, into the boundless horizons of the Run-Away Game. *Païdium! Païdium* my love!

Gradually, the ranks of émigrés were thinning. Wrangel's men had dispersed; the old were dying off. Some went to end their days in the Russian colony of Ste. Geneviève des Bois and were seen no more about the city. Mosjoukine had died, after a painful decline; the arch-seductor was said at the end to be picking up a meal or a drink as a partner at *thés dansants*. In the Orthodox churches of Paris, the cathedral, like the little place of worship in the Rue de Crimée, the faces were changing, sharpening, for many of the younger generation had married among the French. The rich Slav blood was thinning. There were still a number of Russian taxi drivers, berets crammed low over their unmistakable flat Slav features which proclaimed their origin as clearly as their furry R's. But Paris too was changing; was beginning to abandon itself to the post-Hemingway invasion, finding there was a lot to be said for the dollar.

Few Russian émigrés wished to hear anything I had to recount of the new Russia. They could not accept the fact that it existed – much less that it progressed: it seemed almost indelicate to insist, and was simpler to dwell, with them, entirely in the past.

At the end of a narrow sunless cul-de-sac, le Passage des Trois Sapins, was a small hotel of unimaginable squalor. Here old, brave, desolate Madame Sapojnikov had found refuge, wedging herself into a small room on the sixth floor, taking in dress-making, which she did very well and cheaply. She had run her own *maison de couture* in Moscow; but that was long ago. Now only her needle and thread and her skill, salvaged from the débâcle, attracted a few clients, impoverished fellow-exiles and some ruthless, bargain-hunting, French *petits bourgeois* who were prepared to suffer the six flights of greasy dark stairs where, on every landing, a noisome privy was in constant use by the shuffling, unbuttoned or peignoir'd inmates of the hotel.

I too accepted these disadvantages, attracted not only by Madame Sapojnikov's skill and prices but also by the purely Dostoievskian atmosphere prevailing. It needed no stretch of imagination to believe oneself back in one of those quarters of St. Petersburg where Dostoievsky sets so many of his most wonderful scenes; streets in which I had wandered, imagining, repeopling them, reliving each scene, when I had first visited Leningrad and sought out those desolate areas beyond the Haymarket where, in Dostoievsky's time, the dram-shops were crowded with *moujiks* and drabs, and barrel organs ground out their melancholy airs. Hurdy-gurdies still sounded in the 15ème arrondissement, and I would listen, spell-bound.

'Street music... I love it,' said Raskolnikov, 'particularly when they are singing to a street-organ on a cold dark grey winter's evening, when all the passers-by have pale green sickly faces – when snow falls like sleet, down, straight down, no wind, and the lamps shine... You know?'

'I don't know. Excuse me,' said the unsympathetic stranger to whom Raskolnikov spoke. But I knew, wandering along the Rue Frémicourt, catching snatches of some wry tune, longing for even the doleful St. Petersburg Dostoievsky immortalized, and which a hurdy-gurdy now recalled. In the little hotel where Madame Sapojnikov lived I was immediately able to transport myself to the lodging house where the Marmeladov family played out their tragic and grotesque lives; as it were, to occupy a seat in the stalls.

A vinegary reek – cabbage soup – which perpetually simmered on a gas-ring balanced on the corner of Madame Sapojnikov's marble-topped chest of drawers strengthened this illusion. Through the yellowing net curtains I could peer down into a well-like courtyard where shadowy figures came and went. Sonia, huddled in her thin shawl. Catherina Ivanovna coughing her lungs out, recalling past glories, instilling airs and graces in her bewildered children. Another figure – Dounia? or Sonia again? Though this one is pert, business-like, and scarcely seems likely to be going upstairs to read the Bible. A light floods out from her room on the fourth floor. A man has followed her there. It seems improbable that he will throw himself at her feet and ask pardon for either the sins of the world, or his own, for this is France. This time, the characters have stepped out of their frame. The spell is broken.

But look again! Here is Louzhin, crossing the courtyard, followed by coarse-grained Madame Lippevechzel the German lodging-house keeper and her lover, the Pole, running some crazy errand for Panna Marmeladov. That swaggering figure banging the glass door into the corridor must be Svidrigailov, making for another lodging-house. Perhaps the Hotel Adrianople, where the mice will crawl over his coverlet, rousing him from his erotic nightmares of sly little painted children in his bed. Across the well, through dimly lit windows, the farther side of the hotel always presented itself as some evil dolls' house, where a number of puppet figures went through the motions of living out some sinister life. Although in fact, I never observed anything of singular interest, these figures lent themselves to my own form of dramatization, and the shadows of two men, engaged in lengthy conversation, were at once transposed into the Baron and Kostylev, for sometimes this scene became Gorky's *Lower Depths*.

One young man, wan and solitary, particularly intrigued me. He seldom stirred from a table covered with papers, upon which he occasionally scrawled something, and his attitude seemed one of despair. Raskolnikov himself, brooding over the murder. Any moment now, as I watched, he would get up, walk over to the cupboard, and furtively bring out the fatal purse. But Madame Sapojnikov knew all about him. Removing the pins from her mouth and puffing, for kneeling on the floor to measure hem lines taxed her failing strength, she said he was the physical culture instructor at a neighbouring Lycée, temporarily immobilized by a strained back, poor boy, and was working out a new system of callisthenics. He came from a happy family in Dieppe and was engaged to an heiress from Lille, she added. So I returned to my own fancies, my own Russian transpositions.

While the reek of cabbage soup impregnated my hair and clothing, I would stand patiently through the fittings, my eyes fixed on a postcard of the Imperial Family. Dog-eared and faded, it was pinned above the bed beside a bunch of battered paper roses and a ribboned Easter egg painted with the double-headed Russian eagle.

In the corner hung a small sticky-looking ikon which Madame Sapojnikov would not consider selling. It incorporated Holy Russia, Mother Russia, the shadow, the echo – all that was left to her now.

'And if we make the sleeve raglan?' she panted, reaching under the table for a tattered book of patterns. Raglan? My mind skipped across Europe, down the Danube, over the Dobrudja to Varna (not the Varna I was to know, far ahead, in 1946, under Red Army surveillance), but a muddy or dusty village where, in 1853, the British and French troops were embarking for Crimean battlefields. Had not Lord Raglan commanded the army during that dreadful, unnecessary war? Had not this kind old gentleman battled beside Florence Nightingale to better the lot of his men?

He was a veteran of Waterloo and still absently referred to the enemy as the French; something which piqued the French commanders Canrobert and Pélissier, who were by now fighting beside him.

'Alors, la coupe raglan?' persists Madame Sapojnikov, brandishing her cutting-out scissors, a tape-measure snaked across her heaving bulk. Raglan... the cut had indeed been named after the old leader; it all came back to me. He had lost an arm as a young man serving as Wellington's A.D.C. at Waterloo, and had devised this loose-sleeved garment to slip easily over the stump. When the surgeon had hacked off his arm he had borne it stoically, merely calling back an orderly who was removing it from the room, saying 'Hey! Bring that back! There's a ring my wife gave me on one finger.'

Crimean commanders, many of whom had been in service under Wellington, were all larger than life. The monstrous Lord Cardigan, whiskered, corseted, and cruel, coolly returning to his yacht, after leading the charge of the Light Brigade, to enjoy a champagne supper. On the *other* side – I could not bring myself to think of the Russians as *the enemy*, there was Kornilov, defending Sebastopol, commanding his men to kill him with their bayonets if he should ever give the order to retreat; while Prince Menchikov, commanding at the battle of Alma, had put up a grandstand with splendid optimism, misplaced as it turned out, and invited a number of elegant ladies to follow the battle through pearl-handled opera-glasses.

From the overtones of Crimean Generals my mind moved to the extravagant beauties of Crimean shores, so little suited to battle. Halcyon shores, where the Khan's Palace, the Fountain of Tears and all the marbles and palms of those princely villas the Traveller had known as a child were jumbled in my mind's eye. I began to question Madame Sapojnikov about life in the Crimea. But she had never been there, 'unless you count those terrible days and nights crowded on to the jetty at Yalta, waiting to be evacuated to Constantinople?' She had seen the British warship carrying the Dowager Empress Marie Feodorovna and her suite to safety in England. It had steamed past, quite slowly, inshore. The small black figure had stood alone on deck looking her last on the Russia that had been her country for so long. The people waiting on the quay wept, knowing that she was weeping for them, as for her son and her grandchildren, prisoners; where, she did not know. Tears poured down Madame Sapojnikov's face as she remembered the scene.

Mopping her eyes, she made the sign of the cross towards the old postcard, for, to Madame Sapojnikov, any recollection of the Imperial Family was sacred.

Shifting from foot to foot (the fittings were protracted), I tried to turn her thoughts to happier times – to life in Kiev, her childhood's home. Kiev dried her tears and, recalling those faraway scenes, she waxed lyrical. Through her eyes I saw the gold-starred cupolas of its monasteries and cathedrals shimmering under a Ukrainian sun, fruit blossom hanging heavy over the low-fenced gardens, the white dust of acacia flowers powdering the quiet streets: starlight and moonlight glowing brighter there than anywhere else... This was the region of Gogol's *May Night*, of *Evenings on the Farm at Dikanka*, tales that were always my bedside reading and now I followed Madame Sapojnikov into her childhood, sharing her longings.

'How happy we were then! Everything was so beautiful in those days,' she said. An expression of surprise, of shock even, gathered on her face as she looked round the mean room to which she was committed. But she turned back to her work with resolution, fitting the waist-line with rheumatic but still skilful fingers. 'In the evenings,' she went on, with equal resolution, 'Papa played the violin. Two or three friends used to join him. I remember they often played Schubert... We children were allowed to stay up late and listen. We sat round the table and Mama lit the samovar. Whichever of us had been best at lessons that day was allowed an extra spoonful of jam. Mama made a most delicious preserve from white raspberries. They grew in our garden, beyond the lilac hedge where Agrafina used to hang out the washing... I can still see our pinafores on the line... we wore pinafores, pink cotton ones. Children don't wear them any more. At Easter we had new dresses for the Easter night service – Mama too. Ours were always white silk. We looked forward to Easter night all the year. Papa used to give each of us a little golden egg to hang on a chain round our necks. By the time I was fifteen I had a whole necklace.'

As she described the innocent tenor of their lives, so different to the provincial splendours Madame Marmeladov wished to recapture, tears ran down her kind old face, set now forever in a cast of sadness. But her eyes retained a look of youth. They were the trustful puzzled eyes of an animal alone in an incomprehensible world. Madame Sapojnikov had never acquired the carapace of cynicism. Indeed, I think few Russians do. It is foreign to their nature. They may, particularly when drunk, adopt a cynical tone: but it remains a matter of words rather than actions. In the nineteenth-century spleen and cynicism were the hall-mark of breeding among men of fashion, and Eugène Onegin was their prototype, while Lermontov not only continued the Pushkinian tradition by his *Hero of Our Time* but lived out his own brief life in this wastrel's pattern.

Russian women, however, were otherwise; were, in both fact and fiction, essentially limpid, loving-soft and guileless: the Traveller had always said so and, as I came to know them, I found it true.

~

In spite of all the Russian links and echoes which Paris offered, I could never come to love it. I had many friends there – but I did not love it for itself. Its noblest vistas, most magnificent possessions or wise old grey houses along the Seine left me unmoved. Its spirit was Cartesian: its scepticism, materialism and rationalism were antipathetic to me: and I took comfort from reflecting that I was not alone in this point of view, which appeared so singular to most others.

Tolstoy had been critical of both Paris and the French. 'There is no poetry in this people,' he wrote, and in his journal, during a brief stay in the city he noted: 'Horrible life! Horrible town. Recapitulation of the day. Saw several men of letters, one of whom asked me if one could reach Russia overland! No doubt he took Russia for an island.'

As a detached observer, I came and went unmoved about Paris, something I have since learned to appreciate greatly, for to be involved, to mind too much about coming or going from a place, can be as demanding as human involvements. My roots had been planted in London, but had flowered into an unlikely Slav blooming. No Latin shoots ever flourished there. Even when, years ahead, I was to become French by marriage, I could not adapt myself to Paris as I did so easily in Balkan or Slav cities. And if I have always been aware of some faint, yet persistent atavistic memory pulling me towards all things Russian, as though once I lived a life in some Russian city in happy disorder, so also, I am aware of some vague unease in Paris; as if perhaps yet another life was lived there in well-ordered unhappiness.

The only part of Paris to which I returned with that sense of participation so necessary to the true enjoyment and comprehension of a city, was a strongly-flavoured Arab quarter behind the Mosque, where, once again, I could fancy myself somewhere else – in this case nearer to North Africa, which was then a new horizon of pleasure. Beginning at the Place Contrescarpe, the Rue Mouffetard plunged down towards the Boulevard Arago. This narrow winding street was curiously cheerful; in spite of the sombre tinge of its ancient, scrofulous-looking houses it seemed lit by an African sun. The various shop windows were so many *souks*. Near its end an alley-way led to one particularly evocative small square, being tufted with catalpa trees but to me entirely Slav in its evocation.

Here a peeling yellow plaster building was advertised as BAINS DES ARCHEVÊQUES. BAINS DES PIEDS. DOUCHES. This conjured up a vision I much enjoyed. Here, I envisaged a dim vaporous interior, that of the traditional Russian steam-baths, where *moujik* and master alike stewed away their sins. These vapour baths were first introduced into both Russia and Turkey (where they became the *hammam*), by the migratory Asiatic tribes; they were the custom of a people living in the saddle, generally in arid country, or so the Traveller said. The Bains des Archevêques can have had little in common with either of these more exotic institutions but, I suppose, Orthodoxy catching me unawares, I had at first sight confused Archevêques with Archimandrite. At any rate, the image was fixed for ever. I saw eddies of steam puffing and swirling to reveal, not some flagellant's voluptuous indulgences, monkish expiation, or the traditional Russian peasant's method of stimulating circulation by lashing themselves with birch twigs, but a gathering of solemn-faced long-haired bearded clergy, the black-veiled, black-robed figures of the Orthodox church. Or perhaps the Phanariot priests of old Constantinople? They were sitting ranged side by side, as if at some solemn oecumenical conference, but with their feet plunged in steaming tubs of hot water.

Here, I decided, were the Brothers of some remote Russian monastery; a back-biting sly lot most likely, yet I loved to conjure them, for the Russia they conjured around themselves; silent white wastes; a whiteness, and stillness broken only by the crows that strutted outside the barred windows of the Monastery... black, flapping birds, whose cawing sounded in my ears above the clattering present of the Rue Mouffetard.

Perhaps it was not quite fair to berate Paris for being itself, when it was just that quality which I found so alien that roused me to take refuge in the flights of fancy I enjoyed. Which sent me speeding to the Hermitage of Krasny Yar. No such flights could be arrived at in London; it was too bound up with my roots, my memories and my daily life.

In London, each street or house had its own mythology, was peopled with its own phantoms and the figures of history and literature which were my heritage and which I could neither ignore, nor convert. As a Londoner born, I felt the city imposing itself, obstinately refusing any imaginative transpositions, while at its gentlest, it lulled rather than

199

stimulated. And then, in spite of myself, in spite of my perpetual cravings for the strange or the exotic, I loved its insularity. I loved it, or I left it; but I did not try to transpose it.

Paris was otherwise; it provided the irritant which my imagination needed to take flight. Perhaps this is the quality so often referred to as stimulating; 'Paris is so stimulating,' say its admiring visitors. Perhaps, had I been living in a city more congenial to me personally, one where exoticism prevailed such as Istanbul or Isfahan, my mind would have grown lazy, staying where it was, satiated by actuality, having no wish to take off into some intangible realm of fancy. Yet when later I came to know those particular cities, I never found them stultifying. Limited, yes; but that is another thing. Paris, by the force of its French logic, imposes its own conventions, in varying degrees, or interpretations, so that you must concur or take imaginative flight, as I did, skulking about its streets and boulevards, yet indulging in what Wordsworth describes as 'the inward eye that is the bliss of solitude.'

~

My richer friends knew that I loved Russian food and sometimes they would take me to the now vanished Kornilov's, for a feast; or to *boîtes de nuit* where a desperate gaiety prevailed, everything now become as *ersatz* as the flabby *blini*, and the artificial-satin *roubashkas* worn by anxious-faced men, who sang with mechanical abandon in the many languages learned from their tutors, so long ago, in the big houses where they grew up. They sang in French, Spanish, Italian or German, as well as the expected Russian airs; and, year by year, their voices became more colourless and their embroidered shirts more gaudy, till at last sequins flashed in the limelight that followed them through the exhausting antics of some national dance, and I felt shame for them.

In the humbler kind of Russian restaurants I preferred, there was sometimes, besides a more genuine kind of cuisine, an old tzigane lingering on playing, however poorly, my favourite songs. Such restaurants were dark caverns of nostalgia and regrets; and yet, of pleasure.

In Russian Paris there were a considerable number of small food shops where every imaginable Russian speciality could be obtained, something the exiles of London had been unable to achieve. (At that moment exotic products and foreign foods were little in demand there: it took World War Two and massed Continental holidays to widen the British public's gastronomic horizons.) Passy was the quarter where the best Russian foodstuffs were to be found, for it was here the more prosperous émigrés congregated, and here I came on regular pilgrimages.

No lover ever waited below the window of his adored with more longing, with a more ardent wish to unite, than I, loitering outside the Russian grocers. Flattened against the glass, I would gaze spellbound at the delicacies within; *bublitchki*, great slabs of sturgeon, the noble *koulibiak*, feathery dill, pyramids of Easter *paskha* and the curious wooden moulds in which this rich dish is made. Entering, I would spin out my more modest purchases, in order to breathe the unmistakable, spicy-sour flavour of Russia, a compound of cabbage, salted fish, and poppy seeds.

I would dawdle over the evocative merchandise listening to the deep, dark voices of the Russian customers. The simplest household orders were music to my ears, though applied to the émigrés, the words *simple* or *household* did not ring quite true. They were seldom simple or, if they were, then they were unlikely to possess a household of their own, being generally part of someone else's.

But within this, whatever its style, they lived in their own nomadic fashion, taking with them wherever they went that sense of impermanence, of the tent, even though garnished by the extravagances that are so characteristic of them as a race (volcanoes, extinct, quiescent or in eruption).

So, looking and listening, I spun out my purchases, deliberating between a jar of dill pickles, some *kasha*, or a loaf of that close-textured white bread – manna no less – from the Boulangerie Moscovite, sprinkled with poppy seeds, and to me, a thousand times more evocative of Russia than the celebrated black loaf. I generally came away with a packet of Caravan tea which, although it tasted like hay, was irresistible on account of its wrapping paper. Across a yellow desert a camel caravan plodded towards a Chinese trading post backed by a blue pagoda. Coolies scuttled about, ant-like, unloading the tea boxes, while a scarlet sun sank behind a yellow horizon. *Kiakhta Tea Company* said the label, in Russian, and I ached to have known the little frontier town at that depicted, quintessential moment, before lorries, telephones and the twentieth century were imposed on even the confines of the Gobi Desert.

The last echoes of that Russia were fading fast now; but the longer I dawdled among the Russian groceries, counting over my change, talking with the proprietor, the more I could hear of those diminishing cadences, those Slav voices, dwindling, sounding fainter every year, but still speaking the classic language of their past, as distinct, to the alerted ear, as the spelling, vocabulary and typography of pre-Revolutionary Russia differs from that of the U.S.S.R. today.

Into this outpost of Russian traditionalism, few of the Soviet Embassy personnel penetrated. I believe some of their more trusted Chancery staff were occasionally to be seen there but they were not communicative, and did not dally. There was one aged, shuffling figure who intrigued me particularly. She was the typical *baboushka*, a cotton handkerchief tied round her head, a short padded jacket over her shoulders and an expression of innocence on her potato-like face. She had escaped from the Revolution with the family into which her mother had been born a serf, and her attitude to the Princess, her mistress, was still serf-like in its abnegation.

For many years now she had toiled, receiving preposterously low wages; but as she spent nothing even this pittance had mounted up, until at last the Princess found it worth while to borrow the lot. After some years this had still not been repaid, and her friends at the shop were urging her to claim its repayment. Every time she came in they pressed her to know if this had been done. The mere idea seemed an affront to her.

'Ah! There's a real Princess for you!' she would say, shaking her head, penniless and imposed upon but happy, finding it the proper way for a Princess to behave: the way she had been brought up to believe they should; and happy too that in exile, the familiar pattern should continue. *She* would never have to learn anything about equality. *She* knew her place, and so did the Princess.

These ageing figures from that other world preserved a strict sense of protocol, which nothing – exile, impoverishment, or the years – could stifle. Near the Russian Cathedral there was a café which I particularly enjoyed: it was, I think, called the Café des Ambassadeurs. Here a number of White Russians used to congregate, solemnly nominating each other Governors and high officials of various Russian provinces. Upon the death of one of their rank, further solemn meetings were held to nominate a successor to this unrealizable post, ratified over a *coup de blanc*.

CHAPTER SEVENTEEN

I n those last years before the war engulfed us in 1939 there was still some time left to chase the will-o'-the-wisp of happiness. 'But why should you expect to be happy?' a Russian had once asked me, looking genuinely puzzled. Until then, happiness had always seemed a desirable state, something to be hoped for, worked for, and ultimately achieved... Happy ever after. I had not yet realized its illogical and transitory nature, nor the fact that it could be simplified, or reduced; a matter of food for the hungry, a cessation of pain for the stricken. Happiness, for me, was still contained in this hallucinatory vision of someone else's Russia which I wished for my own.

Although the Trans-Siberian journey – unalloyed bliss, in my eyes – was not to come my way for many years, I believed that one day I would possess it in all its five thousand miles. Gradually it had assumed for me the mystery and power of the alchemist's Arcanum – that inner secret or remedy for which they searched their whole lives through. Meanwhile, there was much else of 'all the Russias' (or the U.S.S.R. to those of a more contemporary mind) which I continued to devour whenever it was economically possible, now playing the Run-Away Game in terms of hard cash. Most people, I observed, visited Russia to see *Communism*: but I still went to see *Russia* – or rather that of the Traveller's Tales. And now, I set my heart on provincial scenes; Voronej, Uglitch, Tula... Why Novocherkassk? Because of the Hetman Platoff and his Don Cossacks. Why Mtsensk? Because of Leskov's *Lady Macbeth* of that province, now become doubly obsessive by virtue of Shostakovitch's music. Kalouga? Because of the Imam Shamyl's years of exile there. Kazbek for Lermontov's grave, Odessa for Pushkin's sojourn there, and for the cruiser *Aurora* too: Nijni-Novgorod, as I still called it, for Gorky's childhood, rather than the Fair, since I came to love this writer increasingly over the years, and through him, to love and understand something of an eternal Russia where each age overlapped, leading towards one that was all new, yet eternal... 'That promised land of the soul, that land we call Russia – it is Gorky who has evoked it, expressed it the best,' wrote the poet Alexander Blok.

Thus by books, as well as dreams or travels, I absorbed my

promised land... Thus, the Ukraine for love of Gogol's *Dikanka*, for *Roussalka* and the *Fair at Sorotchinsk*; Great Novgorod, because of its early history, its churches. Thus the settings of fact and fiction and legend all merged in my mind's eye, confusing what I had read and what I actually saw, often a grey scene, but all of it 'All the Russias' that were the landscape of my heart, peopled by a race which I instinctively loved.

Yet in all my journeys about Russia, one thing eluded me: the countryside. I was never able to have my fill of aimless wandering – of just dawdling. In the U.S.S.R. journeys were arranged with some specific view. However difficult it might be to achieve an outlying city, a dilapidated monastery, or not-yet-restored monument (for once convinced of their historic and artistic worth, the Soviets were unsparing in expense and skill to preserve or lovingly restore their heritage) it seemed almost impossible to achieve a week or two going nowhere in particular – just drifting. Wandering all day in a forest, listening to its soft sounds, following a stream Roussalka might have haunted, sitting on a bench beneath the giant sunflowers of an Ukrainian village or watching the clouds massing over the limitless steppe country, as Turgeniev describes them... these objectives seemed difficult to explain.

It is only through such timeless hours without pattern that we obtain the essence of a land. But any such moments generally had to be snatched, en route for some significant landmark. While they were nearly always interrupted by the exigencies of transport, time-tables, or the pre-arranged programmes, it was, on occasions, these very things breaking down which gave me the unexpected, unscheduled hours for which I longed. But not often enough: it was simply incomprehensible to the official mind that a visitor could wish to contemplate nature – unless on some grandiose, or scenic mountain scale – rather than man's – preferably contemporary man's – handiwork.

This was, no doubt, the result of most visitors being curious to observe Communism, rather than Russia.

~

While I continued to seek out the Traveller's traces, if not with the ardour of my first intoxicated visit, still with enough to preserve much of our double vision, I had now become more selective. I no longer gulped indiscriminately, but began to strengthen my own perspectives, and to the pleasure of sight-seeing added the *volupté* of choosing the precise moment which I thought best for each place. Thus the pearly early morning light that radiated across the waters of the Gulf of Finland showed Peterhof at its loveliest. Then the ornate palace with its numerous pavilions and gardens, its cascades and fountains all sparkled with prisms of brilliance in the morning dew, and there were as yet no visitors, so that mine still being the backward glance, it seemed to have slipped again into its past, to be awaiting the serf-gardeners while, within, the riotous court of the Empress Elizabeth Petrovna snored off the night's excesses. But medieval Russia, the monasteries and convents of Donskoie, or Kolomenskoye, in the curve of the river, turreted Novodievitchy, Great Novgorod should, I thought, ideally be seen in deep snow, in all their austere beauty, with the ravens circling and cawing over the bare trees, black, white and grey, lit by a flash of gold where cupolas and crosses glitter against livid skies.

Pursuing my theory of the time and place, (I no longer hoped for the loved one with any conviction), midsummer noon seemed best for the great houses round Moscow. Archangelskoye, in the green gloom of its woods, or Ostankino, as once I saw it, with its little church reflected, shimmering in the lake, and unexpectedly animated by a foreground of immemorial rustic figures, rather than the giant pylon which, I am told, now dominates the scene. The people I saw there were figures in a landscape – the women charming, bunchy figures in bright-coloured skirts and aprons, the men still wearing their old-fashioned pink or red *roubashkas* and high boots. They were scything and tying the swathes, singing their shrill *chastoushki*. It was a naïve print, one of those *Narodni Kartinki* such as I had seen on the Traveller's Paris walls, come to life for my greedy eyes and ears.

All at once, Conscience stirred. How could I revel in such a scene? How to patronize the living by turning them into stage props. That had been a wicked age of intolerable injustices and inequalities. And penetrating Count Sheremetiev's country house, now become a museum, I found room after room dedicated to exposing such abuses – particularly those of serfdom. The lovely little pillared theatre and musician's gallery reminded us that here the more gifted serfs were obliged to perform. (The Count became so infatuated by one of them that he married her and they lived happily ever after, though this is not stressed.) Sometimes the union of aristocracy and serfdom produced genius: Borodin was the child of a serf-girl and a sixty-year-old Georgian prince, descended from the ancient

Kings of Imeritia. The blend of his blood is echoed in his music, where the traditional airs of old Russia sound beside Oriental cadences which range from the Caucasus to the steppes of Central Asia.

At Ostankino, all the arts had flourished. Long galleries displayed pictures painted by other gifted serfs, in particular a series of remarkable *trompe l'oeil* paintings. But all these serfs were owned, body and soul, by their master, said Conscience, rapping me sharply, as I thought for one fleeting moment how agreeable it might have been to live at Ostankino, attached to such a Maecenas, living rent free on his estates, having no doubt plenty to eat and being trained and encouraged to sing, paint or perform in his orchestra or theatre: in short, to pursue the arts without those harassing pressures of competitive wage-earning known to most of those who pursue the arts today.

So, wandering through the enfilades of gold and white rooms, treading delicately across the burnished parquets that generations of serf labour had tended, I wondered at what point patronage and dictatorship clashed. And then Conscience nudged again, and Taste, too (for it was a very bad painting), as I was confronted by the celebrated canvas, to some viewers *clou* of the whole Gallery, where an unhappy serf mother is depicted as forced by her wicked owner to nourish his thorough-bred greyhound puppies at her breast, while her own infant lies on the straw denied. Conscience won. I could no longer enjoy the illusion which those rustic haymakers had conjured earlier. They were not happy carefree serfs turning the hay between rehearsals of something Beethoven had composed for their master's friend, Count Razoumovsky. They were their freed, much more fortunate, progressed descendants. Any moment now, a collective tractor would lumber up, splendid symbol of such progress, and a lorry would bump them back to their Komsomol Club and a lecture on the rotation of crops. It was all wholly admirable, desirable... And yet... mine was still an uncontrollably backward glance.

~

Whole days; dreaming, unprofitable days of no consequence from Intourist's brisk viewpoint, were spent in the ancient, high-walled Novodievitchy Convent and its cemetery, a national burial ground where all history, all heartbreaks were centred and where, odd as it may seem, I liked to picnic.

I love the atmosphere of Russian cemeteries. They have nothing of the impersonal atmosphere, either pompous or in the nature of a dumping ground, so often found elsewhere. Russian cemeteries are intimate places which invite a continuity, a keeping of company between living and dead; and for all their professed agnosticism, the government supplies, free, a cross for any mourner that desires to place it on a grave.

Beyond the convent garden a path led to the cemetery, a thronged yet peaceful place, bearing great names and small; Dekabrist heroes; great generals; Chekhov; musicians; patriots; a cross section of the whole land. Each grave, in the Russian fashion, was surrounded by a low wooden fence, enclosing it like a little private garden. Here, in each plot, a bench was placed for the mourners to rest beside their departed, while a little lamp glowed at the grave-head. Here, as in so many other ways, one senses the East beneath the Slav. The East too, makes no final, awful severance with death; it is a letting go... a separation, rather than an end. Moslems hold cheerful family picnics round the tombs of their dead, often bringing the departed one's favourite dishes to gratify his shade, while a little hollow in the stone serves as drinking trough for the birds. It seems that the terror of death increases in ratio to its urban surroundings. Death in the fields or the woods is a natural process, but in the city – among bricks and asphalt, under telegraph wires and neon lights – a coffin is an unseemly reminder that all man's mechanisms fail. Death is dolled-up before being quickly shovelled away, and never, never again allowed to remind the living of their precarious state.

In the Novodievitchy Convent garden death seemed as inevitable as autumn and, as I threaded up and down the paths, I wondered if, spelling out the names on the headstones, I would at last come on the Traveller's grave as if, perhaps, he was willing me to that discovery. In a sense it would not have grieved me. I would rather have imagined him in Siberian earth or the Buriat steppes he loved, under some remote cairn placed there by a Shaman. But the Novodievitchy birch trees sheltering the graves were all Russia, all the land he loved, in their gentle, evening melancholy.

Overhead the rooks circled and cawed and shuffled among the branches. Through a gap in the old wall I could see the swans moving slowly across the still lake. It was very quiet, very reassuring here. 'And he says much, who says evening...'

~

Sometimes I would wake to the sound of a storm, with steel rods of rain slanting down over Moscow; not good tourist weather but that, I thought, was the moment best suited to spend in Tolstoy's Khamovnicheski house, the weather when the countrified square wooden building in the little *pereulok*, or side street of an unfashionable quarter of old Moscow, seemed to be more alive, more personal. It was as if the shades of its former inhabitants were all concentrated there, kept indoors by the rain and going about their various occupations, so that I could perhaps catch them unaware. In the yard, the stable door creaked on its hinges and I half expected to see the blunt nose of Tarpan, Tolstoy's dappled grey, appear over the loose-box. The dog-kennel stood empty but no doubt its occupant was snuffling round the large overgrown garden where in winter Tolstoy and his children skated.

The rain lashed down and puddles spread over the yard and I entered the dark narrow hallway with a sense of intrusion, for the curators had restored the house meticulously, strengthening its sense of privacy. There were no other visitors on such a day. Galoshes and cloaks hung by the door as if just removed; on the turn of the stairs a large stuffed bear held a tray of visiting cards between its paws. I turned them idly – Count this, Princess so-and-so, a Marshal of the Nobility, distinguished painters, writers, musicians... 'The Shining Ones' as the family came to describe this élite, as distinct from 'The Dark, or Shadowed Ones', the obscure or nameless peasants and labouring men whom Tolstoy encouraged. These were a disturbing, sweaty lot, in their rank sheepskin *shoubas*; they left muddy footmarks rather than calling cards, and both the Countess and the servants resented such an invasion, for they came at all hours to speak with the Master but naturally did not tip the lackeys who tried to maintain that style to which their mistress clung. Those yellowing slips of pasteboard were eloquent of her way of life, but it was one which her husband sedulously undermined.

He rose at daybreak, as if to emphasize his solidarity with the workers, roused by the hooters of neighbouring factories where they laboured under such oppression. He then chopped wood and fetched water for the household (none was laid on), often going with a sledge as far afield as the Moskva river. He brewed his own barley coffee, made porridge flavoured with dried mushrooms on a spirit lamp, and enjoyed a vicarious sense of achievement – he, the author of *War and Peace* – by making his own boots, instructed by the local cobbler. While eschewing luxury he was, in fact, indulging in the most refined of all luxuries – selective simplicity – but then inconsistency was ever part of the giant's extraordinary nature.

At last his self-imposed asceticism reached the point where, playing Chopin (he was a good pianist and passionately fond of music himself), he wrenched himself away from the keyboard crying 'Ah – *the animal!*' his face paling with the force of emotions aroused by the Fourth Ballade.

Sometimes, however, the senses could not be denied and, although forswearing meat and alcohol, he was still overcome by appetites; for his wife, upon whom his lusty vigour had imposed thirteen pregnancies; and for pickles. Next to his sombre study with its worn leather upholstery deepening the gloom, I found a little stairway, five or six steps, most conveniently leading to a cupboard-like stillroom where huge jars of pickles and preserves were ranged, as once they had been stored there from the estate at Yasnaya Polyana. Now they were faithfully replaced by the curators, a detail of infinite evocation. I was told that Tolstoy would often leave his desk, that rail-topped desk at which he wrote *The Kreutzer Sonata*, *Resurrection*, and *The Death of Ivan Illyitch*, to seek some irresistible mouthful.

Outside the double windows the rain still lashed down, and I imagined just such an overcast day here fifty or more years earlier; in the school-girlish bedrooms of the daughters, one of them, Maria, typing Tolstoy's manuscripts (her mother had recopied *War and Peace* by hand seven times); the servants bustling to and from the outside kitchens, and, in that claustrophobic bedroom which this loving and hating couple shared so disastrously, the Countess seated at her desk, doing the accounts, making endless crocheted quilts, or recording in her journal how she dreads another pregnancy, how she fights for the publication rights of her husband's works, which he is determined to renounce. How she will plead with the Tzar himself to lift the ban on some of her Levovitch's most provocative writings... Poor, pathetic, bewildered, maddening Sonia, clinging, quarrelling, harassing her husband, infuriating him, as he infuriated her, to the point of madness.

The old house in Moscow speaks of all this most poignantly. Little things, telling of great. The calling cards by which she set such store – the pickle-jars he could not resist... I envisaged the giant tiptoeing, like a greedy boy, his home-made boots creaking, as he moved clumsily, guiltily, from a bite of salted cucumber to a spoonful of cherry jam. Sublime and childish Tolstoy! So loving to mankind, so often cruel to his wife. All the tragedy of their lives together is in that bedroom with its two pillows, side by side. 'I will tell the truth about women when I have one foot in the grave,' he told Gorky. 'I shall tell it, jump into my coffin, pull the lid over me and say "Do what you will, now."' And Gorky added 'He gave a look so wild, so terrifying, that we all fell silent.'

But such bitterness vanished when he and his wife grieved together over the death of their last-born, the adored little Vanya, a celestial seeming child, with whom the sixty-year-old Tolstoy would talk on equal terms. He was anguished by this loss, while Sonia railed against God and the whole world, banging her head against the wall, wailing and lamenting. Tolstoy tried to console her with unusual tenderness: but the incorrigible egoist still sounds in a letter of this time: 'I have never loved Sonia so much as now, and that does me good,' he wrote. The family kept Vanitchka's nursery as a shrine; there were no more children.

To me, this Moscow house is far more revealing of the whole tragic epic of Tolstoy's private life than Yasnaya Polyana. There, Tolstoy was sustained by the countryside he loved. Something of Pan remained in the patriarch. He knew great joy there. But in either house the Countess buzzed noisily, trying to obey the man she adored, to indulge him and protect him from himself and from those she believed were destroying him: and also to preserve the heritage of her children, for she was hysterically possessive. She only achieves the true stature of tragedy at Astapova, the obscure wayside station where the eyes of the world were turned on Tolstoy's death-bed. While vast crowds assembled there she, his wife, was locked out, flitting round the station yard, a desperate wraith. When she came too near the house they pulled down the blinds.

These were some of the thoughts that were in my mind one rainy day as I went through the silent yet eloquent house where everything told a tale of terrible intimacy. Had a tourist, a foreigner from another world and age, the right to intrude here, I wondered? Had I the right to see so much that his friends and contemporaries never knew?

Perhaps the veneration in which I held Tolstoy was justification. For me it was not just another visit to another museum – the thing to do: nor did I feel the same degree of emotion exploring Chekhov's house, Dostoievsky's, that of the Boyar Romanov, or the Palace of Tzarskoe Selo, where personal relics of the last Tzar reach the apogee of intimacy. Pushkin's house? But Pushkin is something apart for me, whom I *love*, rather than venerate. He is Mercury, to Tolstoy's Jupiter.

There were other more collective shrines I visited, poring over them for long hours of speculation, indulging the old yearning to trace my Traveller. The various Museums of the Revolution provided such a hunting ground. Surely, here among the photographs of street battles, of crowds listening to a street orator, I would at last come on one loved face? These blurred, mostly unskilled photographs impaled history with a terrible intensity, catching sweeps of the emptying city, crowds scattering before a cavalry charge, leaders conferring in the lee of an upturned tank. Crowds spellbound by the eloquence of a great leader; crowds looting, laughing; crowds surging across the immensity of the Red Square, each one with a face, a destiny, with features offered for my microscopic inspection. The camera had transfixed them, waving up at the photographer, lying dead in the snow, or rebuilding their shattered land. But for all my searching, nothing revealed the one face I sought.

So I would move on, or rather backwards in time, to study perhaps the features of the young Dostoievsky serving his Siberian sentence. He wore uniform and looked comparatively unravaged: it must have been taken after Baron Wrangel had materialized to ameliorate his lot at Semipalatinsk – after his experiences in The House of the Dead. Here was the persecuted Petrashevsky group; here a forlorn street in Chita where the Dekabrist wives had lived. Siberia! I *must* reach it! But still the authorities frowned on my request – still, it seemed, people were sent, rather than went, to Siberia. Balked, I turned southwards.

Though hardly reluctantly, with cities such as Kazan, Orenburg or Astrakhan to be achieved. The curiously-flavoured Tartar port of which I had heard so much from both the Traveller and Aunt Eudoxia, during that faraway summer in Corsica, had always lured me. They described it set on the flat, fly-infested sandy banks of the Volga, three miles wide here, where the big river-boats moored and the green bellied melons were stacked, and where fur-capped Tartar fishermen brought in their reeking loads of caviare. Over all rose the pagoda-like Tartar mosques, gaudily painted, and bell-hung, they said.

Now it was the turn of my mind's *ear*; I heard the clear, humming sound of bells – not the bronze tolling of Russian Orthodox Church bells, but something higher in pitch, at once shrill and silvery, a sound that was wholly Asiatic, befitting the fluted roofs and temples from which it issued.

I was resolved to make the journey to Astrakhan by steamer, down the Volga, from Kazan, another Tartar city enshrined in my mind's eye as being violently picturesque, and the centre of the old Tartar families, the Mirzas, or Mongol-blooded princes. Kazan, where the young Tolstoy had enrolled at the University to study Oriental languages in preparation for a diplomatic career, the city where both Gorky and Chaliapin had spent some years of their youth, living in the same street of the poorest quarter, unknown to each other... Besides, I had read the most alluring accounts of Kazan by an English author who made the journey in 1852. But *'Savez-vous ce que c'est de voyager en Russie? Pour un esprit léger, c'est se nourir d'illusions...'* I heard again the Traveller's maddening, ironic tones, quoting the detestable de Custine. But I remained obstinately nourished on the Englishman's descriptions and still anticipated some brilliant agglomeration of pagodas and pinnacles, with bright-coloured buildings reflected in the river, all Asiatic splendour, perhaps even outshining Vassilii Blajennii in their strange and savage beauty, and worthy of this ancient capital of an ancient Kingdom. The inhabitants, I had read, were held to be particularly handsome, the women going about unveiled, wearing their beautiful national costume with particular grace; the well-to-do Tartar ladies enveloped in emerald green taffeta cloaks resembling the Persian woman's *chaddor*, their faces splendidly painted, their little flat embroidered caps tinkling with golden ornaments, like the ribboned *bouti* I had received from the Traveller so long ago. The soft, bright-coloured slippers of the Kazan ladies emerged from bell-shaped skirts hitched over the pantaloons worn by every conventional Moslem woman. 'Orientalski morals,' as a Bulgarian Orthodox peasant once remarked to me. 'Tzigane-Moslem women all wear *chalvari*. *Our* women don't need trousers, to keep virtuous.'

And then, there were the mysterious Tchouvass, a tribe inhabiting these regions whose origin no one has rightly traced. They were said to be a mixture of Mongolian and Finnish stock, but referred to the Devil by his

Arabic name of Shaitan. The men wore peculiarly shaped high black felt caps, the women elaborate breast-plates, a kind of Amazonian armour of riveted coins; both men and women wore their hair in dishevelled snake-locks, and were known to worship idols. All my ethnographic blood was up – I would drift from Kazan to Astrakhan, following the sluggish yellow current, seeing these and other strange peoples and the territories Stenka Razin once commanded.

Unfortunately, this programme appeared highly suspect to the authorities and quite incomprehensible to those enthusiastic interpreters who were fitfully detailed to accompany me. Gradually, I was learning what an increasingly stern discipline of mind was required to pursue illusions such as those I cherished.

Vanished flavours are as hard to recapture, or to preserve, as illusions. *'De se nourrir d'illusions...'* De Custine, thou shouldst be living at this hour! At Kazan, tugs raced up and down the great waterway, radios blaring from the deck head: no one wore emerald green taffeta cloaks, and where were the breast-plates of the Tchouvass?

But Astrakhan did not require so violent an effort of imagination. By its setting, its landscape alone, it retained a strongly Tartar flavour, and being remote in its sandy wastes, it was possible to visualize it as it had been when Hommaire de Hell, the French geologist, was exploring the surrounding deserts in the 1840's. Over the whole place, an oily, fishy odour hung like a pall. It was disagreeable, but since it derived from the caviare one could eat there so cheaply, it was worth enduring.

In an old-fashioned shack-like restaurant, 'Red Star and Flower of the Steppe' (I fancy the *Red* had been added), sitting on a fretted wooden balcony above the river where the steamer docked and the melons were still stacked as the Traveller had described them, like green cannon-balls in an arsenal, I simmered in the heat of noon, eating great dollops of caviare from a painted wooden spoon and (remembering his agate one) knew it was the only way to savour this delicacy. Even two modest spoonfuls are worth half a dozen mouthfuls on toast. That particular day I was alone; alone with the Traveller's shade, that is, for I was also left alone by the Intourist personnel and he always appeared when they disappeared. Had I won their confidence at last or did they guess that quantities of caviare would anchor me fast, and that I would feel no temptation to wander unwisely?

Far away I could see the herons along the sandy banks and overhead a solitary hawk circled and plummeted. There are many kinds of wildfowl hereabouts. The red-breasted goose, which breeds in northern Siberia, migrates south to the Caspian in winter, and in March the cranes fly northwards, from Central Africa. They cross Palestine and the Sea of Galilee, northwards again, to Russia, reaching Southern Central Asia first, as I have seen them, beside the storks, perched on their enormous, turban-like nests, topping the mosques of Bokhara. On, eastwards, to Astrakhan and farther north again, even to Siberia these aerial migrations continue. 'For the stork in the heavens knoweth her appointed times and the turtle and the crane and the swallows observe the time of their coming...'

There were other migrations in these regions. As the sun declined westward over the salt wastes where only the wildfowl now lived, I remembered 'the Tiumene Prince', a Kalmuck ruler of whom Hommaire de Hell writes in his accounts of his travels in Southern Russia – the same, I discovered, as that intriguing character whom the Traveller had described to me in Paris, who had raised his own regiment and fought beside the Russian army in the Napoleonic campaigns, pitching his tents, at last, along the Champs Elysées as once his ancestors had pitched their *kibitkas* across Asia. In the historic migration of the Kalmucks in 1771 (which inspired Samuel Coleridge), vast numbers of them had fled from the restraints which the Empress Catherine II imposed with increasing severity. The great migration headed north, making for the confines of China: but some fifteen thousand of the Horde had remained, betrayed by an unusually mild season when the Volga had not frozen over and they were unable to cross.

In 1814 it was the Noyon, or chief of this particular Horde who had so much impressed Paris. Hommaire de Hell has described him in 1840, returned from the wars to live in state, in a pagoda-like château he had built on a sand-bank island up the Volga. Here he lorded it over the local society of Astrakhan, surrounded by a mixture of European luxury and barbaric opulence, slaves, dancing girls, grand pianos and bows and arrows; when he rode out, it was in a satin-lined landau, the work of French carriage-makers. The Prince was something of a *magnifico*, a Lorenzo di Medici figure: painter, philosopher and musician as well as a warrior. Scientific research interested him and he was particularly genial to the French geologist and his wife. The Prince was not cut off on his Volga island for steamers called regularly, depositing everyone of note who came through the region. Madame Hommaire de Hell describes the Kalmuck's pagoda-palace as exquisite without, but, alas, rather too European within. (But then she was quite besotted on the east and never willingly ceded the smallest flick of local colour for comfort, an attitude with which I was in sympathy). Dinner, served on Sèvres porcelain, was a mixture of French and Russian cuisine – nothing Kalmuck – no yak-fat stirred into tea. Champagne flowed, as they toasted King Louis-Philippe and the Tzar Nicholas I. Next day, three hundred guests were convened and steamed up the river from Astrakhan to watch wrestling matches, contests of wild-horse roping, and all the barbaric leapings and langorous pantomime of Asiatic dances...

For years I had longed to know more of this fabulous figure and, on one of my later visits to Moscow, in the archives of the Historical Museum, among souvenirs of the Napoleonic Campaigns, maps, prints, Bagration's spy-glass, Kutuzov's orders of battle and such, I came on a pastel sketch of three Asiatic figures whose cast of countenance and Caucasian tunics intrigued me. *'Tiumenev Princes: Serbedjan, Batyr and Tzeren by Hamplen'*, said the label, briefly. And here, unexpectedly, my chase had ended.

One, I knew, must be 'the Tiumene Prince' of Paris: but which one? Two were sketched wearing identical high fur-bordered caps and caftans; the third was seen in profile, the flattened Kalmuck features very marked. One figure was placed more in evidence, being seated, or rather crouched, in the Asiatic fashion, on a satin-covered *bergère*. He wore a medal of the Tzar Alexander I round his neck and beneath his long, snake-like locks, pearl-drop earrings dangled exotically. His expression was curiously remote, as if lost in some dream of distant horizons, which no doubt he was recalling during the *ennui* of the sittings. The third figure was as exotic, but less remote; and he seemed younger. Was he a son or a brother, I wondered? His dress was more strictly that of the Caucasian *tcherkesska* (a costume adopted by most of the Asiatic volunteers in the Russian army), the chest barred with silver braid, on the lines of cartridge-cases, and he fingered a long dagger, the Caucasian *kindjal*. With his hair falling round him like sleek plumage and his wide-set slit eyes also gazing intently into some far distance, he seemed strangely familiar. But not so strange, for his eyes were the eyes of all Asia.

215

Suddenly I saw they were the eyes of both the Traveller and Kamran – my loved and lost Russian family – that looked through me and beyond, from this mysterious drawing.

Since in my imagination Tzeren Norbo became Kamran, and Sergei, who had faded from my mind, did very well as the figure in profile, I now identified Prince Serbedjan with the Traveller. There was so strong a look of both in these Kalmuck warriors, that I plagued the Museum authorities until I obtained a photograph of the drawing which, from that moment, assumed the value of a family portrait.

That the Traveller had Kalmuck blood I knew; Aunt Eudoxia had revealed that his father had descended from the Torghut Horde. This was enough to inflame my fancy. Could this, I wondered, be why the bells had always been rung, and the Metropolitan in person come to the Gates of Kiev, whenever the Traveller's great-grandfather had arrived there? (Although Kalmucks worshipped at Lamist Buddhist shrines and were therefore unlikely to rate a ceremonial orthodox welcome). The Traveller had never been forthcoming over his great-grandfather's precise status, although he sometimes mentioned his more exotic forbears. But beyond sketching the migratory habits of the Hordes, he had not particularized.

Had anyone so colourful as this Tiumenev Prince been of his family, I thought he would have enlarged on him: but there were curious withdrawals in his nature and he would often withhold a seemingly straightforward piece of information, or suppress some link in a chain. As Aunt Eudoxia had said, he always enjoyed secrecy for its own sake.

PART SIX

THE BORROWED LOVE

Ici-bas, tous les lilas meurent
Tous les chants des oiseaux sont courts
Je rêve aux fleurs qui demeurent toujours – toujours.

Ici-bas, tous les hommes pleurent
Leurs amitiés et leurs amours.
Je rêve aux couples qui demeurent toujours – toujours.

Sully-Prudhomme

CHAPTER EIGHTEEN

E aster in Paris is one of the clichés of tourism. Organized insouciance, at so much per head, transforms the city into a huge tourist trap where the visitors court pneumonia in their determination to eat outside, under bleakly flapping awnings, to the fury of the waiters and the indifference of the chefs, who know this sort of custom is not worth bothering about. Paris is best in August, when the Parisians are for the most part away and those who remain seem to have called a truce to their usual activities of exploiting or intimidating the foreigners. But at Easter-time they are there in strength, closing in for the kill.

'What does one do in Paris at Easter?' I remember asking the Traveller, on my first rapturous visit.

'Leave it, of course,' he had snapped, but for reasons I never discovered, spent the following three weeks there showing me something of it.

Easter-time always renewed my hunger for him; those weeks had seemed to belong to us especially, as no other hours, past or to come, could ever do. So, in whatever country I chanced to find myself at Easter, I would search out the Russian church, going to the midnight service in a spirit compounded of self-dramatization, thanksgiving and mourning.

'Never say with grief, he is no more
But rather say with thankfulness – he was.'

These lovely lines, addressed, I think, to the memory of Pushkin – or were they by Pushkin himself? – were uppermost in my mind whenever I remembered the Traveller.

Fifteen or more years after I had first spent Easter in Paris beside him, found me there again. Once more I was going to the midnight service at the Russian Orthodox Cathedral in the Rue Daru. Russian friends had invited me to a party later but there would be no more Gypsies, I knew. The Gypsies were fading, fading fast. Those who remained had been absorbed into troupes which performed in expensive night-clubs catering to an international clientèle who listened carelessly, called for 'Black Eyes' and more champagne, and went on chattering. Nevertheless, the Russian exiles continued to make much of the occasion, one way or another, fasting or feasting. By now I had lived among them all enough to be aware that, for the Easter midnight mass and after, evening dress was considered proper. When the Traveller had initiated me into my first Russian Easter he had not followed custom to that extent, nor had he instructed me to wear anything particularly festive. At that moment I doubt if I had so much as a schoolgirl's party-dress in my baggage: certainly Mademoiselle Lavisse would have been opposed to the idea of buying any finery for the occasion.

Now integrated into the exiles' magic circle I held to their traditions with a convert's zeal. Thus Madame Sapojnikov was concocting an elaborate toilette of blonde lace which, in the fashion of that moment, swept the ground, was very décolleté and, we both thought, particularly becoming.

During the fittings I was again indulging my passion for Madame Sapojnikov's Russia – that vanished, chaotic, comic, dramatic, touching and generally ineffectual world that charmed me. She had once made the Trans-Siberian journey under particularly enthralling circumstances, and I was never tired of hearing her description.

It had all happened long ago – in her heyday when, as one of the best established Moscow *couturières* she had received a splendid order to make, and deliver personally, *twenty* elaborate toilettes for the wife of a wealthy merchant in Harbin.

'Twenty! It was such a chance! I knew it would lead to a lot more work... Besides, I liked the idea of starting a connection with the Far East. I always wanted to travel.' Madame Sapojnikov wheezed alarmingly nowadays. Life in Paris, after years on the sixth floor of the same dingy little hotel, was taking its toll. But as she pinned and snipped she gathered momentum, like the train she was recalling for my delectation.

'It seemed a whole way of life – we all got to know each other so well... At night we used to get up concerts or dances, even. There was plenty of room; why, the saloon car even had a grand piano. Oh yes! We knew how to enjoy ourselves, in those days.'

For the twentieth time I listened, entranced, to Madame Sapojnikov recounting how she had not trusted her precious dresses in the luggage van.

'I reserved an extra compartment for them. I could afford that sort of thing then. Even so they piled up to the ceiling. Clothes took up so much room at that time. All my boxes were pale mauve – the tissue paper was lilac-coloured too. I had half a dozen great big hatboxes with me as well. The sort of hats worn then needed enormous care... There was one, I remember, covered in bunches of sweetpeas with green tulle butterflies, so becoming... And the hat pins, I remember one pair of jewelled dragon-files... But you don't want to hear that again,' she would say deprecatingly.

'Oh, but I do – please go on. I love the part about the Japanese General. It's so like *Shanghai Express*.'

Madame Sapojnikov looks mystified, for she does not go to the cinema and has never heard of Marlene Dietrich. But she embarks on the whole story once again.

Soon after the train had crossed the Urals the Japanese General had discovered she had all those lovely dresses in the second compartment and, being anxious to ingratiate himself with the blonde adventuress farther along the train, he had approached Madame Sapojnikov most civilly and made her an offer for some of the clothes. Of course, she refused, even though he had been very generous in his terms. When he saw Madame Sapojnikov was not to be persuaded he had bowed and smiled and bowed again, in a most pleasant manner, and backed away to his own compartment saying how much he regretted her decision. But while Madame Sapojnikov was in the restaurant car, having dinner – 'ah! how delicious those dinners were, caviare and champagne every night; there was always some man to offer you caviare and champagne then – and the little tables looking so festive, lit with pink shaded lamps, and outside, the snow-covered forests rushing past...' She falls silent, remembering her happy hey-day, and I do not like to intrude. But presently she takes up the tale... While she was in the restaurant car, the Japanese General had forced her compartment and slashed open the lilac dressboxes with his sword, helping himself right and left.

'Yellow rat!' hisses Madame Sapojnikov, lunging with her scissors. No one had dared to stop him – one of the attendants had tried and had an ear sliced off for his trouble. He had rushed down the corridor screaming. He had nearly knocked down Madame Sapojnikov as she was returning from the dining car. When she saw the disorder in her compartment she fainted. All those lovely dresses in heaps on the floor! Hat-boxes ripped open, tissue-paper everywhere, and half the things missing! It was only some hours later when everything was put to rights and the General, who was now locked in with the adventuress, had promised the Controller (through the locked door), to settle the damage in the morning, that Madame Sapojnikov noticed the attendant's sliced-off ear lying there on the floor!

Madame Sapojnikov gives a dramatic rendering of herself, discovering this grisly object. 'I shrieked! The man next door rushed in and threw it out of the window. Of course he ought not to have done that, but I was too upset to stop him. When the poor attendant heard we had found his ear and thrown it away he was most upset. I remember he flung himself down on my bunk and sobbed. He had bought a bottle of vodka and meant to pickle the ear as a souvenir. So I got up a little subscription for him – even the General contributed – and we ended up drinking the vodka and singing... It became quite a gay party... Yes, life was like that, then.' Madame Sapojnikov drags to her feet and pads across the room to remove the cabbage soup from the gas-ring, before it overboils and floods the chest-of-drawers.

~

Easter eve found me once again in the darkened Cathedral of St. Alexander Nevski. The atmosphere was claustrophobic. The crowds were wedged, immobile, unable to advance or retreat. There was none of that drifting, shifting concourse of the usual Orthodox service. Only those in the front rank were able to prostrate themselves in prayer or go from one miraculous ikon to another. The brooding silence of the Easter night vigil hung over all, so powerful that it seemed to reverberate in the shadowy dome, silence pressing on silence, stilling alike the muttering of the priests, invisible behind the iconostas, and the rustling of the congregation, as they passed lighted tapers across the church from hand to hand, shimmering garlands threading through the gloom. Incense drifted heavily, mingling and overcoming the wafts of expensive scents worn by the more affluent women – and men too, for a love of strong perfumes was an Oriental trait shared by Russian men. Incense and perfume; sacred and profane; on that night they were met in good measure.

As the hour of Resurrection drew near the tension mounted: there was a quality of expectancy, of urgency about the vast throng; they seemed to simmer, standing there so rigidly. Behind the iconostas, remote from the world, the mystic rituals continued, glimpsed from time to time, when a bearded, black-robed figure came or went, the brief opening of the gilded doors revealing the dimly-lit inner sanctuary where more black-robed figures moved in their hieratical pattern, and a line of long-maned heads were bowed in prayer.

Soon, very soon now, the clergy would emerge in all their panoply, to circle the building three times and then proclaim the Resurrection. But first, all was darkness, stillness. I felt myself sway with exhaustion. I had been standing several hours and, moreover, fasting. Most of my friends had observed the strict Lenten fast of Orthodoxy and I had joined them, though my denials were half-hearted beside their rigours, just as, beside their shining faith, mine was pinchbeck. Indeed, my presence in the cathedral that night, like all my other Easter attendances, was more in the nature of a remembrance service.

The sense of expectancy was becoming suffocating. With only salted fish and *kasha* in my belly since morning my head began to spin and I sagged against the surrounding throng. I had become separated from my friends but I thought I saw Nadia's auburn head beside a pillar, against which I longed to lean. With rising panic, I wondered what would happen were I to faint. But standing long hours in church was one of the things all Russians, even the most fragile or aged, were able to achieve. It would not do to falter.

The candle I clutched was beginning to waver, spilling hot wax over my hands. Across the nimbus of light it cast the long dark faces of the ikons seemed to merge with the broad pale faces of the exiles, a shifting mirage of Byzantine and Slav; a mirage where my eyes still searched, almost automatically, for one long-sought face that once had been beside me there.

Suddenly, with the impact of a blow, Byzantine and Slav and Tartar formed into one gigantic and blinding vision. In what seemed a clap of thunder and a blaze of light I saw that face before me. As I gazed, the vision dissolved, the light dimmed, and I saw the Traveller in the flesh, standing there, only a few yards away! His features were lit theatrically, as by footlights, from the glow of the candle he carried. The slit eyes were restless, ranging over the crowd, sliding towards me, and then, as if drawn by the violence of my desire, fastened on me. I saw him start in recognition. Forgetful of my whereabouts I tried to call his name but the words were strangled in my throat. I must have leaned forward towards him, for at that moment my candle set light to the lace Madame Sapojnikov had draped across my bosom so gracefully. There was a smell of singeing, but I continued to stand there transfixed, staring; as in a dream I felt someone snatch my candle, while someone else beat out the smouldering lace. There was a murmur of disapproval at the disturbance but only my immediate neighbours had been aware of the danger. Once this was averted they turned again towards the iconostas and were absorbed in their devotions.

As if returning to consciousness after an anaesthetic, I seemed to circle outside myself, disembodied. At that moment I was aware of the Traveller forcing his way through the press towards where I, or my *döppelganger* body stood. With a sense of enormous effort, the bemused, the dispossessed, I managed to return inside my waiting shell. I must be there to receive him. He was within an arm's length of me now, his face still lit dramatically by the candle he carried. Now he had reached me. 'Outside!' he muttered, seizing my arm.

Dragging me after him, he fought a way through the crowd, going against the surge of bodies pressing forward. There were angry exclamations, scowling faces and complaints as we struggled towards the door.

At last, dishevelled and panting, we faced each other under the dim bluish light of the porch.

I stared at him, uncomprehending. He seemed taller, younger... and where was the Chinese-bald skull? Hidden now beneath a close black cap of hair.

'Mamasha! Don't you know me? Oh Mamasha darling... darling...' It was Kamran.

How long we stood there I do not know, but almost at once, it seemed, the crowds began to pour out, making way for the procession. They swept us before them, stumbling down the steps into the forecourt. The bells clanged overhead among the stars. The crowds were crying out the joyous Easter salutation. *'Christos Vosskress!* He is Risen! Verily He is Risen!' they cried, exchanging the triple Resurrection kiss. Below the sound of the bells I heard the Traveller's voice once more: *'The Resurrection kiss – you swore it me!'*

Kamran pinned me against the wall and, hunching his shoulders against the pressure of the crowd, continued to kiss me, greedily, angrily, as tears of love and disappointment streaked my face.

~

So began our strange relationship. Did I love him? Yes, for a past we had shared briefly, and for a certain reckless joy we now found together. But what I loved and sought in him were the echoes of his father. Did he love me? Yes, for the same shared memories, and for a sort of pride of conquest. His father, whom he had loved from afar and admired so unquestioningly, had loved me. So now, in possessing me, he came nearer to his father. Each of us were reaching for a ghost.

His moody young face, which had grown so heartbreakingly like that of the Traveller, would darken as we kissed.

'You always thinking of Papasha. Don't lie – I am seeing!' And furiously he would try to make me forget.

Our friends were bent on separating us. Exasperated, we would take refuge in an obscure little hotel where, ostrich-like, we believed ourselves unobserved. Locked in our wildly-papered hide-out, we ignored the half-hearted attempts of a sullen *femme de chambre* to do the room. We would send down for relays of *café complet*, which was cheaper and more convenient than going out to meals; a shuttle-service of trays were alternately placed outside, or collected from, the threshold of our door by an even more sullen *valet de chambre*.

The bilious gloom of a premature autumn in northern France was uninviting and the shutters remained permanently closed. A bead-fringed bed-side lamp was nourished by a current as fitful as the heating which regurgitated through the aluminium-painted radiator. A curtained alcove contained a large bath where the hot tap sometimes lost control so that a jet of scalding water would suddenly gush out noisily, jerking us from the langours by which we were possessed. On the rare occasions when we opened the shutters we could see, across the narrow street, a house with florid *dix-huitième* balconies inhabited by Adam Mickiewicz. A plaque commemorated his sojourn there: ADAM MICKIEWICZ – POÈTE POLONAIS. 1798-1855.

'Pole!' spat Kamran with the same scorn his father had shown towards that nation. But Kamran was speaking in echoes, becoming once again his father's shadow, and I would tax him with this.

'*You've* got no reason to despise the Poles,' I would say, annoyingly. 'You aren't even a full Russian yourself! Poles are quite as good as Kirghiz, Kalmucks or Bashkirs, I'm sure. Besides, Mickiewicz is different – and he was a friend of Pushkin's.' But Kamran did not want to be drawn into such discussions. It might have shown up his ignorance of anything concerning nineteenth-century Russia. This was a region where he could not follow me, where he knew I had been led by his father, a region in which I, an interloper, was more at home than he, the expatriate. Here the Traveller and I had enclosed ourselves, barricading ourselves against the present, against intruders, against himself, too. So now he sulked, too proud to show any interest. Presently one of us, exasperated, would pick a quarrel, the sort of violent quarrel which is in itself an act of love, and the fourth or fifth breakfast tray of the day would crash to the ground, dragging the slippery yellow eiderdown with it, brioche flakes and buttery knives adding to the disorder.

Kamran had only the vaguest recollections of Russia; for him it was a blurred passage of time from which a few figures or incidents emerged briefly. Tobolsk, his birthplace? Nothing. Some long journey with dromedaries and horses and bright-coloured tents... A Kirghiz camp I suggested? Perhaps – he was not sure; he thought he had made a journey from some place a long way off, and that his mother had been waiting for him in a big town. She was pretty. Her eyebrows met across in one dark line, and she wore her hair in long black plaits – many of them; he used to play with them; each one had a gold coin attached. His father? He thought he had seen him for the first time much later, in Vienna. He recalled his fat Russian *nianya*, a summer of happiness running wild in the country, playing in a field where huge yellow sunflowers were tall as trees above him. Then a long indoor winter in a city where snow lay banked round the houses and he had been ill... A lot of people coming and going, trunks being packed, his *nianya* crying; then, no more Russia. School-days in Vienna, learning to speak German – later a Lycée in Paris and, in Rome, the death of his mother whom, it seemed, he did not mourn greatly. In France he had lived much among Russians, but already he was very far from his roots, and seemed indifferent when I showed him the portrait of the Tiumenev Princes, and Tzeren, his double. Russia remained deep in his blood; no Russian transplants wholly; they adapt, but a Slav core always remains untouched or, perhaps uncorrupted. Kamran knew nothing of Russia's history, legends or literature, nor the tempo, or texture of its daily life – yet he felt himself an exile.

But he was an exile without memories.

Gradually, I perceived that Kamran craved such memories – that he envied that rich store of remembrance which sustained and linked the older exiles and which constituted a whole country he could not share with them. Gradually, he turned towards his unknown roots. From a rag-bag jumble of hearsay and casual knowledge he would select something and question me. I think he felt easier admitting his ignorance to me than to his compatriots; and then he knew that my own collection of rag-bag learning had been acquired from his father – that father who had always held him at arm's length, for the Traveller had plainly not wished for the obligations of sustained family life.

So Kamran would question me. 'Who was Poltava?' he would ask naively, and I would describe the battle. Or, 'Have you read book called *Dead Souls?*' 'Were Strelzi good or bad?' 'What is story of Roussalka?' 'Did Papasha know Petrashevsky people?' 'Tell about Ilya Mourametz.' Now it was I who was the teller of tales, I who told of a thousand forgotten things belonging to his roots... of the curious street-names in old Moscow, the street of the Pug-Nosed, the street of the Louse-Eater... of churches which evoked Babayaga, and Mousourgorsky's Great Gate of Kiev, St. Nicholas on Chickens' Feet, or the church of the Nine Martyrs on the Cabbage Stalks, a name still redolent of the refuse-strewn alleys of old Moscow. It was I who evoked for him the medieval wooden city which retained something of a nomad Asiatic encampment about it, and where the kites still circled overhead. Before the eighteenth-century, houses were torn down or erected on a whim, thousands of carpenters being steadily at work to still that migratory itch which was so marked a characteristic of the Russians. It was I who told him of Stenka Razin, the brigand, seated in his ivory and silver chair high on the cliffs above the Volga where he could lord it over the reaches he terrorized:

'In the night, beyond the Volga
The robber gangs flocked round their fires...'

The quotation came from *The Robbers*, an unfinished poem by Pushkin, but Kamran knew nothing of Russian poetry, could not savour it through my Anglicized versions, and was too lazy to read it, for any length, in the original. Despairing, I would turn to legends or songs of the people: one, to me, conjured all the romantic wildness of the brigands' boat:

'The crew were Cossacks and the sails were silk.
At the helm, the Hetman with his gun.

At the prow, the captain with his lance.
On the deck, a tent of velvet
Shelters caskets filled with gold.
On them, stretched on silken carpets
The Hetman's doxy sleeps,
A creature fresh as blood and milk,
All beauty, all desire...'

But Kamran was not to be won and, having questioned the exact meaning of 'doxy' (I see, yes, so you are being my doxy – no?'), he liked me to recount the mysteries of Russian history; of the belief that Alexander I had not died, but vanished to become a monk. Princess Tarakanova's fearful end intrigued him, for he had seen a picture of this young and beautiful pretender to the throne of Catherine II, trapped in her dungeon, surrounded by rats, as the waters of the Neva rose round her. Kamran was partial to strong meat; what he preferred in the history of the Strelzi was not the motives of their rising but the drama of their end, in particular, the manner in which the leaders were strung up outside the windows of the Novodievitchy Convent, where they hung, blackened and rigid, turning idly in the wind, all winter long, their frozen boots tapping against the windows where Peter the Great's sister, Sophia, who had been inculpated in the plot, was immured for the rest of her life.

Sometimes I would edge my stories eastwards, towards Siberia, telling of Jenghis Khan's banners over which, it was believed, no bird could fly; how the escaping convicts used to burn off their brand marks, enduring further agony for the chance of freedom. Or I would launch into a homily on the Trans-Siberian, telling how it had, from its inception, played a dominant role in Siberian life.

'It's not just that I want to make the longest train journey in the world,' I would explain: 'don't you see – it's the country's life-line. It has known so much history. Well, it's about the most romantic thing imaginable,' I would end, lamely, for it was clear my eloquence did not stir Kamran. But undaunted, or self-indulgent perhaps, I would return to my theme, telling how, by this life-line, a whole new population of settlers flowed eastward into the emptiness, each turn of the wheels bringing them closer, they believed, to their hopes of new life and prosperity. Westward, the riches of Siberia were exported along these same rails. The long, long passage knew births and deaths; wayside stations saw meetings and partings; anguish and even joy travelled on these trains, like dread, and the rattle of the convicts' chains. During the Revolution terrible battles raged for possession of each section of the line. Roughly plated with iron sheeting, railway carriages became armoured cars. Within, supreme commanders planned their campaigns from these ambulant G.H.Q.s.

Often, a briefly appointed leader would live out his whole command from one, never reaching the scene of battle, his route hampered by snow and blocked by mined tunnels. The carriages became martial courts and execution cells too as they rolled across the country, slowing down or accelerating, attacked or attacking, carrying their secrets within their steel walls.

In Siberia, battles were lost or won on trains rather than in the field, where diminishing numbers of soldiers sometimes waited forlornly for reinforcements that never came, that had perished, en route, when their train was dynamited; or as they deserted, one by one, dropping from the train as it headed for battle. Thousands of such deserters, growing more and more uncertain of what they were fighting for, made their getaway from the troop trains and took to the *taïga*, on the run, as once the escaping convicts had done.

But epic battles left Kamran unmoved. One of his favourite stories was that of the French prostitute from the Pont au Change who had found her way eastwards to become interpreter at the Mongol Court...

Asia! Asiatic Russia...! Siberia! The old magic. 'Don't you ever want to go back?' I would ask Kamran, hoping we might share something of the same romantic longing.

'No, this is good,' he would reply, content to spend the hours in love and idleness. 'All the time you thinking about Siberia, Mamasha,' he said, 'you always wanting to love in the *taïga*. I am loving to love *anywhere.*'

There was no answer to this. And so, engrossed for awhile in loving, 'emparadised in one another's arms', I stifled my longings for the Siberian journey.

But then, perhaps a love affair is a journey in itself – a journey into the heart of another. Sometimes a journey of no return.

~

Even in Paris, in Paris of the late thirties, our meetings were few and difficult. We had no money and far too many friends who disapproved and interfered. Some had known the Traveller; some had known my place in his life. Kamran was his son; then, he had no job, no future (unreliable, they implied, like his father). He did not even have a proper passport – his father had never bothered to attend to anything practical like that. Then, I was a married woman – at least I had been married, and the matter of my divorce had never been regulated. Where was my husband, anyhow? It was all very unsatisfactory. It would be a nice mess if this forgotten husband were suddenly to reappear and cite Kamran. Damages... Costs... They muttered and prophesied, witch-like, round the cauldron-samovar. There was a lot of gossip and our relationship was condemned as thoroughly unsuitable. Though what precisely this term implied was never classified. What has suitability to do with the emotions?

'How I am caring what they thinking?' said Kamran, who now wildly suggested that I should try to free myself from my long-forgotten marriage. 'And if we are marry together,' he continued naïvely, shaking a wing of black hair from his eyes, 'then they couldn't say not one thing.' But when I pointed out that this was unlikely, he scowled, calling them all the names with which the Russian language is so richly endowed.

'So they say things then, the something sons of somethings. Bloodee bloodees. You were always so loving of the Tartars – so O.K. I am learning incest was the religion of the Tartars. Marco Polo tells so.'

I had lately persuaded Kamran to join a Franco-Russian library and to catch up on some of the reading his unsettled childhood had denied him; in general, he showed a preference for the Simenon books, or something like *Nana*, which of course he should have read at school. Now, as if quoting Scriptures to his own ends, he read from Marco Polo's Travels triumphantly: 'the sonne marrieth sometimes all his father's wives except his own mother.'

'See? I copy it out for you.' Ingenuously, he proffered an envelope scrawled with his rather childish handwriting.

'I see. All the same, I'm not free, and I wouldn't dream of marrying you if I was. It wouldn't do.' I heard generations of Anglo-Saxon convention sounding primly in my voice.

Overweening conventions! They have us in a stranglehold from the cradle to the coffin. Sometimes a surge of violence liberates us for a while, for good or ill, but the voice of convention rather than conscience is ever with us. Even when, every twenty years or so, these conventions change or shift, their force does not abate and they din themselves in every ear. You *must* be respectable. You must *not* be. Either way, we are aware of their impositions.

And so I did not make this improvident, imprudent marriage, and thus was spared much trouble and also, perhaps, missed much delight.

CHAPTER NINETEEN

Years had passed and we were still together; together and apart, for although my visits to Paris were frequent, I could no more install myself there than Kamran could install himself in London. I earned my living in London, while Kamran was working, but scarcely earning, with a firm of French architects. Even the little hotel that had harboured our first transports was now beyond our means, or rather beyond Kamran's means, for he was adamant in refusing my proffered share. 'What we eating and where we loving is business of me,' he said, something of the Traveller's arrogance sounding suddenly.

What we ate, being mostly *pommes frites*, presented no problem, but where we loved was another matter. Kamran was sharing a room with two other struggling architects who, he assured me, were prepared to go out whenever I visited him, a project I found disconcerting. I myself was in very low financial waters and had gone to stay with an English family out at Versailles. They had never known the Traveller and, I thought, could not criticize my affection for Kamran. But I had not reckoned with the strength of British principles. They might be living in France; they might have wine with their meals and breathe garlic fumes with the best of their neighbours; they might be aware that Kamran was my lover; and, as such, he might sometimes make the journey out to Versailles and dine *en famille*. But set a foot upstairs, in my room – certainly not. There could be none of what Mrs. Aphra Benn described as 'the midnight's kind admittance'. Nor was the weather conducive to evenings spent out of doors, in the park, so that it seemed our emotional life had come to a standstill. We would sit glaring at each other, estranged by this transplanted, but omnipotent British family life. Today, the bastions of such prudery have been stormed, and we should no doubt be encouraged to make free with the drawing-room sofa.

'But why does he call you Mamasha?' asked my hostess. Ah! Why...?

'You *must* stop calling me Mamasha,' I said, next time we met. 'It's not suitable – not now.'

But Kamran brushed the suggestion aside.

'You are Mamasha for me for evertime. Then, I am believing it is more exciting to be making the love with my father's mistress... I am reading of François I and Diane de Poitiers... Also, as I say to you before, incest is Tartar religion. I am very much religious,' he added, between embraces snatched in the shelter of a jasmine arbour, out of sight of the house. I remembered the Traveller's postscript to his last letter: 'Be kind to Kamran...' It was not hard to obey.

~

For a while, I tried to improve his English, but it made little progress. Generally we spoke a jargon of mixed French and English richly laced with Russian. Sometimes his misuse of English was particularly graphic. As we crouched under one raincoat, waiting for a summer storm to pass he hugged me close:

'Thus is cuddleful, isn't it – no?'

'"Cuddleful?" What a ghastly word. Where on earth did you pick that up'

He smiled engagingly. 'Once I had the happiness to love a blonde lady in Windsor Park. She was married with the professor from Eton school. She liked the cuddle.'

I shuddered. 'Papasha would have preferred you to have found a respectable French tart in Soho – a real pro.' I spoke severely of the dangers of casual or amateur involvements.

'Papasha always said English amateurs are more in gratefulness,' replied Kamran with finality.

Kamran telephoned me at Versailles to say he had found a solution to one problem, at least.

'Come to Paris tomorrow. We shall eating *blini* to celebrate. I am finding good place for us. Not *maison de passe*... You will see!'

Pride rang in his voice and, intrigued, I promised to join him.

He was at the station to meet me, his dark slanted eyes smiling impudently over a large bunch of lilies of the valley, which he explained were not so much an offering of love as a symbol – a traditional offering of this day. 'Is first day of May – you have forgotten? May-day in Moscow? The Red Flag? There will be big workers' meetings, music, big talking, here too.' And calling me Charlotte Russe, he suggested I should show my solidarity by joining them. Charlotte Russe... the old name, recalling the Traveller's bantering tone.

I plunged into my bouquet, side-stepping both memories and politics.

The *blini* were not particularly good, but neither was the restaurant – we knew it well and went there because Dadya, or 'Uncle' Plotnikov as the proprietor was called, kept prices low and portions large for his favoured clientèle.

My bouquet was immediately seized and plunged into the water jug by a beaming Dadya Plotnikov. Perfume swam round us, enclosing us in a romantic aura, isolating us from the blasts of cooking emanating from the stove in the back room where, behind a bead curtain, Dadya Plotnikov's brother could be seen doing the cooking in a singlet and battered cap.

'You do not speak – what you thinking?' asked Kamran, who could show himself jealous even of my thoughts.

I did not tell him that his bouquet had reminded me of his father, and how, long ago in Corsica, he had carefully instructed his sons on the finesse of flower-giving – the kind of flowers suited to the winning of this woman, or another. For example, in *le temps des lilacs*, he said, it was more *recherché* to give white lilac – only white – especially to married women, who particularly appreciated being treated in a bridal manner. Orchids, on the other hand, were for *jeunes filles* -they might be sufficiently naïve to think them deliciously evil – *les fleurs du mal*.

Kamran and Sergei had listened to their father's helpful suggestions with respect. The Traveller's slit eyes had been intent, below frowning brows: he was wholly concentrated on the importance of his theme.

'Believe me,' he had finished, 'it takes considerable sophistication to appreciate jonquils. If you are after a well-known actress or ballerina be sure to send some modest little bunch of country flowers – it's worth taking a lot of trouble to get them – she'll notice them at once, among all those sheaves of long-stemmed roses and gladioli – and then, also, she'll think you think of her as *younger*, more *innocent* than she is. It never fails.'

When I taxed him on his revealing such a knowledge of flower names he merely said that a man should know how to order from the florist as well as from the wine-merchant.

Suddenly I remembered how he had come to meet me at the Gare du Nord that faraway Easter, bringing bouquets for myself and Mademoiselle Lavisse.

I stood again on the grimy platform, watching him come towards me through the crowds. '*Pussinka Moyia* – at last !' he had said.

O Aesop! there *are* fields of amaranth this side of the grave! There *are* voices of which the echo is never stilled!

'Now for surprise,' said Kamran, ardent and urgent, pushing me out into the dazzling May sunshine. 'It is very quickly near here – you will see – no one find us there – it is our Gallantry Bower!'

I stopped in my tracks. 'Gallantry Bower! What d'you mean? What do you know about Gallantry Bower?' I shook off his encircling arm.

Seeing my look, Kamran became defiant.

'Is what you and Papasha call your hide love place in Corsica – yes?'
'You *knew?*'

'Silly Mamasha darling. How I not know? You always walk away so secret like criminal peoples so Sergei and I follow sometimes. How am I knowing about pretend-game, making the love in Mongolian *yurt* and on Trans-Siberian? But you are always so wanting the pretend Siberia I think you will like *our* Gallantry Bower, *our* pretend... A Kirghiz *kibitka*, like my mother's people, if you like it so. We go now.'

The pride in his voice had given place to an aggressive note.

Waves of fury engulfed me. I hit out at him with the bouquet. 'You spied on us! *Voyeur*! Filthy *voyeur*! Your own father too! How dared you! I never want to see you again. Don't explain. You've spoiled everything.' I hit him once more, for good measure, and leaving him standing gaping in the sunshine, rushed blindly away, diving into the nether regions of a Métro which conveniently presented itself at the end of the street.

Chaâtelet, République, Belleville, Porte des Lilas – the train was grinding its way under Paris towards some destination I did not know or want. Mairie des Lilas – the end of the line. With a sense of surprise I emerged into the same strong sunlight in which I had left Kamran standing bewildered, the lilies of the valley scattered at his feet. Somehow, I had expected the weather to change with my mood; it should have been grey, chill, for already I was overcome with a sense of desolation. I sat on the noisy terrace of a brasserie, waiting for the interminable *café filtre* to fill my cup and wishing passionately that it was a *tchai-khana* in Russian Turkestan – the kind the Traveller had so often described to me in his tales. But he had gone, and with him, his tales; and now Kamran was lost too. With a sense of abandonment that verged on panic I turned inward, into that other world of fantasy that always waited for me, that was only a sigh away.

I scuffled in my bag and tugged out the chunky little red volume which alternated with Herzen's Memoirs as my daily reading. My affection for Baedeker's *Russie 1895* (French Edition) which rivalled and often contradicted that other treasure, *Murray's Handbook of Russia for 1893*, was mystifying to my French and Russian friends. They constantly reminded me that it was out of date. But then I, too, was out of date, keeping company with a ghost who had known Russia at that time. Apart from the fact that the Russia of which Baedeker writes is no more and that present-day guide books suggest enormous itineraries and cover distances which are only realizable by the use of jet planes and fast cars, there is another, striking difference.

These earlier guide books are all obsessed by the same question – how to pass the time (when of course, the real problem is how to stop it passing so quickly, especially if one is in the faraway realms on which Baedeker and his kind dwell). But on that particular May-day of desolation at the Mairie des Lilas time undeniably seemed to drag. So, ordering another *café filtre* I opened my guide book and took flight to Russia, to St. Petersburg, 1895...

The magic never failed. Paris faded; the spire of the Admiralty gleamed before me, the old familiar smell of sun-flower seeds, wet leather and salted fish assailed me. I was home, safely home...

Emploi du temps, says Baedeker, listing his suggestions – all of them, to me, mouth-watering prospects, but it is clear Baedeker doubts his reader's abilities to pass the time in Russia without his aid. Murray goes further and devotes a long passage to eating, counselling and explaining the typical Russian cuisine for adventurous British stomachs. Is there, perhaps, a faint trace of cynicism to be detected? Of patronage, perhaps? In listing *Botvinia* merely as 'a soup of a green colour,' or describing *Porosionok pod khrenum*, cold boiled sucking pig with horse-radish, as 'not a pretty dish but very eatable', and dismissing various local cheeses warily, 'should the digestion or habit require them', we can also detect a dyspeptic note. Murray follows up this gastronomic section with one headed SANITARY PECULIARITIES, and I imagine the editors sitting back, a good day's work done. That will keep the tourists busy! After the red pottage (or the green soup?), the exceeding bitter cry. Just let them try out those dishes. They have been warned, and then, if they feel poorly, we have listed reliable pharmacies and doctors too, say Murray's editors complacently, going off for a mutton chop at their club.

But Baedeker knows his French readers are not to be fobbed off with any suggestions about eating as an *emploi du temps*. They have been brought up in the noble traditions of the French cuisine and for them eating is not an *emploi du temps*; it is a whole way of life, a whole civilization. They are not to be distracted by picturesque *plats*. They must be given other suggestions for passing their time abroad. But so insistent are the editors on this *emploi du temps*, this pressing question of how to pass the hours, that I begin to envisage numberless tourists, all raging with boredom, all pacing up and down the confines of the variously graded hotels throughout the world. In cities and remote provinces alike, the same ennui, the same gnawing preoccupation – how to pass the time? At the Hôtel de France, the Imperial, de la Poste, du Commerce, the Schweizerhof, the Victoria, or, for bold travellers in southern Russia, '*Cafés Tartares en face de la Gare. Malpropres*'. The *emploi du temps* here will probably be how to obtain insecticides but the preoccupation of the editors is always the same: how to pass the time. In Russia? They wouldn't have to tell *me*.

~

Slowly, reluctantly, with a drug-addict's sense of unreality, I returned to the present, to France, to the brasserie at the Mairie des Lilas. And as the French here and now sharpened round me, coming back into focus, I perceived that a petulant wind had sprung up round the terrace, slapping at the table cloths, flapping at the awnings, driving the *garçon* inside to comb his oily black locks into place again. Everything was bleak, lonely and sad. I knew that, however outraged I might be by Kamran's clumsiness, I could not shut him out of my life for long. There was, I knew, no future for us – yet how much past!

And so it was not long before we were together again, and Kamran conducted me with ceremony to his own version of Gallantry Bower.

This was revealed as the back-room of a small furrier's shop owned by a blue-chinned Armenian named Armin Nourbarian originally from Baku. He had been a wholesale furrier in Moscow and Kamran's mother, of an extravagant nature, had often ordered furs from him, still craving the extravagant snow-leopard or black fox pelts prized by the Hordes from which she stemmed. Towards the end of the Revolution, as she was proceeding southwards planning to board a boat at Odessa, she had encountered Monsieur Nourbarian speeding southwards with the same intent and fortified by a large consignment of fine furs. Kamran's mother was not one to let such an occasion pass and had obtained at bargain rates the sort of fur wrap she believed would be suitable wear for the journey to Constantinople, the chill nights on board, the treacherous climate of the Bosphorus and its social distractions.

As things turned out, the coat (Persian lamb, trimmed with ermine, and made up while waiting for a boat at Odessa), had been no use, for the departure had been more tricky than anticipated. Crawling under some barbed wire behind the harbour, the coat had become inextricably hooked and, after desperate struggles, Kamran's mother had been thankful to be cut free with a pair of nail scissors and to proceed without it.

'Who cut her free? Papasha? Was she with Papasha?' I pressed, believing I had stumbled on another piece of the jigsaw. But Kamran was vague on that essential point. He had run across Monsieur Nourbarian again by chance but the furrier appeared to cherish a warm regard for the son of his former client, 'so elegant a lady, of such rich taste'. He was now happy to offer Kamran hospitality of the nature he sought.

Southern climes had impressed their ardours on Monsieur Nourbarian. He found it the most natural thing in the world for Kamran and me to spend long afternoons in the back room. Here on a springy couch consisting of a heap of rather rank third-rate pelts, lamb and fox, we resumed our ghost-ridden romance while Monsieur Nourbarian, all understanding, would put up the shutters and hang a notice on the door saying CLOSED OWING TO SUDDEN DECEASE. This device came to be used so regularly that Monsieur Nourbarian appeared to be in a perpetual state of bereavement, and at last the sign lost all meaning for his few customers or those idle friends who were forever dropping in.

They would batter on the door, shouting jovially, 'Hey! Armin Nikolaivitch! Here we are! Don't keep us waiting! We know what you're up to all right!' And Monsieur Nourbarian, revelling in a borrowed aura of intrigue, would tip-toe down the *colimaçon* stairs from his room above, his collar and tie loosened suggestively, his sallow face oiled over with smiles, a finger on his lips, to admit his visitors, and with a comprehensive shrug indicate the romantic situation, which might be taken to involve either himself or some unrevealed Paolo and Francesca.

Stretched on the pelts and surrounded by dusty scraps of fur and paper patterns we watched, with some apprehension, the frowzy velvet curtains which divided our hide-out from the shop billowing with each fresh arrival. The atmosphere was not conducive to the softer passions and soon we were quarrelling once more. This was no substitute for Gallantry Bower, and we both knew it.

Sometimes, overcoming my opposition, Kamran would try out his own make-believe. Hauling the sheepskins over us like a stifling wigwam, he would say: 'This is dog-sledge. We are crossing frozen river' or 'Now we are in Trans-Siberian train...' But it was no good, for I knew, and he knew, he had never travelled on the legendary train and could tell me nothing about it that I did not already know. It held no significance for him – certainly none of those mystical attributes with which I had invested it; for him, it was only a way of pleasing me, part of a ritual that his father had liked to follow, and so he endeavoured to do likewise. Soon a shadow would fall between us and we were quarrelling again. But Kamran knew very well how to make up, and in his most wheedling manner he would say:

'Mamasha darling, don't you want that I love you in hut in *taïga?*'

How close the echoes: almost the same voice, almost the same question. The rank sheepskin gloom gave place to the scented green twilight of the maquis where one star shone overhead... a star that had not granted my wish. I knew now that I should never make the journey on the Trans-Siberian with the Traveller... Yet his whisper sounded down the years:

'*Pussinka moiya*, don't you want to be loved in a Mongolian *yurt?*'

I sat up and pushed the sheepskins away, demolishing Kamran's hut in the *taïga*. But he pulled me down again, laughing, loving, teasing, beguiling.

'No *taïga?* O.K., anywhere you are saying, only not so cross-looking, Mamasha *moiya*.'

It was easier to lie there listening to the soft Slav syllables, catching sometimes the echoes of another, dearer voice.

~

As time passed, the strain of material conditions and frequent separations told on our relationship. Our quarrels were more frequent, our happiness more rare. I found myself resenting my lost journey to Siberia. I had given up the substance for the shadow; or perhaps one shadow had been sacrificed to another.

In my heart I believed Kamran could have told me something of his father's fate or whereabouts. But he was vehement in his denials.

'I am telling to you, he just vanish like that! For me, too. My mother is dead. I don't know more to tell. He never coming to see her either. Always you were the lucky. How much I am thinking to find him too.'

But this I doubted. Kamran was a possessive lover. Even a ghost tormented him. He would not have been prepared to relinquish me, now; not even to the father of whom he had stood in such awe.

'And Sergei?' I would needle him, harping on the family. 'I always had a weakness for Sergei... Perhaps Sergei will come back one of these days, looking for you – after all, you're his half-brother.'

'Come back – why he come back? To what person? We was different families. His mother Georgian. Mine Kirghiz. I think he went in South America to become gigolo.'

'You've got it wrong. That's where they came from.'

'So, why speaking of Sergei now? Why thinking of him like he is in Siberia with Papasha, perhaps, and you go there and find them. Me – I am not enough?'

He stormed at me, young, urgent and brutal in his desires, and indeed for a while Kamran was all.

But neither of us could long forget the link which had brought us together, and now, kept us together long after we should have parted.

I had become a double prisoner, of memory and the flesh: and when at last the means and the permits to make the ardently desired Trans-Siberian journey seemed likely to materialize, I backed out. Kamran could not go with me. He had no money, no permits, no regular passport. And I could not leave him. Kamran at his most seducing had wound himself round my heart, and so, enmeshed in loving, I let the journey go.

~

Kamran the Asiatic could be cruel. In his possessive moods he displayed a sure aim, as if, galloping across the Gobi on his shaggy Mongol pony, he had pierced my heart with a lance and gone on with his white teeth that were so unmistakably Asiatic, so much part of his heritage. After one of our more stormy meetings, he struck:

'How much strange,' he said, his dark face carved into a mask of malice, 'how you still thinking about Papasha, still loving him much, after many years... I think when you was together, he was still feeling very very in love with your mother.'

I was too much taken aback to feign awareness, indifference.

'You not knowing? Is it possible? Why he was terrible in love with her. Long, long time ago... in Normandy or somewhere... Aunt Eudoxia tell me. So they never tell you? I am thinking when she marrying with someone else, and time going on, and he losing her, he begin to find some her in you... And then, you loving him so strong, and losing him, you finding something like him, in me... It is making the circle – so – isn't it?'

I could not reply. I did not know what was Kamran's malice or spiteful invention, and what was truth. I was never to know.

~

Gradually the gaps between my visits to Paris lengthened. There were distractions in London. Kamran was sinking back into his old habits of rootless apathy, reverting perhaps to his Kirghiz ancestry or grubbing along in the old student pattern of disorder and fecklessness. When I chided him he shrugged with fatalism.

'How you expecting me to find fortune here? Where? Tell me! And for what I make fortune? For you, perhaps? For you to go and buy ticket for Siberia for finding Papasha? Yes?' His voice was unusually bitter. Lately he had seemed too apathetic to care about anything, personal relationships, or even ghosts. I remembered the Traveller's words, 'emotions need feeding'. Kamran often went hungry.

But abruptly all was changed. With the offer of a job in Germany an unwonted energy transformed him.

'In Germany? You can't be thinking of accepting!'

'Why not? It's very important architects people. They are building much now. And they pay me good. No work, no fortune here. And you, Mamasha, you always saying you hate to be living in Paris.'

'But Germany,' I repeated, stunned. 'Nazi Germany! I wouldn't set foot in the loathsome place.'

'I am not asking you to put your feet there,' replied Kamran, working up to a fury which was met by fury.

Soon after I returned to London, while Kamran left for Berlin. I was never to see him again; the war took care of that. Like his father, he vanished from my sight – yet he, too, remained in my heart – echo of an echo...

PART SEVEN

THE JOURNEY DONE

The whole seems to fall into shape
As if I saw alike my work and self
And all that I was born to be and do.
A twilight piece . . .
So free we seem, so fettered fast we are!

Robert Browning

CHAPTER TWENTY

London in wartime: now the Run-Away Game was replaced by hide-and-seek with bombs. Shelters, sirens, gas-masks and black-outs – such was the texture of daily life. The war gathered momentum. London was full of Allied troops, strange uniforms and languages, each man making the most of his brief leaves, enthusiastically aided by Englishwomen, a number of whom had travelled little or not at all before the war and now discovered some of its joys without leaving home. Poles, Czechs, Belgians, Dutch, Norwegians, Yugoslavs, the Americans, the Free French, all were among us... But no Russians. Once, once only, I sighted three dashing figures, some military delegation I supposed, in the familiar long grey overcoats, high boots and fur caps. They were striding up and down under the arcades of the Ritz as I was coming out. Through the revolving doors I saw them and, goggling, went round and round with the doors, rotating in a sort of treadmill of longing, at each turn feasting my eyes on this hallucinatory vision. Alas! They were joined by a chunky-shaped civilian who shepherded them into a War Office car which shot away leaving me bereft.

~

Long ago, one of my Russian friends from the old days in Paris – was it Vassili, Mistislav, Nicolai, Boris, or Dimitri – had said 'You must only marry Slavs. Only they will suit you. Make you happy? That's another thing. No one but a Russian will provide you with the *extravagant* emotional climate you want. Only our sort of natures – people call them unstable, chaotic – but always vibrant, will satisfy you. A romantic English love would be too composed. Latins? Too facile. French? Too self-conscious about loving – too organized about living.' Now the words came back to me, but were soon forgotten, for those were not marrying times, I thought.

But on a night made restless by incessant bombing, at a party for Free French airmen on leave in London, I observed one of them who seemed rather aloof from the rest. He was sitting in a corner, hunched over a bowl of salted almonds, which he was attacking with concentration. At that time salted almonds were an exotic rarity and I saw our hostess casting anguished glances in his direction. Something in his long dark brooding face seemed familiar, yet I could not place him, nor imagine where I had seen him before. Our party exploded into a night-club and still the singular stranger baffled me until, listening to his voice, his boot-deep tones, beneath the wail of the saxophones, I suddenly realized he was Russian. The sombre features were those of an ikon, the voice unmistakably that of a Slav. Free-French or no, this man was a Russian. Wearing the identical blue uniform of his *copains* he remained irrevocably Slav. I was not deceived. A year later we were married – in a Registry Office. Once again the golden crowns of the Orthodox Church had eluded me. But no passports, no Free French uniform or decorations could make my husband a Frenchman, any more than my newly-acquired nationality could make me a Frenchwoman. Changelings we both remained, and for a time well matched.

As a child of exile he had grown up in France, subjected to his mother's passionate conviction that France was all. Over the years I watched him striving to absorb and be absorbed by a country which, psychologically, could never be truly his, while I strove to preserve in him the eternal Slav I craved.

He had been moulded by the will of his mother to become a Frenchman, and now he encountered my determination to retrace our steps eastward into my own chimera and the profound roots of his nature.

~

As the years passed we settled and unsettled ourselves about the world, for my husband was now in the French Diplomatic Service, but I still gravitated towards everything and everybody Slav, and fostered the habits of domestic Russian living to which both of us were accustomed. Successive glasses of tea and salted cucumber punctuated the day, although our habit of sitting for a long moment in silence, on the threshold of our home, before leaving for a journey, a traditional Russian observance, was apt to make the drive to the airport or station a tense race against time. I still sometimes succumbed to the tyranny of the *domovoi* and surreptitiously left provisions for him by the door, and when we had Slav-born servants this was always understood. There were other nationalities who came and went in our kitchen, but I do not recall them: they played no part in my life, as did the Slavs.

They come back to me as I write. Maddening, lovable, funny, and often pathetic creatures, making uproars and *blini* with equal ease; imposing their family dramas, recounting singular episodes of their past, of long ago and far away, of the Ukraine, the Macedonian mountains or those Caucasian fastnesses which were so much part of my mind's eye. Generally, it seemed. they had survived unimaginable trials, being harassed, if not regularly raped, by Cossacks, Turks, Bashi-Bazouks or Kurds.

Such sagas made all the difference to daily life; and there was, I believed, some current of understanding which flowed between myself and all the Slavs who worked for me. Perhaps it was because they never bored me, however much they tried my patience by their inefficiency. Sometimes I hit them, but this was accepted in the light of a colloquial gesture rather than an act of violence; I was, in fact, talking their language. They were not the kind of domestics, nor did they have the training customary to those obtained through Registry Offices.

However much in moments of social stress I believed I wished for those discreet, efficient figures who are the image of a good servant, I knew that I could not have endured their conventions any more than they would have tolerated my ways. Even if you come by this archaic breed, to keep them you must live in the traditional pattern which suits them. Our habit of writing half the night and requiring meals on trays at unpredictable hours in equally erratic settings, so that a roast might be enjoyed in the bedroom or a yoghourt and black coffee at the dining-room table, was something which the more bourgeois hirelings always found unacceptable.

'You'll never get good service if you don't dress for dinner,' a shrewd old lady once told me. 'And by that I don't mean *dressing-up*,' she added, deploring my weakness for exotic costumes. But, in the matters of the exotical, I was out-done by the kitchen, where crude ikons were propped among the saucepans and the preparation of every dish was accompanied by incantations or imprecations of an ecclesiastical flavour, all the Saints of the Orthodox Calendar being summoned round the stove, with a smack of magic added. Sometimes these incantations were of a markedly poetic nature, beginning and ending ritualistically, as they had been handed down, generation by generation, the length and breadth of peasant Russia: 'I, servant of God, Marfa Petrovna' (or whoever voiced the spell) always prefaced each specific incantation, which was likely to bear on the rising of a soufflé or the expulsion of some insect plague. The ending was always the same. 'I, servant of God, Marfa Petrovna, will bend myself like the young moon. May my words be strong, be powerful! Here be lock and key on my words. Amen! Amen!'

The last phrase was accompanied by the pantomime of turning a key in the lock. After which it seemed the matter swung between God and the Devil and nothing had been left to chance.

Such local colour was deepened by bunchy aprons, heads tied up in gaudy kerchiefs and feet as bare as they had been in the *izbas* of their origin. Sometimes, catching sight of them padding across the parquets, linoleums or moquettes of urban living, I saw instead the rich black earth of the endless steppes, and knew how idle it would be to imagine such feet could be crammed into shoes, any more than the big fist now proffering the *kasha* and mushrooms could ever be encased in gloves. But I welcomed the spectrum of local colour which the Slavs imposed and I was grateful for their special quality of warmth; it was the cosy glow of some traditional family *nianya* – the Russian family into which, by some mischance, I had not been born.

Marfa, Anna, Liouba, Natasha... the bright-coloured figures, toddling like Matrioshka dolls, gather again as I write. Katyusha getting out of her own warm bed to bring me *borshch*, when I had been writing far into the night. Liouba lingering to talk, taking a robust enjoyment in describing how the Cossacks had swept down on her village – how, searching for an escaped criminal in the name of the Tzar, they had ransacked the place and, of course, raped her elder sister, a cousin, and her mother. Liouba, flinging herself at the chest of drawers and hurling the contents to the ground as, with an imaginary sword, she turned over the dishevelled heaps of my stockings and underwear and pantomimed the repeated rapes with graphic gestures.

'Barinya! They were devils! Terrible devils! Bad people! But so handsome! So strong! Such *men!*'

She melted at the memory and looking out of the window on the perspectives of civilization, spat angrily.

Masha, describing street-corner dentistry in the Tashkent of her childhood, where the Uzbegs hung their extracted teeth on the tombs of saints as votary offerings. Irina, explaining the intricacies of her

Finnish-Tungus ancestry, while telephones shrilled unattended or I answered them absently, for with such counter-attractions at hand all else paled.

Raiina telling my favourite story of her Don Juan uncle and the Tzigane dancing bear which mauled his fiancée.

'Ah! Gospodja! If you had seen my uncle Pencho when he heard the news! She was the fiancée he didn't want to marry, if you remember Gospodja?'

'Perfectly. Do go on.'

'Well, my mother sent me running off to tell Uncle. I found him at the inn, behind the Rose Mosque... I remember he gave me a whole *leva* – that was quite a lot of money then. We had a party that night. Everyone in our street came. The wedding was put off, of course. Tears of joy ran down Bai Pencho's face. *How happy we all were!* Uncle danced till morning! Ratchinitzas! Horos! The Wedding Horo! All the dances you love, Gospodja.'

Twirling a kitchen cloth she performs a few ritualistic steps.

'So what happened?' I ask, forgetting to reprimand her for having short-changed me over the fuel bill.

But this is what Raiina has been counting on; now she can finish the story comfortably. She squats on her hunkers, smiling her broad, flat smile. 'Well, they put the Tzigane in prison – because it was his bear, and he hadn't watched what it was doing...'

'And then?'

'Then they put the bear in the Zoo. But he was so unhappy without the Tzigane he wouldn't eat and lost his fur, so they decided to lock the Tzigane up with the bear, in the cage. The bear was happy. So was the Tzigane. He got regular meals, he didn't have to work and he was out of doors. Tziganes can't live indoors, you know. They kept each other warm at night too... Everybody used to go and see them and push food through the bars. Sometimes we took flowers for the Tzigane, because the bear smelt rather strong. We would have taken cigarettes but he wasn't allowed to smoke. After all, he was in prison,' she adds primly.

Once again I am spellbound, accepting every shortcoming.

~

Old Katerina exercised a particularly potent charm, for she had lived in Siberia, which of course compensated for almost every lapse. 'Ah! *Priroda! Krassivaya priroda!*' Nature! Beautiful nature! 'What beauty in the Siberian countryside!' the sly old thing would say, knowing I cared more to hear about the Siberian landscape than laundry problems. 'Such air! Siberian air... it smells of mushrooms and apples... And at night – the moonlight over the snow...!' She was off, waxing lyrical to distract me from her lapses.

Now I am in one of the many ill-equipped kitchens of the leased houses in which we lived. I am trying to ensure that eight people who will soon be arriving for dinner will be well fed. Katerina is at her most inept today, standing the white wine near the stove under the impression it should be *chambré*: on the other hand I have just rescued the Bordeaux from the refrigerator. Someone has sent me a bunch of lilac and, as I arrange it, my mind crosses continents and seas to a lilac thicket in Koursk... Koursk, where the celebrated Fair is held the tenth week after Easter, or so *Murray's Guide Book* said in 1893... Koursk, where my husband's family once lived; but Romain can tell me nothing of it; his is not the backward glance. He finds no fascination in those accounts of provincial life by nineteenth-century Russian writers which are my passion and my drug. Now Katerina is trying to distract my attention from the butter which she has left in the westering sun, so that it is a rancid pool. She knows exactly how to proceed with this manoeuvre.

'When we travelled on the Trans-Siberian train,' she says importantly, 'I kept the milk in a bag, outside the window. When we needed some, we chipped off a piece... And where I taught school,' she adds hurriedly, seeing my eye still fixed angrily on the butter-pool, 'there was only one W.C. for the whole street. At night we used to go along to it wrapped in bear-skins. From our house it was quite a long walk.'

Above the clatter of the saucepans I hear the rattle of chains as the convicts crawl across the prison yard... My steam-filled kitchen fades, dissolving into a snowy waste... Siberia! SIBERIA!

Suddenly I am Albina Megouria, the Siberian heroine. I have followed my husband to some forgotten outpost, sharing his sentence. My two children die but I live on, for him, for the day when I can achieve his escape... I plan, I wait... I am crafty in my loving. I have perfected my plan and contrived to hide my husband in a crate which everyone believes to contain the children's coffins. The long journey begins... day and night, over the boundless snowy tracks, a white world of silence and dread. Only one Cossack guard accompanies me, for a widow-woman with her children's coffins is not much to bother about. We reach the frontier post too late to cross that night but, beyond, I see the glimmer of the little town where I shall be free... where my husband can rejoin me, where we can turn westward, towards a new life together... The Cossack climbs stiffly down from his horse; I offer him a drink at the *traktir*. As he crosses the yard, Bijou, my little dog, whom I have kept close to me all the way, slips the leash and bounds towards the crate. Frisking and yapping, Bijou proclaims to all the posting house that there is something of interest, something he knows well, inside the crate. The Cossack guard turns back from the door of the inn to see what all the noise is about...

The door bell shatters this dramatic reverie... 'My little God! The guests!' says Katerina, crossing herself as she takes a look at the roast. Laboriously, I return from Siberia, from inhabiting the body of Albina Megouria and go to welcome my guests. Eight *doushi* – eight souls, says Katerina picturesquely: ten, with ourselves. With four courses and all those glasses, I calculate the washing up will go on far into the night. The hireling help will leave early and Katerina will give notice once again.

The Traveller used to say we all made far too much fuss about washing up in London. Nomad Mongolians, he said, just licked their plates clean. I wonder how such a suggestion would be received by the company.

~

Perhaps one of the least considered aspects of diplomatic life – of life *en poste* in an Embassy – is the strain imposed on the digestion, until either ulcers prevail, a state proclaimed by the number of pill-boxes placed beside the diner's plate, or by a resistance, which once reached, might be described as a variation of Diplomatic Immunity. Invitations to an endless round of complicated meals are interspersed by a mosaic of cocktail parties, the whole structure assuming infinite intricacy and preserving a curiously early nineteenth-century flavour, harking back to the days of Talleyrand and Metternich when diplomacy was indeed conducted across the dinner-tables of Europe, a sort of bickering family party where Africa, America, and much of Asia simply did not enter into anyone's calculations. Congress waltzed in Vienna, and for a century afterwards inside information continued to be obtained via the key-hole, rather than some electronic device. But now that politicians – and even Heads of State – are jet-propelled backwards and forwards in time and space, making and, unmaking treaties as soon as they land (after journeys from which doctors assure us, the human system needs thirty-six hours before returning to normal) there really seems nothing left for the professional diplomats to do – except eat. So back to the dinner-tables.

Like the diplomatic menus (which seldom retain an interesting national flavour and follow the sole, chicken and profiterole circuit), *placement* inclines to monotony. But this is due not so much to any lack of imagination or social daring as to the implacable rulings of protocol. One does not trifle with protocol. Thus, unless there was some new blood of a corresponding ranking, I would constantly find myself allotted the same dinner-partner, until, over a season, this began to assume almost matrimonial status. Having once found a topic of mutual interest such as I recall doing at one post with the Albanian Minister (our topic generally being Bashi-Bazouks), we were able to resume our conversation each evening at the point where we had left it the previous night. And were some passing visitor suddenly to replace the familiar figure at my side, it lent all the zest of bigamy to the evening.

~

Wherever we went, the snow-bound horizons of my inward-turning eye remained the preoccupation of my life. No place, no person changed this. Abroad or at home (and with our years of wandering the two became indistinguishable) I was for ever seeking my elective affinity, listening, below the overtones of daily life, for some ghostly Slavic cadence: the bells, sounding from Kitej, perhaps. Once, these overtones sounded loud and clear, becoming the tune to which I danced for two halcyon years. This was while Romain and I were *en poste* at the French Legation in Sofia.

Bulgaria! The coloured wings of love and perhaps illusion, for they go together, are, for me, for ever spread round this country where I was so happy. Bulgaria was the archetypal Balkan country; itself, and yet more than half-way to Russia. The desired horizons came closer: here I found echoes, or rather, transpositions of the beloved.

Beautiful, haunting, Bulgaria! I have never been back. I am told that the Black Sea coast we knew as a deserted paradise is now teeming with giant hotels. Do the summer visitors ever go inland, deep inland, to Tirnova, the old capital, to the Pachmakli and the heart of the country I knew so well, that cost me so dearly to leave, that I remember with love, with tears? I write of Bulgaria with such emotion because, although it was not part of my whole life, as Russia, it was part of my heart, and has remained so.

~

Wherever I went – in the New World, as in the old – East, West, New York, Mexico, I would catch myself still wondering if, one day, the Traveller would appear, djinn-like, as in my nursery. Magic of magics! Would I find him sitting opposite me in the Brooklyn subway? Or would he be the driver of some Tunisian *fiacre*, that I hailed at the Bab Souika? Would he be stooping to peer at me impudently, below the canopy, his sly slit eyes glinting with malicious amusement at the trick? Would I recognize him among the Indians of Guatemala, pacing with the stone-faced Quichés at some religious festival? Would his face be glimpsed there, wreathed in the eddies of copal-smoke from some Pagan altar? No: this was not his setting. Neither the High Sierras nor the Deep South, nor the pagodas of Bangkok or the deserts of Arabia were his: though I thought he could be in Asiatic, Moslem Russia, in Bokhara, or a village in the Pamirs, perhaps. And when I reached Samarkand and installed myself in some *tchai-hana* where, beneath gigantic plane trees, I drank bowls of green tea and watched the sun slanting low over the turquoise minarets, he seemed very close. I recalled how he would quote Gérard de Nerval's *Voyage en Orient*, where the author deliberates, voluptuously, on where best to pass his declining years...

'*Oui, soyons jeunes en Europe tant que nous le pouvons, mais allons vieillir en Orient, le pays des hommes dignes de ce nom, la terre des patriarches...*' The passage goes on to deplore the increasing equality of the sexes in the West so that, for men, it was already becoming a lost battle for supremacy. The Frenchman toyed with the idea of retreating to the East: '*il faut que je m'unisse à quelque fille ingénue de ce sol sacré qui est notre première patrie à tous...*' 'Life-giving', 'reviving', 'poetic'... he waxes lyrical over the East but I fancy it was the *fille ingénue* of whom he was thinking: which was probably why the passage remained one of the Traveller's favourite quotations.

In my turn, as I came to travel more widely, I too fell under the spell of Islam. For me, the traditional ways of Moslem life, like its beliefs and traditions and trimmings, were all infinitely seductive, all beauty and harmony. From Turkey to the Sahara by way of the Middle East and Central Asia, the various Arab and Moslem civilizations held me in thrall. Gradually they merged into one fixed star, a glow to which I turned, and return, whenever I can. But Russia has remained the Pole-star by which I chart expeditions, both about the horizon of my mind or in the flesh: all else remain sorties from base.

And, in spite of Gérard de Nerval, I still believed the Traveller had turned northwards; I thought he would be somewhere along the mysterious frontiers of Outer Mongolia and Siberia; and there I knew my longings would at last bring me.

~

Meanwhile, there was America: or rather, the Americas, for there were as many as All the Russias of my mind's eye. In the United States, where we lived for several years, I found many Russians absorbed, in particular, into the mosaic of New York life. Gradually, the centre of émigré gravity had shifted west across the Atlantic. Writers, the world of ballet and musicians, were now centred there, as once in Paris. But it was another ambiance to that of the original exiles I had known. The succeeding generation, and those who had adapted successfully to the American pulse – whether a cross-section of the intelligentsia, professors, princes from St. Petersburg, musicians or Jewish furriers from the Pale – all had become competitive. Here, no one drifted; few Oblomovs survived in the New World any more than in the new Russia of the Soviet Union.

The Russians of New York City were a less closely-knit colony than in Paris, having become more truly absorbed. The American melting pot is a powerful dip. There were, however, two groups which remained comparatively unaffected, putting their separate ideologies above personal advancements. On the East Side, the Soviet Delegation to the United Nations went about their work aloof; on the West Side, the offices of the Tolstoy Foundation cared for the old or needy and those of their compatriots who had fallen by the way.

Since everything concerning Tolstoy has always seemed to me in the nature of a sacred revelation, my meetings with his daughter, the

Countess Alexandra, were, to me, the confrontation with an oracle, and the modest little Japanese restaurant off Broadway where we met became a temple. Bowls of green tea and mysterious dishes of seaweed assumed mystical properties, as I listened to her memories of the gigantic figure who had dominated her life. This heroic woman was created in the same mould; burly, with her father's bumpy potato features and the same small penetrating eyes that radiated goodness, understanding and intellect. In spite of a shapeless old overcoat and an equally battered fur cap stuck anyhow on her grey head, she had the same air of high breeding which struck everyone who met Tolstoy, the *barin*, the *seigneur*, disguised in peasant clothes.

'So you know his daughter Alexandra?' said a Soviet delegate to the United Nations, at a New York dinner-table; and he looked severe as he spoke of the Countess Alexandra's 'bigoted views' and her work, heading the Tolstoy Foundation, for which he had no sympathy.

'She is our enemy, you know,' he added. And we both smiled. As if any child of Tolstoy's could be regarded as an enemy of any Russian, anywhere.

~

The threads of Russian life that were interwoven in America sometimes glittered, and sometimes barely gleamed. Every encounter with Russians – even those of New York's café society – held the promise of some peculiar significance. Similarly, I searched, and sometimes found, reflections, or cadences of my elective affinities in the most unlikely places such as Los Angeles, at Hollywood and Vine.

Driving along Sunset Boulevard towards down-town Los Angeles – the *wrong* end of Sunset I was often reminded by those who had never been there – I discovered a forgotten quarter of modest little streets and gardens isolated by two great sweeping free-ways. Here a small Russian colony lived lives as by-passed as this section.

The grocery store, the watch-mender and the laundry signs read – 'Popoff's Great-Guy Groceries', 'Sosnovsky's Snow-White Washings', and '*Shtochass* Watch Repairs' – this latter I particularly enjoyed for, literally, '*shtochass*' in Jewish-Russian patois reads 'what o'clock'. The snug little shacks and bungalows, each with their porch with its rocker and tea-table adorned by a large samovar, were gathered round a diminutive Russian village church with stumpy pillars framing the porch and a toy-like belfry, where one large, out-of-scale bell clanged assiduously. Giant sunflowers rose above the low white palings and, for me, it was the Ukraine. On Sundays, after mass, the bearded, long-maned Pope and his flock gathered in a large whitewashed room, a sort of parish hall. The samovars steamed valiantly, misting the glass over large portraits of the last Tzar and Pushkin. This was a Hollywood interior with figures, a little-known one, which I remember as fondly as all the turquoise swimming-pools, the flood-lit palms and extravagant households of Beverley Hills which I enjoyed so greatly during the four years my husband and I lived in Los Angeles.

At that time I was writing *The Sabres of Paradise*, gnawing away at the dry bones of Arabic transcriptions or ferreting out some obscure detail of Russian-Caucasian warfare. Romain, having captured the *Prix Goncourt* with his *Racines du Ciel*, had just completed *Lady L.*, and was plunging into *La Promesse de L'Aube*. It was a busy and productive time for both of us. Brews of tea succeeded each other and cups of black coffee and chocolate, Romain's favourite stimuli at that time, were dispersed about, or upset, among cushions and piles of manuscripts balanced on sofas and chairs. Outside, the humming-birds darted and zoomed about the terrace, dive-bombing the flowering vines, and were watched longingly by our cats. Over all, recordings of Caucasian or Arabic music (to which I liked to write) sometimes floated out, surprising those who came to the Consulate-General on French affairs.

One night, staying in a country house up the Hudson River, where so much of the landscape recalls the old estates and wide, still, river reaches of the Russian provinces, I tasted strangely exotic yet subtle food, unlike anything I had ever known. It was not, I thought, so much an unplaceable national cuisine as an evocation of a profound past, which stirred some atavistic memory I could not trace. Something with aubergine? With nutmeg, unnameable spices and cream... This was not *haute cuisine* as we generally know it: it was immensely intricate and yet bold. I tried again to analyse it. Here was suavity and opulence too, without in any way being the cuisine of stuffed peacocks and *pièces montées*.

'Ah! that is Vassili's secret,' said the Princess, my hostess. 'He has been with us ever since he left Russia, during the Revolution. He was a kitchen-boy at the Winter Palace... He must have learned all sorts of curious dishes there.' She added that he seldom admitted anyone to his kitchen, and preferred to work without assistance, jealously guarding his secrets.

For this was the cuisine of Byzantium, no less.

When, later, I was fortunate enough to be admitted to his confidence, and saw the old man among his pots and pans I knew that I was in fact watching some of the last rituals of the Paleologi palaces. No doubt much of the Russian Imperial cuisine derived, like their Court ceremonial, from Byzantium, being originally transported to the Kremlin (along with the double-headed eagle and the first roses), by the Paleologi princess Zoë, become Tzarina Sophia.

Thus echoes of that Russia which was both my city and my solitude sounded for me even in the New York of the nineteen-fifties.

CHAPTER TWENTY ONE

The Traveller's last letter had said: 'Granting our wishes is one of Fate's saddest jokes,' and so it seemed, for only when my marriage broke up was I at last able to make the long-desired Siberian journey. Since I was no longer anchored to any person or any place, and the Siberian spell still held, I turned northward. Now, as if in a mood of conciliation, Fate made everything easy. All the difficulties which had impeded me for so long melted away; all that had been unrealizable was suddenly within reach.

'You *want* to go by train?' they asked me at the Intourist Travel Bureau in Paris, fearing the blasé western visitor would find the immense journey – the longest train journey in the world – tedious.

'But from Moscow you can fly to Irkutsk in eight hours.'

I know. I know: and the train takes five days and another three and a half on to Vladivostok. A whole week... a whole week on the Trans-Siberian train – on *my* train, our Gallantry Bower that should have been... No, I shall not find it tedious. *Païdium!* Let's go,' I said, and they did not argue any more.

~

Over the years when I had planned and replanned this journey, I had seen myself making it exactly as the Traveller had done when he used to vanish from my nursery. For him, it had begun at Dover, and from Paris he had taken the North Express, via Berlin, and the Russian frontier at Wirballen, to St. Petersburg, from there reaching Moscow and the Trans-Siberian train. He never went direct to Moscow, by the Paris-Warsaw line. 'No one goes direct to Moscow,' he said scornfully, dismissing the Warsaw-Moscow route as the merchants' way. The North Express linked Paris and St. Petersburg directly and was, he explained, considered the only way to travel to and from Western Europe. Besides – even people who didn't live in St. Petersburg preferred to go through the capital, see their friends, the ballet, and hear what was going on...

The North Express had a cachet all its own. Its character was entirely different to that of other celebrated trains, the Orient Express, or of course, the Trans-Siberian; it had neither the reputation for intrigue which coloured the former, nor that odd mixture of drama and monotony peculiar to the latter. It was regarded by its regular passengers as a kind of exclusive club on wheels, where the attendants, like faithful club servants, studied each passenger's whims. 'Everyone knew everyone else, the food and wines were excellent – yes, there was nothing like it anywhere else,' he concluded nostalgically. But I was never tempted away from the Trans-Siberian chimera and now, eager to hasten this longed-for consummation, I cheated, flying from Paris to Moscow via Prague, thus sacrificing something of the gathering momentum the gigantic journey deserved, and which even the despised Moscow-merchants' route would have provided.

Not that the plane – a Russian jet – lacked atmosphere; drama, even. A victorious football team were returning home in triumph and, ignoring the customary injunctions about safety belts, which indeed no one had reminded us to fasten, immediately plunged into a recapitulation of the match, tackling exuberantly as we shot aloft. A massive carved side-board, baronial-Kremlin in style, blocked one end of the plane and on it glasses of tea and a large samovar shifted uneasily, while a loud-speaker relayed folk-songs. Early descriptions of Russian trains (no doubt not including the North Express) always told of samovars and tea-tumblers rattling ceaselessly to the rhythm of the wheels, while passengers turned corridors and dining-cars upside down stamping wildly to the accompaniment of accordions and balalaikas. Russian jet travel, I perceived, maintained these characteristics.

That night, in Prague, I crossed the statue-lined bridge to wander about the old town. The Street of the Necromancers (where, so long ago, the Traveller had assured me I would find spells to wing me to Siberia) was shuttered and deserted. The few shadowy figures that flitted, furtively I thought, from one ill-lit alley to the next, were each Cagliostro, the Golem, or Nostradamus casting those spells in which I had believed so ardently, as a child; and perhaps, still did. 'Black Magic or White? You must believe in one or the other, or else this world is far too finite.' The Traveller had said this as he lit a candle before some wonder-working ikon in the Rue Daru. Which magic, I wondered, was at last granting my wish; was now winging me towards Siberia? I willed my gratitude towards both shrines.

~

Next morning, flying over the rain-sodden plains of the Russian frontier zones I shut my eyes, the better to concentrate on the great train that awaited me in the Yaroslavsky Voxal – 'the Siberian station' – where I used to stand yearning at the barrier. Soon, I too would be one of that purposeful throng surging on to the platform; soon I would be settling into my compartment – my world for a week. 'O fair house of joy and bliss!'

The plane tilted steeply, and beyond the wide wing span I saw the silvery loops of a river, spinach green clumps of forest, straggling, toy-like villages, and here and there, the blue or gold onion-dome of a little lost church, a pin's head, marking the map-like expanses. Russia once more.

And Moscow again. My taxi sped away from the airport through fine but characterless avenues of new housing developments and, suddenly, the Kremlin rose before me in all its barbaric beauty. The spectacle never palled, always intoxicated anew. 'Innumerable circumstances concur to give to Moscow an Asiatic air beyond any Town I ever saw,' wrote Miss Wilmot, a century and a half ago, in a letter home, extolling 'the glittering crescents beneath the Cross... Globes of Gold blazing among the Sunshine... Gaudy Belfries... stupendous Palaces guarded by roaring Monsters.'

A fair description of the Kremlin, even now.

~

'In Russia, it is always the unexpected which prevails,' wrote another, less enraptured visitor. And so I was to find it, on the threshold of my Siberian odyssey. The train was due to leave on a Friday night and I had arrived at the Yaroslavsky station in a mood of mystical fulfilment. All day I had told myself – still incredulous – *'Tonight I shall sleep on the Trans-Sib! It has come to pass at last!'* At the station, puffs of smoke were lit by livid greenish lights which bleached the faces of the crowds converging on those barriers that now, at last, admitted me. Children wailed, unwieldy bundles of bedding were dragged through the throng; passengers reeled under loads of provisions, bulky paper parcels and string bags full of gigantic watermelons (No longer any peasant qualms about St. John the Baptist's severed head, I thought). Beside such baggage, my own, especially my dressing-case, looked startlingly streamlined, although in Western Europe and the United States, a particularly luggage-conscious community, it struck me as shabby. Chekhov had known how to travel light. When setting out for Sakhalin, to study conditions on the dread penitentiary isle off the north eastern Siberian coast, he had departed with a sheepskin coat, a pair of top boots, and a knife – 'to cut up sausages or kill tigers', and, we suppose, some writing materials, for he set down his grim findings at some length.

I was travelling soft, having stipulated a first-class compartment to myself. Seeing the third and fourth class carriages overflowing with humanity, I did not regret this indulgence, and shuddered remembering the Traveller's descriptions of conditions he had seen, in his youth, in the *fifth* class wagons, which had no windows, and one of the diversions had been betting on which flea or bug would cross a given line first – the race lit by a ha'penny dip. On my first journeys about the U.S.S.R. I had often travelled hard, in the most hugger-mugger manner, finding it enthralling – and clean enough – although on occasions I had the impression that the Traveller's shade did not share my enthusiasm, sometimes even abandoning me for the duration of a journey, and only reappearing, by his own djinn-like means, when our destination was reached.

But this journey was different – was *our* journey, to be made in conditions he would have approved, in first-class luxury, alone (or together) or not at all. I had promised myself that, as soon as I had settled the baggage into my compartment, I would walk the length of the platform to where the monster engine stood, fuming to be off. I wanted to see and remember every aspect of the train which had so long possessed me and which now, at last, I was to possess.

Every detail was to be studied lovingly: its carriage work, the look of the restaurant-car, the cook's galley, the peculiarities of the wheels, the pistons and the engine, its typical funnel-shaped stack, its buffers, and the faces of its crew; all must be imprinted in my mind's eye for ever. Like the place names of its route, running along its side – SVERDLOVSK – NOVOSIBIRSK – KRASNOYARSK – IRKUTSK – HARBIN – VLADIVOSTOK – everything was part of the magic. It was my bow of gold, my burning arrow of desire.

At the door of wagon No. 7 ('Seven, the mystic number of all Asia,' the Traveller's voice reminded me) a brown bear stood on its hind legs, a furled red flag tucked into its shaggy side. The guard, I supposed, finding it quite in keeping with my pumpkin coach. I placed my ticket in its outstretched paw, but alas! as it consulted the passenger list, it revealed a human face, and spoke, rather than growled. The full-length fur coat had misled me. It was to be the first of several deceptions.

I was now conducted to my compartment along a crimson-carpeted corridor, all burnished brass and dark woodwork, where already a small wood-stove crackled, heating up water for the samovars, and little shaded lamps burned cosily beside banquettes being made up into beds. This was as the Traveller had described it, and I felt him pushing me forward towards our Gallantry Bower.

Compartment A.14 said my ticket. 'In here,' said the porter, ripping open the door to reveal three ladies disposed about three of the four berths: two were already in various stages of déshabille. The porter asked forgiveness and edged my luggage in among them.

'No! No! There must be some mistake,' I said, my agitation mounting as several attendants now converged on the scene, countermanding my orders to move the baggage to the compartment reserved for me.

'But no one wants a whole compartment to themselves – not all across Siberia,' they said winningly. Speaking excellent French one of the ladies – the fully-dressed one – now introduced herself as my guide, to be attached to me throughout my journey.

'Please call me Olga,' she said. Fighting down my fury, I suppose I glowered, for the other two passengers appeared affronted.

'These are Cultured Citizens,' said Olga, making introductions in the silky manner of an accomplished hostess. I bowed. The ladies, already ensconced in the upper berths, smiled widely and bowed, spilling over the edge. But it made no difference. My whole plan lay in ruins. I had requested and, I thought, obtained a compartment to myself when, some weeks earlier, I had arranged the details of my journey in Paris. On arrival in Moscow I had understood all was in order, so that now I felt aggrieved.

I might have realized that I would not contrive to go to Siberia unaccompanied. It seemed that even the *wish* to go there was still suspect, or at least worthy of observation. My guide appeared an agreeable girl, in fact I could have taken a liking to her under other circumstances, but when, much later, we became friends, I learned that my favourable first impressions had not been reciprocated at the time. At that first meeting she had found me an extremely capricious, incomprehensible and indocile Capitalist figure. Moreover, she suffered from claustrophobia, and this interminable train journey represented, to her, unrelieved suffering. But she had her marching orders: 'Olga Maximova, accompany this visitor to Siberia.'

'You must find me another compartment at once,' I said firmly. But there was, it seemed, no other available.

Time was running short, I saw by the platform clock, and the brown bear began to show signs of agitation, looking anxiously from face to face as the arguments continued and I was being more firmly wedged into the compartment.

'Then I shall not go. Please get my stuff out of here at once!' I said, renouncing all Siberia with a wave of the hand; and I felt the Traveller's shade nudge me approvingly. (He was always a *scandalist*, Aunt Eudoxia had said.) But how could we have kept our tryst in a four-berth compartment crammed with ladies in pyjamas and hair nets, stoking boiled sweets?

Overcome with remorse at my seeming incivility, I now tried to draw the ladies into an all-embracing farewell smile.

'I'm afraid it wouldn't do for me to share with you – You see I have insomnia – I keep the light burning all night and play my radio – hot *jazzki*,' I said wildly, hoping to soften my rejection. Although my Russian was as rudimentary as ever, the ladies followed my trend and responded warmly.

One patted my hand: 'I too cannot sleep,' she said. 'We shall play chess all night long, all the way to Vladivostok.'

Clutching my dressing-case, I left the train.

Olga Maximova followed me hurriedly and now expressed the liveliest concern. Renouncing the journey? It was unheard of! 'But why do you not like to share a compartment? It is with *ladies*, after all.'

I said I would prefer gentlemen, at which piece of levity she shrugged off the struggle, reminding me that there might be no more places available on any Trans-Siberian train for weeks to come, and certainly no compartment to myself. My visa would expire while I waited... And as for tonight – since I had quit my hotel room and Moscow was full to overflowing, where would I sleep tonight?

'The lady might go on the Peking Express, the one that leaves on Tuesdays,' said the brown bear, taking his snout out of his fur collar, his little eyes bright with good-will. Ignoring the furious glances of Olga Maximova, he went on to say there were often whole compartments empty on that train.

'Only it goes on *Tuesdays*,' he added in a melancholy tone.

I pointed out that it was all the same to me, which day of the week I went to Siberia.

'Ah well! If you are prepared to leave on a Tuesday...' said Olga Maximova. Unexpectedly, she had now exchanged bureaucratic briskness for Chekhovian vagueness. But she promised to do her best for me. In her eyes, I think I had assumed a peculiar significance – that of some Capitalist cross which she must bear for the sake of her Communist faith. Besides, I was a visitor; and I have always found the Russian people most sweetly disposed towards the stranger in their midst.

Contrary to her predictions, I passed a comfortable night back in the hotel. No one had yet registered the fact of my departure; I took my key, went upstairs, exchanging the customary badinage with the two dragon-figures who were always presiding over the lobby, and finding my room in the disorder in which I had left it, fell back into the crumpled sheets in a mood of mixed triumph and anti-climax. Once again, the Trans-Siberian train had eluded me, but I had not betrayed the Traveller's tryst.

~

Although I was irked by this turn of events, I abandoned myself, with a certain sense of adventure, to the three extra days in Moscow. There is a secret pleasure attendant on *missing* a scheduled departure, for the unexpected hours suddenly at our disposal come as some bonus, uncharted hours, stolen from orderly living to be enjoyed with the sharpened sense of unreality. The heightened colours of this sudden vision make us aware of how much we take for granted ordinarily. Now, while we should be many miles away, we return like revenants, to familiar scenes; or to search out places and people which pressures of time denied us earlier. Now, perhaps, we lie again in the lover's arms after all the farewells had been said, living a whole romantic episode anew... meeting, loving, leaving, all over again.

In my own case, there was now time to search out an old friend, one of the exiles I had first known in Paris, beside the Traveller, and who, I learned, had returned to the country of her birth. I believed she might have been able to tell me something of the Traveller's whereabouts, but I had never succeeded in tracing her during my former visits to the U.S.S.R. It was only on the eve of my departure on this latest journey that some of her former friends, the old exiles of Paris, become a spectral band in their colony at Ste. Geneviève des Bois, furnished me with an address in Moscow from where she had written to them. A letter from Red Russia! This, in their eyes, constituted both a miracle and an affront, and they handed me her letter almost as if its touch could sear. It seemed she lived content; she did not vaunt a Utopia but she was *home*, working as a translator for she possessed many languages. That she was content, the spectral band found inadmissible; that she had gone home to die was, perhaps, understandable. '*Mat Rossiya!* Mother Russia,' they sighed, and crossed themselves, looking towards the little pasteboard holy images that adorned their quarters.

When I had first known her in Paris she kept a book shop specializing in Russian and Oriental material, where over the years I spent much time and money. In retrospect, I have small doubt she had other fish to fry in the murky little premises where the shelves were stacked three-deep in a wildly unclassified richness. She was generally to be found in an inner room even darker and more murky, piled with Oriental manuscripts, catalogues and tattered books, forgotten cups of tea and stale rolls mouldering among them.

I often arrived to find her in earnest conversation with some unplaceable individual who would bow politely, and take himself off forthwith.

'He's really the Khan of Avaria,' she might say, making my mouth water at the perspectives such a title evoked. Or: 'That man who brought in the bundle of books last time you were here, would have interested you. His father has a lot of papers concerning the Petrashevsky affair.' But she never introduced them. A decrepit cat – a Siberian grey called Boris, which she had contrived to carry out of Russia with her in the exodus – occupied the only armchair, draped, like its owner, in a frowzy shawl. Over the years Boris had faded away, his memory perpetuated by a son, named Loris (after that Loris-Melikoff who had played a considerable part in the Constitutional reforms which were on the point of being realized when terrorists' bombs shattered both the Tzar Alexander II and his liberal dreams).

Both cat and woman peered myopically through a haze of cigarette smoke which hung over everything. Although my friend's shoe-uppers gaped from the soles and the nails of her beautifully shaped hands were black-rimmed, she always puffed her cigarettes through a long gold and enamelled holder. This she waved over the jumbled stacks like some diviner's wand, to produce treasures I had despaired of finding. Sometimes, when I took myself off for a more frivolous involvement, after long hours of concentrated grubbing, she would eye me critically as I prinked before the broken slice of looking glass hanging crooked beside last year's calendar.

'You should never arrange yourself for any man – they must know you as you are, clean or dirty, pretty or plain. All the rest is just posturing,' she would say, stabbing the air with the cigarette-holder so that it glittered, now become a witch's wand and she the witch, binding me to the intellectual life and a shiny nose.

When I had returned to Moscow this time the preparations for my journey had been all-absorbing and, raring to go, I had forgotten about her; but now, with this unexpected time-bonus at my disposal, I decided the finger of fate was pointing to the address I had obtained in Ste. Geneviève des Bois.

~

The old Yakimankaya quarter was familiar to me as being where the Traveller's family had lived for a while. On earlier visits I had sometimes gone there, to wander about the quiet streets that sloped down from a brisk modern thoroughfare. These backwaters were lined with low houses shaded by trees, their little gardens heavy with lilac and sunflowers. As the daylight faded behind the lovely bell-tower of Sved Ivan Voina, St. Ivan the Warrior, and the lamps glowed from its porch, lighting the way for a straggle of the pious who still assembled there for vespers, I would peer in at the uncurtained windows of the shabby houses round about. They were still charming in their harmonious proportions, and I would wonder which had known the Traveller's youth. Spying in, through pots of geranium and verbena, I would try to reconstruct a vanished way of life – not because I admired it particularly, but because it had been his. The rooms I saw were brightly lit, their graceful form unchanged beneath the darkened paint-work. Some still contained the traditional brass-bound white tiled porcelain stoves. Sometimes a pretty chandelier still hung from the ceiling, but it was unlit; beside it, a single bulb hung, starkly functional. Such a chandelier, I thought, must once have lit a family dinner-table – focus, or altar of family life round which the Central and Eastern Europeans always gathered, not only to eat, but to spend whole evenings, uncomfortably, in upright chairs, playing chess, drinking tea or sipping wine. It was a calm domestic pattern frequently broken by the fury of political arguments, which, unlike English family life, were allowed to penetrate the home.

Transposing the scene now before me, I imagined such a dinner-table, with its imposing silver samovar steaming gently and, among the family ranks, my Traveller; a rumpled fidgety schoolboy, a smartly uniformed lieutenant, and finally, a blasé black-sheep, straining to be off to join his mistress – myself – at some Gypsy cabaret.

Coming back to earth, it seemed that the windows into which I now peered were so many stage settings where the players all wore the same costume and acted out an identical scene. At the table, now piled with books rather than dishes, a samovar still stood; a young couple were bent over their studies, for further qualifications and night-classes were something most citizens desired in the U.S.S.R. On a high matressed bed, often curtained, in an alcove that did duty as bedroom, a child or baby slept. In another corner, the *babushka*-figure of tradition, head bound by a flowered handkerchief, a mother or grandmother, prepared supper on a small stove. In some rooms, the furniture, generally Beidermeyer in style, was arranged with more taste than others: usually there were pictures, snowscapes, or prints of Red Armies on the march. Ornaments ranged from plasterbusts of Beethoven or Lenin to models of aeroplanes; always there were flowers and books.

In one such room I believed I would now find my friend the bookseller, unchanged, for such a witch could not have grown old or died. She was immortal, pickled in nicotine. But would she remember me – receive me, unannounced? Or would she, witch-like, know I was arriving? Would our meeting be wise – for her – for me? I decided to chance it.

The house looked much like all the others but perhaps even more dilapidated. I tugged at a contraption of wire and string which jangled furiously. All Yakimankaya, I felt, must now be observing me covertly, while the forbidding grey-uniformed Guards stationed outside the French Embassy, on the main thoroughfare nearby, might abandon their posts to investigate my noisy, unorthodox conduct... 'Strangers do not make sudden, unaccompanied calls on citizens,' a voice seemed to hiss in my ear, and a sense of guilt and apprehension now began to make itself felt. So much for the conditioning to which those who visit the Soviet Union are often exposed by others who disapprove – such persons being more often *without* the frontiers than within, I have observed.

The door was opened by a young woman wearing boots and a pinafore and carrying a baby.. She smiled and seemed in no way surprised, replying to my Russian in her English. 'You have brought the books? No? Then you wish to speak with my grandmother? She is above in her work. Enter please.'

I did so. The room was much like the others but knee-deep in newspapers and manuscripts in all languages, Greek, Spanish, Hebrew, Arabic... Lying on the ledge of the stove in a state of stupefied bliss lay a cat – another, younger-looking Siberian grey. My old friend now appeared and greeted me without surprise. She seemed quite unchanged by the years: the same frowzy shawl and steel-rimmed spectacles, the same witch-like regard; but the wand had vanished, and her shoes were stoutly sewn.

She accepted my visit, like my forthcoming journey and its object, as entirely natural.

'I always thought you would come back here. Why didn't you come to see me before? If you are still looking for *him* you've left it late. I've lost sight of him for a long while. Of course he returned here for good. Neither of us ever belonged anywhere else... All the rest was play-acting...'

'You mean he really was -' I stopped, and caught myself looking over my shoulder towards the door.

She laughed sardonically. 'Spying? Is that your idea? Then why don't you say it? Are you afraid of the big black bogy Tcheka? If our police bother at all with a minnow like you, they'll know by now that you are not worth troubling about – just *toquée*, love-sick... Besides, you know enough Russian not to be needing interpreters every inch of the way. What mischief could you get up to, anyhow? If only you tourists, especially the Americans, would realize that half the time what you all think of as surveillance is really quite benign – the means of organizing vast numbers of inarticulate foreigners who have come here just to follow the fashion – or to go back and say we live like savages. Snap-snap with those cameras, forever trying to photograph the broken-down remains – never the new, and the fine – or else posing each other in front of our historic monuments... Grinning pygmies! We have to organize them somehow, or else they'd say we were lazy and inefficient and want their money back. Why, I'm told a lot of them can't even find their way to the lavatory, let alone get themselves to a museum or know what they see when they get there. The Kremlin jewels and a bottle of vodka are all they recognize.'

She spoke with a peculiar bitterness, but softened suddenly to offer me plum-brandy, and I ventured to ask what had happened to Loris.

'Oh! I managed to get him back here, at the end of the war. That was really far more of an undertaking than getting Boris out, during the Revolution... As a matter of fact, it was one of the things that decided me to return.' She paused, waiting for me to digest this statement, but as I said nothing, she continued: 'You see, I couldn't find another Siberian grey to mate him with in Paris, so that was that. He was over eighteen when he died. He's buried under that lilac bush.' She looked beyond the tight-shut steamed-up windows. 'That's his daughter, Doris,' she added, indicating the soporific animal on the stove, 'but it's almost as difficult to find a mate for her in Moscow. She's only had one litter of kittens. Times have been hard for man and beast here; there are not many animals about, as I dare say you've noticed. I'm lucky to have Doris.' She patted the animal lovingly.

When I recounted my difficulties in leaving for Siberia she looked thoughtful. 'Siberia – yes, that might be troublesome... I suppose you still hope to find your old beau? "Journeys end in lovers' meeting". What incurable romantics you English are! A revolution would have changed that... Never mind: you must go – it's part of the pattern. We all have one we must follow. I can't help you much – but I could give you the name of a man in Irkutsk who might be able to tell you something. He's Serbian – an old friend – he used to make the best explosives, but something went wrong.'

'With the bombs?'

'No – with him. He got religious mania or something – anyhow he stopped making them. They sent him away... Now he mends all the clocks at a factory or some such place outside Irkutsk. I believe he's become quite esteemed there. I hear of him occasionally – 'by slipper post'. That's what it used to be called in the old days, when the ghetto Jews in their felt slippers had their own means of transmitting news they weren't supposed to know... It wouldn't be any good writing to him from here, but if you are going there you might manage to see him. Why not? You found me.' She scrawled something on a piece of paper.

'Here's his address.' She burst into a cackling laugh – a witch, up to her Abracadabras again.

'So I'm playing Cupid at last! And by the way it might be wiser not to talk about this idea with other people. They might not show sympathy. When you get to Irkutsk, write to him – in English – he understands it well. Say you've seen me. Suggest a meeting place. Where? I don't know – I've never been to Irkutsk. You'll find a suitable place, I'm sure... You'll have to show some initiative, you know.'

She glared at me crushingly through the steel-rimmed spectacles. 'Be sure to address the envelope in Russian though. You can do that? Good. And don't post it from the hotel. Put it in a street letter-box yourself, after dark.'

My sense of the dramatic and the romantic now being amply satisfied I took my leave, overwhelmed with gratitude.

'Don't thank me – I've learned something too – about personal relationships. I've always put politics first myself.' But her remark did not ring entirely true, considering her devotion to the Siberian greys.

~

I was never to see her again. Next morning, when I returned to leave some of the soap, fountain pens and malted milk tablets I had been assured in the West would be so welcome in the Soviet Union, no one answered the bell. The house appeared deserted, the curtains drawn, as if to discourage callers. I left my goodies on the doorstep and hurried away through the quiet streets towards my sky-scraper hotel on the big new boulevard.

~

The Peking Express is so named because its last lap is a diversion of the direct Moscow-Vladivostok route. Beyond Baikal a line swerves south-east to run by Outer Mongolia, edging Manchuria to Harbin, and then plunges south to Mukden, where the Chinese Eastern Railway runs directly to Peking. The whole Far Eastern project had only become feasible after China ceded the Ussuri provinces to Russia by the Treaty of Peking in 1860 (the Treaty of Aigun had given them the Amur provinces in 1858). Then at last Russia awoke to the necessity of completing a line which stretched from coast to coast, spanning this colossal territory. But nothing was done about it for another thirty years. And even then, for some time, there was only a single track line.

It was a fearful undertaking. The engineers were confronted not only by expanses of permanently frozen soil that had to be blasted, but by the frustrations consequent on employing Chinese coolie labour, where every coolie had to be taught even the most rudimentary use of technical equipment by means of interpreters who could not be obtained in sufficient quantities and hindered the work by graft and sedition. Moreover, construction was constantly threatened by attacks from the dreaded Red-beard bandits, the Hung-hutzes, as well as both Chinese army units and Boxer rebels, burning bridges and destroying completed sections of the line. When at last these dangers were overcome by large detachments of Russian troops being sent there to protect the railway, Asiatic cholera and bubonic plague spread along the line, ravaged the labour camps and threatened Harbin. After Homeric efforts this completed Chinese Eastern section was lost to Japan in the Russo-Japanese war of 1905 and only in 1916, after a series of further campaigns, frontier disputes and treaties involving China, Manchuria and the Japanese once more, did the Trans-Sib at last run throughout on Russian soil.

But all across Siberia, until Baikal, the Peking Express is identical with the Trans-Sib of my desire, so that I did not feel cheated. In all events, I planned to make the unbroken run as far as Irkutsk and, there, either to pick up the Vladivostok train of my original plan, or go about the Trans-Baikal provinces which had been the heart of the Traveller's Tales or, perhaps, to find the Serbian one-time high explosive expert and, through him, be led yet farther afield.

The whole immensity of the Trans-Siberian route was made fitfully, in merging sections. The Western Siberian line links the Eastern, and that with the Trans-Baikal, and its off-shoot, the circum-Baikal loop beside the lake, or inland sea. There is the South Ural diversion, the Kuibyshev line, the northern route from Chita to Vladivostok by Khabarovsk, and the Turkestan-Siberian – or Turk-Sib, linking the Central Asian provinces, its line laid in blood during the Civil War.

All these sections have taken half a century to compose, and are still, at certain seasons sometimes augmented by river transport, though the rivers run, for the most part, north and south, while most transport is needed east and west. All these complicated arteries of communication, stemming from the main Trans-Sib blood-stream, had been a matter of sharp temptation to me as I pored over Russian sectional maps and realized that, by doubling back on my tracks, side-stepping, hanging about wayside halts and relying on uncertain timetables – a prospect which did not intimidate me – it would have been possible to obtain a far more comprehensive Siberian journey than by remaining rooted in one train, moving inflexibly eastwards. But after all, it was the *train* I had wished above all to know, so I renounced all the rest.

Though not without lingering regrets. Several longed-for cities had to be sacrificed. Two of these were of a particular, personal significance to me. Tiumen, east of the Urals, had been, I supposed, originally the headquarters of that Kalmuck Horde over which my Prince Serbedjan Tiumenev had ruled. Then, in the province of Tobolsk, near Semipalatinsk, 'the Tartar Province of the Seven Tents', the Traveller had wooed and won the Kirghiz beauty, Kamran's mother; and Kamran had been born in Tobolsk. Putting aside such family interests, I referred to a tourist handbook. 'Province Of Tobolsk: 439,859 square miles' was not an enthralling opening. I possessed more lively snippets of general information.

There were two towns in the city of Tobolsk. Nijni, the low, and Verkhné, the high, with its historic buildings dominating the bluffs above the Irtysh. In this river Yermak the Cossack, conqueror of Siberia was drowned, fatally weighed down by the splendid armour and royal mantle Ivan the Terrible had bestowed as a mark of gratitude for the conquest. Here the Swedish prisoners taken at Poltava built 'the Swedish Tower', and went on to build churches and monasteries in eastern Siberia. Here the Stroganov family founded their fabled fortune trading glass beads for ermine pelts from the gullible locals. Here trading centres, where Bokharan and Chinese caravans converged, imparted a note of violent colour in the monochrome setting of snow and leaden skies which, for most of the year surrounded Tobolsk, where even in June the temperature sometimes falls below zero.

Here, until 1892, reposed the bronze bell of Uglitch, which had been exiled to Siberia by Boris Goudenov after being publicly flogged and its tongue removed for sounding the tocsin which roused the town's insurgents. Tobolsk was one of the great forwarding centres for the convicts sentenced to Siberian exile. At Tobolsk many of the Dekabrists ended the tragedy of their lives, after surviving sentence in the mines of Chita far further east. Here is the Znamenski Monastery, oldest in all Siberia, where Kerensky had planned to banish the Emperor Nicholas II to a reasonable exile in 1917.

Twenty versts to the south, I recalled, the Traveller's note-book told of strange ruins – the remains of Sibir, ancient capital of the Kingdom of those Siberian Tartars or Mongols from whom the Traveller's ancestors had sprung – in the saddle, armed with bow and arrow and lance, as I saw them: a marauding horde streaming across Asia to steal one's heart away.

But renouncing Tobolsk and other historic towns en route was the price I must pay to possess the Trans-Siberian journey in all its unbroken mileage; to savour, fully, the drama of the train that had thundered through my nursery so many nights, so long ago.

CHAPTER TWENTY TWO

Tuesday's train is fair of face, I told myself, going down the platform to install myself in solitary state. The Traveller, I decided, was obliged to linger behind at the barrier to deal with the luggage; he would be joining me on the train, no doubt. But even before I reached my compartment a vague feeling of disappointment clouded my spirits. This train left Moscow in the afternoon, and a pale late autumn sunshine lit the platform so that there was none of the drama of a night-time departure. Nor did the crowds seem so archetypal. They were less urgent; their baggage was less bulky; some bedding and string bags were being hoisted through the windows, but there was not a samovar to be seen.

Nor was there a guard in the likeness of a bear. A neat young woman in a beret and top boots replaced the shaggy figure I had found so sympathetic. As for the engine, the mighty monster was not at all the kind my mind's eye had cherished all these years. Where was the funnel-shaped chimney stack typical of earlier Russian rolling-stock? In its place, I saw a stream-lined, blunt-nosed funnel-less diesel. Not a puff of smoke issued from its sleek bulk. It did not fulminate as its predecessors had done when I pined for them from behind the barrier.

Now, with every verst we sped eastwards I would be obliged to overcome reality, and imagine the diesel engine replaced by one more traditional. It was with a sense of betrayal that I returned to my compartment, only to be confronted by yet another disillusion. Authority had proved implacable on the point of companionship. If I must wander about Siberia, then it would be better, from all points of view, not to make a lonely excursion...

Olga Maximova was already installed; she smiled gravely and was, I saw, prepared to make the best of what she too considered an unfortunate situation. It was not her fault she was to be imposed on me and by her presence would certainly banish the Traveller's shade; nor could I be blamed for approaching this journey in a spirit unlike that of other tourists. Ultimately, we overcame our sombre start, and I like to think she remembers me with the affection and esteem I reserve for her. But relations were strained until it became evident that neither of us were going to bother the other unduly. I was a self-reliant traveller, able to order my meals and enjoy some exchanges with fellow-passengers, and to spend timeless stretches either glued to the window or plunged into romantic reveries of the country as earlier travellers had known it. This was not the Siberia Olga Mazimova had counted on revealing to me; indeed, her knowledge of the past was as limited as my awareness of the present and we spent some time correcting each other's inexactitudes or lapses.

Olga Maximova suffered her claustrophobia stoically and, finding me self-sufficient, took to her bed, or bunk, for most of the trip, an arrangement which suited both of us. I would wake, dress, go to eat one of those timeless meals which merge one with another on this train and return to find the same log-like silhouette hunched beneath the blankets in a paralysing emotion composed of both claustrophobia and mortal boredom, from which she would surface dutifully to prime me with some vital statistics on lead ore, mining output, or collective agriculture.

But that first afternoon we had not yet established our respective ways. Resigned, but mournful, I observed our undramatic, almost stealthy departure, sliding out of the station as smoothly as a liner launched from the slips. There was no chugging, no straining, no blasts of a self-important whistle; no sense of power. What should have been, for me, a moment of supreme achievement passed almost imperceptibly.

The train had settled into its loping stride (one thousand miles an hour, I was informed by a patriot who, like myself, had no head for figures) as we streamed through the birch-woods heralding the golden-domed complex of Zagorsk. Great Zagorsk, the medieval monasteries and cathedrals once known as the Troitza, the Convent of the Trinity of St. Sergei, was famed as the 'loveliest of all the holy Russian citadels', and so I thought its rich jumble of rococo and medieval when first I visited it, some years earlier. And so I still thought it, seeing it now from the train, high on its hill, its crimson, pink and pistachio green walls glowing in the westering sun, and the five lofty domes of the Uspensky Cathedral (the highest for Christ and the lesser for the Evangelists) glittering above the tomb of Boris Goudenov. We were barely a half hour out of Moscow but once this patriarchal seat had been the object of prolonged and arduous pilgrimages for rich and poor alike. While some trudged for days, their feet encased in *lapti*, birch-bark wrappings, the Court made a splendid showing in gilded, sable-lined coaches, with tumblers and dwarfs to while away the tedium of the journey. The Traveller told me of the little boy who was to become Peter the Great who went there in a miniature golden coach pulled by dwarf horses, with dwarf outriders to complete the cortège, a splendour for which my infant heart had yearned in vain.

Zagorsk vanished, the setting sun crimson behind its glittering gold belfries, and the birches thickened along the track; we were running through sparse woods now. Birches, always birches fringing our route – the *baraba*, or birch steppes beloved of Russian writers. Viatka would be the next landmark. Viatka, where Herzen had spent two years of political exile as a young, bruised idealist. Now was the time to consult the Traveller's little black note-book, the treasure he had bequeathed me on my twenty-first birthday and which, naturally, I had brought with me on this journey. But it was not to be found. With hands made clumsy by agitation, I searched for it frenziedly. It had been in my dressing-case in Moscow, protected from the face-creams in a plastic bag. I had been re-reading it in voluptuous anticipation the night before I made my false start, before renouncing the four-berthed compartment. It *could not* have vanished! But it had, and in a rising gale of panic I emptied my suitcases on the floor and fought down a desire to pull the communication cord. In an effort to hide my tears from Olga Maximova, I continued to pack and unpack incoherently. At that moment I thought the note-book lost or mislaid, dropped from the dressing-case or left behind in the hotel; but later, it seemed more likely that it had been removed by some persons curious as to its significance among my belongings. In any case, without it, I now had to rely on my memory. Deceptions and frustrations again. Neither the Traveller nor his shade nor even his notes would now accompany me, when at last I made the journey for which I had waited half my life away.

These gloomy reflections were interrupted by the arrival of our attendant offering glasses of tea, fresh-brewed from the stove-samovar, or *batchok*. There was one at the end of every corridor; ours was labelled The Titan, and it steamed furiously throughout the run. This tea-making ritual, and a passionate polishing of every available metal or wooden surface, seemed our attendant's chief occupation throughout the trip. He took a proper pride in his train and looked puzzled, hurt even, when I confided my regrets regarding the diesel engine. He thought this innovation particularly fine but, anxious to comfort me, promised a steam engine – the real, funnelled kind – at Omsk, 'or Tomsk at the latest'. Engines were often changed en route, he said soothingly. And was it only my imagination that later, harnessed to the more classic form, our train ran differently? Its loping gait seemed accentuated; its blasts of steam and smuts, its lonely wail as it raced on through the night all reassured me. It was still the great Trans-Siberian train of legend, a nine-day wonder journey – only *days* to cross the expanse of Asia that had taken Bering six years; which sometimes took the tragic prisoners two years, to stumble in chains to the halfway forwarding houses, such as that House of the Dead which Dostoievsky knew.

The lands through which we ran, hour after hour, day after day, and all through the night, they too were much as I had envisaged them. Rarely, a fierce glow lit the horizon; blast furnaces; some huge works such as the Traveller had never seen, their stacks rising like cathedrals of a new faith. Factories, armaments, unknown industrial plants, new installations, like the towns, both old and new, mostly lay miles from the railway. When the Tzar Nicholas I had originally discussed the route of the first Petersburg-Moscow railway he had cut short the experts' suggestions, and taking a ruler drew a straight line from one point to another.

'Gentlemen, the tracks will follow this line,' he said, and the engineers knew better than to argue. This high-handed principle was repeated when, during the reign of his grandson, the Tzar Alexander III, the project of the Trans-Siberian line at last materialized. Thus, as the long steel ribbon of rail unwound westward from Vladivostok, it ran through swamps and forests, across raging rivers piercing the almost impenetrable *taïga*, seldom swerving to touch a city, so that most of them lay ten miles or so from the station or wayside halt which served them.

In the words of an Imperial edict, 'having given the order to build a continuous line of railways across Siberia to unite our rich Siberian provinces with the railway system of our Interior,' the Tzar Alexander III commanded his son, the Tzarevitch, later Nicholas II, to lay the first stone of the East-West Eastern line, at Vladivostok, in 1891. The young Grand Duke had been removed from the hot-house atmosphere of a love affair with St. Petersburg's *prima ballerina assoluta* Mathilde Kshessinskaya, for the more bracing distractions of a world tour aboard a man o'war. From the Far East he put in to Vladivostok and ceremoniously trundled the first wheel-barrow load of Siberian earth; that earth over which, twenty-seven years later, he was to trudge his bitter path to the 'House of Special Purpose' at Ekaterinburg.

As we sped eastwards the stations we passed were singularly pretty – coquettishly so, as if in a man-made effort to counteract nature's desolation. The fretted wood-work of the *izbas*, like *cottages ornés*, and the fanciful little gardens with pebble-work and rustic log trimmings were strongly Victorian in flavour, but with a bold use of colour, bright blue or orange washes picked out in white paint. Sometimes an over-life-sized topiary bear in some local clipped shrub competed with an aluminium-painted statue of Lenin striking a commanding attitude. But the topiary bear won, for his eyes were invariably made of the semi-precious stones so plentiful in Siberia. It was these flashing amethyst or topaz peepers, rather than Lenin's upraised arm, that seemed to galvanize the railway officials, who were to be seen trotting about so zealously, like lesser bears, in their full-length furry overcoats, blowing whistles or blasting on curious curved horns recalling Beowulf, as they stood to attention and waved us on our way in a flutter of red flags. The train, I observed, was still accorded ceremonial. If it was no longer the most luxurious train in the world it was still the most fabulous, as it snaked forward into the five thousand miles of its tracks, ever farther, into 'a waste land where no man comes, or hath since the making of this world'. Or so such vast emptiness sometimes seemed in its infinity.

Sometimes an eagle circled overhead, and now I saw marmot colonies – the Pharaoh's mice of my childhood dreams. They sat perked up on their haunches just as the Traveller had described them, appearing astonished as the train thundered past. In all these years, more than half a century (and no one could calculate how many generations of marmots this would represent) it seemed that the train still took them by surprise. As we slowed to a halt in the middle of nowhere I was able to observe them more closely, for the other side of the track they stood their ground stoutly. Catching several pairs of beady bright eyes through the window, I saluted these brave little animals, remembering they were immortalized by Tarbagan, my Marmot Hero of nursery days, he whose bow and arrow shot down some of the twelve suns blazing on high. Marmot colonies have their own ways of transmitting news, and know what is happening in other, faraway colonies: they are aware of climatic changes long before mankind, and the Siberians regard them as the most reliable barometers.

Crossing the Volga, as I had always been told, was regarded as a moment of nationalistic fervour when every man on the train stood up and doffed his cap to Mother Volga.

But had anyone done so, as we rumbled over the bridge? Not in the restaurant car, at any rate, where, at that historic moment I found myself; as I happened to be, also, when we entered the tunnel, at Zlataotist, where Europe ended. AZIATIKA said a large notice beside the track, as we emerged from the tunnel. Asia! Asiatic Siberia. Siberia! Siberia won!

The waitress had put down a clattering tray of glasses and rushed at me, gripping my hand. 'That's your first handshake in Asia!' she said affectionately. Russians are gregarious by nature, and a train journey is, first of all, a social occasion. I ordered drinks all round.

'Siberia! The Great Highway of Revolutionary ideas!' I quoted Maurice Hindus as I took my first look at the landscape of my inner eye and was accorded a smile from Olga Maximova, who perhaps thought this rousing phrase was my own.

~

Suddenly we were running through a man-made belt of prosperity, a pastoral world. Snug villages huddled down under beetling roofs, the *izbas* brightly coloured, each window massed with a green curtain of plants and surrounded by the traditional *nalichniki*, delicate lace-like carved framework, painted white, to strengthen the lace-paper illusion. Trim gardens topped by gigantic late sun-flowers already singed by frost. Curious bee-hives, waggish wooden figures of birds, cats or bears for the most part, as primitive as African sculpture, where the bees swarmed in and out through holes cut in the eyes, or the belly. But to each *izba*, however traditional, its own aerial and television installation. What did they watch, in the long black nights of a Siberian winter, I wondered? Yet there was nothing forbidding or lonely in these lost villages. They looked peaceful, snug, very sure of themselves, and I preferred them to suburban Siberia, those straggling new town developments on the outskirts of some towns.

Birches, always birches fringing our route. I used to think them insipid until I saw them massed in silvery columns, graceful as the captive Princesses in the kingdom enchanted by the Firebird of legend and ballet. Riders. Lone riders rounding up grazing cattle with a long pole and lariat in the Mongol manner described to me by the Traveller. Horses, singular little horses, horses of the steppes – those small, shaggy creatures whose ancestors had trotted in victory to Paris; toy-like, blunt-nosed little horses. Harnessed to farm wagons they looked rat-sized, more fitted to pull a pumpkin coach.

To the few Siberian citizens (an unexceptional, husky lot usually wearing *oushankas*, ear-flapped fur caps) who were about the stations where we stopped and rushed to buy sun-flower seeds, sweets, or to gulp intoxicating mouthfuls of northern air, the train seemed an everyday spectacle, and they were obviously of far more interest to us; or rather, to myself, for I was, I think, the only foreigner, or tourist from the decadent west, on that particular run. Though, as we all clambered down to stretch ourselves, at each of the three-a-day stops, we presented a strange enough spectacle, for our clothes ranged from overcoats to striped pyjamas, chintzy peignoirs and singlets and shorts for a few athletic types who exercised vigorously. Two whole carriages were reserved for a group of officers of the Vietnamese army, returning from a course in Moscow no doubt, tiny, beautiful creatures, a lesson in neatness and elegance. They had exchanged their uniforms for well-pressed boiler suits, appearing in claret-red for meals, while emerging on to the platforms in dark blue ones for a gruelling round of gymnastics, and a curious battledore and shuttlecock routine, spinning and bouncing with india-rubber exuberance. Throughout, they retained that air of *soigné* distinction so apparent among the peoples of the Far East. I remember reading somewhere that in the official Indonesian language, trains are called 'snob-containers', and I wondered if these Vietnamese warriors found the Trans-Siberian such, and were making particular efforts to live up to it. But I came to the conclusion they were born *soigné* as a race; even their bone-structure made all the rest of us look lumps of very common clay. As we ran forward – or was it backwards – into another time, losing or gaining on the clock each twenty-four hours, nothing disrupted their exercise, their meals, or their immaculate appearance.

But for the rest of the passengers, a timeless lethargy prevailed where, imperceptibly, hours and days and meals merged. Thus, for those who had begun the journey in Moscow it ought by now to have been, let us say, Friday lunch time but mysteriously appeared, in the restaurant car, to be Saturday breakfast; while for those who had got in at, perhaps, Omsk, it was supper time – though which day of the week they were at, one could not guess. The degree of licence in clothes was no help in the guess-work either, for while some wore pyjamas throughout, as their *tenue de voyage*, others wore them, more classically, only on going to bed, just as one was, oneself, getting up. In any case, the restaurant car provided an endless, nameless meal (the menu being printed in Russian and Chinese) composed of basic dishes which were available the clock round and could be constructed as the passenger chose. This system is held to be an expression of Russian *laissez-aller*, for punctuality, like set times for meals, is apt to irk; thus some perpetual *plats* are ever simmering at the ready, in both restaurants and restaurant cars. Since tea was served with every meal on our train, the addition of caviare could make it either an exotic breakfast or a fish tea, while a meaty *borshch* transformed it into lunch or dinner. After such a spread, a glass of Armenian brandy proffered by a late-comer to the train might appear in the nature of a liqueur to some, while to others at the same table, a pre-breakfast apéritif. The Traveller had not mentioned this puzzling aspect of life on the train.

Once, there had been no restaurant cars attached to the Trans-Siberian, or any Russian trains, and passengers had to make-do until the next stop. But, in return, station buffets were excellent and even stylish: in the provinces, it was quite the thing to go and dine at the station buffet; besides, watching the passengers coming and going broke the stagnation of provincial life. We read of waiters in evening dress, six course menus and *champagnskoye*; also, accounts of the ruthless military descending to commandeer the buffets' entire resources for their mess, so that nothing remained for incoming trains with mothers and small children aboard but salted fish and vodka. But Heaven was high and the Tzar far away as the old proverb ran, and military abuses were seldom punished. Nowadays, I thought, station meals were no temptation, but train menus were generally good. With the flexibility of food vouchers, which were currency, I usually contrived to trade-in all the rest of the menu for caviare.

'Nearly a week on the train – whatever did you eat?' I have often been asked since. The reply, 'caviare', always seemed to annoy my questioners.

Whenever I had imagined this journey into my mind's eye, the Traveller and I had not gone to the restaurant car; we were always locked in our compartment with love and caviare: perhaps, once, we made a sortie to the library car, to hear some velvet-voiced choir collected from the 'hard' wagons; or, if it was a Sunday, I might steal out while the Traveller slept, and join the kneeling crowds packed into the chapel car, to kiss the ikons and receive the blessing of some itinerant Holy man before returning to my lover's side.

After such reveries, now augmented by Armenian brandy, I would collect my thoughts, telling myself there could be no more sighing, no more backward glances. Today, pilgrims reach Mecca in air-conditioned buses, and man goes to the moon in a capsule. Sigh no more, lady, sigh no more. But sighing, all the same, I would lurch the train's length, pausing, sometimes, en route, inveigled into a 'hard' compartment where concertina players endeavoured to rock and roll in the restricted space at their disposal. Most of the hard class had, I observed, taken pains to make things cosy. There was always a jam-jar of flowers on the side table; for, however modest their means, passengers bought bouquets all along the route; a bottle of something for passing visitors; books, and of course, concertinas, balalaikas or guitars were in abundance. I saw no pets; unhappily, they are not encouraged in the U.S.S.R. But passengers have the right to travel on the Trans-Siberian with one bird cage, it seems.

On reaching my compartment I generally found Olga Maximova, who showed a positively sublime indifference to the flesh-pots, still huddled beneath the blankets. But gradually, the baleful stare with which she used to greet me was becoming benign. Our friendship was ripening in an aura of mutual *laissez-aller*.

'It was good eating?' she would ask.

'- and drinking,' I would reply, climbing dizzily into my berth, for what might be either a morning nap or an afternoon siesta, my brain steeped in Armenian brandy and charged with Siberian history. The significant names of our route were dinning in my ears with the clatter of the wheels, till at last they seemed to merge with the clank and rattle of chains – the fetters worn by untold thousands of convicts herded into their barred prison wagons attached to the Trans-Siberian, crowded inside the cage-like structures that covered the decks of the ferries and steam-boats transporting the convoys northwards to further miseries; fetters dragged by the convicts plodding along the Vladimirka, the great Siberian highway across the Urals; unhappy phantoms who had passed this way, into the desolation which Leskov has described so hauntingly:

'...a handful of human beings torn away from the world and bereft of the slightest shade of any hope for a better future, drowning in the cold black mud of the unpaved highway. Everything around them was hideous to the verge of horror: the never-ending mud, the leaden sky and the sodden willows that had shed their every leaf and the raven with its feathers all ruffled, perching among their starkly outflung branches. The wind would now mourn, now rage, then wail and roar...'

The prisoners' journey was often protracted by climatic conditions. Sometimes, those proceeding to the extreme north were obliged to wait at Irkutsk until winter hardened the ground, which was otherwise an impassable bog. And only in summer could certain convoys reach their destination, travelling by barge, drifting slowly along the great rivers, crammed into their cages. Only on the ferry boats, used for a short crossing, were the prisoners uncaged; otherwise suicides, escapes, mutinies, and the sort of fight to the finish, such as that of Leskov's *Lady Macbeth of Mtsensk* and her rival would have been frequent.

There were others, less wretched, who crossed the Urals as settlers, pioneers in a new land, but, the Traveller had said, they are neither dramatic nor sinister, you don't find them interesting. *Touché*. I saw Siberia in other terms: though there was great drama in these bands of settlers who pitted themselves, puny, unprivileged and unprepared, against the violence of Siberian nature. Yet, as if that nature had come at last to love its conquerors, it was to yield unimaginable riches. The black Siberian earth bestowed sumptuous harvests: the mines revealed fathomless treasures.

Tobolsk and Omsk had been two of the largest forwarding centres from where, under the Tzarist regime, convicts were sorted and dispatched to remote labour camps deeper into the Siberian wastes. Here they were often torn for ever from their families, some of whom had contrived to accompany them so far. Here, scenes of unimaginable grief and suffering were everyday life, as the prisoners were marched off in five-pound iron leg-fetters, their heads grotesquely half-shaven, some branded across the face, this grey phantom procession had stumbled across the Urals, fifteen miles a day, their diet a watery soup and black bread, and such small extras as they could obtain from the peasants on the way. There were four main categories of prisoners (many of whom were convicted without trial): *Katorzhniki*, hard-labour criminals; *Poselentzi*. penal convicts; *Silni*, banished persons; and *Dobrovolni*, women and children who went into voluntary exile and followed their men. But having got so far, they were not always able to continue – sometimes their strength failed, or, by careless administration, they became separated and then for ever lost all trace of each other. Sometimes they had not been able to buy the goodwill of the guard and were deliberately herded into opposing columns, and began their march, north or east, a thousand miles farther, to the appalling Kara or Nertchinsk silver mines beyond Baikal. In leg-fetters, with boots that had rotted over the months, their wretched clothes hanging on them in clammy rags, these tragic columns marched, died by the way, or prayed for death.

~

As we moved farther east, I began to realize how much the loss of the Traveller's note-book meant to me. Confronted with the actual towns and regions that had been only names, anecdotes or historical data brought to life by the Traveller's handwriting and, I thought, graven in my mind, I now found everything fusing in a hallucinatory jumble. Was it at Omsk or Tomsk that the mysterious monk, Feodor Kouzmitch, in all probability none other than the Tzar Alexander I, expiated his sins – parricide among them – as a hermit, during the last years of his long life? Now I had to rely on my memory, for history or colourful details did not seem to be Olga Maximova's strong point. Nor did she have anything to say when I told her that, while English children's first notions of Siberia came from reading Jules Verne's *Michael Strogoff*, it could be considered as a rather accurate description of the country and conditions at that time. Verne had obtained much data from his friend Elysée Reclus who, in turn, had received it from his fellow-idealist Kropotkin – and few were better fitted to describe Siberia than he.

Sverdlovsk was on us before I remembered that, to the note-book, it was Ekaterinburg of dark memory. But the note-book had been kept before the Revolution cast its own light and shadow, transforming people and places, imposing new connotations, heroic or sinister. From the train window, Sverdlovsk seemed a thriving modern town slashed by a fine main boulevard. In vain I raked the cement sky-line for old roofs, searched for rising ground, crowned by the domes of an old church, which might have served as a landmark to locate the 'House of Special Purpose', the Ipatiev house where the Romanov family were shot down in the cellar.

Had I left the train and gone to seek the setting of this holocaust, it would have been difficult to convince Olga Maximova that I did not go in a spirit of reverential mourning. The Tzar and Tzarina were wilfully blind rather than evil. But who has the right to be so blind? In the words of one historian, their reign (for they became an indivisible force of obstinacy) 'went from one pogrom to another', the culmination of Romanov misrule. Even so, the Tzar had long retained a mystical significance for his people: he was *Tzar Batioushka*, their Little Father – God's anointed, for Holy Russia. But by 1905, the year of tentative revolution, such beliefs were beginning to be questioned.

As the Romanovs stumbled into the train that was to take them to their Siberian prison, I wondered if the Tzar recalled that jewelled conceit that had been made for him by Fabergé's craftsmen in 1900. The Great Siberian Easter Egg, as it was known, was the apotheosis of those exquisite extravagances for which Carl Fabergé was famous, and which the Imperial family in particular enjoyed exchanging among themselves and their friends to mark some event of significance, whether national or domestic. The Trans-Siberian Easter Egg was an especial treasure: it commemorated the train's through run. Moscow to Vladivostok, and the route was engraved round its enamel circumference. Inside lay a tiny model of the train. Uncoiled, it measured about twelve inches; the carriages were made of gold, the engine in platinum with rubies for headlights. It was a perfect working model and could be wound up to chug along for several inches. We can imagine it snaking its way across a malachite tea-table at Tzarskoe Selo, among the *petits-fours* and tea-cups, coming to a stop before a lace-edged napkin; as now, the ex-Emperor's train crawled to a standstill at some wayside halt in the Urals and the Imperial suite – forty or more persons in all – drew down the blinds to avoid prying eyes. At that moment, the Tzar was still surrounded by a considerable suite, something that is now forgotten, overshadowed by the stark drama of their end, in Ekaterinburg. But at first, after the abdication, being dispatched in all honour by Kerensky, to what he believed would be safety at Tobolsk, they travelled in some style.

Two ladies in waiting (and their *femmes de chambre*), two equerries, or gentlemen-in-waiting (and their valets) did not seem unreasonable to the Provisional Government; nor did two doctors, two tutors for the Imperial children, a lady of mysterious function, described as *lectrice à la Cour* and her two maids, a barber, a wine steward, the *maître d'hôtel*, five footmen, three chefs and their three aides, a number of *femmes de chambre* and *valets de chambre*, the *valet de pied* of the Grand Duchesses, and Nagorny, the sailor who was the puny little Tzarevitch's devoted attendant. Fifty trunks crammed with household comforts followed the exodus of what was, after all, the last remnants of the Byzantine Court.

It was rather in the terms of some Byzantine mosaic of splendour that the Romanovs were still seen by the majority of the peasants. The driving necessity behind the Revolution was slow in permeating the more remote villages: they too had their visions, but in terms of the old *skazki* or fairy tales. For them, the Tzar was still a legendary being, beyond merely human comprehension – perfectly expressed by a Siberian peasant, of whose words we have a transcript. Eudoxia Semenova had been commandeered by the local Soviet to scrub the floors at the 'House of Special Purpose' – the merchant Ipatiev's house – on July 15th, and was therefore one of the last people to see the Imperial family alive. Confronted by the trapped, tragic little group – for at Ekaterinburg the suite of fifty had by now been reduced to half a dozen – she describes her astonishment; for reality did not tally with fact. Her words, spoken later to the Court of Enquiry, speak for legions of simple country people at that time, to whom the Tzar was *Gosoudar* or, more warmly, their Little Father.

'As God above is my witness, Sirs, I often used to dream of seeing our Little Father. And once, in a dream, I saw all our *Gosoudars* together in golden robes, surrounded by a golden light, with flowers falling all round them, I don't know from where. There was music and flags, and the bells rang without stopping... Our own *Gosoudar*, Nicholai Alexandrovitch, was just as I had always known he would be – a giant – a fine-looking giant. The Tzarina was one of our real rosy Russian beauties. She walked like a Queen and her voice was like a flute in Paradise... The *Nasliednik* – the heir to the Throne, the hope and pride of our nation, was a strong and happy cherub, a blessed child. As for the Princesses, they were the most perfect beauties you ever saw. One was preparing herself, as God had ordained, to become wife to the King of England. The second, to marry the King of France, and the third, the King of Germany.'

It was this innocent and radiant vision that most of the faraway peasants still cherished at that time. It was the townspeople and industrial workers who envisaged the Romanovs otherwise.

~

And in that waiting hour at that desolate wayside halt going towards some unknown destination, did the Tzar remember the many chances he had been given to understand his people's needs? The crowds converging on the Winter Palace that winter Sunday in 1905 had come singing hymns, carrying ikons and banners, to speak with their Little Father; but his Cossacks had shot them down.

When the Moscow-Kazan railway workers joined the strikers' movement and ran supplies to the rebels it was General Orlov, a particularly close friend of the Imperial couple, who restored order by ruthless military force. Three hundred strikers were killed, seventy shot out of hand, and a station-master who did not – or could not – provide a requested train was hung.

Meanwhile, the Trans-Siberian line was also in rebel hands, and only reduced to submission by equally violent measures. The strikers had been abetted by numbers of disillusioned soldiers returning from defeat in Japan. At last two special troop trains, each controlled by a General, set out simultaneously, from points East and West, stopping along the way to flog and execute the rebels ('Never forget – Russia loves the knout!' wrote the Tzarina, ruthless but perceptive, in one of her admonitory letters to her husband). By the time the two Generals met and, over a bottle of champagne, congratulated each other on the success of their joint expedition, the strikers' moderate demands were heard no more. The strike had occasioned particularly severe casualties in Siberia since for a while chaos had prevailed, with unqualified men taking over the engines, so that fatal collisions were daily occurrences and order, at any price, seemed desirable to the passengers along the line. As no doubt it seemed to the self-engrossed Imperial couple in the fussed-up middle-class suite in which they lived aloof at Tzarskoe Selo. The Tzar Nicholas II and his wife Alexandra Feodorovna represented a hated system and thus it was inevitable they should have perished with it.

Everything about this dark Siberian drama is poignantly obsessive; it has the inevitability of a Greek tragedy; moreover, it is surrounded by a strange pattern of coincidence and prophecy. It was in the Ipatiev convent at Kostroma that the Romanov dynasty had begun and, three hundred years later, it was in the Ipatiev house at Ekaterinburg that it perished. 'In my end is my beginning'. When the Imperial family had been taken under guard to their first Siberian imprisonment at Tobolsk, part of the journey was by boat, and as they followed the slow windings of the river, passing the little white houses of a village on the banks, Pokrovskoie, they must have recalled the words of Rasputin 'the Siberiak' their adored *staretz*, or Holy one, 'Our Friend', who had foretold that one day, willing or unwilling, they would pass by his house. From St. Petersburg, the notion of visiting such a remote Siberian village must have seemed improbable. But it had come to pass, like so many of the *staretz*'s pronouncements. They must, then, have remembered another of his prophecies; that when he died, their days would be numbered. Now Rasputin's body lay in a little chapel the Tzarina had erected in the park at Tzarskoe Selo, and the Romanov family were going towards their own burial place, in a mine-shaft beyond Ekaterinburg.

CHAPTER TWENTY THREE

A s the train loped on its way towards Tomsk I thought of another, earlier Romanov, the Tzar Alexander I who had found *doushevny mir*, the peace of the soul, in Siberia: or so it is believed. The Tzar's end is surrounded in mystery and the belief that he did not die in 1824 at Taganrog but reappeared, ten years later, at Tomsk, as the holy man or *staretz* Feodor Kouzmitch is still firmly established in the countryside; and elsewhere too, for it is one of those enigmatic episodes which break through the rigidity of fact, and are so shot with colour and threaded with conclusive details that they become obsessive.

All that day I was recalling the strange story. Worthy and unworthy subjects alike obtain obsessive power by the mystery surrounding them. Was Naundorff the Dauphin? What really happened at Mayerling Who was the Man in the Iron Mask? Was there a Monster of Glamis? What of Anastasia? In Moscow I encountered a distinguished historian who seemed astonished at my interest in her. 'But why do you foreigners puzzle so much over Anastasia? If one of them escaped...? It's of no consequence to us now.' His tone was authoritative, his lack of interest unfeigned, unlike so many of his fellow countrymen who showed a lively interest in anything concerning the Romanovs, the Yussoupov-Rasputin drama, and other episodes over which a veil has been drawn. Was Yussoupov still alive? Truly? Living in Paris? How? And was it true the last Tzar's sister had gone to America...? These were the *coulisses* of history; in the U.S.S.R. it seemed the limelight fell on more immediate issues or those far further away in time.

~

Below the roar of party leaders, relayed on the loud-speakers, a persistent humming sounded. One late lingering mosquito was travelling with us, and zoomed round hungrily. I remembered how the Traveller had described the particular fury of Siberian mosquitoes. They had caused fearful malarial epidemics among the workers constructing the line. In summer, he said, one saw linesmen and working parties all wearing gloves and heavily veiled straw hats, like elegant Edwardian lady motorists.

We decided to move to the restaurant car while Mikhail, our attendant, dealt with the mosquito. He was partial to spraying all the compartments and corridors with particularly vigorous perfumes; but they had evidently not overcome our mosquito. Russians share the Asiatics love of scent, and manufacture many kinds. I asked Mikhail their names; some were flowery, Silver Lily, and Lilac; some were not, Red Moscow and Kremlin being, I thought, almost as oddly named as another, *Pikovaya Dama* – Queen of Spades – generally considered of ill-omen, as in Pushkin's tale of that name. Mikhail let me sniff at his store of bottles, but *Pikovaya Dama* was not among them. It might have been just the thing to finish off our mosquito.

~

'Do you know what Siberia produces in one hour?' asked the engineer, beaming across the dining-table. Fortunately I was not expected to reply. 'Six hundred tons of steel, 500 tons of laminated iron, 700 tons of mineral iron, 21,000 metres of cotton material, 6,000 cubic metres of wood, 15 million kilowatts of...'

His voice glowed with pride and Armenian brandy; I held out my glass for some more 'insanity drops', as the Buriat-Mongolians referred to alcohol. However impressive, I have always found statistics exhausting. But after another revivifying nip of 'insanity drops' I was able to marvel at descriptions of the new town of Akademgorodok – miracle concentration of scientists near the science-city of Novosibirsk; where Nuclear Physics, Cytology, Cybernetics, Solid State Physics and Geophysics are all household words. We were now joined by Olga who beamed, finding me at last responding to developments of which she was justly proud. Trotsky had called Siberia the accentuation of Russia's backwardness – one railroad cutting across a wasteland. But now? Now it is surely the essence of Russian progress.

Akademgorodok was begun in 1957 and endowed as a privileged, first class community, in order to persuade a scientific intellectual élite to disperse from the overcrowded Russian cities and settle there, beyond the Urals. But there is no sense of exile. It lies in a beautiful countryside with skiing, hunting and swimming too, in the short but torrid Siberian summer. I was told that the opera-house is larger than Moscow's Bolshoi (a city's status, I noticed, is apt to be reckoned by the size of its opera-house), and all the best companies come there. There are cinemas, super-markets, amateur concert-groups and many clubs. The scientist society live in comfortable modern 'kottedgi' set among the birches. There is a special *Wunderkind* school for children from all the ethnic groups of the U.S.S.R. who show an outstanding scientific turn of mind, infant seismologists or mathematical prodigies from the Ukraine, junior physicists from Samarkand, and such.

I thought of another, earlier intellectual élite: the Dekabrists. They too had formed schools – the first in Siberia, when at last their prison sentence was commuted to Siberian exile. The brilliant tuition of these lost men was such that, when some of their pupils were later admitted to the universities of Moscow or St. Petersburg, they far surpassed the other students. Thus were they avenged, for from the young intellectuals they had formed came the seeds of a stronger, better organized spirit of revolt, which at last swept the way clear for the new Russia I now saw around me.

~

All that night the train was racing through the nursery once more, speeding on its way past the rocking-chair, through the rosy-patterned walls, carrying me to Siberia... the blue pin-point light in the ceiling of our compartment had become the little winking ruby glow of the *lampada* hanging before my first ikon – the one which the window-cleaner had found so alarming, so long ago... The hunched up form on the other berth was no longer Olga Maximova but Nanny, and I was back in my own bed, imagining the Siberian journey. The bed was swayed with the loping rhythm of the train and I drew the covers over my head as I heard the wolves howl; with a shriek, the mighty engine gathered speed, putting distance between itself and the terrible pack that streamed after us... Now we were in a troika... I threw out my sable muff, hoping the leader would fall on it and so lose speed; on and on through the darkness we raced eastward... Now the wolves were gaining on us. The Traveller was about to fire his last shot...

A violent crash woke me. Where were the wolves? There was no forest, no nursery nor any ikon to be seen. One of the suitcases had fallen off the rack; Nanny had given place to Olga Maximova, who stirred uneasily, and slept again. Wolves or not, the train was now hurtling along, and the rest of the baggage shifted uneasily. The hiss of steam alternated with a regular high-pitched wail from the engine, as if pushed beyond its endurance. Gradually, these sounds wore themselves into a soothing cacophony to which, dozing, I fitted names – the magical Siberian place names that seemed always to have sounded in my inner ear... Omsk and Tomsk and Tsitsi*ha* – Krasnoyarsk and Pokro*va*... The words rhymed with the train's rhythm and lulled me to sleep again until, abruptly, we came to a standstill and the absolute stillness woke me as surely as a clap of thunder. Down the line I could hear the metallic tap, tap – tap, tap, tap, of a linesman testing the wheel caps, a reassuring sound, breaking through the tense silence of the steppes which pressed round us.

On that other journey – the one I had made almost every night, and which started from the nursery – the Traveller and I always lifted a corner of the blind, to see the wicked, phosphorescent gleam of eyes – those wolves again – as the pack skulked on the edge of the forest... It had been a particularly delightful moment, snug in the train rather than a troika, although that too had a thrilling charm all its own when racing for life across the snows... Tap tap... Tap, tap tap sounded the linesman's hammer. It came nearer, was outside, and slowly receded, the length of the train. To its staccato beat I was fitting another song, one of the Mongol herdsmen, *The Lord of the Arrows*. The nomads of the Gobi desert used to sing it round their camp fires, the Traveller had told me as we lay together in the Corsican *macchia*. That *macchia* and the Outer Mongolian wastes that were drawing nearer now seemed to merge. 'For I am the Lord of the Arrows said he...'

'The Khan! The Khan!' tapped the hammers.

'The son of the Khan!'

'The daughter of the son of the Khan!' they echoed.

'The veil of the daughter of the son of the Khan.'

'The breeze from afar that lifted the veil of the daughter of the son of the Khan.'

'The flowers that perfumed the breeze from afar that lifted the veil of the daughter of the son of the Khan.'

'The Lord of the Arrows whose passion so perfumed the flowers that they scented the breeze that lifted the veil of the daughter of the son of the Khan.'

'The marriage of she for whom the Lord of the Arrows perfumed the flowers that scented the breeze that lifted the veil of the daughter of the son of the Khan...'

~

It was morning: we were snorting to a stop. We were at Tomsk.

CHAPTER TWENTY FOUR

N ow the days and nights were merging, like the forests and steppes that slid past endlessly. 'Monotony is the Divinity of Russia,' wrote de Custine, and I wondered what he would have thought of Siberia. For long stretches there was no living thing, no sign of life in the unchanging emptiness.

Like the desert, it might have been monotonous, had not this very nothingness stimulated the imagination to fill it with a mosaic of figures and events that had animated its vastness. Now I thought of the vanished note-book and its comments with an increasing sense of loss. Dostoievsky, I told myself, must have passed this way, freed from his years of Siberian sentence. Had the note-book told something of this? From the House of the Dead, I see him making southwards in a *tarantass*, cutting across this very stretch we now traverse, heading for Semipalatinsk where, basking in the torrid sun of a brief Central Asian summer, he will tame lizards with saucers of milk in company with the liberal-minded young Baron Wrangel, Administrator of the province, who admires his writing and offers him hospitality.

Eastwards lies Kiakhta, once the great caravan centre on the Chinese border (that Kiakhta of the bright-coloured packets of tea I used to buy from the Russian Grocery shops in Paris). Here the merchants endowed their church with solid silver doors studded with diamonds, rubies and emeralds. And away, far away to the north west, beyond that ridge of firs, lie the black diamonds of Kuzbass, the coal basin – finest coal reserves of all the U.S.S.R. Between there and the Urals, raw materials are scattered as prodigally as the precious stones in the merchants' silver door: black diamonds, coal; green diamonds, timber; white diamonds, the cotton fields; liquid diamonds gushing from oil wells – in particular, the rare 'white oil'. Magnesium, gold, silver and natural gas all abound here, while at Mirny, centre of the diamond industry, the mines are said to exceed, in their concentration, the output of any in South Africa.

These were some of the rich harvests now yielded by Siberian earth; it was as if, so long neglected, a dumping ground for convicts, 'cess-pool of Russia in Europe', or exploited for the benefit of the feudal few, the earth was responding lavishly to each fresh mark of confidence it received from a new regime; while seeing the great rivers harnessed to hydraulic plants and mighty barrages, one could almost fancy they now flowed with more force, surging towards their man-made goal more joyously. They had flowed furiously or listlessly, these great Siberian rivers, the Irtysh, the Lena, the Ob, the Angara (into which four hundred and fourteen tributaries flowed): but their character was wholly different to the rivers of central and southern Russia, the Dnieper, the Volga, the Don. *Could Quiet Flows the Don* have been written around a Siberian river? They too have their still reaches, but they are more primeval. On their way from the frozen north they have reflected so little of human life or habitation: they have carried timber rafts, and convict barges, their decks overloaded with iron cages holding the prisoners. *Shamans* or priestly sorcerers were said to dwell among the rocks but few villages were reflected there; few lovers have trysted by their banks in the pale sun of a northern midnight; few children have splashed in their shallows.

When I aired this romantic view of the rivers' character to Olga Maximova she listened sympathetically. Gradually her chill materialism was thawing and, sometimes, she now followed me some of the way into my mind's eye.

Even now, aboard the diesel-drawn Trans-Siberian, I still saw the country, like the rest of Russia, through a romantic, nineteenth-century filter which, of course, she could not be expected to share. My fellow-passengers had only to mention the existence of tigers in the Trans-Baikal provinces, and my mind instantly presented a series of highly-coloured flash-backs, stemming from the illustrations to that old edition of Atkinson's *Travels in the Region of the Upper and Lower Amoor* with which the Traveller had started off my nursery book-shelf, some particularly romantic ones depicted the tragic idyll of Aï-Khanum the beautiful, and Souk, a young chieftain of the Horde, the *Kara*, or Black Kirghiz (from which Kamran's mother stemmed...). The restaurant car faded, the gravy-spotted table-cloth with its crumbs and ash trays and collection of shifting tinkling glasses, containing tea, vodka, Caucasian wines, and all the aftermath of our dinner disappeared, like the faces of my companions; the lonely wail of the engine slipped imperceptibly into a lower key, becoming the wind howling round a mountain pass...

The lovers are fleeing from the wrath of Aï-Khanum's father, but their pursuers gain on them. Souk fights them off single-handed (illustration of the slant-eyed Tartar brave flourishing a battle-axe as the enemy close in). After overcoming every danger and hardship, the lovers reach the fertile lowlands at last and, locked in each other's arms, believe their troubles are past. As the sun sinks, Souk goes hunting wild game for their bridal supper, while Aï-Khanum, a devout Moslem, rashly spreads her cloak in a clearing beside the lake and prostrates herself in prayer, praising Allah for his protection – at which instant she is seized and carried off by a ferocious tiger which has been prowling in the tall reeds near by (illustration of the meek beauty, with down-cast eyes, flowing locks, Turkish trousers and a pair of singularly Victorian-looking bootees. Behind, staring fixedly at the artist rather than his prey, the Siberian tiger skulks in the reeds). A fearful shriek pierces the dusk, but when Souk reaches the clearing there is only Aï-Khanurn's blood-stained cloak. Souk curses himself for having left his beloved to go looking for food. The tiger, disappearing into the marshes with his own supper, is never tracked down, nor are Aï-Khanum's remains. Atkinson does not tell us what happened to Souk...

'You are silent. Of what you thinking?' inquired a young Red Army major, shattering my reverie.

'Of different kinds of big-game hunting,' I reply evasively, an answer which satisfies him as being thoroughly comprehensible.

~

Sometimes, our train followed a huge curve, sidling forward so that as I leaned out I could see the whole of its impressive length; and, when the sun shone, it cast a shadow, a long, shifting shadow, flickering over the pale grasses of the steppe. Sometimes, it was a shadow that was of particular moment to me, for when our diesel engine was replaced by the older, more traditional kind, I saw the silhouette of that high, funnel-stacked engine of tradition, the engine of my mind's eye, racing ahead, eating up the miles, puffing smoke, wailing its lonely wolf-like howl, at once puissant and toy-like – the engine that had raced, each night, into my heart.

As we rolled east, our rails ran parallel with a wavering track threading across the desolation. This was once part of the dreaded Imperial *trakt*, the Great Siberian Post Road, trudged by legions of convicts and persons of all degree. Here came pilgrims, 'the God-praying ones', hardened criminals, vagrants, politicos, and such as that noblewoman who had been found guilty of extracting the jewels from one of the Church's most precious ikons. While appearing to kiss it with particular ardour she had, in fact, been engaged in biting out the best stones, and now, stumbling among this doomed band, expiated her cupidity in bitterness.

Along this *trakt* came the composer Alabiev, for whom the song of the nightingale sounded above the clanking of chains; and sounded for me, once more, above the rattle of wheels, spinning me back through time to a shuttered salon in a Corsican hotel, where the Traveller and I are playing duets at an old-fashioned piano inhabited by mice...

Along this way, more lately, came other minorities, uncooperative ethnic groups, or throw-outs from the Stalinist régime, heading towards those labour camps such as Solzhenitsyn described in terrible detail in his *One Day in the Life of Ivan Denisovich*. But the old note-book had not spoken of labour camps; though they were, in a fashion, a repetitive pattern in Russian history. It seemed better not to question Olga Maximova about this recurring pattern and since, for my mind's eye, the twentieth-century Siberian scene remained out of focus, I returned to the earlier ages it saw so vividly. The Traveller had been too closely involved, perhaps, to evoke the contemporary Russian scene which was still barely forming when he vanished: perhaps what he knew of it made him as hungry as I for more remote and romantic visions. Perhaps not. In any case the note-book had concentrated on purely historic or personal perspectives; nothing political was apparent. Thus my own peep-show vision remained a period piece, and I preferred it that way.

~

Here comes a swaggering figure, all evil, with fur *papakh* set rakishly over his fleshy, sly face – the Ataman Semienov and his Manchurian bandit troops, a most unfortunate choice for the Allies to have sustained in the Siberian campaigns of 1918-20.

Now we overtake a rambling line of children – spectral figures – the *bezprezorni* or homeless ones, refuse of the Revolution, hunting in packs, stealing and killing to survive, vicious, ruthless desperados of all ages, knowing no laws, yet forming their own fraternity, the elder children wonderfully protective towards the younger. Thousands of these *bezprezorni* roamed Russia, terrorizing as they went. Many who went southwards, towards the Crimea or the Ukraine, survived and were at last rounded up, to be successfully reclaimed by new systems of re-education; harsh ones, but not without idealism. Punishment, it was soon found, only hardened these desperate young creatures. Of the thousands who went north into Siberia, many did not survive the rigours of the climate. Those who did grew up to be absorbed into the new land, participating in its struggles and reaping its rewards. Today, they rank among its most responsible citizens.

Our train runs through a dense forest, and the road is lost to view. Daylight is blotted out, and for a while there is no sky to be seen above the branches of the towering fir trees. Abruptly, without any thinning of the trees, we emerge as from a tunnel. Once more the steppes stretch ahead to infinity and beyond; and, once more, the *trakt* keeps us company.

Here, going against the east-flowing tide of humanity comes a solitary figure, that of a frail young girl, in a borrowed sheepskin pelisse, *la jeune Sibérienne*, whose case aroused great interest at the time and inspired Xavier de Maistre's story, the same which my mother donated to my first Siberian bookshelf in the nursery.

Now her solitary figure is replaced by a band of revellers, it seems, all wrapped in furs, roundabout figures, singing lustily. They are the six Kamchatka virgins that the Empress Elizabeth commanded to be brought to St. Petersburg, wishing to acquaint herself with her furthest peoples. The virgins set out on their immense journey in the charge of an officer of the Imperial Guard, but some months later, on arrival at Irkutsk, barely half-way, all six were in a noticeably interesting condition. The officer in charge was, as may be imagined, severely censured by the Governor, and no doubt the Kamtchatka ex-virgins heard the sharp side of his tongue too. But there was nothing to be done about it; the caravan was obliged to put up at Irkutsk until all of them had been brought to bed safely. At last the journey was resumed, the ranks increased by six little additions. Alas! such was the force of habit, such was the vastness of the lands they traversed, that on arrival in St. Petersburg, they were all in the same condition again. History does not relate what the Empress said, nor what punishment she inflicted on this enterprising officer.

Here, spattering the mud bridle-high, I see a *sotnik* of Cossacks at the gallop, escorting the *britchka* of Count Muraviev, Governor General of Eastern Siberia from 1847 to 1861. He sits muffled in his cloak, sunk in some dream of Imperialistic expansion, planning those long-sighted moves by which Russia will acquire from China the Far-Eastern territories through which my train will presently run.

And along this same route I am now travelling – a way that has known adventurers, anarchists, explorers, patriots, mystics, the fine and the wicked, oppressors and oppressed – what may follow?

So the endless horizons of time and space dissolved, one with another, and I sat in my corner seat watching the expanses of this haunted landscape, expanses where, it has been said, the only hills are those made by the exiles' graves. Now they were thinly veiled by a fringe of birch trees, 'the cold-place loving birch', as it was described by William Browne, a seventeenth-century poet, in his *Britannia's Pastorals*. The delicate striped saplings were shivering and swaying in a cold rain that whipped round them. I remembered the hideous purpose they had sometimes served in

Siberia. Cattle thieves were shown no mercy; Siberian peasants would rope a horse-thief by his hands and feet to two birch saplings they had bent together – when released the trees sprang back and the thief was torn apart between them.

Once, as I gazed out across the nothingness that was the central steppe region, the bands of phantoms which I summoned gave place to a small procession of Soviet citizens wending their way towards a distant church, its cupolas lonely on the vast sky-line. This was a funeral procession, the traditional white coffin carried on a ramshackle *telega*, the mourners plodding after.

In former days, the funeral rites prescribed for taking a coffin by rail were of such protracted ceremonial, with priests in their purple vestments, choristers, ikon bearers, candles and incense, that at last, only one coffin was permitted to each train, throughout its entire run. Otherwise, the rituals of Orthodoxy would have undermined those efforts which railroad companies were making with determination, but little success, to overcome the natural indifference to timetables displayed by the Russians as a race. Travellers of earlier days recount how the Trans-Siberian would dawdle so that passengers climbed down, picked flowers and regained their places without any rush. For some years, trains appeared to run when they would, or could. Hopeful travellers congregated at the wayside stations with their bedding and provisions, and settled down to wait unprotestingly.

On one occasion, the presence of the living delayed a train's run as much as that of any dead. There had been extraordinary scenes when the twenty-one-year-old Spiridovna, hailed by the terrorists as their heroine, was transported by the Trans-Siberian to serve a life sentence in a far Eastern Siberian prison.

In 1906 she had succeeded in killing General Luzhenovsky, a monster of brutality and tyranny, whose crimes were widely known, but went unchecked by those in authority. 'The assassin Spiridovna' was condemned to death but, owing to the violence of public opinion in her favour, her sentence had to be commuted to life-imprisonment (as in the case of Vera Zassoulitch, another terrorist of tender years, who in 1878 fired on the chief of St. Petersburg's police). Indignation swept Russia, and reached out even across its frontiers to Trafalgar Square, where a meeting of The Friends of Russian Freedom met on a Sunday in July 1907, with

Cunningham Graham denouncing Russian (Tzarist) tyranny to enthusiastic crowds, among whom, it chanced, were my mother and the Traveller. Many years later he described to me the meeting and told me Spiridovna's story. It seems that he and my mother had set out for a pleasant afternoon at the National Gallery among the Italian Primitives, but found themselves part of a mass protest meeting. The subject being of particular interest to the Traveller, they had stayed to the end.

Feelings had run very high in Trafalgar Square, as well as in Moscow. There, outside the dread Butirky clearing-house prison, where the young girl was detained and tortured, crowds gathered below her cell window, demanding her release and chanting revolutionary songs. Although dispersed by Cossack *nagaïkas*, they returned again and again. As Spiridovna was put aboard the Trans-Siberian, she addressed the crowds that surged round acclaiming her. 'Comrades, we shall meet again in a free Russia,' were her parting words, as she was thrust into her barred compartment for the journey to her prison, beyond the sinister mines of Nertchinsk.

But what should have been a prison journey became a triumphal progress. Mysteriously, at each stop, cheering crowds were assembled. News was brought that her Moscow prison persecutors, Avramov and Zhdanov, had met justice at the hands of the mob. At Omsk and Krasnoyarsk the frenzy mounted. The engine-driver was stoned, the Marseillaise was sung and red flags waved; the prisoner addressed the crowds from behind her bars as offerings rained through them, kopecks, five-rouble gold pieces, flowers and fruit. At each halt it seemed more likely she would be rescued and the guards were trebled. But they too, seemed infected by the extraordinary circumstances, and soon Spiridovna was holding receptions, regally, from the steps of her wagon. Yet she did not try to escape, nor did the feared rescue take place. An acceptance of suffering has always been a marked Russian characteristic. And then, perhaps, everyone realized that Siberia was prison enough. Where could she have gone – who could have hidden her, for long?

At Kurgan scraps of paper were passed up – 'Write something for us,' yelled the crowd, hysterical in their admiration for the young heroine who had slain the dragon. All along the route she addressed them with noble words. By then the stops were getting longer and longer, the train's schedule more and more wild, but, since the station-masters were one with the crowds, nothing was done. Now people ran beside the tracks shouting encouragement to her, or once again stoning the unfortunate engine-drivers. One hardy grey-beard, who had survived a prison sentence in Siberia to settle on the land, raced beside the train for eight versts, lifting up his grandchildren who proffered flowers.

'Take them! Take them, little sister,' he shouted, above the hullabaloo. 'All their lives they will remember for whom they picked them.'

And perhaps they did; perhaps they are still living somewhere in Siberia, still glowing from that brief encounter. One thing is certain. 'The assassin Spiridovna's' journey was seldom if ever equalled on the Trans-Siberian; certainly not by the Tzarevitch Nicholas Alexandrovitch, returning westwards, after opening the line at Vladivostok some fifteen years earlier. Siberia reserved its really royal welcome for the revolutionary.

~

Once again it was the stillness which woke me – as insistent as the rhythm of running wheels. The train had stopped. Peering out I saw clouds racing across the moon's face. So brilliant was its light that they scarcely dimmed this silvery northern midnight. It was my last night on the train, for I had finally decided to break my journey at Irkutsk. Too many places were being sacrificed for the image of the train's fabled run and the shade of a lost companion who had not materialized but who still could – who might – somewhere. Perhaps he had been waiting for me in one of those towns along the route, which I had by-passed. Or, in Irkutsk, we should come face to face, quite simply, in the street, with no more ado. The place, and the loved one... but the time? I never thought of time where we were concerned. I was for ever in my twenties, as I had been when last we were together. He might have been twenty-five or more years my elder, but for me he remained without age, the unchanging Djinn of my nursery. I could not envisage him 'tied up to the pier of old age' in Turgeniev's moving phrase. Pathos was not for him '...For I am the Lord of the Arrows said he'.

~

When I announced to Olga Maximova that I had decided to quit the train at Irkutsk and see something of the city before proceeding to

Verkné Udinsk and beyond, in short, to break the run in its entirety, she received the news with enthusiasm and began listing a number of engineering achievements, educational ventures, geological institutes and kolkhoz in the vicinity, all of which were triumphs, to be seen to be believed. So she thought them, and so, no doubt, they were; yet I knew that many other magnets would be pulling at me, among them the Outer Mongolian border-land, perhaps to find there the Lamaserai where the Traveller had spent a year among the saffron-robed bonzes, nursing a broken heart. Was he withdrawn there, for ever, from life? There was a letter to post in Irkutsk, too; a letter I did not know how to write to a man I did not know, proposing a meeting at some place I had not yet seen; to question him about a long-lost love – though this project was now assuming an almost mythical aspect, like my old friend the witch at Yakimankaya. Had it not been for the address she had given me, lying snug in my wallet, I should have thought it all a dream.

And then, I was side-tracked by the most beguiling accounts of a natural mud spa high on the northern shores of Baikal which functioned, it seemed, as much for the wild animals of the vicinity as the few locals and fewer visitors. From time immemorial, seals, reindeer, foxes and bears, all the creatures of the *taïga* where it edges the arctic tundra, had come south to wallow trustingly in its curative mud. The presence of a handful of humans had not, until now, appeared to discourage them, I was told. Today, game laws are very strictly enforced in Siberia, and the inhabitants do not rush about slaughtering with the indiscriminate zeal of some other countries. The more I thought about this primitive spa, the more I had a fancy to go there and wallow beside some lolloping seal. Beside such attractions, what could the Monte Catinis, the Bad Gasteins and the other spas of Europe offer? Rheumatic complaints, said Olga Maximova, responded particularly to this mud cure. I had not imagined seals to suffer from rheumatism but then, Baikal seals are a breed apart – of enormous size – and their presence in the lake has always baffled scientists, for Baikal is an inland sea and no one has ever explained how the seals got there in the first place.

Then, there was the magnet pull of Chita, eastward, beyond Verkhné-Udinsk, where the Dekabrist Princesses had at last been able to rejoin their convicted husbands and share their fate. There I would see for myself the miserable but now historic little street named for them,

Damskaya Ulitza, Ladies' Street, where they lodged, these once-pampered young women, in a wretched *izba* too cramped for them even to stretch out full length on the floor, for there were no beds in the beginning. The Traveller had often recounted Princess Volkonskaya's reunion with her husband, a man she had not loved, but who represented every political idea she cherished. After the terrible journey she had undertaken and the hardships she had survived, when at last she entered the pestilential cell in which he rotted, she first knelt to kiss his fetters.

The Dekabrist wives inspired some of Pushkin's most beautiful verses, and were worthy of them. How, I asked myself, could I presume even to think of such women from the softness of my first-class compartment? How idle to imagine I could ever comprehend anything of Siberia and its dramas from such a cocoon.

'Prête-moi ton grand bruit, ta grande allure si douce
O train de luxe!
Tandis que derrière les portes laquées
Dorment les millionaires.'

Even if there were no millionaires on this train, I was, figuratively, among them. Factually, I was journeying across Siberia, a journey few people of my acquaintance had made; actually, I was still playing the Run-Away Game – certainly not coming to know Siberia as once I had believed I would. I had confused the issue, glimpsing the country while brooding over the Traveller's loss, comfortably, in my first-class compartment. But could I have done what the Dekabrists' wives had done? Could I have crossed those terrible wastes, by slow and agonized stages, to join him – even to learn more of the country that had held my imagination for so long?

The Traveller's words came back to me: 'You're such a romantic creature, *Pussinka!* I wonder, would you have followed me to Siberia in the classic manner...? But then, wouldn't that be because you were more in love with the *land* than the man...?' Again I heard the mocking voice: 'I believe you're more in love with the train than me!'

My spirit may have been willing, but O my flesh was weak! Only when one has seen the immensity of the Siberian steppes, or those implacable stretches of the *taïga* can one begin to measure the abnegation and courage of the *dobrovolni* – those who voluntarily followed the prisoners into exile here.

Time and soft living had overtaken me and now, it seemed, I was in fact more in love with comfort than anything else, content merely to watch a new world through a window.

'*Et vous, grandes glaces à travers lesquelles j'ai vu passer*
La Sibérie et les Monts du Samnion...'

Through a gap in the steamed-over windows of our compartment I could see the shadowy outline of trees surrounding the track. *Taïga* – primeval forests rising above, and interwoven with dense thickets, covering marshy land where the deeper earth remains perpetually frozen. The buffeting wind that soughed outside our windows and sent the clouds racing overhead could not stir the *taïga*. It was locked within itself, hostile, menacing. Here (until the advent of helicopters) no human being had ever penetrated profoundly, for it is estimated that the *taïga* covers over four thousand miles from east to west, and about one thousand five hundred from north to south. Hunters and fugitives and wild animals, too, always kept close to the few rivers that thread through the density. Even on the fringes where our train ran, a way had been forced with epic endeavour.

~

Olga was sleeping heavily, cocooned in blankets. I lowered the window cautiously and leaned out, breathing the icy resinous air, catching, I thought, some rustling or muttering where the *taïga* thickened. I remembered how my Russian friends used to tell of the mushroom-gathering expeditions of their childhood, in the great forests of Central Russia, and how the peasants believed that storms in the forest were battles of the *Lyeshei* or Wood Demons – Pan-like figures who lived in the deepest glades. Squirrels and mice, said the peasants, were their captives, and the yearly migrations of these little creatures were transactions of *Lyeshei* – gambling debts repaid in furry currency – two thousand or more mice wagered against a hundred squirrels. The *Lyeshei* were perilous to man; every peasant or hunter knew that. They lay in wait for wanderers in the forest, seeking to obtain their souls in exchange for granting a wish.

And what if, at that very moment, the *Lyeshei* were gathering at the edge of the clearing, huge figures from a Vroubel painting, with wild, pale magnetic eyes, willing my soul away for a wish? It would have gone gladly, I thought, if they could have conjured the Traveller to my side on this, my last night on the Trans-Siberian.

But as if to reassert its own, more positive powers, the train gave a sudden jerk, shook itself to life, and with a shriek, began speeding towards Irkutsk, leaving the *Lyeshei* and their spells far behind.

CHAPTER TWENTY FIVE

As we drew near to Irkutsk I lurched my way to the dining car for a farewell breakfast. The train would be going on by the circum-Baikal route and the usual nameless meal was being served for those to whom it was lunch, or supper time. I listened, for the last time, to the special sounds of my Trans-Siberian – a whistle, an infinitely lonely wail, and the rattle of tea-tumblers in their metal holders, shifting uneasily as they had done all the way across Siberia. Leaning from the window, straining for a first view of Irkutsk, I watched once more the shadow of our train racing alongside and, seeing far ahead that our engine was the majestic high-stacked kind puffing smoke self-importantly, I rejoiced that it was this, rather than the soulless diesel that should bring me at last to Irkutsk.

Leave-taking was an emotional moment; my 'Fair house of Joy' that had done its best not to disappoint! From the platform I reached up to pat its heaving flank – for so its metal sides now appeared to me. There were many farewells to be said. I had found friends the length of the train. 'Come back! Come back!' they cried, pressing sweets and flowers on me, as if I was leaving a house where I had been a welcome guest. The cooks leant out of their galley waving dishcloths with the majestic enticement of Queen Tamara from her Caucasian keep. Our car-attendant rehearsed me, once again, in the current Mongolian for 'good morning' – 'I love you' – 'thank you' – useful phrases he had assured me, when teaching me, en route. The Vietnamese army, who were proceeding to the Chinese frontier and were now frisking about the platform performing their ritual gymnastics, stopped in mid-somersault to wish me well, as I wished them, going towards the cruel war that lay ahead.

Olga Maximova, released at last from her claustrophobic torments, beamed as she shepherded me towards the station's main building, a handsome structure adorned with formal parterres and busts of national heroes. While the good-byes were being said she had assumed the gratified yet deprecating air of a parent whose child has done well at the end of term celebrations.

Driving to the hotel, along wide, tree-lined boulevards flanked by massive, rather over-ornate buildings redolent of taste at the turn of the century, interspersed by contemporary cement functionals, I remembered that Irkutsk used to be known as the Paris of Siberia. Beside the *izbas* and village settlements or wandering outskirts of industrial developments we had passed en route, it was infinitely urban; though the sky-scraper developments of other cities are discouraged here, on account of the severe earth-tremors which occur regularly, said Olga Maximova, apologetic that Nature had been so unaccomodating towards progress.

For the limitless regions lying around and beyond, Irkutsk had always been a magnet, with something of splendour in its legend. The city's arms were a curious animal, a *babyr*, heraldic, yet seeming plausible, as if some creature likely to be encountered in the *taïga*. In the old prints or carvings its paws and ears were those of a wolf, while its tail was that of a fox. In its mouth, it held a sable. It was of Chinese origin, I was told.

Second generation Siberians, settlers, or the children of reformed prisoners, those who survived sentence to strike it rich on the Lena gold fields, and merchants, grown fat on commerce, rarely made sorties to Moscow or St. Petersburg, though they traded with all the big cities within and without the Russian frontiers. For themselves, they preferred to import sumptuous trimmings to impose on their provincialism. Their newly built houses were resplendent with chandeliers, satin covered, gilded furniture, billiard tables and mechanical pianos. Luxuries such as kid gloves, French millinery and champagne, and engravings of Landseer's paintings found their way here; but, while living it up, these native pioneers clung to earlier ways, and were sometimes said to ignore the comforts of their grandiose canopied beds, preferring to sleep on the floor, fully dressed and covered by their *shoubas* – probably sable-lined.

Some of these Siberians developed a strong sense of civic pride, built churches and became patrons of the arts, endowing orphanages, theatres and an opera-house to which they cajoled the best artists. A flavour of gold-rush days persisted, however, and gambling saloons and their brassy girls abounded. Yet according to one visitor, around 1900, a positively frenzied ennui gripped its inhabitants. Even the hazards of lawless living did not dispel this. Some citizens were in the habit of firing off revolvers from their bedroom windows before turning-in, to remind possible marauders that they were armed. But perhaps it was also to shatter that nerve-wracking stillness that descended on the provincial capital where, through those interminable winters, the nothingness of *taïga* and steppe and tundra closed round.

Looking about me, I thought the town remarkably thriving, lively and orderly, its streets controlled by buxom policewomen. Everywhere, I saw posters announcing performances of ballet and opera, specialized exhibitions or visiting orchestras. The Hot-Jazzki Boys from Tiflis were announced for the next night and I promised myself a rich mixture, with the Tadjik Folk Opera from Tashkent for my first evening in Irkutsk. 'Now welcome pleasure' as the hedonistic Harriette Wilson used to say. I had already planned my menu for dinner: *omoul*, the 'satin-fleshed' fish from Baikal which had rejoiced the Abbot of Krasny Yar in Melnikov-Pertcherski's book on the Old Believers.

'*Omoul* first – then Siberian apples, please – the transparent kind.' I sat in the overheated, noisy restaurant fulfilling some of my dreams, and having looked up the Russian for transparent – *prozratchn*i – expected to be served this local delicacy. 'Apples or oranges?' asked the waitress (oranges are confusingly called *appelsini*). There were to be no nuances. The room was overpoweringly hot and noisy, crowded with a preponderance of reddish-brown faced diners – Mongolian medical students from the University, I learned, and others, in from Ulan Bator for a football match – Irkutsk v. Buriats United.

The Mongol Hordes! But where were the saffron robes and Torghut boots described by earlier travellers, mine among them? I thought of the Hordes in that remote past when they conquered Moscow and held week-long feasts, Homeric junkets, their tables and benches being supported by the prostrate Muscovites, many of whom died under the weight of huge platters and hogsheads of liquor, as well as that of their sprawling conquerors. The Mongols round me in the dining-room looked a mild lot by comparison, though no doubt seen out of context – in a Western snack-bar, say – they might have appeared formidable. They were eating modest platters of *pilmeni* and discussing 'futbol', their usually impassive faces glowing with enthusiasm and bottled beer. The word Shamanite spoken with fervour, recurred constantly, and I was surprised to find the youth of Outer Mongolia and Irkutsk too, were still invoking their primeval forms of worship. But Olga Maximova informed me otherwise. 'Shamanite' was the latest catch-word, a newly-coined adjective expressing anything fabulous, from a pass at 'futbol' to a record harvest. It derived, admittedly, from Shaman, those priestly witch-doctors whose magic had once been so powerful a force in these regions. But they were no more, she stated firmly.

The Twist, I discovered, was of passionate interest to the young of Irkutsk, as well as those from Outer Mongolia. Since Western visitors were a rarity it was not long before I was approached to demonstrate the latest variations. Dialogue, in a curious mixture of tongues (I did not try out my three Mongolian phrases), was conducted with infinite civility.

'Excuse please you one English Madam?'

'English by birth, French by marriage,' I reply, cashing in on both nations.

'You reading Napoleon Bonaparte? You reading John Stuart Mill?'

'Constantly.'

'You do tweesting?'

'Well, not constantly...'

'You loving Siberia much?'

'MUCH.'

'You tell words of English tweest song on pick-up machine?'

'I'll try...'

And hanging over a tape-recorder that had been left in Ulan Bator by an *Amerikanski* archaeologist, I did my best to distinguish words and phrases from a sound track that had collected all the dust of the several Gobis in its passage to Irkutsk.

'It says "Baby! Let's twist! Baby! Let's twist again!"' I announced, before it spun into a particularly gritty passage... Asiatic dust... the reddish dust of the Gobi, where no tree or flower lives, and only the many coloured stones, mauve and orange and gold, nourish the eye... On a spiral of desert dust, I was whirled far from the Twist-entranced Mongolians, far away, eastwards, down the ages, to Karakorum, where Jenghis Khan ruled in terror and majesty. I heard the clash of cymbals and the wild strains that accompanied the Mongol armies on their march. The Traveller's note-book told that, when they swept across the Danubian provinces, they brought with them musicians from Northern India, for the savage rhythms they played stimulated the troops to even more furious conquests, and such music was the origin of the Hungarian gypsy music we know today. Around me was all the panoply of the Tartar camp. I saw the silken banners and horse-tailed standards and the white chargers tethered to gold or silver posts...

Then slowly, I spun forward in time, to regain the hotel lounge with its leatherette club sofas and dark veneered walls. As they came into focus I saw that a coloured photograph of the Kremlin over the buffet hung slightly askew and the buffet was massed with festive beer bottles. I dislike beer at any time but now it seemed particularly out of place. All Mongols should be drinking their 'insanity drops', I thought; and for the Siberians there should be the ritual Siberian punch. I knew the recipe by heart.

'Three bottles of champagne, one bottle of vodka, half a bottle of brandy, four glasses of curaçao, sugar, sliced apple, grated nutmeg, the zest of a lemon: soda water *if desired*. Stir well and set alight.'

The flat, brick-brown Mongol faces and the pale Slav ones were smiling widely, even on beer. They wanted to know all about Pop music; it was not every day they encountered anyone likely to unravel such tape-recordings. But although I proved inadequate and the tape deplorable they were insatiable.

'No more wording? Always "Baby let's Tweest"?'

'Well, farther on it says "Let's Twist again Baby...:"' I began to feel cornered as they pressed round, all talking at once. Cruel in my desperation I told them the Twist was out – old-fashioned, already forgotten; that everything was Rock now, or the Madison, which had been the rage when last I was in San Francisco. It was a fatal move. They flung themselves on me.

'ROK? MADISOUND? Please? Sing Madisound please! Dance Rok!'

They were off again. And no doubt my rudimentary versions of both appeared as exotic a spectacle, to them, as the dislocated neck jerkings and fluted quarter-tones of the Tadjik Folk Opera appeared to me.

The evening broke up late in an atmosphere of cordiality. In spite of her principles, it was clear that Olga Maximova had enjoyed it greatly. But later she confessed she had been obliged to revise her opinion of me. She had thought me more serious-minded.

'On the train you spoke much of the Dekabristi. You read Herzen. I admired your culture. But in Irkutsk I see you are more interested in the Tweest.'

'I'm much more interested in the Mongolians,' I told her, and she seemed satisfied that I spoke the truth.

~

I thought it better to see something of the outlying country, as well as getting my bearings about the city, before I ventured to send my letter to the Serbian clock-mender. The Intourist Bureau had thoughtfully provided me with a map of the streets but it was not going to be easy to allay Olga Maximova's lively curiosity as to my activities, however innocent they were in fact. As a sop, I allowed myself to be swept off on a round of uplifting visits to collective agricultural experiments, schools and hospitals and community centres, all of which, once faced, I found of absorbing interest. No one could be unmoved by achievements such as the new 660,000 kilowatt Power Station; nor remain indifferent to accounts of another, even mightier, in construction at Bratsk; a monster, to produce 4.5 million kilowatts – whatever that might mean. But it was in such mysterious terms I was learning of Siberia's industrialization programme.

Yet to me nature remained more impressive. Standing beside the primeval stretches of Baikal, where the Angara flows from it, I thought of Thomas Beddoes' lines:

'The loud rocky dashing
Of waves, where Time into Eternity
Falls over ruined worlds...'

I had hoped to avoid being confronted with the Angara Dam, for I dreaded to see progress imposed on the lovely landscape I knew so well from both the Traveller's descriptions, and the romantic engravings that adorned my copy of Atkinson's Travels. But when I saw this stupendous achievement I forgave Olga Maximova's insistence. All the same, I mourned the disappearance of the age-old landmark, Shaman-Kamen – the Shaman's Rock; now only one craggy tip remained above the encroaching waters. Soon that too will have vanished, and with it, the heart of Buriat legend, home of all Shamanist sorcery and sacrifice since the beginnings of this land.

Baikal – the Holy Sea of legend, 'the inland sea', is the world's largest fresh-water lake and would take five hundred years to empty, said Olga Maximova, the voice of knowledge. Its depth, at present soundings, is 5,315 feet; its clarity such that, in fine weather, it resembles some Pacific lagoon, its limpid turquoise waters revealing objects 130 feet below.

But in bad weather it lives up to its reputation for terror. Within a few moments, under lowering skies, it can produce giant waves eighteen feet high which dash over the darkened waters whipped by the dread *Gara* or mountain wind from the north. Hardly less furious is the *Koultouk*, or south-west wind, and the *Bargouzine*, which rages across the lake from east to west. Such are the storms and the waves which have inspired so many of the old Siberian songs.

When furious Baikal rages to the rocky shores -
Even the beasts of the *taïga* dread its coming...

Another, the song of the escaping convict, urges the *Bargouzine* to speed his raft across the lake to freedom. I had known them all from the nursery, and now, following the lake-side, heard them again.

When covered by its six-month-long crust of ice, Baikal is particularly treacherous. In spite of ice which attains a depth of six feet or more, it will suddenly crack asunder, without warning, leaving an icy canyon, perhaps fifteen miles long, and wide enough to swallow whole sledges, trading caravans and anything crossing the lake at that moment. Such were some of the facts and figures with which Olga Maximova primed me, adding that all the scientific data I could wish for was awaiting me at the Limnological Institute up the lake-side, at Listvyanko. But doubting my stamina for such exactitudes, I first made for the fishing villages, where sombre granite cliffs are fringed with pines and lonely little settlements of wooden dwellings are gathered in the shelter of narrow valleys running inland, to avoid the inclement open lakeside. Tradition was upheld by a few remaining small wooden churches, with green cupolas: progress, by bewilderingly-fitted meteorological stations checking the hour to hour vagaries of the weather. It is from these regions that the Laïka dogs were chosen for the lonely Sputnik voyages they endured in the interests of science, those who survived becoming Dog Heroes of the Soviet Union. I encountered some of them, strong, shaggy creatures; golden eyed and loyal-looking; they were guarding the little stockaded gardens of their owners. It was clear they were not accustomed to casual pattings, but they looked well-fed. In the Traveller's notes I remembered reading that, before the commercialization of caviare, the Buriat and Yakute fishermen set no value on it; they had not learned to salt and prepare it, and so threw it to the dogs.

We had walked a long way; the lake-side road stops at Listvyanka, where the ice-breaker ferry boats and hydrofoils put in for passengers or freight, plying across the lake to Trans-Baikal territory. We were following a precipitous path winding round the crags and cliffs that continue northwards, volcanic in formation, with basalt and lava-like coarse granite to rejoice geologists. As the day became more overcast, and the path more precipitous, and we scrambled for a foothold, clutching at rocks and blasted pine boughs, I thought how much the Traveller (who always stressed his abhorrence of nature as much as walks) would have detested this outing. A piercing, chill rain spat down, and the choppy waters assumed a sullen greyness. However much I had longed to find him, or believed his shadow accompanied me, I knew it would not be on this sort of expedition.

But I pressed on, longing for seven-league boots, to stride me to Olkhon Isle, forty miles up the north shore. The straits that separate it from the mainland are known as the Little Baikal and, to the Buriats, this was the most sacred part of the Holy Sea. Gigantic and curiously formed rocks tower above the water, pinnacles of 1,200 feet, rising before the few boats that venture near, for the island is honeycombed with caverns, arches and inlets where the waves surge and roar and form whirlpools. There is a tradition that Christ visited this part of Asia (perhaps there is a connection, here, with another Asiatic legend, that He passed through Afghanistan, after His supposed death on the Cross). The Buriats believe that He ascended one of the highest rocks on Olkhon and surveyed the great expanses of water and land. After blessing the mountains and woods, northwards, He turned south, and looking across the lake towards the Trans-Baikal province of Daouria, said: 'Beyond this lies nothing.' Which, the natives believed, accounted for the sterility of the region. Deep inland, lies Chita and Nertchinsk, where prisoners serving their sentence in the mines no doubt concurred with the natives' view.

Eastwards from the lake lies Birobidjan, where there had been plans to found a new Israel. Here around 25,000 Jews were to pursue their own way of life far removed from even echoes of those persecutions and indignities they had once suffered in Russia, and with which they had become permanently associated. But nothing came of the scheme: the Jews showed a lack of interest – Olga Maximova could not say why. Today, all Jews have Soviet citizenship and a nationality, being Estonian, Uzbeg, Ukrainian or other Jewry. The pogroms that were so terrible a part of Tzarist rule are no more: although I have heard that a certain prejudice is still remarked. The habit of centuries dies hard.

~

The weather had turned really disagreeable, and by common accord we turned back, towards the little inn at Listvyanka, where Olga Maximova promised the best *omoul* in all Siberia; and the best *rastegai*, added Russlan, my driver, who had accompanied us on this expedition. I called him Russlan because I could never remember his own name and, his wife being called Ludmilla, it seemed the simplest thing to do. This allusion to Pushkin's poem *Russlan and Ludmilla*, combined with humming an air from Glinka's opera of the same name, delighted him, as well as earning his respect for my cultural depth. Russlan, who at eighteen was fighting at Stalingrad, was a third generation Siberian and knew many of the legends or old stories I had learned from the Traveller and which Olga Maximova, the young Moscovite, did not know: I was even able to steal a march on him by telling him how, long ago, the *narta*, or dog sledges had runners made from long strips of whale jaw-bone – a system peculiar to Siberia, and unknown in the Arctic. Later, American traders introduced metal runners, known as 'iron bones'. Such exchanges of what my father would have called useless information were a great bond between us, and Russlan displayed an especial patience when I used to stop the car every few miles, a habit which exasperated most drivers, to get out and look at some unscheduled aspect of his homeland; perhaps a little church where I hoped to find interesting ikons, or some particularly beautiful stretch of forest leading deep into the *taïga*.

Majestic, and sombre, the giant Siberian conifers, which are at their darkest in summer, stretched ahead into realms of blackness. *Tchern*, a derivation of *tchorny*, black, is the local name for such forests. Here I fancied I might catch sight of bears, or lynx – or even the *babyr* of Irkutsk's armorial bearings. 'Only last week a huge bear came down into the centre

311

of the town,' Russlan told me. 'It went right up to the policeman on point duty and stood on its hind legs – that's a very dangerous sign; that's when they are going to attack. But the policeman thought it had got out of a circus and was just doing its tricks, so he went on directing the traffic. It wasn't till the bear ripped at him that he understood. He had to shoot it...'

I saw there was, perhaps, a case in these parts of the world for arming the police.

Stories about animals, forest laws, Shaman legends, village lore; these were my meeting ground with Russlan, and like picnics and country expeditions, simple pleasures we could share. Once, while Olga Maximova waited discreetly in the car, we broke every law of forestry and, with the aid of a spanner, dug up a very small fir tree that I hoped to transplant to France as an evergreen keepsake.

Brave little tree! It survived the long journey home, concealed in a sponge-bag, for the various frontier customs generally object to foreign plants. Repotted and cherished it lived for some years on my roof-top terrace in Paris, but although it remained green, and sprouted miniature cones, it did not thrive there. At last it was transplanted, all over again, to a Thames-side garden, where, among the roses and honeysuckle, it grows; slowly, but still, it grows, and is treasured. Each time I go to England, I see it, and remember the Siberian *taïga* of its origin.

~

Chudodie Baikal! Miracle-working Baikal! 'You must come back to Baikal in June,' said Russlan, skipping statistics of the lake's scientific potential which he knew bored me, to tell how, at that moment, briefly, the lake is covered with pink flowers, a kind of lily. This is known as the Blossoming of the Holy Sea. But its depths blossom strangely too: here among other extraordinary fauna are those emerald and violet-coloured shrimps I had coveted for my nursery aquarium; or those spherical fish which live at a depth of fifteen hundred feet, producing ready-made young rather than eggs (they eat their progeny in hard times) and burst or melt away if by accident they surface, encountering different pressures and daylight. This, and other seemingly wild statements of Russlan's were later confirmed and enlarged upon by the Director of the Limnological Institute, displaying his exhibits with true passion.

Atkinson's treasured book told of all this, and more besides. I was

back, refuging in the school lavatory, avoiding compulsory hockey...
CHAP. III HOW TO CROSS THE DESERTS OF ASIA, I read, but of
course, I knew it all by heart... 'Early in the morning I found the chieftain,
Joul-bar, directing arrangements for our long ride... Twelve Kirghiz were to
be my attendants... men on whom I could depend, who had a knowledge
of the country...' Yes, Atkinson had passed this way: he wrote
intoxicatingly of the Eastern Siberian scene; of crossing the lake at the very
point where I now found myself.

Leaning over the ship's rail, I thought of its ancestor, the first
powerful steam ferry, which was ordered from Newcastle shipyards in
1898. It was constructed in sections and dispatched, in 7,200 separate
packages, by rail to Krasnoyarsk. At that time the Trans-Siberian line ran
no farther: from there the packages were carried on a sledge or *soudna*, a
river barge, so that it is not surprising to learn that when the Russian
engineers waiting at Baikal (where there were no shipyards) began to
assemble the various parts, some were missing. Far more surprising, the
boat was nevertheless assembled and triumphantly launched the
following year. During the Civil War it perished, being destroyed by the
Czech forces allied to the White Armies. Russlan told me that its stack can
often be glimpsed, far below, becalmed there during the half-century of
convulsive change that has ensued on land. Such were the intriguing
pieces of information that Russlan fed me.

In some telepathic manner we were always able to communicate. I
followed the Russian he spoke more easily than that of more sophisticated
citizens and, in return, he seemed to understand my efforts at
conversational Russian, although these were often eked out by thumb-nail
sketches, or primitive mime. He did not bother much with dates, 'in time
of grandfather's father' would indicate anything earlier than the
immediate pre-Revolutionary era. I secretly enjoyed such an approach, for
Olga Maximova's professional exactitudes, though necessary, sometimes
lacked the personal, or vivid narrative nature of Russlan's information.
Russlan was one of the many simple Russian people I encountered on my
travels, whom I shall always recall with respect and affection.

~

As we drew near to the farther southern shore, I could see a train
following the cliff face by the edge of the lake, where rocks rose sheer from

glassy waters. It emerged and disappeared through a series of tunnels, following the circum-Baikal route my train must have taken, after leaving Irkutsk, before plunging inland towards the Chinese frontier. This section of the line had been particularly cruel on the workers; it was constantly sliding into the lake, while blasting operations caused many deaths. When the scheduled time was exceeded, the authorities became fretful, and soldiers from local battalions were commandeered and formed into working gangs, like the convicts or Chinese coolie labour. The troops had no say – military discipline was inexorable. It was barely fifty years since army reforms had reduced the twenty-five years' army service which earlier Tzars had maintained. The commandeered troops, it was said, worked an eighteen-hour day, hauling sleepers and construction material, after which they were lined up for military exercises. But then, the legacy of positively maniacal militarism, so cherished by Paul I, and by his son Nicholas I, was still a force with which to be reckoned in Russia.

It is recounted that when Nicholas II, as Tzarevitch, was visiting Siberia in 1891, an equerry was dispatched from the capital, post-haste across all Russia in Europe and all Russia in Asia, to Vladivostok on the Pacific rim, being instructed to take no rest by day or night, so urgent was his mission. He accomplished the journey by sleigh, *britchka*, and on horse-back, at the gallop, in record time, after which he collapsed and was for some while under treatment in a mad-house. But then, the matter had been of the utmost urgency. The Heir to the Throne had just received regimental promotion and, said General Staff Headquarters, it was essential that his new insignia and epaulets should reach him without delay.

There were, it seems, no aspects of Russia's past, whether trivia or great sweeps of history, which did not point to the inevitability of its Revolution. Everything came back to that one inescapable fact. Everything spoke of the abuses and misrule this people had always endured. Revolutionary Bakunin was succinct, writing in *La Reforme*, in 1845:

'Despite the terrible slavery which crushes it, despite the blows which rain on it from every side, the Russian people is in its instincts and habits altogether democratic. It is not corrupted, it is only unhappy... The moment is perhaps not distant when the risings will be merged in a great revolution: and if the Government does not make haste to emancipate the people, much blood will be spilt.'

~

I climbed the main stairway of the beautiful colonnaded white mansion that had been built by a parvenu Siberian merchant to became the residence of successive Governors, Count Mouraviev-Amursky, my childhood hero, among them. His visionary approach to his post was matched by his energy: not only had he acquired the Amur provinces for Russia (thus gaining his title) but been among the first to urge the construction of the Trans-Siberian railway. In Irkutsk Mouraviev had surrounded himself with a staff of exceptional young officials who shared something of his large views. He was both an idealist and a man of action: a despot too, but a benevolent one.

His statue, a stocky, side-whiskered figure, still stands in the little park near his house overlooking the Angara. The Traveller remembered that in his youth all loyal Siberians removed their hat to this statue; but I saw no such pious gestures. The memory of this remarkable man, to whom Siberia owes so much, seemed tolerated, but not venerated. I was glad to think that once I had placed flowers on his grave in the Paris cemetery where he lies, far from his Siberian achievements. The elegant white mansion from where he had ruled so imaginatively was pitted with shell marks, memorial to a violent battle between Red and White forces during the Civil War. Today it holds the city's Scientific Library, and the Regional Archives – particularly rich ones, I guessed, sniffing longingly at the files.

One of the greatest Siberian libraries is now in the possession of the Library of Congress, at Washington. It was sold by its founder, Gennadius Yudin, in 1907, at a purely nominal figure 'for the purpose of strengthening the ties and understanding of the two peoples.' Such was the wish of this self-made man who attained wealth by his distillery at Krasnoyarsk, and set about amassing everything pertaining to Siberian and Russian history, ethnology and the fine arts. Yudin's dream of unity between Siberia and the United States of America had also been in Mouraviev's mind, some fifty years earlier. In his *Memoirs of a Revolutionary* Prince Kropotkin writes: 'In Mouraviev's own study, the young officers, with the exile Bakunin' (who was also Mouraviev's cousin) 'among them, discussed the chances of creating the United States of Siberia, federated across the Pacific Ocean with the United States of America.'

The pleiad which surrounded Mouraviev during such visionary discussions, and others on a more realizable level, were to prove some of

315

the most remarkable men of their age. Count Ignatiev, triumphant diplomat, brilliant rogue in the game of international banditry, who obtained vast concessions from the Chinese and is remembered chiefly for his Central Asian acquisitions; young General Kukel, who became chief of the Governor's General Staff and who was presently to obtain the even younger Peter Kropotkin the future 'anarchist prince' as his aide-de-camp, and with him to plunge into a programme of administrative reforms. Here too was the youthful Baron Wrangel, an equally cultivated and advanced administrator, he who befriended Dostoievsky at Semipalatinsk. These were men who could keep pace with their chief, and in Siberia, were the right men, in the right place. This was Siberia, where, for good or bad, the *excessive* qualities of Russia reached their apotheosis.

~

'Which was Mouraviev's study?' I asked, as I went through the beautiful rooms with their high porcelain stoves and splendid Bohemian glass chandeliers, turquoise blue, or ruby red, where the lofty windows overlook the wide river. I wanted to see the setting for this co-radiation of imaginative administration: also, to visualize the background for some of the fateful encounters that had taken place here before and after Mouraviev's tenure. For a while, his successor was able to continue the liberal tradition: but generally, both before and after this era, the climate of Government House was inflexibly reactionary.

The rooms through which I went were now lined with bookshelves and the students worked at long tables. I envied them the possibilities of their studies here, for Irkutsk is, naturally, rich in first-hand material on the Dekabrists. I wondered which of them had come to this house? Not in their earlier days, when they were shackled, far away; but those intrepid women who followed them in the years between 1825-1830, battled, fragile yet steely, pitting themselves against one of Mouraviev's predecessors, a man of very different kidney. Such men saw to it that every opposition and humiliation confronted these women. They automatically forfeited their titles and possessions. Nor could they ever return to Russia so long as their husbands were serving Siberian sentences. Their children lost their names, or the right to attend schools: those born in Siberia were automatically classed as the children of serfs. To most provincial administrators, as to the Tzar, the slightest liberal sympathy spelled anarchy, and like him they followed the celebrated dictum: 'I prefer injustice to disorder.'

Nicholas I's savage death sentence on five of the leaders stunned the nation. Hanging was not then practised in Russia, and the gallows were clumsily knocked together. It was only when the five condemned men saw this rickety contraption before them that they lost hope. No experienced hangman being found for the task, the authorities had been obliged to summon one from Finland. Even so, things went wrong. The ropes gave way as the prisoners were strung up, and they crashed into the pit below, breaking their legs and arms. 'Unhappy Russia! They don't even know how to hang properly,' said Mouraviev-Apostol, as he lay waiting for death. At last their broken bodies were hauled out and strung up all over again, efficiently this time.

~

Over the years the Tzar maintained his implacability. Siberia must finish off the rest of the rebels. Those whom he had not hung remained dead, in his eyes. When, eighteen years later, Prince Sergei Volkonsky's daughter Hélène attended the opera in St. Petersburg with her uncle, her youthful beauty caught the Tzar's attention.

'Who is that charming young creature?' he asked.

'My niece, Sergei's daughter, Sire.'

'Indeed? The dead prince's child?'

'But my brother is not dead, Your Majesty – he is in Siberia.'

'When I say someone is dead – he *is* dead,' was the Autocrat's reply.

'At what do you look?' Olga Maximova asked me, as we went down the steep stone stairway of the Governor's mansion. I was observing how the stone was worn away, in two trough-like depressions, unnaturally deep, I thought, for a house only built in the early part of the last century. But then I remembered the ceaseless file of exiles that had climbed them to plead for justice, for mercy, for life itself. The years of enlightenment and compassion had been as brief as the tenure of office held by Mouraviev and his successor; before and after stretched years of bitterness. Hopes barely raised and soon dashed have a heavy tread, and stones, like hearts, were worn away in Siberia.

CHAPTER TWENTY SIX

A s befitted a capital city Irkutsk possessed its own standards. I observed that certain things were not done – were not *Siberski*. I liked this word: it had an air of local pride about it. Above all, it was not *Siberski* to dwell too much on the immediate past of Stalinist purges and labour camps. The citizens were proud of their present and the all-absorbing future for which they worked and they liked this to be admired. But since I had come five thousand miles or more to indulge the historic and personal interests so richly represented in Irkutsk, I continued my usual pattern of rationing visits to contemporary achievements, and went my own way.

In the forgotten old churches of outlying villages I still found ikons which bore beautiful names and were counted miraculous. St. Praskovia and St. Innokenti were ever present, being Siberian saints; St. Innokenti was the country's patron saint. A handful of old women humped into shawls, were usually shuffling and snuffling round, busy with cleaning rags or candles. Sometimes they were dispensing the little funeral cakes which are ritualistically eaten in memory of the departed. It is the custom of both the Greek and Russian Orthodox church that the coffin remains open till the moment of burial, and in the U.S.S.R. I became hardened to glimpsing these still faces, waxy and remote, wreathed in bright paper flowers, being carried through the streets or placed in the churches, surrounded by little groups of mourners. There was a practical side to this, too. Since funeral parlours appear to be rare in the U.S.S.R. and housing shortages still acute, with teeming families crowded into two-roomed apartments, the dead lie more peacefully in quiet dark churches until the earth receives them.

Some of these old village churches were particularly beautiful in their mixture of simplicity and splendour. Their thick, low, white or ochre washed walls and dark woodwork were confounded by the glitter of sumptuous metal-cased ikons, some three or four feet square, shimmering in the glow of coloured *lampadas*. When I asked the old women the names of the various saints they mumbled them for me with a furtive air. The Virgin, 'Countenance of all Sinners', 'Of all Consolations' or 'Joy of the Afflicted' seemed particularly suited to their Siberian setting and the long history of suffering they had consoled. Here in Siberia, as in the Kremlin or the Church of the Old Believers, which houses some of Moscow's richest ikons, the Russian people's innate love of splendour is evident. In the past an oriental passion for jewels was always remarked by visitors to both the Court or merchant society, and it was maintained in extravagant religious ornamentation. The Virgin is sometimes mantled or netted in a lattice of pearls, her jewels worthy of Sheba's queen, her background cloth of gold or hammered silver, while crucifixes bleed rubies for blood or are crowned in emerald thorns. It is an idiom more barbaric or Eastern than the purely worldly splendours of so many Catholic images; while the diamond-studded crowns and jewelled copes still worn by the Patriarch and high clergy are worthy of a coronation. (Even in a more purposeful, less colourful contemporary scene, something of this unbridled love of splendour is to be seen in the Moscow metro – surely the most refulgent of any, anywhere.)

'A very old painting – probably a Byzantine saint,' said Olga Maximova, rather dourly I thought, when I lingered in the Znamenski Monastery, admiring the curiously crowned Virgin of Feodorofskaya. On leaving I picked my way over a handful of beggars crouched on the steps, supplicating silently.

'They could all have work, if they would,' said Olga Maximova, glaring at the log-like figures. 'They are begging, because they think some God is going to give.'

The ethics of begging proved a lively subject for further discussion in the restaurant that night.

Once, I was told, Irkutsk possessed thirty fine churches and not a single factory.

'Then beggars were inevitable... but now – Now we have over a hundred factories at Irkutsk.'

'And two churches?'

'You criticize us for that?' yelled the stranger who was eating at our table. He sounded truculent but as he was obliged to shout above the vibrant tones of the *tchang* and the *temir komous*, curious instruments native to Tadjikstan and now being demonstrated fortissimo by members of the Tadjik People's Opera *Ansamble* also staying at the hotel, no doubt his combative tone was not directed at myself.

I hastened to explain that I just happened to find old churches and ikons more aesthetic than factories. But I could see this was not considered really *Siberski*, so I listened with an air of enthusiasm while he told me of the latest kind of *yurts* being manufactured for the Buriat-Mongolian encampments across the Gobi. The supporting poles (which come in three sizes), are now made of fibre-glass, while the former felt coverings are replaced by foam plastic, an excellent protection against the snow... But the snows of yesteryear – where are they?

~

In the sad autumn days, with their whipping winds already hinting snow, Siberia had a melancholy that would soon give way to beauty, I was assured. Winter would crystallize the scene to a white world glittering under those blue and radiant skies which all Siberians vaunt. This is another aspect of their pride, along with size and extravagance. 'In Siberia,' says the proverb, '100 miles is an ordinary distance, 100 roubles an ordinary sum, but a day without sunshine is extraordinary.' Nevertheless I was content with the grey skies I found there; they were in keeping with my mood.

Long wet afternoons, when even Russlan's enthusiasm for picnics in the *taïga* flagged, were spent in the Historical Museum or meeting with persons connected with the city's historical background. With them I followed the changing pattern of the centuries and the land.

In this Museum, ethnographic, historic, political and economic developments were interwoven. Here were reconstructions of Siberia's prehistoric beginnings, the dwellings and customs of the primitive tribes, the epic of Cossack conquest, of explorations and colonial expansion or the merchants' trading ventures along Chinese shores, following the exotic tiger-lands of the Amur. Here, as might be expected, I found whole sections devoted to the convict settlements, the Lena goldfields, the Alexandrovsky forwarding prison and many more such terrible records. Here were grim photographs of prison life on Sakhalin, of which Chekhov wrote in his *Travel Notes from Siberia*. The yellowing old prints of this island, which lies off the extreme north-east coast, show a forbidding coastline rising sheer from the sea, to heights bare of anything but the prison buildings and the stark huts of settlers, usually former prisoners working on the land.

As might be expected, a whole section of the Historical Museum (a turreted crimson building, robber-baron in style), was devoted to the Trans-Siberian, its founders, its construction, its first run, and the vicissitudes of its branch lines. Here were photographs of the various types of engines and cars used over the years. Here were pompous officials in tight gold-lace uniforms standing beside Chinese dignitaries in silken robes, with massed bands blasting away on a bunting-hung platform, celebrating the opening of the Chinese Eastern Line, in 1887. Here were pictures of elaborate compartments such as I had not imagined, such as the Traveller had not described, which, by their resplendence had lost all the drama of train travel. Lace curtains, mirrors, Moorish-brothel style alcoves and painted and carved ornamentation vied with tasselled trimmings, and an *art nouveau* bathroom where, by some feat of stabilization, the water could not flood overboard, however much the train bucked.

One lavish model had been originally designed for the Paris Exhibition of 1900 with the purpose of inspiring confidence in possible Western passengers. There was also a dining car, expressed in similarly fantastic terms, where arm-chair travelling Parisians could feast to the accompaniment of mechanical swaying and rattling, while roll after roll of scenic canvas raced past the windows, depicting steppes, mountain peaks, raging rivers, and whole Kremlins, gold-domed and gorgeous, to emphasize local colour. (What bliss, could I have installed this in the nursery, long ago, to lend zest to my simple suppers! But could it possibly have heightened those exotic perspectives once conjured for me, from an eider-down *yurt*?)

In the section devoted to the Civil War were photographs of the armoured trains – *broneviki*, improvised by using sheets of ironplating and layers of sand bags, with gun-turrets mounted on the roof of carriage or box car. These ambulant forts were much used in the fierce battles which raged between 1917-1920, when the Trans-Siberian was the prize life-line for which Red and White forces struggled. But while the White forces were sustained by Allied aid, for French and British troops fought beside them, and were later joined by American forces, 9,000 strong, plus 17,000 Japanese, the Reds fought on alone, ill-equipped and poorly organized.

'When the trains stop, that will be the end,' said Lenin; but somehow, the trains ran. Although the Trans-Siberian's last through-run,

Vladivostok to Petrograd was in February 1918, the various sections operated fitfully, controlled first by one side and then the other – but still they ran.

Then there were the Czech Legions, who played a leading part in the history of Siberia's revolutionary years, and here was photographic documentation. After the Bolsheviks signed peace terms at Brest-Litovsk, in the winter of 1917-18, there was the question of repatriating 50,000 of them, all well-equipped. The rest of the Allied forces had withdrawn from the Russian-German front. President Masaryk counted on Allied support to obtain a return of Slovakia and other provinces formerly crushed under Austro-Hungarian rule. It was therefore agreed that his armies should be withdrawn from Russia to fight on the Western front. But the Ukraine was blocked by German troops, thus there was no way out except north through Siberia and Vladivostok. In the spring, the exodus began: but as the Legions flooded into Siberia, suspicions and incidents multiplied. The Bolsheviks feared they were to be used as a spearhead of an Allied invasion of Siberia; the Czechs doubted the Bolsheviks would allow them to leave with all their equipment and arms intact. They violated Soviet terms by secreting arms and, at last, bloodshed broke out and some of them were arrested, while an order went out to the Red Commissars that any Czech found with arms was to be shot. The Legions imagined their German enemies were behind this and they promptly formed into bands of guerrilla fighters, joining with the White partisans. It was now that they seized rolling stock, converting the trains to *broneviki*, using them as the spearhead of an attack, or for fighting rear-guard actions. Most celebrated among them was the Little Orlik – or Eaglet, and now I saw photographs of it in action, racing across the snows, its gun-turrets blazing.

The Czech Legions, fighting their way out of Siberia to regain their homeland, at last liberated from Austrian domination, had a clear view of issues. They no longer wished to be embroiled with either side, Red or White; they wished to return home and, at last, anyone who hindered them was an enemy. Their *esprit de corps* was the outstanding factor in their survival and this sense of brotherhood was the same spirit which had sustained their ancestors, the Hussite Brethren. Troops addressed their officers as Brother General, Brother Captain. There was discipline, but no protocol. The particular quality of ingenuity displayed by the Czech Legions became famous throughout Siberia. Although they arrived from the Western front well-equipped, they knew how to turn the simplest assets to advantage, in contrast to the feckless extravagance of Kolchak's men, or the stoic endurance of the Red troops who, for some while, fought on with little or no equipment or food.

It was the Czechs who first plated the railway carriages with rough iron sheeting, thus converting them into armoured cars. And there was something almost housewifely, thrifty and cosy, in the manner in which they converted the box-cars – *teplushki* – that became their barracks (forty men to a car), into snug quarters. Here, during the latter part of the campaigns, they painted flowery or symbolic designs on each car, achieved curtains, hot water and, above all, devised heating systems.

To the homeless, half frozen, starving bands of refugees that wandered hopelessly across the land, displaced local villagers or the hunted bourgeoisie escaped from Russian cities, such *teplushki* seemed paradise. In the desolate forest clearings, they might come on a siding where a string of such box-cars glowed with warmth, oil-lamps and the flicker of stoves, where men stirred cauldrons of soup... All Paradise was there. But no flaming swords barred the entrance. The Czechs responded generously to the miseries around them.

At one point, these Legions controlled most of the rail, from Penza to Baikal, supporting the counter-revolutionaries all along the way; they even seized control of the gold reserves of the Bolshevik Government, which had placed them for safety at Kazan. The situation must have seemed hopeless to the impoverished and encircled Bolsheviks. Beyond Baikal power then lay in the hands of another enemy, the Japanese-supported Ataman Semenov, that flamboyant and sinister individual who for some while contrived to be in the good graces of the Allied Command. He was of mixed Russian and Mongolian blood and had proposed to raise a Buriat-Mongol regiment, a plan to which the harassed Provisional Government of 1917 had agreed. Thus, the moment of the Revolution and Siberian campaigns found him in Trans-Baikalia, commanding a rather small force but looting and feathering his own nest vigorously. His headquarters were over the frontier, in Manchuria, at the crucial junction of the Trans-Sib and Chinese-Eastern line, where he lived dissolutely, in considerable style.

Among the White Russian commanders fighting alongside, rather than with him, was the fanatic Baltic Baron, General von Ungern

Sternberg, whose reputation for cruelty, as I remembered the Traveller saying, equalled that of the Ataman. But with this difference: while the Ataman indulged purely personal sadistic fancies, the Baron's fury was inspired by a sort of mystical fervour, a belief in his divine mission to cleanse the world of the Soviet Anti-Christ. Together, these two terrible men raged about Siberia and the Outer Mongolian border country, joining forces with the White armies against the common enemy.

As I hung over records of these Siberian campaigns, it seemed the warm, lemon-scented air of a Mediterranean evening fanned round me again; the brown wooden show cases, the old photographs and ragged banners of the Red Army faded, and I was on the veranda of a Corsican hotel, where, in the golden afterglow, I listened to the Traveller (or was it Aunt Eudoxia?) telling of Ungern Sternberg's belief in divination by the Tarot cards. He had been deeply involved in the shadowy world of Asiatic necromancy, often guided by the prophecies of lama and shaman. The manner and hour of his death being foretold, he showed a fatalistic disregard for his own life or that of anyone else. Wearing Chinese robes over his uniform, his heavy Russian army epaulets attached, he stalked – death in person – about the Mongolian city of Urga, or Ulan Bator as it is today, revolver in hand, executing his prisoners horribly, consulting various oracles in the scarlet and gold temples that flowered in the wastes, ticking off the days of life or carnage, left to him.

This extraordinary character had always interested me; he was the stuff of the Teutonic knights and dreamed of founding a military monastic order which would expunge the last Communist from the face of the earth. He boasted that his family sprang from Attila's Huns and had, throughout the centuries, continued in the way of violence. He maintained discipline among his troops with ruthless efficiency, just as he suppressed cholera epidemics, or any others which threatened, by shooting all the victims. This bizarre man contracted an equally curious marriage, allying his arrogant Baltic noble's blood with that of a daughter of Yuan-Shi-Kai (then President and Dictator of China), thus identifying himself even closer with the Asiatic hinterland that fostered his legend. He dreamed of a Buriat-Mongol Empire on the borders of Siberia – perhaps to overlap and control Siberian territory – and ranted of Buddhist prophecies, the Apocalypse, Karma, and Satanic communism which would precede the final destruction of mankind. In the name of a saviour he played on his undoubted powers of second sight, assuming god-like status among the superstitious soldiery. But when, at last, crossing into Soviet-held territory at the head of eleven thousand cavalry, he fell into a trap and was beaten, all this mystic ballast was destroyed by the methodic procedure of a Soviet military court. The Baron's ravings were coldly cut short; deflated, he listened stonily to his death sentence. He had known it would come for so long. In June 1921 he was shot – it is said, on the exact date predicted by the necromancers.

His fellow adventurer the Ataman Semenov also met his end, if not his deserts, at a Soviet military court. He was less dedicated than Sternberg, except in the matters of slaughter. Rapacious and ferocious, he enjoyed combining the business of battle with the pleasures of looting and indulging his sadistic whims. To ensure that the massacres he so frequently organized should not begin to pall on his troops, he allowed them to choose the manner of each day's executions. It lessened the monotony when the population of whole villages were successively put to the sword, poisoned, hanged, or burnt alive. It lessened opposition too.

But it was unfortunate such a man was counted as an ally by the Allied Command; though to the Japanese (in whose pay he was, since they had designs on Manchuria and reckoned on his aid) his methods seemed quite in order. As a mark of especial esteem they allowed him to paint the Imperial Japanese emblem of the Rising Sun on the railway carriages he used. As this brigand steamed furiously about Eastern Siberia he was accompanied, or followed, by his dread 'Independent Brigade', a guerrilla band largely made up of Mongols and Buriats, and which numbered only about two hundred Russians – White Russians, who still hoped the monster they followed fought to restore the monarchy to Holy Russia.

Here in the Museum's archives I studied the faces of these Siberian freebooters: Sternberg as pale-eyed and fanatic-looking as the Traveller had described him; the fleshy Ataman, with heavily moustached muzzle like some nightmare beast of prey. Here were finer faces, peaceful in death, or flash-lit, tensed – in some underground hide-out of an illicit printing press. Red partisans and White; local heroes or villains; a firing squad, victims and executioners. Bodies piled dead on a snowy battlefield beside a wrecked section of the Trans-Siberian, the crows circling overhead, as lonely in these vast skies as the dead in the vast steppes below. Here was a women's Army battalion, exalted Amazons, padded in their sheepskins till they looked like spherical toys toddling to battle; but there was nothing playful in the arms they carried with such assurance. Here was a fiery politico, though his appearance, seated at a desk and wearing pince-nez, was not inspiring. Here were the dark, strange faces of men from Turkestan, Inner Mongolia or the Caucasus, who had found their way north and joined the battle. This was heroic Siberia as I had heard it described by the Traveller. Would my search at last end here – a fleeting glimpse on a shadowy picture, rather than a name on a tombstone or a recounted memory?

Now a cold, tight-lipped face stares out – austerity personified, Admiral Kolchak, briefly the self-appointed Supreme Ruler of the White Government, and part of the Siberian legend. How an Admiral of the Russian fleet came to be in command of White Army forces in Siberia is too complicated a story to tell here. Suffice it to say that the Admiral assumed power from entirely disinterested motives of patriotism – to save Russia, he believed – but never for personal aggrandizement. He never succeeded in winning the whole-hearted support he had hoped, either of the Russian people or the Allied Command. He was out of touch with the former, while the latter held back from committing themselves to interior Russian political issues. Did the Admiral really represent the country as a whole? Could it be that the Bolsheviks were more representative? The Czechs settled the matter by handing him over to the local Soviets and he was shot at Irkutsk, one February night in 1920, his body disappearing beneath a hole in the ice.

~

I was keeping the Dekabrist souvenirs in the Museum for a last treat: they were something I had been waiting to see most of my life and now, confronted by the pathetic relics, I felt tears come to my eyes. There were no overtones of horror here – no branding irons, no chains; but there were some pieces of delicately wrought iron, bracelets and rings made by Bestoujev from the prisoners' fetters, when at last they were removed. The wives had clamoured for these romantic keepsakes, and some wore their Dekabrist wedding rings till they died.

When, in 1830, the Dekabrists were moved to new quarters at Petrovsky Zarod the Tzar's spiteful rage was apparent. He had authorized the architect's plans; but there were no windows. In the obscurity of these icy rooms (the prison was on the edge of a swamp) their life continued. They read by sitting at the doors opening into the corridors; there was a debating society and a music society; they held chess contests, and in the short summers, cultivated flowers and vegetables (and were the first to produce tomatoes there). Children were born; the beautiful Anny Mouravieva died, and was buried beside the prison stockade. Such milestones marked the slow passage of time.

Nine years later the hard core of the Dekabrists was released. Their new place of residence, as 'free Siberian settlers' (for they could never go home), was allotted to them by the authorities in St. Petersburg in an apparently haphazard manner, no doubt by indicating a spot on a map, some remote village, or wretched little town, or even a Buriat trading encampment as it sometimes turned out to be. Then their true sentence of exile began; there was no more of that comradeship that had sustained them for so long. They were forbidden to move from their allotted places. Their children could not attend school, being listed as serfs. They were even deprived of the right to a patronymic. Thus the son of Prince Sergei Volkonsky was merely inscribed as Sergeiyiev.

The new, 'free' life closed round the Dekabrists like further prison walls. Yet gradually, these proscribed men whose heroic aura dazzled the Siberians were becoming the country's aristocracy, forming a centre of cultivation new to Siberia. 'Our princes,' said the Siberians, welcoming those who now lived among them.

Both the Volkonskys and Troubetskoys were fortunate, being placed at Irkutsk, where they lived in some style, their establishment at last numbering twenty-five servants. These two families presided over local society, and invitations to their musical soirées were much coveted. When the Princess Marie attended a concert or the theatre (although still listed officially as the Criminal Volkonskaya), she was given such a tumultuous welcome that at last the Governor-General was obliged to forbid the wives of Dekabrists appearing at public functions.

In 1849, another band of persecuted liberals, 'the Petrashevsky' came this way, Dostoievsky among them. They were an intellectual and scientific élite, while the Dekabrists had been largely a military aristocracy. But they were linked by their ideals, and a living chain was forged that white winter's day when the wives of the 'freed' Dekabrists rallied to them at a stopping place outside Tomsk. The women went alone, for their husbands were proscribed from an encounter which would have been construed as a political manifestation. But the wives contrived to be there, waiting by the snowy *trakt* with food, warm clothing and books, and by their presence they transmitted something of the courage that had sustained them when they had first passed that way.

~

'Don't you want to see where the Volkonskys lived?' asked Olga Maximova, and she led me to a quiet backwater in the old part of the city where streets of ornate little wooden dwellings had not yet been destroyed and were dug snugly into the earth, half buried below the wooden pavings. All the houses hereabouts date from before the great fire which ravaged Irkutsk in 1879. Afterwards building in wood was forbidden, being replaced by stone; though the fire was so fierce that it devoured many stone buildings too. The Volkonsky house, which appeared to be portioned out in tenement-like flats, was large and two-storeyed, of the usual weathered grey timber, with the typical fretted decorations round the windows and doors. A high stockade lay between it and the little street running beside a small square or plot of unkempt bushes and tall old trees. Beyond rose the graceful white belfry of an old church – now a warehouse for government publications. The Volkonsky stockade was pierced by a wide arched gate, giving on to a courtyard with out-houses and stables. Beside the gate, facing the square, was a little bench, the usual street bench that is an immemorial part of the Russian scene, seeming to demand a Chekhov dialogue or one of those tangled monologues in which Dostoievsky characters luxuriate.

It was very quiet here in this unfrequented quarter, and suddenly I knew that this would be the right place to meet the Serbian bomb expert – if he would come – if my letter ever reached him – if I could contrive to post it unperceived. The historic associations of the house would provide me with a good reason for mooning about there; I could sit on a bench without exciting curiosity, it seemed; and so could anyone who came there to meet me.

I was still weighing up these possibilities as Olga Maximova led me down other quiet streets of low wooden houses, and stopped before one of more importance, of weathered grey wood, similar to that of the Volkonskys. This was where the Troubetskoys had lived; it too was now inhabited by several families, but was far more dilapidated, and an overpowering odour hung about it from a near-by plant for salting fish. There was a project of turning it into a Dekabrist museum, said Olga Maximova. I hoped the salting works would be removed elsewhere, for it was destructive to nostalgic reveries.

That night, pleading letters to write, I went up to bed early and composed the fatal missive; brief and to the point and yet a cry from the heart, I thought as I sealed it; and then I wondered if it was not all a mistake... I heard again the Traveller's smoky tones quoting Browning. 'Where the apple reddens never pry...' But the fruit of my longings had never reddened: my curiosity remained as sharp and green as ever.

CHAPTER TWENTY SEVEN

All next day I went about with the letter in my handbag (best not leave it about my room) and wondered when I would find a suitable place to post it unobserved. I knew better than to put it in the hotel mail box or be seen by Olga Maximova posting letters elsewhere. She would of course have offered, and expected, to take charge of them for me, and been very much surprised to see one addressed in Russian. I was still carrying the letter in my bag that evening when we set out to attend a Mongolian wrestling contest held at a near-by youth club. Olga Maximova looked resigned when I opted for wrestling rather than a concert by pupils of the Irkutsk Conservatoire, but she went along with good grace; it was at least an example of contemporary life, even if not a cultural manifestation.

As we joined the crowds surging into the building I noticed a most conveniently placed letter box just outside and managed to get jostled towards it by the crowd while Olga Maximova was showing her official pass at the door. With one lightning thrust, I had the letter in the box and was worming my way back to her before she was aware of my activities.

Now it only remained to wait; to reach the suggested rendezvous outside the Volkonsky house alone. Or perhaps, to be followed and arrested? It would be difficult to explain what brought me there; but it was not, I felt, a hanging matter, and I could hardly be sent to Siberia since I was there already. So I took my place for the Mongolian wrestling match in a mood of achievement, rather than anxiety.

I would have preferred to watch Mongolian wrestlers in their true surroundings, the Gobi wastes of my childish imaginings where, seated before a ceremonial *yurt*, in company with the Kutukthu, I watched my own stable of champions winning every contest. But even here, in a stream-lined Siberian building, the wrestlers and the whole ritual was sufficiently exotic. The sport seemed much like that which I had seen in Turkish villages where, on Fridays, crowds circle a field to watch a number of local contestants; they wear the traditional leather knee-breeches and are soused in oil, which renders them eel-like in their adversary's grip. These Mongolian wrestlers were lean and muscle-packed rather than muscle-bound; and there was none of that comic pantomime which makes all-in wrestling in the West a naïve spectacle with cooked-up dramatics, good man versus bad.

Wrestling is by origin an Asiatic sport, and here the Mongolians were following an ancient tradition in all its classic purity. They opened with the curious ritualistic caperings, *alchik-balchik*, the Turkish wrestlers called it – I did not discover if the Mongolians used the same word – by which the contestants warm up. Every move or gesture had its significance, and dated, probably, from the encampments of Jenghis Khan. Flailing their arms above their heads, they were recalling the eagle's wings; arching their torso, they told of the tiger's strength, and slapping their thighs (but not at all in the playful manner of Tyrolean folk dancers) they were recalling the beating wings of a mighty bird of prey. They wore soft leather topboots, and a minute and bright coloured satin *cache-sexe*, while their arms and shoulders were covered by a bolero-like garment, fancifully embroidered, which left the rest of the body bare. They were handsome men, with black cropped heads and bodies like polished ivory, and they bore proud titles which their trainers vaunted. Darkhan Avraga signified a champion of three years running; Arsalan, the lion; Nachin, the falcon, and so on.

'You have such contests in your country?' asked the man in the next seat, a medical student who spoke good English and was explaining the finer points to me. He seemed surprised when I tried to describe the antics of characters such as the noble Boy Batman from Outer Space versus the sinister Killer – Gorilla – a morality play more than a sport, in the Asiatic sense.

~

For several days past, during which time I was alternately cast down and elated, thinking of my letter, I went about Irkutsk with one eye on the clock. I had not asked for a reply. I had simply said that I would be outside the Volkonsky house at six o'clock on a certain day and that I would wait there for one hour. This meeting might lead to complications, I thought, and found myself a prey to all the dark propaganda I had heard over the years; but it would not do to be fobbed off by second-hand fears after crossing half Asia for facts.

The Traveller's revenant had been strangely absent during my time in Irkutsk; it was as if my actual arrival in the country we had so often entered together in our dreams had broken the thread by which he used to join me. Perhaps my journey to Siberia, like my determination to discover what had become of him, had been an invasion of privacy.

Meantime, I was to be consoled by other kinds of facts. A distinguished Siberian, Professor of the Faculty and specialist in Dekabrist history, had invited me to visit him at his home. To this rendezvous I could go without qualm.

The Professor lived in a stark cement block, on the edge of the city: but the windows looked out on 'the Street of the Dekabrists' – the road they passed along, en route for their first prison in the mines. I wondered if the Professor had been allotted this flat by chance, by the rulings of a housing committee, or if he had chosen it for its romantic associations. The broad, benign face smiled: the leonine head nodded.

'Naturally. Sometimes at night I fancy I can hear them, dragging their chains...'

The Dekabrist mystique, I saw, was something to which the Professor admitted, in spite of his academic stature, and I settled down to an afternoon of unalloyed bliss. But his book-lined room, like the shelves of the City Archives, presently reduced me to a mood of acute frustration and remorse. Why had I never learned to read Russian properly? The Professor spoke in a rapid manner with which even the interpreter could not always keep pace. German, his second language, was no help to me, and although it was evident he read French and English easily, he refused to speak either, except when we came to an impasse. Moreover his tendency to mispronounce 'historic', a word which occurred frequently, as 'hysterique', 'this hysterique moment,' or 'a hysterique figure' caused some confusion. But nothing could detract from the range and riches of his knowledge, and I hung on his words in any language.

'You know much of our past – how do you come to know of Radistchev or the Passek family?' he inquired flatteringly, and added, 'this is not usual knowledge for tourists,' at which I felt myself cast down, being taken for one. I had never seen myself as such in Russia. There, I remained a returning exile.

Now the Professor was talking of Tolstoy's projected novel on the Dekabrists and his reasons for dropping it. Originally he had planned it as a vast historical canvas to immortalize the movement and the men. He had known two aged survivors, but although for many years obsessed by the theme (it was before he began *War and Peace*) he at last abandoned it. Because, said the Professor, Tolstoy had grown out of sympathy with revolt, or force. Iconoclast he might appear, at different times, to different people, but he became fixed in his abhorrence of violence. The growing terrorist movement in Russia (which derived from the Dekabrist stand) had no support from him.

From the top of a rickety step-ladder the Professor was amassing books to substantiate his views. Pamphlets and quarto volumes crashed down on the head of our interpreter, who was steadying the ladder.

'Tolstoy is always labelled universal,' said the Professor, from the heights, where he swayed dangerously. 'But he is above all profoundly *Russian*. He distrusted foreign influences such as French liberalism which influenced the Dekabrists. He came to judge them as setting Russian against Russian... He even went so far as to say the whole movement had no roots – no Russian roots, that is.'

The Professor looked distressed, for his loyalties were sadly divided here.

'Then what about Pushkin?' I reminded him of the poet's love for French traditions, and his craving to be allowed to travel there. 'Do you consider him less Russian for that?' I pressed. 'And he was entirely in sympathy with the Dekabrists, his friends.'

'*Pussinka* – don't Arg!' The Traveller's voice! The old familiar command! So his shade had joined me at last, here in the Professor's study – was here, somewhere, among this concentration off Dekabrist data he would have loved. I looked round the room, half-believing he would materialize – in that armchair – beside those bookshelves...

'You have lost something?' asked the Professor, who was plainly not to be side-tracked from justifying the Dekabrists.

'Remember this,' he continued, looking down over his spectacles, at once owlish and imperative. 'Remember! It was only through amassing material for the projected Dekabrist book that Tolstoy found the subject of *War and Peace*. And *War and Peace* is not only the greatest achievement of our literature, but the greatest novel in *any* language,' said the Professor with finality; and it was clear that for him this masterpiece must be chalked up to the Dekabrists.

He climbed down and proposed tea.

A curtain which divided the room was now drawn back and the Professor's sister was revealed in the manner of a conjurer's assistant, beside a table piled with surprises. The immemorial samovar dominated an array of cakes, *piroshki*, pies and fancy breads, while there were seven different kinds of jam – home made, from special Siberian berries, *brousnika*, *smorodina*, *rassetki* and such.

'All must be tasted,' said the Professor, as I began this agreeable experiment, to the evident satisfaction of his sister, who had whispered to the interpreter that she had feared I might be one of those dieting Western ladies she had read about, who would not do justice to her spread.

'She should worry,' I replied, a colloquialism unknown to the interpreter, who collected it with enthusiasm.

Except that she wore an amber necklace and had tied her head up in a handkerchief of Bokharan silk, the Professor's sister appeared indistinguishable from her brother; the same broad, beaming face, the same large presence. While she filled and refilled our glasses of tea and the samovar puffed and hummed, the Professor and I continued talking with our mouths full; he, waving his glass of tea dangerously to emphasize a point or using a spoon as a book-marker. When at last I was torn away by the exhausted interpreter I realized I had been the recipient of an entire academic address, delivered to, and for, myself alone. Coming down to earth after this heady triumph, I found the Professor's sister pressing a pot of the *brousnika* jam into my hand, while he presented me with one of his own books on Siberia. Russian hospitality! Russian friendships! How fondly I shall always recall such meetings.

~

All next day was spent visiting a faraway *kolkhoz* where, to Olga Maximova's surprise, I showed unexpected stamina, going from one end of the huge farms to another, being shown over schools, workers' clubs, collective milking plants and administrative headquarters with a brief pause for refreshments in the kitchen of a partisan heroine of World War Two. I was determined that when, later, I returned to the hotel, it would seem quite natural that I was exhausted, and would ask not to be disturbed while I napped till dinner-time. It would all be to the good, too, I thought, if Olga Maximova was also exhausted and napped in her room instead of sitting in the hotel foyer, as she liked to do. That evening, at dusk, I meant to keep my uncertain rendezvous outside the Volkonsky house. I think I knew, in my heart that the Traveller was dead; but I wanted to know all that his friend could tell me of his life since I had lost him.

Through the ginger velour curtains which sagged so dankly, I watched the afternoon fading to a flat, greyish light; in half an hour it would be dusk. Time to go. I got stiffly off the bed – the *kolkhoz* outing had certainly been taxing – and putting on my sheepskin jacket, which was more in the idiom of a Siberian *touloup* than my other, a conspicuously foreign top-coat, I left my room and, with conspiratorial tread, passed Olga Maximova's door.

'A breath of fresh air before dinner – I've such a headache,' I told the desk clerk, but she was deep in accounts, and hardly looked up. They were used to me in the hotel by now, and regarded me with a certain indulgence. My morning tea was always brought to my room; a concession perhaps won because I did not nag for brand-name breakfast foods or Cokes. And then, I had stayed with them long enough to admire the city and its surroundings in gratifying depth. I strolled, apparently aimless, along the boulevards until well out of sight. Then, plunging across the main thoroughfare, I hurried into the old section of unfrequented streets where the high wooden pavements ran beside ditch-like streams bridged by planks, and the little wooden houses were sunk so deep in the earth that the windows were only half-visible, peeping up with a sly air. From inside, passers-by must have appeared as a procession of disembodied boots. My feet now joined them, hurrying on. I wondered if, to a watcher in the windows below, this procession of passing feet revealed anything of their various purposes – supper, the loved one, a political meeting? Or if, seeing the feet dawdle or drag, something of that mood was also communicated to the watchers? My own urgency, I felt, must have been apparent in my steps.

I pressed on, rehearsing what I would say if I found anyone waiting for me. Rounding a corner I saw the white belfry of the old church turned book warehouse; another corner rounded, and I was in the little square, and there was the Volkonsky house, its bleached grey façade and uncurtained windows staring down at me. There was no one about. The big gates still gaped open and, except for a waddle of ducks, there was no sign of life in the yard. I sat down on the bench to wait and watched the grey dusk thickening, turning bluish as an old-fashioned street lamp flickered and settled into a feeble glow. It was very quiet, very still; not a leaf moved, on the brown-tipped trees. Faraway I heard the screech of brakes, the sound of impatient motor horns, and the wail of a distant factory siren, but here, where the Volkonskys had lived the last years of their exile, it was as if such sound had no relation to fact; the impact of the past, of the Volkonsky legend was far more real. Remembrance drifted round the little square and I wondered what echoes the Dekabrists had heard each time the diminishing band of ageing rebels met there. The sound of the Tzar's cannons opening fire on them that decisive December day on the Senate Square? The tolling of a bell and the roll of drums heard in their cells, in the St. Peter and Paul fortress, as their companions were led out to be hung? The rattle of chains?

The drama of those lives rose round me so vividly that I was taken unaware by approaching footsteps. A figure had crossed the square and, emerging from the shadowy half-light, stood by me, before I brought myself back entirely to the present. I looked up, and saw a small man with thick spectacles peering down at me. He wore a peaked cap and a leather jacket, and the inevitable high-boots. He smiled, a wide, silver-capped smile, and held out a bony hand.

'Let us talk,' he said, and sat down beside me.

~

I suppose that the introduction from my Yakimankaya friend removed any reserves he might otherwise have felt, talking to a stranger, a foreigner from suspect shores. In any case he seemed to understand my hunger. He spoke slowly, at some pains with his English and, as he hesitated, searching for a word, his face took on a troubled look; he seemed anxious not to fail me.

It was almost dark now; the slow northern twilight lingered in a greyish smudge westwards but from an upstairs window of the Volkonsky house an unshaded electric bulb was suddenly switched on, lighting the bench where we sat. Its acid glare fell on the old Serbian and I saw that his eyes, behind the thick lenses, were brown and soft – ox eyes, ruminative and peaceful; unlikely eyes for a terrorist.

He had known the Traveller for many years and in many places he said.

'In Belgrade, in Geneva, Paris... London too. You knew him in London – yes? He came back to Russia when his work in the west was finished. He could not stay away for ever... not for anyone...'

He turned his slow, ox-stare on me, speculatively. 'He belonged here. His work, his believing, it was all here.' I began edging towards exactitudes. Where was he now?

'You thought to find him? It is difficult to find people here. So big a country... They go away. They vanish. It is best not to look for them.' He broke off, and taking an apple from his pocket, split it carefully with a pen-knife and offered me half. Munching, and greatly daring, I asked if my love had been involved in counter-espionage work – a double agent.

'Double-man? No. He was single-minded. *Absolute!* Yet he became sad for many things, I think. For many people, too. That is why they sent him here. But first he had done much work well. Dangerous work, for he was becoming known in too many places.'

So there it was at last. All the old, half-formed suspicions were confirmed. A spy.

'I always thought – my family – we always thought he couldn't possibly have really been spying... he seemed so obvious, he was so *openly* mysterious, if you know what I mean?'

He smiled indulgently. 'Ah! But that was his tricking! He took much trouble to appear just what he was... Naturally, if he was a spy, he could have covered up better – or so people thought... It was simple – so – and it worked very well for many years... But in the end it became necessary to return to Russia. And then, when he was back, he was not always wise. He was *têtu*. It is not wise to be *têtu* here. He criticized much, so one day he is sent to Siberia... Oh no! Not to a labour camp. He was well-liked. He had high friends... No, they sent him here to be far away from the West. He spoke good Chinese and he knew the Mongolian and Buriat dialects. He worked mostly on frontier administrative posts. Soon after he came here they sent me, too, and so we meet again. It is a good life here. It is quiet on the *kolkhoz*. Good food, too. Siberia is a good country.'

'Yes, he always said so. He told me a lot about its history, and the sort of life lived here when he was a young man. The family had mines, and a house somewhere near Omsk, I believe. Did you know that?'

'I did; but all that has gone. When we meet again he is telling me he is an exile – an exile in his own land. I ask him, where do you want to be? Then he told an English saying – perhaps you know it? "Home is where is the heart". "My heart," he said, "is not here any more..." And then, he was not always clever. He spoke what he thought too much. And he went often to church too. Not many people doing that here. I tell him, this is foolishness – and always he laughs, saying all men must have a vice. When he was at a meeting – the sort we have here, local politics, he was quickly in *ennui*, and he would go away very loudly. Often I fetched him back. I always knew where to find him. In the church!' (*Scandalist!* He was always a *scandalist,* Aunt Eudoxia had said, laying out the Tarot cards that faraway summer in Corsica.)

The old Serbian carefully collected the core of his half apple and mine and wrapped them in a piece of paper, tidily, before throwing them away, over the Volkonsky fence.

'Your friend often went to the Znamensky church,' he continued. 'You know it? Very beautiful... Always the same thing. He lighted three candles and watched them burn down. One time I asked him "are you praying? " He answers "No." Then why three candles, I say? For what are they? And he tells me: "For the man I was, and the man I am become, and for one person I love."'

'And then?'

'Then one day, he goes away and I never see him again.'

'You mean he died?'

'I don't know. The war came then and a lot of people disappeared. He went to the German front as interpreter. I worked in an armament factory. I heard about him once, though... At the end of the war someone came here who told how he was taken prisoner by the Nazis and then escaped with

Russian soldiers from an Austrian prison camp. They joined up with partisans in my country – in Serbia... Yugoslavia they call it nowadays.

'He was badly wounded and getting not so young any more, so when the fighting is finished the partisans took him to Trieste and put him on a Russian hospital ship leaving for the Black Sea. All the way across Venezia Giulia province, he was saying he wants to stay in Trieste and go to the British Military Mission there. He said they would help him to get to England... Perhaps he was in delirium... he kept telling there was someone he must find in London. But he was very ill, so they put him on the boat going to Odessa. The man who told me all this was on the same boat. It was a beautiful one. Very luxurious it was, he said. It had been built for Roumanian pleasure cruises, those Roumanians think much about pleasure. We don't. But some of the Russian boys took door-handles off the cabins for souvenirs. This man had one – he put it on the door of his *izba*. It looked nice. He kept it well polished, too...'

Darkness had thickened round us and across the little square patches of light appeared from the half-buried houses set below street level. They glowed and winked like the eyes of crouching cats. Two old women shuffled past, mumbling together. They eyed us from the shawls that were wound round their heads. Near-by an accordion sounded, accompanying one of the sad songs of Russian longing. The old Serbian began to speak again, and I held my breath, waiting for some ultimate revelation that would crown my journey.

'That is all. All what I know for certain,' he said apologetically. 'I do not think you will find him. Why try? Perhaps he is dead. Perhaps not. He was badly wounded... and remember, that is twenty years past. He was not being young any more, last time we were together. Now he would be old, like me... Here we do not know much what is happening outside. Siberia is still many miles, many days away from everything. Yet now people are flying here in one day. You have been in an airplane? I have not... Once I was asked to make a special kind of bomb to explode in an airplane... But I told them no. I told it would be against my principles. The passengers take enough risks flying. It would not be fair. But I was not understood. That is why I am sent here to work on the *kolkhoz* clocks. But as I told you, I am happy.'

A silence fell and then, as if to close the subject, he added: 'I never hear anything more of your friend... but like you, I remember him.'

A chill gust of wind stirred the trees and a few late leaves rattled to the ground at our feet. My companion turned up the collar of his sheepskin jacket.

'You do not find it cold? Why you did not say we meet in the hotel? It is more *gemütlich* there.'

A tinge of longing sounded in his voice and I realized that he would have enjoyed the club sofas and an Armenian brandy after a copious dinner in the overcrowded dining-room – the world, the flesh and the devil, beside *kolkhoz* living. How could I have been so inhospitable – so blind, too? I might have known that, if he was able to join me at all, this cloak and dagger rendezvous would not be necessary.

'You mean we could have met there, at the hotel?' I asked.

'Why not?'

It seemed an anti-climax to suggest returning there together now, but I made the gesture.

'Thank you, but it is late. A friend will drive me back to the *kolkhoz*. I must not keep him waiting.' (Or fail to report our conversation to the proper quarters, perhaps?)

From the far side of the square two men were walking towards us; their footsteps sounded softly on the unpaved ground. They passed us slowly, and did not look in our direction, which was odd, for in Siberia everyone is of interest to everyone else – especially people speaking together in a foreign language. Their footsteps died away, and they vanished into the darkness. The Serbian explosives expert got to his feet stiffly.

'Time I am going,' he said, and took my hand, and smiled, and went away, melting, like them, into the darkness, leaving me alone.

The Traveller had always been an elusive figure, and it was in keeping that he should remain so, recalled only by echoes, even in Siberia.

Suddenly I wanted to leave. Chita, the reaches of the Selenga, like the Mongol frontiers faded... It was time to leave my sigh-away, die-away realm: time to go back from where I had come, westward, westward again, across Asia into the fret and fume of the European cities that are, *au fond*, my home. I recalled the words of Komensky the Quietist: 'Return! Return whence thou camest, to the house of the heart, and then close the door behind thee.'

In the house of the heart there is room for all Siberia, all memories.

~

Olga Maximova was thoroughly put out when I told her I had decided to cut short my Siberian stay.

'You want to leave, now? But your permit to stay in Vladivostok has just arrived. This is quite a rare privilege! Your accommodation has been reserved. I do not understand.'

She spoke severely of capricious travellers and a change of plans. As it was equally unlikely she would understand a change of *heart*, I remained silent. Nor could I explain to Russlan who had been planning further, mouth-watering local expeditions, and assumed an air of sad denial.

On the morning of my departure he was waiting by the car with a basket, 'for our *taïga* tree to travel in' he explained, hovering anxiously as we packed it. Then he thrust a small parcel into my hand. It was a painted wooden spoon, one of the charming red and gold peasant spoons of tradition.

'For goodbye from Siberia,' he said. I have used the spoon ever since; it has taken its honoured place on my table beside the knife and fork of Shamyl the Avar, a treasure donated to me by the great Imam's descendants.

~

On the way to the air-field I looked once again at that primeval landscape which had been for so long my heart's desire. It was a desolate stretch of open country merging with the thinned-out edges of the *taïga*, marshy patches that would soon be frozen hard. The first snows had settled and lowering skies pressed round. A sleigh came racing towards us, flashing past in sprays of whiteness. Looking back, I saw it dashing northwards into the icy wastes. The little shaggy horses plunged forward bravely, and I could hear the jangle of bells. For a brief moment I had glimpsed the silhouette of two figures in the sleigh, a man and a child crouched down under their heavy furs. The man's head, in a fox-skin cap, was bent over the child's hood. They seemed to be talking intently, oblivious of the nothingness into which they sped. I wanted to ask Russlan to turn the car and go after them... But then I saw their sleigh left no tracks across the snow; the Traveller and I were making another of our journeys into the mind's eye.

ABOUT THE AUTHOR

Lesley Blanch was born in 1907 and educated by her own reading and by listening to the conversation of her elders and betters. She has always wanted to travel and never cared to sit still, unless it was for the opera. Her love for Russia came very early in life, as anyone will understand when they read *Journey into a Mind's Eye*. She was married to the French diplomat and fellow writer, Romain Gary (or Kacewgary) from 1945 to 1963.

Publications include *The Wilder Shores of Love* (1954), *Round the World in Eighty Dishes* (1956), *The Game of Hearts* (1956), *The Sabres of Paradise* (1960), *Under a Lilac Bleeding Star* (1963), *The Nine Tiger Man* (1965), *Journey Into the Mind's Eye* (1968), *Pavilions of the Heart* and *Pierre Loti: Portrait of an Escapist* (1983). Although renowned for her best-selling *The Wilder Shores of Love*, which studies the attraction exercised by the East over mid-nineteenth-century European women and which has been translated into over a dozen languages, Lesley Blanch herself considers *The Sabres of Paradise* her finest work. This study of the life and times of Imam Shamyl, the Muslim hero of the Caucasian wars of independence, draws together her two great loves, Russia and the Islamic Middle East, and examines the enduring conflict and connections between the two cultures.

ELAND

61 Exmouth Market, London EC1R 4QL
Tel: 020 7833 0762 Fax: 020 7833 4434
Email: info@travelbooks.co.uk

Eland was started in 1982 to revive great travel books that had fallen out of print. Although the list has diversified into biography and fiction, it is united by a quest for the defining spirit of place. These are books for travellers, readers who aspire to explore the world but who are also content to travel in their mind. Eland books open out our understanding of other cultures, interpret the unknown, reveal different environments as well as celebrating the humour and occasional horrors of travel.

All our books are printed on fine, pliable, cream-coloured paper. Most are still gathered in sections by our printer and sewn as well as glued, almost unheard of for a paperback book these days. This gives larger margins in the gutter, as well as making the books stronger.

We take immense trouble to select only the most readable books and therefore many readers collect the entire series. If you haven't liked an Eland title, please send it back to us saying why you disliked it and we will refund the purchase price.

Extracts from each book can be read on our website, at www.travelbooks.co.uk. If you would like a free copy of our detailed catalogue, please write to us at the above address.

'Just before midnight the church doors swung open and in a flood of colour and candlelight the glittering procession emerged to circle the building three times, chanting. The long tapers they carried sparkled on the sumptuous brocaded vestments and the diamond-studded crowns.'

LESLEY BLANCH

Journey into the Mind's Eye

Lesley Blanch was four when the mysterious Traveller first blew into her nursery, swathed in Siberian furs and full of the fairytales of Russia. She was twenty when he swept out of her life, leaving her love-lorne and in the grips of a passionate obsession. The search to recapture the love of her life, and the Russia he had planted within her, takes her to Siberia and beyond, journeying deep into the romantic terrain of the mind's eye.

Part travel book, part love story, Lesley Blanch's *Journey into the Mind's Eye* is pure intoxication.

'One of the finest books about Russia ... one of the best travel books of its generation.'

PHILIP MANSEL
SPECTATOR

'If you are interested in Russia – if you are interested in love – this haunting book is one to read and re-read.'

PHILIP ZIEGLER

'the perceptions of a fine writer ... all cast upon a gorgeous Russian canvas.'

KEVIN MCGRATH
HARVARD REVIEW

Travel/Biography

ISBN-13: 978-0-907871-54-5
ISBN-10: 0-907871-54-2

9 780907 871545

UK PRICE £12.99

2. As above.
3. Keddie, *Triumph of the King,* p.61.
4. Henry, *Commentary,* vol. ii, p.480.
5. *New Geneva Study Bible,* Thomas Nelson Publishers, p.590.
6. Henry, *Commentary,* vol. ii, p.892.

Chapter 28
1. Spurgeon, *Treasury,* vol. ii, p.29.
2 As above, p.30.

Chapter 29
1. Kaynor, *When God Chooses,* p.220.

Chapter 30
1. Henry, *Commentary,* vol. ii., p.491.

Chapter 31
1. Keddie, *Triumph of the King,* p.94.
2. As above, p.95.

Chapter 33
1. Henry, *Commentary,* vol. ii, p.504.
2. As above, p.126.
3. R. T. Kendall, *Jonah: An Exposition,* Zondervan Publishing House, p.85.

Chapter 34
1. Keddie, *Triumph of the King,* p.124.
2. As above, p.126.

Chapter 35
1. Keddie, *Triumph of the King,* pp.133-4.

Chapter 38
1. Keddie, *Triumph of the King,* p.160.

Chapter 40
1. Henry, *Commentary,* vol. ii, p.539.
2. Charles Spurgeon, *The Treasury of David,* vol. i, p.371.

Chapter 41
1. Keddie, *Triumph of the King,* p.172.

Chapter 42
1. A. W. Pink, *David,* vol. ii, p.204.

Chapter 43
1. Keddie, *Triumph of the King,* p.189.

Chapter 44
1. Cited by Keddie, *Triumph of the King*, p.203.
2. As above.
3. As above, p.212.